The First 100 Temples

CHAD S. HAWKINS

The images of temples included in this volume are available as fine-art prints from Deseret Book Company and other distributors of LDS products. For more information, contact Chad Hawkins Art, Inc., by telephone at 801-544-3434; by FAX at 801-544-4122; by mail at P. O. Box 292, Layton, UT 84041; or by email at artist@integrity.com

Library of Congress Cataloging-in-Publication Data

Hawkins, Chad S., 1971–
The first 100 temples / Chad S. Hawkins.
p.   cm.
ISBN 1-57345-921-6 (hardbound)
1. Mormon temples.   2. Church of Jesus Christ of Latter-day Saints—History.
I. Title: First hundred temples.   II. Title.

BX8643.T4 H38   2000
246'.9589332—dc21
00-051409

Printed in the United States of America   72082-6793
10   9   8   7   6

For my sweetheart, Stephanie

8 December 1994, Salt Lake Temple

and our children

Contents

Preface

It is an incredible milestone in the history of The Church of Jesus Christ of Latter-day Saints to have one hundred temples operating throughout the world. Certainly it is evidence that the Lord is pouring out blessings upon the earth. Elder Bruce R. McConkie observed that this season of rapid expansion is a sign of our Savior's second coming:

"For the day will come when temples will dot the earth, for the great work of the millennial era centers around and in these holy edifices."[1]

"We are living in one of the most significant and important epochs in the history of the Church and in the history of God's work among His people. We are living in the greatest era of temple building ever witnessed," said President Gordon B. Hinckley in 1985, when there were in operation thirty-six temples of The Church of Jesus Christ of Latter-day Saints. A mere fifteen years later, he dedicated the one-hundredth temple.[2]

I have delighted in creating artwork that features the temples, incorporating within the drawings various images to help viewers find deeper meaning in these representations of the temples. I have used images that are respectful, meaningful, and appropriate to each temple, researching and visiting temples all over the world to learn their history and capture their individual settings.

Researching, drawing, and painting the latter-day temples have blessed my family and me. What started out as a pastime and then a means to finance my mission has evolved into my career, instead of dentistry as I had planned. Soon after my drawing of the Salt Lake Temple was first printed, I began receiving invitations to speak at church gatherings, including seminary firesides, youth conferences, and institute devotionals. These unexpected opportunities have also greatly blessed me, because they have allowed me to share documented stories and other information about temples, always with the hope that listeners will be motivated to perform more diligently temple work for themselves and their kindred dead.

My most memorable speaking experience occurred in 1994 at a Salt Lake City high school seminary morningside. As I ended my talk by emphasizing to the youth the importance of a temple marriage, I asked Stephanie, my unsuspecting wife-to-be who had accompanied me to the presentation, to come up to the front of the group of more than five hundred students. I told the audience that I was looking forward to being married in the temple and that I wanted to introduce them to the beautiful young woman whom I hoped to marry there. As Stephanie turned a few shades of red, I dropped to one knee and asked her to marry me. Amid the sighs of the crowd, I heard a yes.

The greatest source of happiness in this life comes from the love that prevails in a gospel-oriented family. The gospel of Jesus Christ gives us the knowledge that if we remain true to our temple covenants, we can become exalted families. I have sweet memories of singing Primary songs about families being together forever and have always had a testimony of this doctrine, but when I first held my newborn son Jacob in my arms, the eternal nature of families took on an entirely new meaning for me. Reflecting on that precious moment helps me to more fully understand President Gordon B. Hinckley's words that the temple "speaks of the importance of the individual as a child of God. It speaks of the importance of the family as a creation of the Almighty. It speaks of the eternity of the marriage relationship. It speaks of going on to greater glory."[3]

Preparing this book, which comes in answer to queries regarding the pairing of stories from my talks with my art, has strengthened my testimony of sacred things. It has been an incredible privilege to research documents and papers about the temples and to spend time with numerous individuals from around the world whose faithfulness has helped make the first one hundred temples a reality. During our interviews for this book, individuals bore testimony, expressed deep emotions, and shared sacred experiences. Always we felt the presence of the Spirit.

I have organized the temples chronologically by their dates of completion, selecting and preparing the materials with a prayer in my heart and doing my best to document and accurately represent the facts as I have understood them. Many stories have been included here, and still more are recorded privately in the hearts and minds of those who experienced them. I have attempted to convey the strength of testimony of those whom I have interviewed. My hope is that readers may also feel the Spirit and thereby have their testimonies of this marvelous work strengthened.

The day before the Kona Hawaii Temple dedication, I had the privilege of interviewing Kona Hawaii Stake president Philip Harris. Telling in considerable detail how grateful the members were that the Lord had answered their prayers by blessing them with a temple, President Harris emphasized: "I believe that gratitude is best expressed by our actions. The only way we can thank Father in Heaven for this blessing is to wear out the temple by use."[4] I could not agree more wholeheartedly.

As we commemorate the landmark occasion of the dedication of the one-hundredth operating temple, may this book serve as a tribute to the sacrifice and commitment of those who labored in countless ways to make temples "dot the earth." And may this book edify and motivate us all never to take temples for granted, so that we may become, as President Howard W. Hunter admonished, an increasingly temple-attending, temple-loving people.[5]

Key to the First 100 Temples

K. KIRTLAND
N. NAUVOO

1. ST. GEORGE UTAH
2. LOGAN UTAH
3. MANTI UTAH
4. SALT LAKE
5. LAIE HAWAII
6. CARDSTON ALBERTA
7. MESA ARIZONA
8. IDAHO FALLS IDAHO
9. BERN SWITZERLAND
10. LOS ANGELES CALIFORNIA
11. HAMILTON NEW ZEALAND
12. LONDON ENGLAND
13. OAKLAND CALIFORNIA
14. OGDEN UTAH
15. PROVO UTAH
16. WASHINGTON D. C.
17. SÃO PAULO BRAZIL
18. TOKYO JAPAN
19. SEATTLE WASHINGTON
20. JORDAN RIVER UTAH
21. ATLANTA GEORGIA
22. APIA SAMOA
23. NUKUʻALOFA TONGA
24. SANTIAGO CHILE
25. PAPEETE TAHITI
26. MÉXICO CITY MÉXICO
27. BOISE IDAHO
28. SYDNEY AUSTRALIA
29. MANILA PHILIPPINES
30. DALLAS TEXAS
31. TAIPEI TAIWAN
32. GUATEMALA CITY GUATEMALA

33. FREIBERG GERMANY
34. STOCKHOLM SWEDEN
35. CHICAGO ILLINOIS
36. JOHANNESBURG SOUTH AFRICA
37. SEOUL SOUTH KOREA
38. LIMA PERU
39. BUENOS AIRES ARGENTINA
40. DENVER COLORADO
41. FRANKFURT GERMANY
42. PORTLAND OREGON
43. LAS VEGAS NEVADA
44. TORONTO ONTARIO
45. SAN DIEGO CALIFORNIA
46. ORLANDO FLORIDA
47. BOUNTIFUL UTAH
48. HONG KONG CHINA
49. MOUNT TIMPANOGOS UTAH
50. ST. LOUIS MISSOURI
51. VERNAL UTAH
52. PRESTON ENGLAND
53. MONTICELLO UTAH
54. ANCHORAGE ALASKA
55. COLONIA JUÁREZ CHIHUAHUA MÉXICO
56. MADRID SPAIN
57. BOGOTÁ COLOMBIA
58. GUAYAQUIL ECUADOR
59. SPOKANE WASHINGTON
60. COLUMBUS OHIO
61. BISMARCK NORTH DAKOTA
62. COLUMBIA SOUTH CAROLINA
63. DETROIT MICHIGAN
64. HALIFAX NOVA SCOTIA
65. REGINA SASKATCHEWAN
66. BILLINGS MONTANA

67. EDMONTON ALBERTA
68. RALEIGH NORTH CAROLINA
69. ST. PAUL MINNESOTA
70. KONA HAWAII
71. CIUDAD JUÁREZ MÉXICO
72. HERMOSILLO SONORA MÉXICO
73. ALBUQUERQUE NEW MEXICO
74. OAXACA MÉXICO
75. TUXTLA GUTIÉRREZ MÉXICO
76. LOUISVILLE KENTUCKY
77. PALMYRA NEW YORK
78. FRESNO CALIFORNIA
79. MEDFORD OREGON
80. MEMPHIS TENNESSEE
81. RENO NEVADA
82. COCHABAMBA BOLIVIA
83. TAMPICO MÉXICO
84. NASHVILLE TENNESSEE
85. VILLAHERMOSA MÉXICO
86. MONTRÉAL QUÉBEC
87. SAN JOSÉ COSTA RICA
88. FUKUOKA JAPAN
89. ADELAIDE AUSTRALIA
90. MELBOURNE AUSTRALIA
91. SUVA FIJI
92. MÉRIDA MÉXICO
93. VERACRUZ MÉXICO
94. BATON ROUGE LOUISIANA
95. OKLAHOMA CITY OKLAHOMA
96. CARACAS VENEZUELA
97. HOUSTON TEXAS
98. BIRMINGHAM ALABAMA
99. SANTO DOMINGO DOMINICAN REPUBLIC
100. BOSTON MASSACHUSETTS

Kirtland Temple

In a revelation given 27 December 1832, the Lord commanded the Prophet Joseph Smith to build the first temple in modern times (D&C 88:119–20). Kirtland, Ohio, located about twenty-five miles east of present-day Cleveland, was then the headquarters of the Church and the place of gathering. Even though the fulness of temple ordinances would not be restored until later, the Lord's house in Kirtland would nevertheless provide the setting for remarkable spiritual experiences and for the restoration of vital priesthood keys.

In June 1833 the Lord revealed to the First Presidency of the Church a vision of the temple and the manner in which it should be built. Second counselor Frederick G. Williams described this revelation: "We went upon our knees, called on the Lord, and the building appeared within viewing distance, I being the first to discover it. Then we all viewed it together. After we had taken a good look at the exterior, the building seemed to come right over us, and the makeup of the Hall seemed to coincide with what I there saw to a minutiae."[1] President Williams later testified that the completed temple coincided in every detail with the vision given to the First Presidency.

For three years the Saints concentrated their efforts on building what they called the "Lord's house," bringing to pass the vision of the First Presidency. These Saints, who had sacrificed their homes, farms, and businesses to gather in Ohio, were so poor that "there was not a scraper and hardly a plow that could be obtained among the Saints" to prepare the ground for the foundation of the temple.[2] Edward Tullidge recorded: "With very little capital except brain, bone, and sinew, combined with unwavering trust in God, men, women, and even children, worked with their might . . . all living as

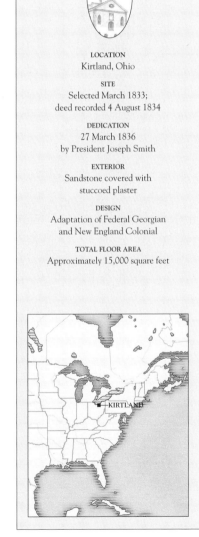

LOCATION
Kirtland, Ohio

SITE
Selected March 1833;
deed recorded 4 August 1834

DEDICATION
27 March 1836
by President Joseph Smith

EXTERIOR
Sandstone covered with
stuccoed plaster

DESIGN
Adaptation of Federal Georgian
and New England Colonial

TOTAL FLOOR AREA
Approximately 15,000 square feet

abstemiously as possible, so that every cent might be appropriated to the grand object, while their energies were stimulated by the prospect of participating in the blessing of a house built by the direction of the Most High, and accepted by Him."[3] As the Saints sacrificed and struggled to build the temple, they also had to deal with persecution from outsiders. President Heber C. Kimball and Elder George A. Smith recalled that sometimes the Saints "worked with a trowel in one hand and a gun in the other."[4]

The women were equally busy in the endeavors of building the temple. Emma Smith directed the women in sewing clothing for the workmen. President Heber C. Kimball later said, "Our wives were all the time knitting, spinning and sewing," noting that they "were just as busy as any of us."[5] Joseph Smith, observing a group of sisters doing handwork on furnishings for the temple's interior, commented, "You [sisters] are always on hand. The sisters are always first and foremost in all good works. Mary was first at the resurrection; and the sisters now are the first to work on the inside of the temple."[6]

The sandstone exterior of the temple was covered with a stucco finish that master builder Artemus Millett declared was inspired. Discarded pottery and glassware were crushed and added to the stucco mixture to make the temple walls glisten in the sun. Newly discovered natural cements also added to the mixture rendered the stucco quite weather resistant, and indeed, it lasted with only minor repairs until 1955.[7]

The temple's unique interior featured two main spaces, one above the other. The lower hall was a chapel used for praying, preaching, and administering the sacrament. The upper hall was used for educational purposes. At either end of both halls were tiers of pulpits facing each other. On the west

Kirtland Temple

Holy Father, we ask . . . that thy glory may rest down upon thy people, and upon this thy house, which we now dedicate to thee, that it may be sanctified and consecrated to be holy, and that thy holy presence may be continually in this house . . . and that this house may be a house of prayer, a house of fasting, a house of faith, a house of glory and of God, even thy house.

—FROM THE DEDICATORY PRAYER

side were seats for officers of the Melchizedek Priesthood, the highest row being for the First Presidency. On the east side were the pulpits for officers in the Aaronic Priesthood.[8]

Spiritual outpourings in the Kirtland Temple began in January 1836, two months before the temple was dedicated. As the brethren anointed each other with consecrated oil and pronounced blessings in the upper west room (in the attic), they experienced revelations, ministering of angels, and visions. Joseph Smith recorded: "The heavens were opened upon us, and I beheld the celestial kingdom . . . also the blazing throne of God, whereon was seated the Father and the Son" (D&C 137:1, 3).

Elder James E. Talmage wrote in his book *The House of the Lord:* "The dedication of the Kirtland Temple occurred on Sunday, March 27, 1836. The early hour of 8 a.m. had been set as the time for opening the doors; but so intense was the interest and so eager the expectation, that long before the time hundreds had gathered about the doors."[9] The seated congregation numbered nearly a thousand people, twice the usual capacity of the building; still others held a separate service in a schoolhouse west of the temple. At the meeting Church leaders were sustained, the dedicatory prayer (D&C 109) was read, a choir sang "The Spirit of God" (a hymn written for the temple dedication by William W. Phelps), and the sacrament was administered. Joseph Smith and others witnessed heavenly messengers during the service. Finally, the congregation stood and pronounced the Hosanna Shout.

The dedication ceremony initiated a week of spiritual experiences, which many of the Kirtland Saints recorded in their journals. On the evening of the dedication, 416 priesthood holders met in the temple. Joseph Smith records that "a noise was heard like the sound of a rushing mighty wind, which filled the Temple, and all the congregation simultaneously arose, being moved upon by an invisible power; many began to speak in tongues and prophesy; others saw glorious visions; and I beheld the Temple was filled with angels, which fact I declared to the congregation. The people of the neighborhood came running together (hearing an unusual sound within, and seeing a bright light like a pillar of fire resting upon the Temple), and were astonished at what was taking place."[10]

On 3 April, the Sunday following the dedication, President Joseph Smith and Assistant President Oliver Cowdery knelt in prayer at the Melchizedek Priesthood pulpit of the temple, behind a curtain that separated them from the congregation. There they witnessed a series of heavenly manifestations. As recorded in Doctrine and Covenants 110, the Lord Jesus Christ appeared and accepted the temple and gave the commandment not to pollute his house. Moses appeared next and gave Joseph and Oliver the keys for the gathering of Israel. Elias then appeared and conferred "the dispensation of the gospel of Abraham" (v. 12). Then, in fulfillment of Malachi's prophecy that the hearts of the fathers would be turned to the children and the hearts of the children to the fathers, Elijah committed to Joseph Smith and Oliver Cowdery the keys of sealing, preparing the way for all future temple ordinances for both the living and the dead.

The building of the temple seemed to increase hostility toward the Church as dissidents joined with mobs and drove the Saints from their homes and the temple. Within two years of its dedication, the temple was in the hands of the Saints' enemies. What had once been a temple of God, in which the Lord Jesus Christ had appeared, became merely a building, distinguished from others only by its wondrous past.

On Sunday, 3 April 1836, the prophet Elijah fulfilled Malachi's prophecy by committing the keys of this dispensation to Joseph Smith and Oliver Cowdery. Hidden in the trees to the left of the temple is a depiction of this sacred event.

. . . that thy holy presence may be continually in this house

Nauvoo Temple

After their expulsion from Missouri, the Saints moved eastward, crossing the Mississippi River and establishing themselves in the swampy village of Commerce, Illinois. They drained the swamps, constructed homes, and renamed their community *Nauvoo*, from a Hebrew word meaning "beautiful." In October 1840, the Prophet Joseph Smith selected a site for a temple. A few months later, on 19 January 1841, the Prophet received a revelation commanding the Saints to build it.

The Saints had lost most of their property in Missouri and were recovering from widespread sickness. As a whole they were depleted physically and monetarily. Healthy Church members who could get work were often willing to work for food alone. Nonetheless, the Church asked men to spend one day in ten working on the temple as "tithing in time." Brigham Young later noted that some of the workers on the temple had no shoes or shirts.[1]

Many skilled craftsmen worked full-time on the temple without guarantee of compensation. One notable example was Charles Lambert, who had recently joined the Church and emigrated from England. Although he had the responsibility of providing for his wife and her orphaned sister and two brothers, he pledged that he would continue to work until the temple was finished, whether he was paid for his services or not. One morning on his way to the temple site, Charles was stopped on the street by a stranger who asked if his name was Charles Lambert. Charles replied that it was, and the stranger responded that his name was Higgins. He continued: "I have heard of your skill as a workman, and want you to go to Missouri and work for me. You are not appreciated or properly paid here. If you will quit the temple and go and work for me

you can name your own price and you will be sure of your pay." Charles thanked the man for the offer but declined to accept it. He bid the stranger farewell, then instantly wondered how the man had known his name and heard of his skill. He turned to look again at the stranger but could see him nowhere—he had vanished from sight, as if the earth had swallowed him up. Charles felt sure that this man had been no other than Satan, attempting to keep him from the work of the Lord.[2]

As in Kirtland, the women of the Church played a key role in building the Nauvoo Temple. Mercy Fielding Thompson told the Prophet an idea that "seemed to be the whispering of the still small voice" to her: "Try to get the Sisters to subscribe one cent per week for the purpose of buying glass and nails for the Temple."[3] The Prophet gave her his blessing, and Assistant President and Church Patriarch Hyrum Smith spoke to the sisters privately and in public, encouraging them to participate. The sisters eagerly paid their portion, many giving a year's subscription in advance.[4] The sisters' efforts to provide clothing for the workmen at the temple site led to the organizing of the Nauvoo Relief Society on 17 March 1842.[5]

Another story of financial sacrifice to build the Nauvoo Temple is that of Joseph Toronto, who emigrated from Europe to Nauvoo soon after his conversion, carrying with him the money he had earned during his service in the Italian navy. Soon after his arrival, he attended a meeting at which Brigham Young pleaded for additional donations for the temple. The building committee then distributed the last of the food and supplies to the workmen, bringing the meeting to an end. Afterward, Brother Toronto gave to President Young twenty-five hundred dollars worth of gold coins.[6]

LOCATION
Nauvoo, Illinois

SITE
Nearly 4 acres

DEDICATION
Privately dedicated 30 April 1846
by Elder Joseph Young;
publicly dedicated 1 May 1846
by Elders Orson Hyde and
Wilford Woodruff

EXTERIOR
Light gray limestone from quarries
near the city

DESIGN
A mix of architectural styles

TOTAL FLOOR AREA
Approximately 50,000 square feet

NAUVOO

Nauvoo Temple

We thank thee that thou hast given us strength to accomplish the charges delivered by thee. Thou hast seen our labors and exertions to accomplish this purpose. By the authority of the holy priesthood now we offer this building as a sanctuary to thy worthy name. We ask thee to take the guardianship into thy hands and grant thy Spirit shall dwell here and may all feel a sacred influence on their heads that his hand has helped this work.

—FROM THE DEDICATORY PRAYER

British Saints made a special contribution to the temple by raising money to purchase a bell for the tower of the temple. When the Saints fled Nauvoo, they carried the bell across the plains with them. The bell now displayed on Temple Square in Salt Lake City is generally understood to be the same bell that once hung in the tower of the Nauvoo Temple.

While the temple was under construction, the Prophet Joseph Smith administered the first endowments in the office above his Red Brick Store on 4 May 1842. More than a year later, in December 1843, after receiving his endowment, Elder Orson Hyde recorded the words of the Prophet: "The Lord bids me to hasten and give you your endowment before the temple is finished. . . . Now if they kill me you have got all the keys, and all the ordinances and you can confer them upon others, and the hosts of Satan will not be able to tear down the kingdom. . . . On your shoulders will the responsibility of leading this people rest, for the Lord is going to let me rest awhile."[7]

The martyrdom of Joseph and Hyrum Smith on 27 June 1844 did not end the construction of the temple, but the Saints for a time were focused solely on defending the temple and their city. Though armed men stood on guard day and night, many homes were pillaged and burned in the weeks following the martyrdom. Faced with this continual threat, the Saints agreed to leave Illinois the following spring. As opposition increased, so did the Saints' desire to complete the temple and receive their ordinances before being forced from Nauvoo. They continued to build the temple as if they were planning to stay and use it for years to come.

So that ordinance work could begin as soon as possible, sections of the temple were dedicated as they were finished. The attic of the temple was dedicated 30 November 1845, and

Under the Prophet Joseph, Nauvoo became one of the largest cities in Illinois and was referred to as "The City of Joseph." In this drawing, Joseph Smith stands to the left of the temple, viewing the stately building and holding the Book of Mormon.

the first endowments were performed on December 10. Many Saints gave themselves entirely to the work of the Lord, laboring both night and day. Temple clothing was often washed at night so that it would be ready for use the next day. During the eight weeks before the exodus, some five thousand Saints received their endowments.

The temple was dedicated in the spring of 1846, two months after most of the Saints had left Nauvoo. Elder Erastus Snow testified: "The Spirit, Power, and Wisdom of God reigned continually in the Temple and all felt satisfied that during the two months we occupied it in the endowments of the Saints, we were amply paid for all our labors in building it."[8]

After the Saints' departure, the mob occupied the temple and made it their headquarters, defiling the building by gambling, drinking, and throwing empty bottles against the beautifully painted walls. Then, on 9 October 1848, after two years of being unoccupied, the temple was set on fire by an arsonist, and all but the stone shell was consumed. In 1850 a tornado destroyed one wall and weakened two others, and the fourth was taken down in the mid 1850s, its stones carried off as souvenirs. Before the destruction of the Nauvoo Temple was complete, the Latter-day Saints had settled in Utah and were already building more temples to serve God.

With reverence for the tremendous sacrifice and faith involved in building the Nauvoo Temple, President Gordon B. Hinckley announced on 4 April 1999 that the Church would build a new temple in Nauvoo—a replica of that building on which the early Saints had labored so faithfully. Of this endeavor, President Hinckley said, "The new building will stand as a memorial to those who built the first such structure there on the banks of the Mississippi."[9]

We ask thee to take the guardianship into thy hands and grant thy Spirit shall dwell here

St. George Utah Temple

The pioneers of southern Utah suffered years of physical hardships as they struggled to establish St. George and other communities. They endured scorching summer heat and heavy spring rains, which frequently flooded the nearby Virgin and Santa Clara Rivers. But despite the difficulties of establishing themselves on the desert frontier, the Saints began building a magnificent temple within ten years of their arrival.

After a selection committee had considered several possible temple sites, President Brigham Young chose a location at the lowest part of the valley. Local Saints argued that the place he had chosen was too boggy—for months after the stormy season the ground could not support even horses and wagons. President Young, however, remained resolute. He reportedly said, "We cannot move the foundation. This spot was dedicated by the Nephites. They could not build [the temple], but we can and will build it for them."[1]

The dedication of the temple site on 9 November 1871 marked the beginning of a great and difficult undertaking for the Saints of southern Utah. Heber Jarvis recorded that President Young said "there would not be any persons who would lose their lives on any of the works on this Temple." Brother Jarvis later declared, "I lived to see this prediction fulfilled as I saw many persons hurt but none of them died."[2]

The Saints wasted no time in starting the construction of their new temple. By 3:30 P.M. good progress had already been made in excavating for the foundation and basement.

In the next weeks and months, workers moved tons of black volcanic rock from the ridges above the town to the temple site to prepare the boggy ground to hold solid the footings and foundation of the temple. With great ingenuity, they used the town cannon to pound the footings deep into the ground. Using a system of pulleys fastened to a team of horses, the cannon, which the workers had filled with lead, was lifted about thirty feet in the air and then dropped onto the stone footings, bouncing three times before coming to rest. This tedious task continued until solid footings were firmly set in the soft ground. This historic cannon had previously been used by Napoleon in his siege of Moscow and was abandoned when his troops left the wrecked city. From there it was somehow taken to Siberia and then to Alaska, finally landing at Fort Ross, California. After their historic march, members of the Mormon Battalion took the cannon to Utah with them. Today, this old cannon is on permanent display on the St. George Temple grounds.[3]

The amount of materials needed to construct a building of this magnitude was staggering. Building the foundation alone cost more than one hundred thousand dollars.[4] Some seventeen thousand tons of black volcanic rock and sandstone were hauled by mule teams to the temple site. Most of the million feet of lumber used in the temple had to be transported from a forest eighty miles away.[5]

During the first three months of 1877, President Brigham Young taught the workers who would minister in the temple the sacred ceremonies, which had been revealed to the Prophet Joseph Smith in Nauvoo.[6]

On 1 January 1877, the lower story of the temple was dedicated by Elder Wilford Woodruff, president of the temple from 1877 to 1884. Baptisms for the dead were first administered in the temple on 9 January 1877, and endowments for the dead were begun two days later. President Woodruff described the occasion as being "the first time endowments for the dead had

LOCATION
St. George, Utah

SITE
6 acres

SITE DEDICATION AND GROUNDBREAKING
9 November 1871
by President Brigham Young

DEDICATION
6–8 April 1877
by President Daniel H. Wells
with President Brigham Young presiding;
rededicated 11–12 November 1975
by President Spencer W. Kimball
after remodeling

EXTERIOR
Red sandstone covered with white plaster

DESIGN
Castellated Gothic style

TOTAL FLOOR AREA
Originally, more than 56,000 square feet
110,000 square feet after remodeling

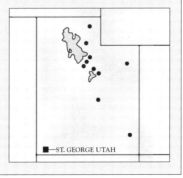

■—ST. GEORGE UTAH

St. George Utah Temple

We thank thee, O Lord, that thy people whom thou hast led to this distant land, and whom thou has preserved by thine own right arm, . . . have been enabled to gather the materials of which this building is composed; to put together and erect . . . a temple, which we dedicate and now consecrate to thee that it may be holy unto thee, the Lord our God, for sacred and holy purposes and that the blessing, even life for evermore, . . . may flow through the ordinances which appertain unto thy holy place, unto us thy children.

—FROM THE DEDICATORY PRAYER

been given in any Temple in this dispensation."[7] After an amazingly short period of five and a half years and much backbreaking effort, the temple was dedicated in its entirety on 6 April 1877 by Daniel H. Wells, second counselor in the First Presidency.

Brigham Young watched the progress of the building with great satisfaction. There was one thing he did not like about the temple, however. He felt the tower on the temple was "short and squatty" and boldly encouraged the members to rebuild it higher. The people, worn out after their nonstop efforts to build the temple, resisted. Five months after the temple was dedicated, President Young died in Salt Lake City at age seventy-six. Several weeks later, on the night of 16 October 1878, a severe storm hit St. George, and the tower was destroyed by lightning. The unanimous feeling of the St. George Saints was that President Young had had his way. The tower was rebuilt taller, thus meeting his original specifications.[8]

Significant spiritual experiences in the St. George Temple have been recorded. Perhaps the best known of these happened to President Wilford Woodruff. He was in the temple late one evening when the spirits of many of America's Founding Fathers gathered around him. He said, "Every one of those men that signed the Declaration of Independence, with General Washington, called upon me . . . two consecutive nights, and demanded at my hands that I should go forth and attend to the ordinances of the House of God for them."[9]

On 21 August 1877, President Woodruff was baptized by Elder John D. T. McAllister for one hundred persons, including

The hidden image reminds us of President Wilford Woodruff's vision of the Founding Fathers and the temple ordinances performed for them. In the bluffs behind the temple are the words "We the people."

all the signers of the Declaration of Independence except two (John Hancock and William Floyd), whose ordinance work had already been done. President Woodruff then baptized Elder McAllister for twenty-one men, including George Washington and his forefathers and all the presidents of the United States for whom President Woodruff had not been baptized, except three (James Buchanan, Martin Van Buren, and Ulysses S. Grant), whose work has since been completed. Sister Lucy Bigelow Young was baptized for Martha Washington and female members of her family and seventy other eminent women. Later that week the men were ordained elders—except George Washington, John Wesley, Benjamin Franklin, and Christopher Columbus, who were ordained high priests—in preparation for the endowment ceremony, which was likewise performed by proxy for them.[10]

President Wilford Woodruff shared his feelings about these sacred events at general conference on 10 April 1898: "I am going to bear my testimony to this assembly, if I never do it again in my life, that those men who laid the foundation of this American government and signed the Declaration of Independence were the best spirits the God of heaven could find on the face of the earth. They were choice spirits, not wicked men. General Washington and all the men that labored for the purpose were inspired of the Lord."[11]

The pristine whiteness of the St. George Utah Temple contrasts dramatically with the brilliant red hills of Utah's Dixie. The temple's grandeur amidst the rugged terrain reflects the sacrifice of a people whose faith and diligence conquered the wilderness and created a mighty edifice to their God.

. . . a temple, which we dedicate and now consecrate to thee

Logan Utah Temple

Excavation for the Logan Temple began on 28 May 1877, just one month after the dedication of the St. George Temple. The prominent east-bench temple site designated by Brigham Young on 15 May 1877 overlooks Cache Valley. The temple is "the spiritual symbol of the valley. It stands in the midst of this very fertile and productive area as a reminder that life is more than the struggle for physical survival or the acquisition of material wealth. It symbolizes a long-range view of things—an eternal view."[1] It stands as a reminder to the Saints of Cache Valley that life's greatest successes come through eternal families and the keeping of sacred covenants.

From the beginning of the settlement of Cache Valley, the Saints had a vision of a future temple on the bench in Logan. Bishop William H. Maughan recorded an event that took place at a religious gathering in Maughan's Fort (later Wellsville) two years before the settlement of Logan: "Brother John Thirkell was appointed orator of the day. . . . He soon got to prophesying and he said there would be a temple built on the ground at Logan. . . . He said he could see these things and could not help telling it."[2]

On 22 August 1863, while in Logan with other Church leaders, Elder Wilford Woodruff prophesied: "Yea, the day will come . . . when you will have the privilege of going into the towers of a glorious Temple built unto the Name of the Most High (pointing in the direction of the bench), east of us upon the Logan bench."[3] Knowing that a temple was to be built on the site on "the bench," the Saints set aside this property and used it as a city park and pleasure ground.

Before building the Logan Temple, the local Saints had generously donated their means and labor toward building the

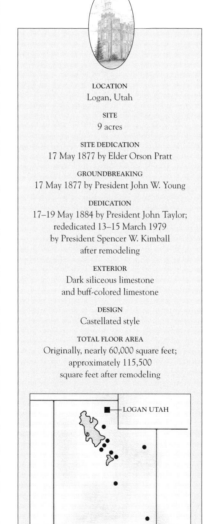

LOCATION
Logan, Utah

SITE
9 acres

SITE DEDICATION
17 May 1877 by Elder Orson Pratt

GROUNDBREAKING
17 May 1877 by President John W. Young

DEDICATION
17–19 May 1884 by President John Taylor;
rededicated 13–15 March 1979
by President Spencer W. Kimball
after remodeling

EXTERIOR
Dark siliceous limestone
and buff-colored limestone

DESIGN
Castellated style

TOTAL FLOOR AREA
Originally, nearly 60,000 square feet;
approximately 115,500
square feet after remodeling

LOGAN UTAH

St. George and Salt Lake Temples and the newly completed Logan Tabernacle. Speaking to the Saints at the groundbreaking ceremony on 17 May 1877, President Young explained that building the temple would require continued great sacrifice: "From the architect to the boy who carries the drinking water and the men that work on the building, we wish them to understand that wages are entirely out of the question."[4]

As the Saints willingly sacrificed time and money to build the temple, God's power was witnessed in the preservation of many lives, including that of nineteen-year-old Brother James, who, in the words of Nolan P. Olsen, "had loaded up about two tons of lumber and headed down stream toward the temple. . . . All went well for a short distance, until the wagon wheel hit a soft spot. The riverbank caved in, dropping the two wheels and throwing Brother James on the bottom of the stream, with his big load upside down on top of him. It took the workmen nearly a half hour to break the binding and to roll the wagon and lumber from the river. Brother James had been under water for this full length of time. They laid his body on the bank, covered it with a blanket and told one of the boys to get on a horse and come to Logan to tell the parents what had happened to their son.

"Before the horse could be bridled, the blanket began to move and Brother James was up on his feet. Evidently his wind had been knocked out as his load went over, and he had not breathed for thirty minutes, and had no water in his lungs. The ice cold water had slowed his body processes, and he had no brain or bodily damage of any kind. He was none the worse for the experience, and reloaded his wagon and brought it on down to the temple."[5]

Logan Utah Temple

We ask . . . that thou wouldst teach us thy will and thy law, and thine ordinances more fully and completely . . . And, as all wisdom dwells with thee, and, as all light, truth and intelligence flow from thee, we humbly seek unto thee for thy blessing to rest upon this house, that it may be indeed a house of learning under thy guidance, direction and inspiration.

— FROM THE DEDICATORY PRAYER

Another manifestation of divine protection was witnessed when high scaffolding that had been supporting three men gave way. One of the men, who fell fifty-three feet, said: "I landed so hard that it bounced my spirit right out of my body. . . . [And when] a worker administered to me saying, 'In the name of Israel's God, we command you to be made whole,' my spirit entered my body and I opened my eyes. After it was all over, they put me in the buggy and took me home. I have testified to hundreds of people as to how I was brought back to life through the Priesthood of God."[6]

Just as the Lord protected the workers as they built the temple, he protected the completed temple from the desecration and abuse of those who would harm the structure or enter it unworthily. One such example of divine intervention took place at the dedication of the temple in May 1884. As President John Taylor watched the large numbers of people enter the temple, he suddenly turned to President Charles O. Card and said that a certain woman coming through the doorway was not worthy to enter the temple. It was discovered that this woman was not a member, and she was asked to leave. She had purchased the recommend from a member for a dollar. President Taylor had never seen this woman before, but the Spirit had whispered that of all the people in attendance, she was not worthy to be there.[7]

The adversary has always tried to frustrate the work of the Lord. Christian L. Olsen lived very near the temple but found that if he mentioned that he planned to attend the temple, something would prevent him from doing so. One evening he

Because the Logan Temple does not have a statue of the angel Moroni atop its spire, a representation of Moroni blowing his trumpet is hidden in the clouds.

said to his sons, "Tomorrow we will finish grinding our molasses, and then I'd like to spend a week in the temple." He woke the next morning to find the main grinding wheel broken. He spent the full week repairing the mill instead of serving in the temple. Twice his corral gates were somehow opened on days he planned to spend at the temple. Instead he spent the days trying to round up his livestock. "Anytime I wanted to go to the temple," he concluded, "I soon learned that I could not say it out loud. I got up, milked my cows, set the bucket down and ran. And then I could get there without any trouble."[8]

A similar story tells of eight girls who began their trek to the Logan Temple one morning at 4:00 to do baptisms. The girls ran into one delay after another every few minutes of their trip. Before they reached Logan, nearly every important part of their buggy had broken down. Despite their early start, they didn't reach the temple that day until 5 P.M., after the font had been emptied. The temple workers who were still there agreed to refill the font, and the girls were baptized for the dead. They said they felt that Satan had accompanied them on their trip that day.[9]

Despite the efforts of the adversary, the Logan Temple has been an important site of latter-day temple work for the living and the dead. From its dedication until 1976, more than 18 percent of all temple ordinances were performed in the Logan Temple.[10] The temple continues to exert much influence for righteousness and contributes greatly to the spirituality of the Saints throughout the region.

We humbly seek unto thee for thy blessing to rest upon this house

Manti Utah Temple

The majestic Manti Utah Temple sits on a hill at the base of a rock mountain and commands a superb view of the Sanpete Valley. The twenty-seven-acre Temple Hill is richly landscaped with hundreds of evergreens and a grass hillside to the south. The temple is one of the best known landmarks in central Utah.

Manti, founded in 1849 by 224 pioneers, was one of the first settlements established by the Latter-day Saint pioneers. In 1854 President Heber C. Kimball prophesied not only that the settlement would succeed, but also that a temple of God would be built on the hill above Manti. "The rock will be quarried from that hill to build it with," he continued, "and some of the stone from that quarry will be taken to help complete the Salt Lake Temple."[1] This prophecy was fulfilled in every detail, as stone from the Manti quarry was used for both the Manti Temple and for decorative tablets at the east and west ends of the Salt Lake Temple.

On the morning of 25 April 1877, President Brigham Young determined where the temple should be built when he took Elder Warren S. Snow to Temple Hill with him. Brother Snow related: "We two were alone: President Young took me to the spot where the Temple was to stand; we went to the southeast corner, and President Young said: 'Here is the spot where the prophet Moroni stood and dedicated this piece of land for a Temple site, and that is the reason why the location is made here, and we can't move it from this spot; and if you and I are the only persons that come here at high noon today, we will dedicate this ground.'"[2]

At the dedication of the temple site, President Young said that if the Saints would build this temple the earth would yield in abundance and there would be no failure of crops in this

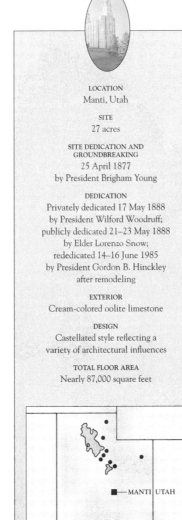

LOCATION
Manti, Utah

SITE
27 acres

SITE DEDICATION AND
GROUNDBREAKING
25 April 1877
by President Brigham Young

DEDICATION
Privately dedicated 17 May 1888
by President Wilford Woodruff;
publicly dedicated 21–23 May 1888
by Elder Lorenzo Snow;
rededicated 14–16 June 1985
by President Gordon B. Hinckley
after remodeling

EXTERIOR
Cream-colored oolite limestone

DESIGN
Castellated style reflecting a
variety of architectural influences

TOTAL FLOOR AREA
Nearly 87,000 square feet

■— MANTI UTAH

stake of Zion. Three years later grasshoppers came in droves, and many thought their crops would be destroyed by the swarms of voracious insects. Within a few days, however, all the grasshoppers had disappeared.[3]

The Saints laboring on the temple worked swiftly and felt protected in their labors. One night Edward L. Parry, the master mason of the temple, was awakened from a very realistic dream in which a man fell from the temple's scaffolding. Brother Parry immediately arose from his bed and went to the site to examine the scaffolding. There he found that an important support rope had worked its way loose. After repairing the scaffolding, he returned home to his bed. Because he heeded the warning, no one was injured.[4]

The most frequent request by temple patrons is to see the beautiful staircases. Two of only three large-scale spiral stairways in the United States constructed without a central support are found in the Manti Temple. Built under the supervision of designer and master carpenter William Asper, the staircases incorporate black walnut railings. The craftsmen formed the railing so well that the joints in the wood are undetectable. Each staircase is wide enough for four men to walk side by side. The staircases, which make six full rotations each, contain 204 intricately fashioned spindles and vertically rise more than seventy-six feet in 151 steps. In 1985, the nearly one-hundred-year-old staircases were carefully inspected and reported to be in excellent condition.[5]

After eleven years of hard work and sacrifice, the Saints rejoiced when the Manti Temple was dedicated in May 1888. Some attending the dedicatory services reported seeing the spirits of early Church leaders. Elder Franklin D. Richards, one

Manti Utah Temple

Let the power of thy Spirit be felt by all who shall enter within its portals. . . .

Grant that it may stand and endure as a monument of the obedience and love

of thy people, and to the honor of thy holy name for ages yet to come.

—FROM THE DEDICATORY PRAYER

of the Twelve, recorded: "When we dedicated the Temple at Manti, many of the brethren and sisters saw the presence of spiritual beings, discernable only by the inward eye. The prophets, Joseph, Hyrum, Brigham and various other Apostles that have gone, were seen, and not only this, but the ears of many of the faithful were touched, and they heard the music of the heavenly choir."[6]

Another remarkable manifestation occurred as a selection by Mendelssohn was being performed. As the music was played, a number of Saints in the congregation heard heavenly voices singing. The voices seemed to be coming from behind or above the congregation, but no one could see another choir anywhere in the room. There was, in fact, no other choir in the entire building.[7]

Because of the importance of the sacred ordinances performed in temples, the Lord grants special blessings that make it possible for his work to be done. President Anthon H. Lund, the second president of the Manti Temple and a member of the First Presidency, related a story of divine assistance concerning vicarious temple ordinances:

"I remember one day in the temple at Manti, a brother from Mount Pleasant rode down to the temple to take part in the work, and as he passed the cemetery in Ephraim, he looked ahead (it was early in the morning), and there was a large multitude all dressed in white, and he wondered how that could be. Why should there be so many up here; it was too early for a funeral, he thought; but he drove up and several of them stepped out in front of him and they talked to him. They said, 'Are you going to the temple?' 'Yes.' 'Well, these that you see here are your relatives and they want you to do work for them.' 'Yes,' he said, 'but I am going down today to finish my work. I have no more names and I do not know the names of those

Hidden in the evergreens below the temple is the figure of Moroni, raising his right hand toward the temple and carrying the golden plates with his left. President Brigham Young said that in ancient times Moroni dedicated the ground on which the temple stands.

who you say are related to me.' 'But when you go down to the temple today you will find there are records that give our names.' He was surprised. He looked until they all disappeared, and drove on. As he came into the temple, Recorder Farnsworth came up to him and said, 'I have just received records from England and they all belong to you.' And there were hundreds of names that had just arrived, and what was told him by these persons that he saw was fulfilled. You can imagine what joy came to his heart, and what testimony it was to him the Lord wants this work done."[8]

Although the chief function of the temple is the sacred work that takes place within its walls, the Manti Utah Temple is also known for the pageant that takes place on its grounds every year. In 1956, temple president Lewis Anderson shared an impression with Glen Nelson, a worker on a new parking lot. Pointing to the south slope of the temple hill, President Anderson said, "I am going to tell you something that you cannot at this time see or comprehend. The time will come when there will be many people gathered here on this site of the temple hill." The Mormon Miracle Pageant, which annually attracts nearly 130,000 people, is a fulfillment of Anderson's prediction. This small production, first organized in July 1967 by Helen B. Dyreng as a stake pageant for Pioneer Day, has continued to grow, eventually hosting some twenty thousand visitors at every showing.[9]

In 1988, during the temple's centennial year, the First Presidency commemorated the occasion by stating: "Our thoughts go back to those Latter-day Saints who first made the trek to Manti. As the first 50 families came into the valley, the hill upon which the temple now stands seems to have marked their destination. . . . One hundred years of temple ordinance work is a great contribution to the Lord's work."[10]

Let the power of thy Spirit be felt by all who shall enter within its portals

Salt Lake Temple

The Salt Lake Temple expresses in stone the religious faith and pioneer endurance of the thousands who built it. It stands as a monument to the beleaguered Saints, who had been persecuted and finally driven from their homes in Ohio, Missouri, and Illinois and across the desolate plains to a valley where they could worship in peace. The Salt Lake Temple, recognized worldwide as an architectural treasure and the centerpiece of nineteenth-century Mormon industry, symbolizes the Saints' efforts to build Zion and establish the Lord's house "in the top of the mountains" (Isaiah 2:2).

On 28 July 1847, four days after President Brigham Young entered the Salt Lake Valley, he chose the site for a temple. The city was planned with the Temple Block at its center, the heart of the pioneers' activities and aspirations. Building this temple required forty years of labor.

During the April 1853 general conference, President Young said: "I have never inquired what kind of a temple we should build. Why? Because it was represented before me. I have never looked upon that ground, but the vision of it was there. I see it as plainly as if it was reality before me."[1]

Ground was broken for the temple on 14 February 1853 and the cornerstones laid with great ceremony on 6 April 1853. The first pioneer company had arrived in the valley only five and a half years earlier, and the Saints were still trying to get a foothold. One who attended the groundbreaking described their situation: "I walked [to the meeting] the morning the ground was broken for the foundation of the Temple . . . on the Temple Block. I went through frozen mud and slush with my feet tied up in rags. I had on a pair of pants made out of my wife's skirt, a thin Scottish plaid. . . . These were all the

clothes I had. It was either go that way or stay home. . . . I was not alone in poverty. . . . There were many who were fixed as badly as I was."[2]

In 1856 Brigham Young sent architect Truman O. Angell to Europe to study classic architectural styles. The prophet told him: "Take drafts of valuable works of architecture, and be better qualified to continue your work and you will increase in knowledge upon the Temple and other buildings, and many will wonder at the knowledge you possess."[3] During his thirteen-month mission, Brother Angell traveled extensively throughout Great Britain and France, visiting many important architectural monuments and preaching the gospel.

In early summer 1858, the United States Army, under federal order to "quell libelous rumors of sedition," entered the Salt Lake Valley. The Saints had left the city and were prepared to burn their property, if necessary, to keep it out of the hands of their enemies. The temple foundation, which by then had been laid, had been filled in with soil and the Temple Block plowed to resemble a farmer's field.

Two years later, after the threat of war had subsided, the Saints unearthed the temple foundation and found that the red sandstone had developed cracks. In accordance with President Young's desire that the temple be "built in a manner that will endure through the Millennium,"[4] this foundation was replaced with one built of granite. With these delays, the walls did not reach ground level until 1867, fourteen years after the cornerstones had been laid.

The tireless commitment that raised the temple walls slowly over the next twenty-five years is exemplified by the story of John Rowe Moyle. A stonemason and farmer from Alpine, Utah, he had been called as a work missionary to use

LOCATION
Salt Lake City, Utah

SITE
10 acres

SITE DEDICATION
14 February 1853
by President Heber C. Kimball

GROUNDBREAKING
14 February 1853
by President Brigham Young

DEDICATION
6–24 April 1893
by President Wilford Woodruff

EXTERIOR
Gray Utah granite from
Little Cottonwood Canyon

DESIGN
Unique six-spire design incorporating
Gothic and classical elements

TOTAL FLOOR AREA
More than 253,000 square feet

SALT LAKE

Salt Lake Temple

O Lord, we regard with intense and indescribable feelings the completion of this sacred house. . . . In past ages thou didst inspire with thy Holy Spirit thy servants, the prophets, to speak of the time in the latter days when the mountain of the Lord's house should be established in the tops of the mountains, and should be exalted above the hills. We thank thee that we have had the glorious opportunity of contributing to the fulfillment of these visions.

—FROM THE DEDICATORY PRAYER

Just as the Salt Lake Temple is built upon a solid foundation of granite, so should we build our lives upon the solid foundation of the Lord's teachings. To depict this, an outline of the Lord's right hand is shown supporting the entire foundation of the Salt Lake Temple.

his talents in building the temple walls. Early each Monday morning Brother Moyle walked some twenty miles north to the Salt Lake Temple site. There he spent the week laboring on the temple until he returned home on Friday. On Friday and Saturday he tended to his farm, and following a restful Sabbath, he began the cycle all over again. But one weekend while working on his farm, a cow kicked him, badly breaking his leg. The best medical advice available was to amputate the leg. While his stump healed, Brother Moyle carved himself a wooden leg. According to family history, he put on the prosthetic leg as soon as he was able and "walked into Salt Lake as was his custom to take up his work, for he had been called as a work missionary on the Temple. And there, the story goes, he climbed up the scaffolding on the east side of the Temple and carved 'Holiness to the Lord.'"[5]

In 1890 as the temple neared completion, Church leaders called John Hafen, Lorus Pratt, and John B. Fairbanks, all promising artists, to travel to Paris and enroll in the Julian Academy. Upon their return to Utah, these artists painted the murals in the endowment rooms of the temple.

The ceremony on 6 April 1892 to place the capstone of the temple marked the completion of the stone work. Some fifty thousand members attended the ceremony, making it the largest gathering to that date in Utah history, a record unchallenged for several decades. Using an electrical button, President Wilford Woodruff laid the stone in place, and the crowd joined in the sacred Hosanna Shout. The choir and some fifty thousand members then joined in singing "The Spirit of God Like a Fire Is Burning," a hymn that had been written for the dedication of the Kirtland Temple fifty-six years earlier. A few days after the capstone-laying ceremony, President Woodruff encouraged the workers to finish the temple's interior by April 6 of the following year.

The angel placed atop the Salt Lake Temple was the first

Dedicated to my wife, Stephanie, this drawing depicts our wedding day. An image of the Savior is hidden in the tree above the newly married couple, his arms lovingly outstretched, blessing and protecting them as they begin their new life together.

formally identified as Moroni.[6] Nonmember artist Cyrus Dallin accepted the commission, and after studying scriptures on angels, he created a heroic upright figure blowing on a trumpet and representing the angel mentioned in Revelation 14:6, declared by President Gordon B. Hinckley to be Moroni, who would bring the everlasting gospel to be preached "to every nation, and kindred, and tongue, and people."[7] The twelve-foot, five-inch statue stands on a stone ball on the 210-foot central spire on the temple's east side.

Forty years of effort and sacrifice to build the Salt Lake Temple concluded on 6 April 1893, the last day of the Church's annual conference, when President Wilford Woodruff dedicated the edifice. The Associated Press carried news of the dedication over its wire service, and newspapers from the *New York Times* on the East Coast to the *Los Angeles Times* on the West Coast ran stories about the completion of Mormonism's most important symbol.

In September 1898 a very sacred spiritual experience took place in the halls of the Salt Lake Temple. President Wilford Woodruff had passed away, and Lorenzo Snow, the senior apostle, worried greatly about his ability to lead the Church through its various difficulties, including its financial debt. After offering heartfelt prayer, he waited for some manifestation from the Lord, but none came. Disappointed, he walked through the celestial room and into the hall leading to his office when the Savior appeared to him and instructed him to reorganize the First Presidency immediately. President Snow later told his granddaughter of this experience and described the glorious personage of the Savior.[8]

Through the years the Salt Lake Temple has continued to be a spiritual center for the Saints. Along with the weddings, baptisms, and endowments that are performed in the temple, it is used for the weekly meetings of the First Presidency and the Quorum of the Twelve Apostles and for solemn assemblies.

Laie Hawaii Temple

A temple in the Hawaiian Islands was the dream of many devoted and faithful Saints in the Pacific from the time the gospel was first proclaimed to them in 1850 by George Q. Cannon. In 1900, while attending the fiftieth anniversary of the founding of the Hawaiian Mission, President Cannon, then a member of the First Presidency, said that if the Hawaiian Saints would be faithful, they would one day be able to be sealed as families for eternity. The Saints saw this as a prophecy that a temple would be built in Hawaii.

This prophecy was partially realized in June 1915, when President Joseph F. Smith dedicated part of the "Plantation of Laie" for a temple. Purchased by the Church in 1865 for fourteen thousand dollars, the sugarcane and pineapple plantation had become the gathering place for the Hawaiian Saints. The property included some six thousand acres with more than three miles of beach frontage, five hundred head of cattle, five hundred sheep, two hundred goats, and twenty-six horses.[1]

Several features of the site presented problems for the workers on the temple. For one, the ground was unstable coral and sand, necessitating a large excavation to provide solid footings for the building. Because large machinery was not available, the entire excavation had to be done using picks, shovels, and blasting powder.[2] The remote location of the temple made it difficult to obtain building materials. Crushed lava and coral were added to the concrete, which was used to form the entire edifice, including the floors, ceilings, walls, and roof.

Even with this innovation, construction often had to wait while the contractors tried to locate necessary materials. At one point, when construction was at a standstill due to lack of

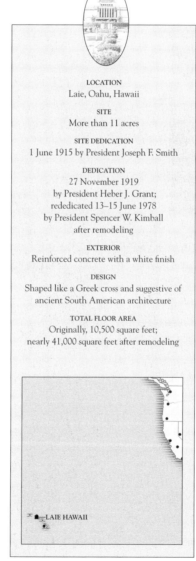

LOCATION
Laie, Oahu, Hawaii

SITE
More than 11 acres

SITE DEDICATION
1 June 1915 by President Joseph F. Smith

DEDICATION
27 November 1919
by President Heber J. Grant;
rededicated 13–15 June 1978
by President Spencer W. Kimball
after remodeling

EXTERIOR
Reinforced concrete with a white finish

DESIGN
Shaped like a Greek cross and suggestive of
ancient South American architecture

TOTAL FLOOR AREA
Originally, 10,500 square feet;
nearly 41,000 square feet after remodeling

LAIE HAWAII

lumber, temple contractor Ralph Woolley prayed for help in obtaining the needed supplies. Two days later during a severe storm, a freight ship became stranded on a nearby coral reef. The captain offered the Saints his cargo of lumber if they would help him unload his ship. The Saints agreed, and thus work on the temple could be resumed.[3]

Raising funds for the temple among the scattered Hawaiian Saints was a challenge that was overcome with faith and ingenuity. The Saints in Hawaii participated in a variety of fund-raising projects, including holding concerts and creating and selling mats, fans, and other craft items at local bazaars. Even though the Saints were already sacrificing a great deal for the temple, the mission president Samuel E. Woolley noted that tithing paid by Hawaiian Saints had increased by nearly one-third during this time.[4]

The temple's interior was beautified with various hardwoods, including Hawaiian koa, a native wood of the islands similar to mahogany. In several rooms, including the baptistry, mosaic tile and marble were used to decorate the floors. Mural paintings by Utah artists A. B. Wright and LeConte Stewart adorn the walls of the various rooms.

On the temple's exterior are four sculptured panels, one on each side of the building, with 123 figures. The friezes, sculpted by Leo and Avard Fairbanks, illustrate four gospel dispensations. The north frieze is of particular significance. It depicts the Book of Mormon dispensation and includes figures representing Hagoth and his companions, who are believed to be among the ancestors of the Polynesian peoples.[5]

The temple is situated on a moderate hill, twenty-three feet above sea level and about half a mile from the shores of

Laie Hawaii Temple

*We beseech thee that no unclean thing shall be permitted to enter here, and that
thy Spirit may ever dwell in this holy house and rest mightily upon all who shall
labor as officers and workers in this house.*

—FROM THE DEDICATORY PRAYER

the Pacific. The grounds are covered with manicured lawn, luxurious ferns, and other semitropical vegetation, with royal palms dramatically lining the final approach to the temple. In front of the temple is an ascending, palm-lined water court consisting of four reflecting pools. The climax to this wondrous scene is a bas-relief panel by Avard Fairbanks of a Hawaiian mother and her three children.

The temple was dedicated on 27 November 1919, four and a half years after the dedication of the site. In the dedicatory prayer, President Heber J. Grant said: "We thank thee, that thousands and tens of thousands of the descendants of Lehi, in this favored land, have come to a knowledge of the gospel, many of whom have endured faithfully to the end of their lives."[6]

Since the dedication of the temple, Saints from around the Pacific have attended the temple for their own ordinances and to perform ordinances for their kindred dead. The rate of temple work slowed significantly when Pearl Harbor was attacked by Japanese forces on 7 December 1941, bringing the United States into World War II. The next day Hawaii was placed under martial law, and the army governed the territory until October 1944. During the war, temple attendance dropped by more than 80 percent. The temple was kept open only by the great faith of its patrons and was used only for a weekly endowment session and for occasional weddings.[7]

Through the years, additions and modifications have been made to the temple, including two wings at either side of the entrance to provide additional office space. Expansion over the years has increased the temple from 10,500 square feet to nearly 41,000 square feet. At one time the white temple was painted pale green to blend in with the landscaping. But most

The first of three hidden images in this drawing, located in the first reflecting pool, is that of the Savior, Jesus Christ. In the second pool are traditional flowers used in the Hawaiian lei—the plumeria and the Cattleya orchid. Finally, located in the third pool, are each of the eight main islands that make up the beautiful state of Hawaii.

people responded negatively, and the original white color was eventually restored to the temple walls. As tourism continued to increase, a visitors' center was built to accommodate visitors from around the world.[8]

In 1988 both the temple and its grounds were beautified. One aspect of the project involved clearing thick plant growth from a pioneer cemetery behind the temple, where some two hundred early Hawaiian Saints are buried. The area has now become the Laie Pioneer Memorial Cemetery.

The beauty of the temple grounds, the serenity of the view, and the "Aloha" attitude of the guides and staff provide a warm welcome to the quarter of a million people who visit Laie each year. Thousands of missionary referrals are received annually from nonmembers who visit the temple's visitors' center and the neighboring Polynesian Cultural Center.[9]

Several firsts in the history of latter-day temples are associated with the Laie Hawaii Temple. It was the first to be built beyond the continental limits of the United States (Hawaii was a U.S. territory from 1900 to 1959, when it became the fiftieth state). It was also the first to be dedicated of three temples of a similar design (the others are the Cardston Alberta, and Mesa Arizona Temples). The temple was also the first wherein living endowments were received by Saints residing in Asian and Polynesian countries.

The Hawaii state motto is "Ua mau ke ea o ka aina i ka pono," which translates as "The life of land is perpetuated in righteousness." The righteousness of many faithful Hawaiian Saints made the Laie Hawaii Temple a reality. Since its dedication in 1919, this temple has represented for them a timeless vision of paradise, white and gleaming, between the emerald mountains and the sapphire sea.

. . . that thy Spirit may ever dwell in this holy house

Cardston Alberta Temple

By 1900 Latter-day Saint settlements had become well established in areas far from Utah and the Church's temples there. In the April 1901 general conference, President Joseph F. Smith stated: "I foresee the necessity arising for other temples or places consecrated to the Lord for the performance of the ordinances of God's house, so that the people may have the benefits of the house of the Lord without having to travel hundreds of miles for that purpose."[1]

Under President Smith's leadership, ground was broken in 1913 for a temple in Cardston, Alberta, Canada, on an eight-acre site set aside for Church use in 1887 by Charles Ora Card, an early settler. The temple grounds were enlarged by two more acres in the 1950s. Although the Laie Hawaii Temple was the first temple completed outside the United States, the Cardston Alberta Temple was the first outside the United States to be announced.

Twenty-four years earlier, in 1887, forty-one Latter-day Saint pioneers, mostly from Logan, Utah, had moved to southwestern Alberta and settled on Lee's Creek, later named Cardston after Charles O. Card. Two weeks after their arrival, Brother Jonathan E. Layne prophesied that a temple would one day bless the Saints in southern Alberta. He said later of this experience, "While speaking, the spirit of prophecy rested upon me and under its influence, I predicted that this country would produce for us all that our Cache Valley homes and lands had produced for us, and that temples would yet be built in this country, I could see it as plain as if it already was here."[2]

A year later, in 1888, while attending a conference in Cardston, Elder John W. Taylor of the Quorum of the Twelve made a similar prophecy: "I now speak by the power of prophecy and say that upon this very spot shall be erected a Temple to the name of Israel's God and nations shall come from far and near and praise His high and holy name." On another occasion Elder Taylor said, "This land will yet become a breadbasket to the world; and in this land a temple shall be reared to the worship of Almighty God."[3] Although these utterances were a source of wonder to these pioneers, the prophecies imbued them with a vision of the future the Lord had in store for his faithful Saints in Canada.

Construction on the Cardston Alberta Temple began in 1913 and was completed ten years later. Many factors combined to make constructing such a large building a difficult undertaking for the Saints in this small community. Progress on the temple was greatly hindered by World War I, which raged in Europe from 1914 to 1918. Canada, as part of the British Empire, was seriously involved in the war. Other factors that contributed to slow progress on the temple were insufficient funding, the severe winters, and the need to transport building materials long distances.[4]

Yet the workers building the temple felt the hand of the Lord guiding their labors. Matthew Leavitt, a worker on the temple excavation, was driving a large plow team when a harness trace broke and a single-tree struck him in the leg. "There was a doctor on the job," Leavitt recorded of the experience, "and he came and examined my leg and found there were no broken bones. He said that a miracle had been performed here, that there was no reason in the world why [my] leg was not cut right off with that severe blow."[5]

The four ordinance rooms of the temple are arranged both practically and symbolically. The rooms are located around the

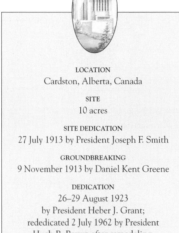

LOCATION
Cardston, Alberta, Canada

SITE
10 acres

SITE DEDICATION
27 July 1913 by President Joseph F. Smith

GROUNDBREAKING
9 November 1913 by Daniel Kent Greene

DEDICATION
26–29 August 1923
by President Heber J. Grant;
rededicated 2 July 1962 by President
Hugh B. Brown after remodeling;
rededicated 22–24 June 1991
by President Gordon B. Hinckley
after further remodeling

EXTERIOR
White granite

DESIGN
Octagonal shape reflecting
ancient Peruvian architecture

TOTAL FLOOR AREA
Originally, more than 29,000 square feet;
nearly 90,000 square feet after remodeling

Cardston Alberta Temple

May thy Spirit ever dwell in this holy house and rest upon all who shall labor as officers and workers herein, as well as upon all who shall come here to perform ordinances for the living or for the dead. May thy peace ever abide in this holy building, that all who come here may partake of the spirit of peace and of the sweet and heavenly influence that thy Saints have experienced in other temples.

—FROM THE DEDICATORY PRAYER

center of the building, each room facing one of the cardinal directions, and each successive room is a few steps higher than the one before. As patrons move through the ordinance rooms, they follow a circular path until they finally enter the celestial room at the center of the temple. Not only is each room higher in elevation than the one before but each is also richer in its materials and decoration. Thus, the architectural arrangement and interior decor of the temple ordinance rooms reinforce the concept of spiritual progression so central to the temple ceremony.[6]

Adding to the beauty of the temple's interior are murals painted by several prominent artists, including Utah landscape artist LeConte Stewart, who is known as the "Master of Mormon Landscape" and the "Dean of Mormon Art." He oversaw all the decorative work in the temple and painted the murals in the creation and terrestrial rooms.

Cardston Alberta Temple architect Hyrum Pope shared his thoughts on temple architecture: "The architecture of a temple of the Lord should certainly be worthy of and in harmony with the genius of the Gospel, which has been restored. . . . It should not be a Gothic cathedral or a classic temple but an edifice which should express in its architecture all the boldness and all the truth for which the Gospel stands. . . . It should express all the power which we associate with God. It should express the refinement which we associate with God for truly art is not a thing which is foreign to God. For all that is great and good that has ever been accomplished by man in the arts and sciences, or any endeavor, is of course of God, and to our minds it seems that a temple should express all these facts."[7]

As the temple construction neared completion, area Relief Society sisters organized a project to raise money to buy materials for furnishings and temple clothing. Each sister was to save the chicken eggs laid on Sunday and then donate either the eggs or their value to the project. By their own labor, the Relief Society sisters thus raised fifteen hundred dollars for the temple.[8]

Hidden in the landscaping to the right of the temple is a depiction of the sculpture of the Savior and the Samaritan woman at the well that adorns the original outside west wall of the temple. In the lower left-hand corner is hidden a silhouette of Old Chief Mountain, which visitors and patrons can see from the temple grounds.

At the dedication of the temple, 26–29 August 1923, so many general authorities attended that Cardston temporarily "became the capital of Mormondom."[9] Elder John A. Widtsoe commented that "it was the first time in the history of the Church that so many of the General Authorities of the Church had been assembled at one time outside the boundaries of the United States."[10]

During the sixth session of the dedicatory services, President Heber J. Grant offered the following counsel to the Saints: "Now, we as Latter-day Saints have everything in the world to be grateful for. We have not only the benefits of the Gospel for ourselves, but we can do a marvelous work for those who have died without a knowledge of the Gospel. . . . And I want to bear my witness here today in connection with others, that the unseen powers, that those who are working for us beyond the veil, never lose their interest in the work of those who are living here upon the earth."[11]

Many temple workers and patrons have experienced strong spiritual manifestations as they have sought to perform saving ordinances for themselves and the deceased. During a sealing of a woman to her children and deceased husband for eternity, President Edward J. Wood, the temple's first president, stopped in the middle of the ordinance and asked the woman if all her children were present. The woman said they were, and President Wood attempted the ordinance again. But again he stopped at the same place and asked if all her children's names were listed on the ordinance sheet. She said they were. After stopping again at the same place, the president asked, "Sister, didn't you ever have any other children?" To this the woman replied that she had a daughter who had died in infancy and whose name had not been included on the sheet. To this President Wood said that he had heard a voice saying, "I am her child." The ordinance was performed again, this time including all the children.[12]

Mesa Arizona Temple

Latter-day Saints settling parts of Arizona in the 1870s eagerly anticipated the time when a temple would be built there. According to James H. McClintock, Arizona state historian in the 1920s, the first donation toward a temple in Arizona "was recorded January 24, 1887, in the name of Mrs. Helena Roseberry, a poor widow of Pima, who gave $5 toward the building of a temple in Arizona, handing the money to Apostle Moses Thatcher. This widow's mite ever since [to 1921] has been held by the Church in Salt Lake. . . .

"Another 'nest egg,' the first contribution received directly for the Mesa edifice, came from another widow, Mrs. Amanda Hastings of Mesa, who, on behalf of herself and children, three years ago [1918], gave the Stake Presidency $15."[1]

By the end of World War I, plans for a temple in Arizona were underway. The recent construction of the Cardston Alberta and Laie Hawaii Temples strongly influenced the planning of the Mesa Arizona Temple. Proposed designs included Spanish baroque elements and a stepped dome in the center topped with a spire and a statue of the angel Moroni. The design that was finally chosen had elegant classical details with suggestions of both pre-Columbian temples and the temple of Herod.

On 1 February 1920, President Heber J. Grant selected the site for the temple at what was then the eastern edge of Mesa. The twenty-acre plot was immediately south of the "Apache Trail" section of the transcontinental highway, an artery that would carry thousands of tourists past the temple each year.

The carefully developed grounds of the temple provide an ideal setting for the Lord's house. The acclaimed gardens include a wide variety of trees, such as Italian cypress, palm,

LOCATION
Mesa, Arizona

SITE
20 acres

SITE DEDICATION
28 November 1921
by President Heber J. Grant

GROUNDBREAKING
25 April 1922
by President Heber J. Grant

DEDICATION
23 October 1927 by President Heber J.
Grant; rededicated 15–16 April 1975
by President Spencer W. Kimball
after remodeling

EXTERIOR
Reinforced concrete faced with
eggshell-colored terra cotta glaze

DESIGN
Modified classic style

TOTAL FLOOR AREA
Originally, nearly 73,000 square feet;
approximately 114,000 after remodeling

MESA
ARIZONA

and citrus trees, as well as a unique cactus garden that features the Arizona state tree, the palo verde.

The exterior of the temple is faced with eggshell-colored terra cotta, glazed like tile. At each corner of the building are sculptured friezes by Torlief Knaphus, based on sketches by A. B. Wright. On the north end of the temple, the sculptures depict the gathering of the elect in the Old World; on the south end the figures represent the gathering in the Americas and in the Pacific.[2]

The temple's internal structure symbolically represents mankind's upward progression back to the presence of Heavenly Father. The design centers on the grand staircase patrons see as they enter the temple doors. Patrons ascend the staircase after they have received instruction and completed an endowment session. They then proceed up the staircase and into the celestial room, symbolizing the achievement of exaltation.

Paintings and other aspects of the temple's design remind visitors that the Mesa Arizona Temple was intended to be a temple for the Lamanites. In the dedicatory prayer, President Heber J. Grant petitioned the Lord to bless the Lamanites "that they may not perish as a people but that from this time forth they may increase in numbers and in strength and in influence . . . and that many of them may have the privilege of entering this holy house and receiving ordinances for themselves and their departed ancestors."[3]

Dedicated 23 October 1927, the temple was important for all members of the Church but especially for Native Americans, who joined the Church in large numbers during the middle decades of the twentieth century. The significance of the Mesa Arizona Temple to the Lamanites is seen in an

Mesa Arizona Temple

May all who come upon the grounds which surround this temple . . . feel the sweet and peaceful influence of this blessed and hallowed spot. And may this building be sacred unto thee.

—FROM THE DEDICATORY PRAYER

MESA
Arizona

experience of a temple worker that took place about two years after the temple was dedicated. The worker told Patriarch John F. Nash:

"'I was sitting in the Creation Room today and there were two old men who were sitting beside me who began to talk very loudly. I reached my hand over and touched one on the knee and at the same time I turned my eyes toward the rostrum, and there stood a Lamanite, a splendid specimen of manhood, clothed only with a loin cloth. He seemed to be looking over the congregation and the room in general. I wondered what it could mean. I looked to see if anybody else saw the same thing, and when I looked back he was gone.

"'What do you think it meant, Brother Nash?' 'Well,' I said, 'it might possibly be this: This Temple is the Lamanite Temple. We have all the Lamanite records here and it has been built especially for the purpose of Lamanites receiving their endowments here, whenever they are ready, and it might be possible that he was sent ahead to look over the building and see how he would like the building and the services that were being performed.'"[4]

A landmark event for the Lamanites and temple work took place at this temple in 1945. Because the endowment had been presented only in English up to that point, it was difficult for Latin American Saints to fully understand and participate in the ordinances. In November of that year, two hundred Spanish-speaking Saints from all over the Southwest and from as far away as Mexico City, Mexico, gathered in Mesa to participate in the first non-English presentation of the endowment. This first "Lamanite conference" was a spiritual boon to the members who participated in it; numerous similar conferences were held over the succeeding years.[5]

Attendance at the temple continued to grow. Finally, it was decided to close the temple temporarily to expand its capacity. After the remodeling was complete, the public was

A full-length image of the Savior Jesus Christ is hidden in the palm trees to the left of the temple, the area of the grounds in which the annual Easter pageant is performed.

invited to tour the building during an open house. The temple was rededicated 15 and 16 April 1975.

Another important tradition began early on Easter morning in 1938, when the youth of the Mutual Improvement Association from the Maricopa Stake presented a sunrise service on the temple grounds. A narrative and choir numbers recounted the story of Christ's life and sacrifice. The service was so successful that organizers made it an annual event, and it has grown to include some four hundred cast members, who present Christ's humble birth, inspiring ministry, and glorious resurrection in dance, drama, and music. The pageant now has a modern, two-hundred-foot-long stage, state-of-the-art sound and light systems, and a soundtrack featuring the London Symphony Orchestra. Even with these changes, however, the message remains the same—to bring people unto Christ by reenacting scenes from the beautiful story of his life. In April 1998, its sixtieth year, the Mesa Easter Pageant attracted more than 120,000 people from all over the world. "People are so impressed by the pageant's excellence that they communicate to their friends that they need to see it," said Douglas Holladay, pageant chairman.[6]

The Mesa Arizona Temple Garden Christmas Festival also inspires thousands of visitors each year. It includes a nativity scene with the scriptural account of the Savior's birth read over loudspeakers. Preparations for the display of 600,000 Christmas lights begin in October. Twenty-five hundred volunteers arrange the lights along pathways and fountains and in the trees.

"There are more and bigger Christmas light displays," said Elder Dale Shumway, director of the Mesa Arizona Temple Visitors' Center. "We distinguish ours by focusing on the Savior as the light."[7] In 1998 more than a million visitors from every state and three hundred countries saw the lights illuminating the grounds of the Lord's holy house in Mesa, Arizona.[8]

Idaho Falls Idaho Temple

The Idaho Falls Idaho Temple is located on seven acres of spacious grounds on the banks of the Snake River in Idaho Falls, Idaho. East of the temple are three ponds continuously flowing from one to another creating three picturesque waterfalls. More than sixteen hundred pine trees add to the serenity of the temple gardens. The temple, rising out of this peaceful setting, projects impressive architectural strength. John Fetzer Sr., a member of the Church board of temple architects, remarked on the spiritual meaning of the temple's outward structure: "Set in its wide, green valley, with distant mountains fringing the horizons, this Temple is visible for many miles and its towering, tapering mass, pointing skyward, seems to tell of eternal values, to symbolize the aspiration and strength of the human spirit, rising above material things."[1]

The 1937 decision to build a temple in the Snake River Basin in southeastern Idaho was the fulfillment of a prophecy made to the pioneers of that area. These Saints had struggled to establish themselves on the harsh, desolate prairie. In 1884 President Wilford Woodruff and Elder Heber J. Grant encouraged them in their endeavors. Standing in a wagon, President Woodruff, president of the Quorum of the Twelve Apostles, said to a small group, "Be not discouraged; be not disheartened, because God's blessing is upon this land." He then foretold the time when the Basin and its inhabitants would prosper and develop into a strong community. "Yes," he continued, "as I look into the future of this great valley I can see temples—I can see beautiful temples erected to the name of the Living God where holy labors may be carried on in his name through generations to come."[2]

At the fiftieth anniversary of the dedication of the temple,

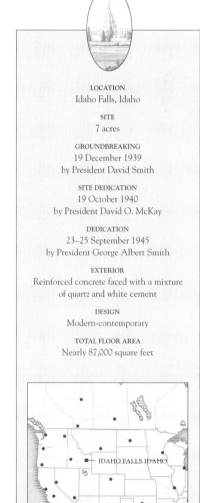

LOCATION
Idaho Falls, Idaho

SITE
7 acres

GROUNDBREAKING
19 December 1939
by President David Smith

SITE DEDICATION
19 October 1940
by President David O. McKay

DEDICATION
23–25 September 1945
by President George Albert Smith

EXTERIOR
Reinforced concrete faced with a mixture
of quartz and white cement

DESIGN
Modern-contemporary

TOTAL FLOOR AREA
Nearly 87,000 square feet

IDAHO FALLS IDAHO

Elder W. Eugene Hansen of the presidency of the Seventy said there was "much friendly competition among the cities and towns in southeastern Idaho for the privilege of having the temple in their community. But once the decision was made the communities rallied together, and it was the cooperative spirit that prevailed."[3]

The location having been decided, each member of the Church board of temple architects was assigned to submit a proposal. The board agreed upon the concept prepared by John Fetzer Sr., who later said that after praying for inspiration "he saw in vision an ancient Nephite temple which he used as the basis for his design."[4] The warm white temple is symmetrical, with bladed pilasters rising up to a final shaft 148 feet high. The temple's exterior design results in vertical lines casting shadows toward the heavens.[5]

The temple's floor plan, which locates the celestial room at the center of the structure, incorporates elements from the Cardston Alberta and Mesa Arizona Temples. To progress through the ordinance rooms of the temple, patrons move through successively brighter rooms on the way upward to the celestial room in the temple's tower, symbolizing mankind's progression back into the presence of God.[6]

Ground was broken on 19 December 1939 by David Smith, president of the North Idaho Falls Stake, and an eighteen-foot excavation was prepared. At just that depth, workers encountered a bed of lava rock, which provided a solid foundation. On 19 October 1940, President David O. McKay, second counselor in the First Presidency, laid the southeast cornerstone, with first counselor President J. Reuben Clark Jr. presiding over the ceremony. The *Church News* related: "An excellent program was rendered during which a group of

Idaho Falls Idaho Temple

For the fertility of this land which, once most undesirable and forbidding, now produces in rich abundance delicious grain, fruits and vegetables, we are most grateful. We too express to thee our joy in beholding great mountains towering majestically toward the sky to inspire thy children to look up, as well as around them, that they might enjoy thy handiwork.

—FROM THE DEDICATORY PRAYER

trumpeters upon the roof of the six-story hospital building a block away rendered in most melodious strains that sacred and cherished number, 'An angel from on high the long, long silence broke.'"[7]

The beautiful walls of the temple sparkle in the sunlight from a two-inch-thick facing of white quartz aggregate and white cement that covers the sixteen-inch-thick exterior walls. These materials were produced by a cement products company operated by the Buehner family of Salt Lake City. When the Church approached the business to provide the materials for the temple, the family enthusiastically accepted. Their excitement stemmed from Brother Buehner's patriarchal blessing, which he had received many years earlier. In it the German immigrant was promised that "he and his sons would help erect temples of this Church."[8] In the years following, the Buehner family assisted in the construction of the Los Angeles California, London England, Bern Switzerland, and Hamilton New Zealand Temples and in an addition to the Cardston Alberta Temple.[9]

The United States' entrance into World War II caused delays in the temple's building schedule. The exterior of the temple was nearly completed, but the interior still needed significant work. As an increasing number of Church members, both men and women, entered the armed forces or went to work in defense industries, a labor shortage delayed or halted most construction projects, including the temple. Wartime restrictions greatly limited the availability of building materials, but steel and other structural materials had been stockpiled for the temple, and most of its marble, from France, Italy, and Sweden, had been imported before the war. A major setback during this period came when it was discovered that mural fabrics in the temple had been damaged by condensation from insufficient insulation of the exterior concrete walls.

Despite the delays and difficulties, however, the temple was completed and then dedicated by President George Albert Smith just one month after the war ended. Not only was the Church able to complete the Idaho Falls Temple but with the

The flowing waters of the Snake River inspired the baptism theme of this drawing. Hidden in the river below the temple are images of five oxen, representing the baptismal font in the temple. The oxen are submerged in the water to represent our immersion into the waters of baptism and remind us of the remission of our sins.

end of gasoline and tire rationing the Saints could attend the temple more easily, making this an important period of revitalization in temple attendance.

In the early 1980s, representatives of the Idaho Falls Idaho Temple district asked the Church to consider adding a statue of the angel Moroni to the temple. The First Presidency approved the request, and on 5 September 1983, thirty-eight years after the temple was dedicated, a twelve-foot statue of the angel Moroni identical to the statue on the Atlanta Georgia Temple was positioned by helicopter on the temple spire.[10]

The blessings of the temple cannot be gained anywhere else on earth. In the priesthood session of general conference in April 1993, Elder Russell M. Nelson counseled: "Brethren, please remember: the highest degree of glory is available to you only through that order of the priesthood linked to the new and everlasting covenant of marriage (see D&C 131:1–4). Therefore, your first priority in honoring the priesthood is to honor your eternal companion."[11]

A tender demonstration of this understanding of priorities took place on a cold winter's morning at the Idaho Falls Temple. An elderly brother and his wife were walking arm in arm to the temple. Rain had made the walkways slick and hazardous. As the couple carefully made their way toward the temple's front doors, the wife gently took her husband's hand from her arm and placed it on the door handle. He opened the door for her and waited for her to enter. The touching scene was repeated at the next set of doors as the blind man opened the door for his beloved companion.[12]

The solid structure of the Idaho Falls Idaho Temple standing beside the flowing Snake River aptly symbolizes the spiritual foundation of a community rich in pioneer heritage and devoted to the eternal goal of linking families in eternal bonds. And as the river nourishes innumerable farms across southern Idaho, so do light and knowledge flow from the "temple by the river," feeding all who will accept them.

Bern Switzerland Temple

The Bern Switzerland Temple was the ninth Latter-day Saint temple to be built but the first to be built in Europe. The temple is located in Zollikofen, a northern suburb of Bern, the capital of Switzerland. Although its design incorporates aspects of temples that had been built immediately preceding it, its exterior architecture and skyline resembles the Kirtland Temple more than any other temple built up to that point. Since its dedication in 1955, the Bern Switzerland Temple has been a mighty symbol for the Church on the European continent.

The Saints in Europe had longed for a temple ever since President Joseph F. Smith, attending a mission conference in Bern in August 1906, said, "The time will come when this land will be dotted with temples, where you can go and redeem your dead."[1] He further predicted, "The time will come . . . when temples of God which are dedicated to the holy ordinances of the gospel . . . will be erected in the divers countries of the earth, for the gospel must be spread over all the world, until the knowledge of God covers the earth as the waters the great depths."[2]

Less than half a century later, in Glasgow, Scotland, on 22 July 1952, President David O. McKay announced that the First Presidency and the Quorum of the Twelve Apostles had decided to build a temple in Switzerland.[3]

Switzerland was the logical choice for the first temple in Europe for many reasons. In the dedicatory prayer for the temple, President McKay gave thanks "for the freedom-loving government of Switzerland, which through the centuries has held inviolate man's free agency and his inalienable right to worship . . . without dictation from any man or group of men whomsoever."[4] Switzerland's constitution, adopted in 1848, guaranteed religious freedom, and the nation's neutrality

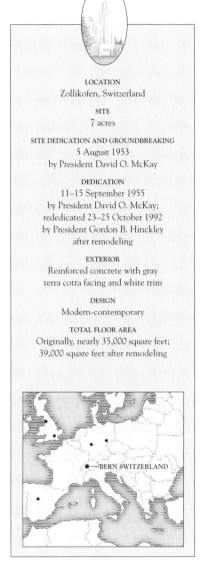

LOCATION
Zollikofen, Switzerland

SITE
7 acres

SITE DEDICATION AND GROUNDBREAKING
5 August 1953
by President David O. McKay

DEDICATION
11–15 September 1955
by President David O. McKay;
rededicated 23–25 October 1992
by President Gordon B. Hinckley
after remodeling

EXTERIOR
Reinforced concrete with gray
terra cotta facing and white trim

DESIGN
Modern-contemporary

TOTAL FLOOR AREA
Originally, nearly 35,000 square feet;
39,000 square feet after remodeling

BERN SWITZERLAND

during World Wars I and II kept it free from the divisive influences in Europe.[5]

Switzerland was also a natural choice for a temple because of its geographic location and diversity of languages. Switzerland is connected to most other European countries by rail, thus making travel to the temple easy for European Saints. Additionally, most Swiss natives are multilingual and may speak Swiss-German, French, Italian, or Romansh. Workers in the temple speak virtually every European language, so that members from all over Europe may participate in the temple ordinances. Because of this representation of people of so many languages and ethnic backgrounds at the temple, Bern Temple president Percy K. Fetzer referred to the sacred edifice as "the United Nations of Europe."[6]

In 1952, President McKay assigned Samuel E. Bringhurst, the president of the Swiss-Austrian Mission, to obtain land that had been selected for a temple site. After several months of negotiations, the Church's bid to purchase the property was denied. Writing President McKay to inform him of the developments, and noting that he was disappointed to have all his efforts come to naught, President Bringhurst wrote that he felt a strange sense of relief and thought things would work out well in the end. President McKay mentioned a similar impression in his response: "My disappointment soon disappeared and was replaced by an assurance that the Lord will overrule all transactions for the best good of his Church, not only in Switzerland but throughout Europe."[7] One week after his first letter to President McKay, President Bringhurst wrote again, this time with better news. He had found an available parcel of land in Bern that was twice the size of the original site and half as expensive. In his letter he noted that all his

Bern Switzerland Temple

On this sacred occasion, the completion of the first temple to be erected by the Church in
Europe, we give our hearts and lift our voices to thee in praise and gratitude.

—FROM THE DEDICATORY PRAYER

Bern

missionaries had "fasted and prayed, and immediately after the property became available."[8]

President McKay arrived in Switzerland in August 1953 to preside at the groundbreaking. The rain, which had been falling for some six weeks, let up just in time for the ceremonies. President McKay announced that this temple would function differently from other temples already built in this dispensation. Rather than moving from room to room, patrons would remain in the temple's one ordinance room, from which they would proceed into the celestial room. Additionally, to accommodate patrons speaking a variety of languages, a motion picture and taped recordings, which could easily be translated into many languages, would be used for the first time. To provide the best technology for the new system, the temple's architect sought the advice of motion picture studios, including M.G.M., Fox, and Paramount. Because President McKay had a personal friendship with M.G.M. film producer Cecil B. DeMille, that studio was especially helpful in suggesting solutions to logistical problems with the new method.[9]

The temple's baptistry is the result of the cooperative effort of American and Swiss craftsmen. Salt Lake sculptor Phil Malan built the casts for the twelve oxen, which were shipped to Switzerland. A particular Swiss foundry was chosen because of its ability to produce sculptures with minute details. The oxen were completed and installed three months before the temple's dedication.[10] At that time President McKay declared that the Swiss temple had the "finest baptismal room of any temple in the Church."[11]

Many acts of personal devotion helped make the construction of this temple possible. One eighty-two-year-old member, Therese Leuscher, sent one hundred francs in half-franc pieces to the home of Swiss-Austrian Mission president Samuel E. Bringhurst with a note stating: "It is my wish that

Left of the temple is an image of the Savior with clasped hands. A dove and an olive branch, symbolizing Switzerland's traditional neutrality, are hidden above the temple.

the Almighty God may accept the temple just as sacred as He did the Kirtland Temple, although I will not be living when this holy building will be dedicated."[12] As she had predicted, this sister passed away before the dedication of the temple. Other financial contributions, large and small, were donated by members from countries around the world.

Workers labored around the clock for several nights to complete the final details as the dedication approached. On 11 September 1955, President McKay dedicated the Swiss temple. After welcoming those present, he said, "I welcome also an unseen, but, I believe, a real audience among whom are former presidents and apostles of the Church, headed by the Prophet Joseph."[13] President McKay later remarked, "The veil between those who participated in those exercises and loved ones who had gone before seemed very thin."[14]

The temple was closed from 1990 to 1992 for extensive remodeling and refurbishing. The changes included adding more endowment and sealing rooms. So thorough were the modifications that the refurbished temple was almost entirely new. Before the rededication of the temple, a public open house was held. Although only about sixty-five hundred members live in Switzerland, some thirty-three thousand people toured the remodeled building.

President Gordon B. Hinckley rededicated the temple on 23 October 1992, with nearly nine thousand members from throughout Europe attending the ten dedicatory sessions. Among his comments during the service, President Hinckley expressed gratitude for "this nation of Switzerland, which through centuries of time has been a land of peace while nations round about have been nations at war." He prayed that Switzerland "may continue to be a land of peace, a land of freedom, a land of opportunity and an example to other nations of the world."[15]

We give our hearts and lift our voices to thee in praise and gratitude

Los Angeles California Temple

The Los Angeles California Temple was built to meet the needs of expanding Church membership in southern California. Situated on a prominent hill, the highest point between Los Angeles and the Pacific Ocean, the temple can be seen from Catalina Island and from ships twenty-five miles out to sea. The property was obtained by the Church in March 1937, and it has since become the site of the temple, a mission home, and a meetinghouse, family history building, temple clothing building, and lodgings for patrons.

One early reference to a temple in California came in a letter of encouragement to the California Saints from President Brigham Young and Elder Willard Richards in August 1847. The message stated: "In the process of time the shores of the Pacific may yet be overlooked from the temple of the Lord."[1] In 1937 President Heber J. Grant announced that the Church had purchased property for a temple on the top of a hill near Westwood Village. The location's legal description dates back to 1542, when it was claimed by "Charles I, King of Spain, and his successors in interest, by right of discovery and settlement."[2]

Although construction of the temple was delayed by the outbreak of World War II, the First Presidency developed plans for the building, which was to seat two hundred patrons in each session. After the war, they directed that the temple design be enlarged to accommodate up to three hundred persons per company. This change, along with the addition of a priesthood assembly room on the upper floor large enough to seat twenty-six hundred persons, made this the largest temple built in the twentieth century, second only to the Salt Lake Temple in square footage. The temple's 257-foot spire is forty-

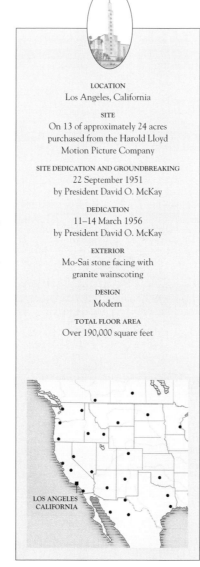

LOCATION
Los Angeles, California

SITE
On 13 of approximately 24 acres purchased from the Harold Lloyd Motion Picture Company

SITE DEDICATION AND GROUNDBREAKING
22 September 1951
by President David O. McKay

DEDICATION
11–14 March 1956
by President David O. McKay

EXTERIOR
Mo-Sai stone facing with granite wainscoting

DESIGN
Modern

TOTAL FLOOR AREA
Over 190,000 square feet

LOS ANGELES
CALIFORNIA

seven feet taller than the Salt Lake Temple's highest spire, and its six levels include about four and a half acres of floor. Its exterior is covered with panels of Mo-Sai stone, made of cement and crushed quartz crystals, so that the walls shine in daylight and glow in the floodlights at night. Some twenty-five hundred panels, each weighing approximately sixteen hundred pounds, cover the exterior surface. The temple's reinforced concrete and structural steel make the exterior fireproof and resistant to Southern California earthquakes.[3]

In February 1952, President David O. McKay encouraged local Saints to bear part of the cost of building the temple. Meeting with twelve hundred ward and stake leaders, President McKay challenged the Saints of Southern California to raise $1 million for the temple. He encouraged them to have the "young people, even the children in the 'cradle roll,' contribute to the temple fund, for this is their temple, where they will be led by pure love to take their marriage vows."[4]

The Saints responded with enthusiasm and generous pledges. When a bishop received a pledge from a deacon for $150, he thought that the young man had incorrectly positioned the decimal. But for two years the boy saved the money from his paper route and lawn mowing earnings.[5] Within three months after the call for donations and pledges, the Saints had far surpassed their goal, raising over $1.6 million.[6]

Much attention was given to the landscape surrounding the temple. At the time of its dedication, the temple was surrounded by more than four acres of lawn and twelve species of transplanted trees as well as ornamental plants, shrubs, and flowers. Because of their great width, twenty-two olive trees had to be moved to the temple site at night under special

Los Angeles California Temple

May all who seek this holy temple come with clean hands and pure hearts that thy holy spirit may ever be present to comfort, to inspire, and to bless. If any with . . . heavy hearts enter, may they depart with their burdens lightened and their faith increased.

—FROM THE DEDICATORY PRAYER

permits. Two of the largest pine trees on the grounds were seventy feet tall. When transplanted, one tree with its soil weighed seventeen tons. The grounds were further beautified by a reflecting pool and a rose garden with roses contributed by the young women of the area.[7]

The building's interior is decorated with eight types of marble, quarried from such diverse places as Vermont, Tennessee, Italy, and France. Original murals are featured throughout the temple. Los Angeles artist Joseph Gibby was commissioned to paint in the temple baptistry a mural of the Savior's baptism by John the Baptist in the River Jordan. As the project neared completion, Gibby spoke with President McKay about a problem he had encountered. "I cannot paint the Savior's face to my satisfaction," he told the prophet. "I need to know his complexion and coloring." Without hesitation, President McKay described the Savior's features.[8]

Millard F. Malin was selected to create the angel Moroni statue for the temple's spire. The nearly fifteen-and-a-half-foot-tall statue was made of aluminum instead of bronze to meet the Los Angeles building code. Still, with gold leaf added, the statue weighed some twenty-one hundred pounds. Malin's angel Moroni has Native American features, wears a Mayan-style cloak, carries the gold plates with his left arm, and with his right hand holds an eight-foot trumpet to his lips.[9]

The architectural plans depicted the statue of the angel Moroni facing southeast, the same direction as the front of the temple. During one of his frequent visits to the temple site, President McKay told the architect and newly appointed temple president that the statue "was not correct in that position" and asked the architect to adjust the statue so that it would face due east.[10]

Public interest in the temple was clearly evident during the temple's fifty-one day open house, when nearly seven hundred thousand people visited the temple. President David O. McKay dedicated the temple 11 to 14 March 1956. The

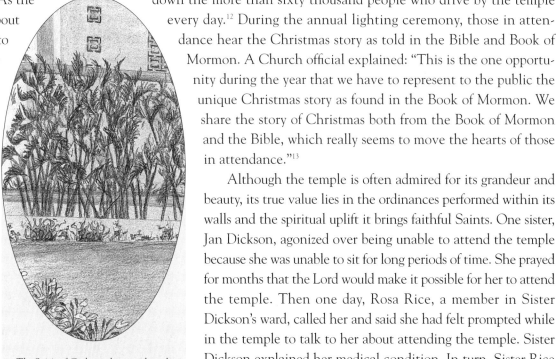

The Spirit of God may be sensed on the peaceful grounds of our latter-day temples. To depict this Spirit, the bushes are drawn as if they were on fire. Flames are also seen along the base of the temple, in the trees, and among the flowers.

proceedings were carried throughout the temple by closed-circuit television. In reference to this technology, President McKay commented, "How easy it must be in the spirit world to tune in on an occasion of this kind."[11]

In recent years, a much-anticipated annual event has brought thousands of people, members and nonmembers alike, to Temple Hill. Each Christmas season nearly half a million lights set the entire grounds ablaze with festivity and celebration. Symbolizing the great light that came into the world through Christ's birth, the lights have been known to slow down the more than sixty thousand people who drive by the temple every day.[12] During the annual lighting ceremony, those in attendance hear the Christmas story as told in the Bible and Book of Mormon. A Church official explained: "This is the one opportunity during the year that we have to represent to the public the unique Christmas story as found in the Book of Mormon. We share the story of Christmas both from the Book of Mormon and the Bible, which really seems to move the hearts of those in attendance."[13]

Although the temple is often admired for its grandeur and beauty, its true value lies in the ordinances performed within its walls and the spiritual uplift it brings faithful Saints. One sister, Jan Dickson, agonized over being unable to attend the temple because she was unable to sit for long periods of time. She prayed for months that the Lord would make it possible for her to attend the temple. Then one day, Rosa Rice, a member in Sister Dickson's ward, called her and said she had felt prompted while in the temple to talk to her about attending the temple. Sister Dickson explained her medical condition. In turn, Sister Rice explained Sister Dickson's situation to the temple presidency, and they gave permission for her to lie on a gurney during the session. Soon Sister Dickson was attending the temple every month. To her friends who made this blessing possible, she said, "Thank you . . . for following the Spirit's prompting, for opening a door I didn't know could be opened."[14]

Hamilton New Zealand Temple

We invoke thy blessing particularly upon the men and women who have so willingly and generously contributed their means, time, and effort to the completion of this imposing and impressive structure. Especially we mention all those who have accepted calls as labor missionaries and literally consecrated their all upon the altar of service. . . . May they be assured that they have the gratitude of thousands, perhaps millions, on the other side for whom the prison doors may now be opened and deliverance proclaimed to those who will accept the truth and be set free.

—FROM THE DEDICATORY PRAYER

Before the missionaries began proselyting among the Maori people in New Zealand, several *Tohungas* (Maori spiritual leaders) told of the coming of the "true religion." In 1879 King Tawhiao of the Waikato said that ministers of the true church would come in the future and would travel two by two. He said, "They will not come to you and return to European accommodations but they will stay with you, talk with you, eat with you, and abide with you."[1] After fasting, meditating, and praying, Paora Potangaroa, an influential spiritual leader of the Ngatikahungunu tribe, foretold that the missionaries would come from the east, travel in pairs, and raise their right arm to the square when performing ordinances. He also said that his people would learn that they were lost sheep of the house of Israel.[2] These are among the many predictions fulfilled with the beginning of Latter-day Saint missionary work among the Maoris in 1881. Several Maoris were baptized in 1882, and the first branch among their people was established in 1883.

LOCATION
Near Hamilton, New Zealand

SITE
86 acres

GROUNDBREAKING
21 December 1955 by Ariel Ballif, Wendell B. Mendenhall, and George R. Biesinger

DEDICATION
20 April 1958
by President David O. McKay

EXTERIOR
Reinforced concrete block painted white

DESIGN
Modern-contemporary

TOTAL FLOOR AREA
34,000 square feet

HAMILTON
NEW ZEALAND

John E. Magleby, president of the New Zealand Mission, made several prophecies concerning the building of a temple in New Zealand. He stated that at some time in the future the Saints in New Zealand would not need a passport to go to the temple.[3] He also declared that "in days to come, Hamilton will be the gathering place of the Saints."[4]

In 1955 President David O. McKay arrived to look for property for a temple site. Of their meeting on the hill west of the Church College of New Zealand, Elder Wendell B. Mendenhall, director of the Church's building program in the Pacific, recalled, "President McKay called me to one side. By the way he was looking at the hill, I could tell immediately what was on his mind. . . . He asked, 'What do you think?' I knew what his question implied, and I simply asked in return, 'What do you think, [President] McKay?' And then in an almost prophetic tone he pronounced, 'This is the place to build the temple.'"[5] Through a series of miraculous events the property was acquired by the Church, and the proposed construction of the temple was announced in September 1955.

The hills where the Church College of New Zealand and the temple are situated were a sacred place to the Maoris and had historically served as a sanctuary from wars. Maori women, children, the aged, and the wounded took refuge there in war time. Traces of this community were discovered during excavation for the temple when bulldozers uncovered a burial ground. The area, located approximately one hundred yards from the temple, was thereafter left undisturbed.[6]

Ground was broken for the temple on 21 December 1955, the first day of summer in the Southern Hemisphere. Work on the temple began immediately, with all of the construction being done by volunteer laborers. Many were experienced builders from throughout the Pacific and the United States who responded to mission calls. Local Saints supported the labor missionaries with food and housing while they worked on the temple.[7] One group of workers decided not to take any days off during a period of particularly heavy rains. Some of them changed their clothes during their lunch break to have dry apparel to work in.[8]

Just as workers on the temple came from many parts of the world, so did the materials from which the temple was built. Timber was shipped from Canada; the baptismal font was built in Switzerland; the finial on the tower was made in London; the marble was quarried and shipped from Italy, Australia, and New Zealand; cement came from the United States; and granite was brought in from Australia.[9]

Workers hurried to finish construction, but it appeared that the building would not be completed in time for the scheduled open house and dedication. Many who had already given their time and energy from dawn to dusk began working even longer shifts. At the peak of the construction, more than four hundred labor missionaries were engaged simultaneously at the neighboring college and the temple. One morning around 2:00, working by the headlights of a truck, a crew of missionaries ran with wheelbarrows of cement to make street curbing so the road crew could begin work the next day.[10] The day before the open house, workers laid carpet and hung wallpaper. Furniture was moved into the temple until 1:00 that morning.[11] Yet the workers agreed that the building project had been even more of a spiritual experience than a temporal one.

Many noteworthy events occurred during the various phases of the building's construction. During the time that the temple's concrete foundation was being poured, many workers witnessed an aberration in the weather. One of them, not a member of the Church, observed: "I have never seen the rain act this way. The rain stops when it comes to this hill. Sometimes the clouds divide and go around the hill."[12] This reprieve from the rains made it possible to work quickly and not lose even one day while the concrete was poured for the foundation.

Soon after topsoil had been spread over the hill in preparation for landscaping, a large storm hit the area, dumping ten inches of rain and washing most of the topsoil from the temple hill. Leaders called on members in the various districts to help fix the damage so that the temple could be finished in time. Some four hundred fifty men, women, and children responded immediately. Within three days the workers had transported all of the topsoil back onto the hill.[13]

During the three-week open house, nearly one hundred thirteen thousand people toured the temple. As the time of the dedication of the temple and the Church College of New Zealand approached, more than six thousand members converged on Hamilton. These Saints enthusiastically greeted President McKay when he arrived with authentic Polynesian dancing and a six-hundred-voice choir number. On 20 April 1958 in his dedicatory prayer, President McKay gave thanks, saying, "We express gratitude that to these fertile Islands Thou didst guide descendants of Father Lehi, and hast enabled them to prosper and to become associated in history with leading and influential nations among mankind."[14]

In early 1986 the temple received three new Maria Theresa Czechoslovakian chandeliers for the celestial room. Each chandelier weighed approximately five hundred pounds and displayed 2,755 pieces of cut crystal. One night, after one chandelier had been hung, temple president Glen L. Rudd woke up with an "uneasy feeling." He said, "I thought to myself, 'something is wrong.' . . . Early the next morning I contacted our temple engineer. He expressed that he too had an uneasy feeling. We went into the temple and looked at the chandelier, and immediately we were able to see that the ceiling was sagging a little from the additional weight it was bearing." Before the other two chandeliers were installed, a structural engineer designed some large plates to correct the problem. President Rudd summarized: "There is no doubt in my mind but what we were impressed by the Spirit of the Lord to the fact that there was a problem and to not hang the other chandeliers until corrections were made."[15]

The Hamilton New Zealand Temple has become an important landmark of Mormonism in New Zealand. It stands as a monument to the Lord Jesus Christ and represents the spiritual inspiration and sacrifice of time, means, and talents of the Latter-day Saints.

London England Temple

An important milestone for British Latter-day Saints came with the construction and dedication of the beautiful London England Temple, located at Newchapel in Surrey. The rectangular temple stands 160 feet high, is faced with beautiful white limestone, and is topped by a lead-coated copper spire. The thirty-two-acre temple site features formal gardens that occupy about one-third of the property. From the time the Church first acquired the property in 1953, it always planned to preserve the estate's formal gardens. Towering oaks listed in a British registry, spacious lawns, an ornamental pond, colorful rhododendrons and azaleas beautify the grounds throughout the year. Temple president A. Hamer Reiser wrote fondly of the natural beauty of the grounds:

"The aromas of Newchapel hover like haloes among the flowers, grasses, shrubs and trees. The fragrances of violets, narcissi, roses, viburnum, spruce and cedar are everywhere. No wonder the butterflies and bees, the blackbirds, thrush, nuthatch, pheasant and waterfowl adopt Newchapel as their special haven.

"The past, the present of all creation are richly in evidence in Newchapel. Time has been liberally vested there: a lovely reminder of the 'lost garden where the world began,' it will henceforward also remind us of the eternal garden to be regained."[1]

The London Temple stands on historic ground that can be traced back to early Christianity.[2] The area around Newchapel was successively occupied by the Celts, Romans, Saxons, and the Danes. Anciently, the property was split in half by the Roman highway that ran between London and the sea. The property was also included in William the Conqueror's *Doomsday Book*, recorded in about 1086, which was instrumental in establishing the feudal system. Old Pilgrim's Way, made famous by Chaucer's *Canterbury Tales*, ran nearby. More recently, the Church rented the horse pastures on the property to Sir Winston Churchill, who had purchased an adjoining estate.[3] Two oak trees on the property—one in the garden and one near the temple—are thought to have existed at the time of Columbus's discovery of the Americas. Before the construction of the temple began, President David O. McKay gave instructions that the five-hundred-year-old tree in front of the temple should not be removed.[4]

The impressive baronial mansion on the grounds, with its flagged floors, hand-hewn oak beams, and wrought-iron fixtures, is referred to as the Manor House and dates back to Elizabethan times.[5] It has served as a home to the temple president and as a bureau of information. In 1985 it became a Missionary Training Center for much of Europe.

After the property was purchased, President David O. McKay and Church architect Edward O. Anderson spent time on the grounds deciding on the best placement for the temple. The site finally selected by President McKay had previously been partially covered by a lily pond, which had left the ground marshy, and the construction engineers feared it would prove unsuitable for the temple's foundation. President McKay, however, insisted that this was where the temple was to be built. Upon further investigation, workers discovered that beneath the boggy ground was solid shale at the proper depth to support the temple. After the discovery, a project engineer commented, "You could build the city of London on that site."[6]

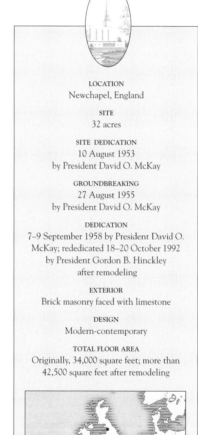

LOCATION
Newchapel, England

SITE
32 acres

SITE DEDICATION
10 August 1953
by President David O. McKay

GROUNDBREAKING
27 August 1955
by President David O. McKay

DEDICATION
7–9 September 1958 by President David O. McKay; rededicated 18–20 October 1992 by President Gordon B. Hinckley after remodeling

EXTERIOR
Brick masonry faced with limestone

DESIGN
Modern-contemporary

TOTAL FLOOR AREA
Originally, 34,000 square feet; more than 42,500 square feet after remodeling

LONDON ENGLAND

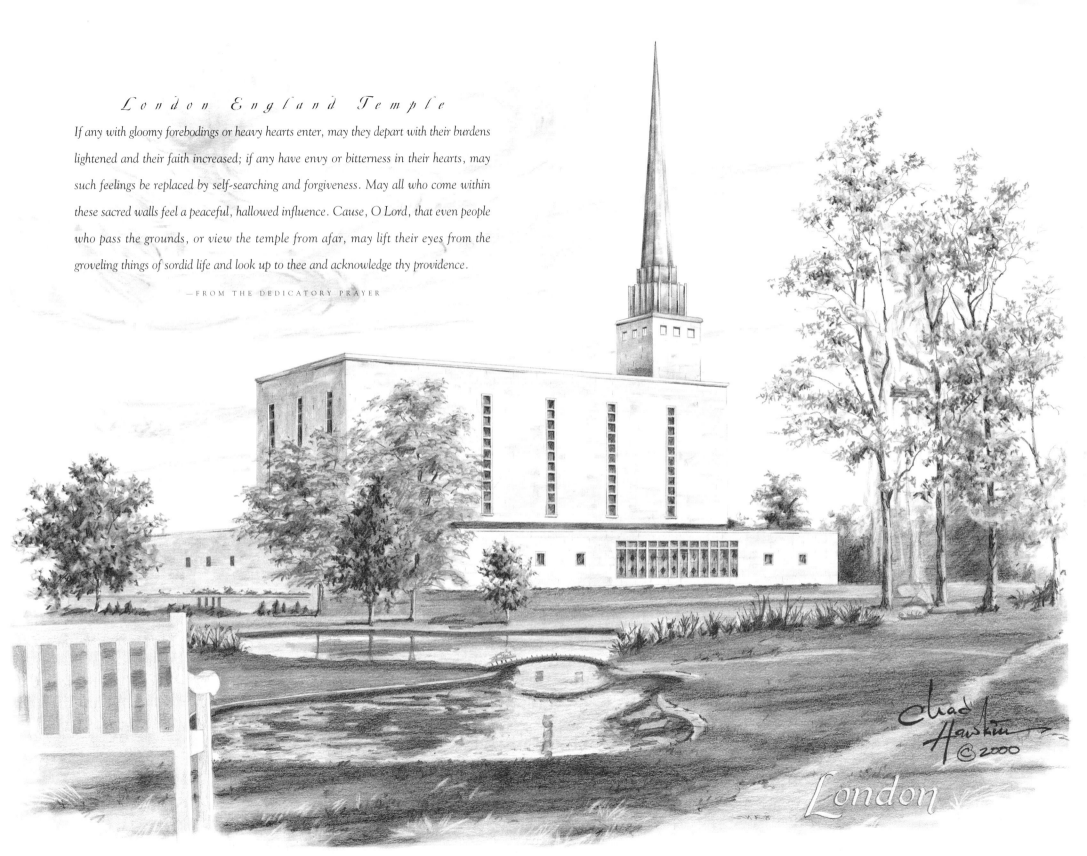

London England Temple

If any with gloomy forebodings or heavy hearts enter, may they depart with their burdens lightened and their faith increased; if any have envy or bitterness in their hearts, may such feelings be replaced by self-searching and forgiveness. May all who come within these sacred walls feel a peaceful, hallowed influence. Cause, O Lord, that even people who pass the grounds, or view the temple from afar, may lift their eyes from the groveling things of sordid life and look up to thee and acknowledge thy providence.

—FROM THE DEDICATORY PRAYER

London

On 10 August 1953, five days after ground was broken for the Bern Switzerland Temple, seventy-nine-year-old President McKay dedicated the site for the London England Temple. Two years later, on 27 August 1955, again visiting Europe, he broke ground for the temple. The services were held under a cove of trees in the garden. The Tabernacle Choir, then on tour in Europe, sang at the groundbreaking.[7]

Fine craftsmen from around England built the temple according to the highest architectural standards of the day. One of these craftsmen observed, "Why, you've put such steel and stone in this building that it might well stand 2,000 years."[8] Summarizing his thoughts on the construction, architect Edward O. Anderson said: "The building of the London Temple recalls stories told about those two fine old temples, the Salt Lake and Manti Temples. The great similarity between them is in workmanship, for they have been built by good craftsmen, who, though of different faiths in the case of the London Temple, have taken great interest in their work. It has been my fortune to work on almost all of the temples in some way, and it is gratifying to say that the workmanship is as fine on the London Temple as on any other."[9]

During the temple's three-week, public open house in 1958, more than seventy-six thousand people toured the temple. Only fifty thousand had been expected, and to accommodate the crowds, the viewing period was extended by several days. On 7 September 1958, four days after the open house ended, the temple was dedicated by President McKay. More than two thousand people filled every available room and listened to the speakers and prayers over a public address system.[10] In the dedicatory prayer, President McKay recognized the fundamental freedoms guaranteed by the Magna Carta: "It

The grounds of the London England Temple are a feast for the eyes. Immaculate gardens, groomed lawns, and evidences of history are visible in every direction. This vignette invites us to step into the scene, rest on the bench, and enjoy the peaceful serenity of the temple grounds. Among the trees is hidden a full-length figure of the Savior.

is fitting that we express appreciation of the signing of the Magna Carta in the County of Surrey, the same county in which we meet today wherein the promise is given that no freeman shall be taken or imprisoned or disseized or outlawed or exiled . . . without proper trial by his peers or by the law of the land."[11]

British Mission president A. Hamer Reiser recognized the hand of the Lord in preparing the way for the London England Temple: "It may seem nothing spectacular or unusual has occurred during the building, but I nevertheless acknowledge the hand of the Lord in every detail. He has worked out His will in very natural ways and brought to pass many, many favourable conditions and factors, that made this project possible."[12]

On 18 October 1992, the London England Temple was rededicated by President Gordon B. Hinckley after being closed for two years for extensive remodeling and refurbishing. A three-week, public open house was held when the work was completed. Advertisements and stories in local and national newspapers, a feature story on the BBC (British Broadcasting Corporation), and some two hundred thousand colored flyers were distributed to every home in the vicinity of the temple. Above a color photograph of the temple were the words, "The last time you could tour this building was in 1958." Beneath the photograph the flyer said, "The next time is for six days during October 1992." Many of the more than fifty-five thousand people who visited this open house had attended the one held thirty-four years earlier.[13] The crowds were so large that some visitors had to wait two and a half hours before touring the edifice. Bryan J. Grant, public affairs director for the Europe North Area, said it was "the best single event in terms of its effect on the general public that we've ever had in Britain."[14]

May they depart with their burdens lightened and their faith increased

Oakland California Temple

The Oakland California Temple rests upon a site that is separate from the noise and bustle of the surrounding metropolis and yet accessible to the millions it serves. The unobstructed view from the East Bay Hills overlooks Oakland, Berkeley, San Francisco, and the waters of the famous bay leading out to the Pacific Ocean through the Golden Gate.

The history of the Oakland California Temple began in the summer of 1924 when Elder George Albert Smith, then a member of the Quorum of the Twelve, visited the San Francisco Bay area. Elder Smith sat on the roof terrace of a hotel with W. Aird MacDonald, a local Church leader. While admiring the view of the bay from atop the hotel, Elder Smith ceased talking and for several minutes gazed intently toward the hills above Oakland. He then said: "Brother MacDonald, I can almost see in vision a white temple of the Lord high upon those hills, an ensign to all the world travelers as they sail through the Golden Gate into this wonderful harbor. . . . A great white temple of the Lord will grace those hills, a glorious ensign to the nations, to welcome our Father's children as they visit this great city."[1]

When this prophecy was made in 1924, the Church in that part of California consisted of only a few small branches, which were struggling to gain a foothold in the community. But the anticipation of a temple in central California brought these Saints hope.

In the April 1943 general conference, President Heber J. Grant announced: "I am happy to tell you that we have purchased in the Oakland area another temple site. . . . The site is located on the lower foothills of East Oakland on a rounded hill overlooking San Francisco Bay. We shall in due course

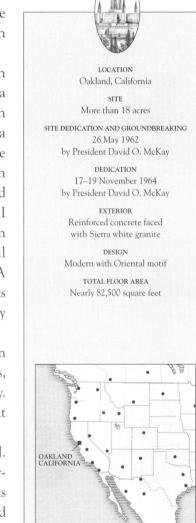

LOCATION
Oakland, California

SITE
More than 18 acres

SITE DEDICATION AND GROUNDBREAKING
26 May 1962
by President David O. McKay

DEDICATION
17–19 November 1964
by President David O. McKay

EXTERIOR
Reinforced concrete faced
with Sierra white granite

DESIGN
Modern with Oriental motif

TOTAL FLOOR AREA
Nearly 82,500 square feet

OAKLAND
CALIFORNIA

build there a splendid temple."[2] A committee was formed and given responsibility to raise funds for the temple. It was suggested for the local stakes to contribute $500,000. The Saints' immediate and generous response demonstrated their enthusiasm for the temple. The San Jose Stake, under the direction of Horace J. Ritchie, raised their entire allotment of $32,000 in a single day.[3] The contributions included the small and heartfelt offerings of Primary children as well as the sizeable contributions of prosperous members. One individual not a member of the Church, made an unsolicited contribution of $3,500.[4] The stakes eventually raised more than $750,000 for the temple.

The Oakland Temple, with two ordinance rooms connected to the celestial room, was the first temple capable of holding more than one endowment session at a time.

The design of the temple's exterior is modern contemporary and has some Oriental influence as well. The towers are perforated and covered in a blue glass mosaic and gold leaf. They present a very striking effect in the sun and at night are illuminated from the spire's interior lighting, transmitting rays of lacy light through the perforations. The second-level roof, with its beautiful garden, provides an incredible view of Oakland, San Francisco, and the San Francisco Bay.

Two sculptured granite panels, heroic in size, are displayed on the temple's north and south facades. The panel on the north depicts Christ and his apostles in the Old World; the south panel shows Christ appearing to the Nephites in the land Bountiful. Lifting and securing the massive panels to the walls of the temple posed an especially difficult problem. The men working on the granite exterior found there was no way to put the twelve-ton panels into place without damaging

Oakland California Temple

This temple . . . is a monument testifying to the faith and loyalty of the members of thy Church in the payment of their tithes and offerings. . . . Accept, O Father, of the contributions from the widow, from the boys and girls . . . May the Spirit that prompted them to give, to serve, be with them throughout their lives, for only by service may they obtain that happiness which passeth understanding.

—FROM THE DEDICATORY PRAYER

Oakland

them. Glen R. Nielsen, a Church member and contractor for the granite exterior, prayed for a solution. "I went to my Father in Heaven with our problem and I asked Him to please show us the way to pick up these panels . . . without accident. One Sunday just before we were going to set the panels I was shown the way we were to pick up the panels. It was as clear to me as if I looked at someone face to face. . . . I knew the exact number of bolts to use, their size, the metal to use and how it was to be constructed."[5]

Careful attention was also given to the landscape around the temple. The attractive grounds feature exotic plants, rose bushes, and citrus trees native to California. Walkways beside fountains and pools of flowing water are flanked by rows of palm trees that direct visitors' attention to the stately grandeur of the temple and lead them to its doors.

During the public open house of the temple, a man arrived in a chauffeured government car and introduced himself as a commander of a ship in the U.S. Navy. He said, "I brought my ship through the Golden Gate early this morning and observed . . . on the foothills of East Oakland, a new landmark which I had not seen before. I immediately berthed my ship and made the necessary arrangements so that I could come here to determine what . . . this new landmark [is]."[6] Some members saw this statement as being a partial fulfillment of Elder George Albert Smith's prophecy that the temple would serve as an ensign to travelers as they entered through the Golden Gate into San Francisco Bay.

When the temple was dedicated on 17 November 1964, most people at the ceremony did not expect President David O. McKay, who had recently suffered a stroke, to offer the dedicatory prayer. His mind was whole, but his physical condition made it very difficult for him to speak or even to stand.

A lighthouse, its beam stretching toward the San Francisco Bay, is drawn among the trees as a reminder of Elder George Albert Smith's prophecy that a temple would be an ensign to ships as they passed under the Golden Gate Bridge from far-flung nations of the earth.

Of these struggles his son said: "His fluency of speech was gone. . . . He hated to talk because nearly always we could not understand him the first time and had to ask him to repeat what he had said." But when it came time to dedicate the temple, President McKay was helped to the pulpit, which he grasped tightly to help him stand, and began to speak clearly and easily to the audience. His son recorded: "[My wife], with tears running down her cheeks, whispered, 'Lawrence, we are witnessing a miracle.' I nodded in agreement. Father finished his talk and, still standing, dedicated the building."[7]

Through the years the Oakland California Temple has been protected from potentially catastrophic natural disasters. The powerful earthquake that shook central California on 17 October 1989 was considered by experts to be the costliest disaster in U.S. history, with damage to the region estimated at $7 billion.[8] But the temple escaped with only a few minor cracks. Two years later, in October 1991, wildfires torched hundreds of homes in the East Bay Hills, causing up to $5 billion in damage. Although the fire devastated the mountain ridge behind the temple, the fire was controlled before it reached the sacred edifice. The temple had been closed the days that the fire burned, and thus no patrons were affected by the chaos that the fire created nearby.[9]

The temple, with its steeples pointing toward the heavens from its seat high on the hills above Oakland, has become a symbol of eternity for those who see it and especially for those who enter its walls. An Oakland California Temple ordinance worker of more than fifteen years stated, "There is an on-going process of learning in the temple. Many of the deeper and more significant principles of life are revealed. Faith is increased. Conviction is attained. A 'nobler estimate of man' is attained. In short, one gets a glimpse of the Celestial Kingdom."[10]

May the Spirit that prompted them to give, to serve, be with them throughout their lives

Ogden Utah Temple

In downtown Ogden, on a corner of the block where the Ogden Utah Temple now stands, is an important part of Utah history. The oldest home in the Intermountain West, a tiny log cabin built by Miles Goodyear two years before the Saints arrived in the Salt Lake Valley, was moved to its present location to commemorate Weber County's first pioneers. Mountainman Goodyear built Fort Buenaventura, a trading post, on the bank of the nearby Weber River. When the vanguard pioneer company neared their destination, President Brigham Young and Porter Rockwell consulted Goodyear on the best route through the mountains. They concluded the trail through Weber Canyon was too treacherous for wagon trains, so they crossed the Wasatch through what is now Emigration Canyon and entered the Salt Lake Valley from the east instead of the north.[1]

The first mention of a temple in Ogden came on 12 December 1920 when Elder Hyrum G. Smith, patriarch to the Church, told the Saints in Ogden that they would one day have a temple. In 1921 President Heber J. Grant inspected potential sites for a temple in Ogden but concluded that the time had not yet come for a temple to be built there.[2] The Saints in the area continued to travel to the Logan Utah Temple to perform their temple work.

During a stake presidents' meeting in Ogden in the early 1960s, President David O. McKay was asked if a temple would be built in that city. Laughing, President McKay responded, "You all know I'm from this area[;] what would the brethren say[?] We need temples all over the world, [so] don't get your hopes up."[3] These remarks caused many of those who heard it to believe that a temple there was still a distant reality;

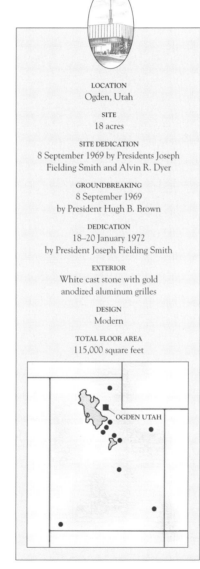

LOCATION
Ogden, Utah

SITE
18 acres

SITE DEDICATION
8 September 1969 by Presidents Joseph Fielding Smith and Alvin R. Dyer

GROUNDBREAKING
8 September 1969
by President Hugh B. Brown

DEDICATION
18–20 January 1972
by President Joseph Fielding Smith

EXTERIOR
White cast stone with gold anodized aluminum grilles

DESIGN
Modern

TOTAL FLOOR AREA
115,000 square feet

OGDEN UTAH

however, President McKay pondered the idea and initiated research on the use of the temples then in operation. The study revealed that 52 percent of all ordinance work was being done in just three of the thirteen existing temples: the Salt Lake, Logan, and Manti temples. Instead of expanding these temples to meet the ever-increasing needs of Church members in northern Utah, the First Presidency decided to build two new temples along the Wasatch Front—one in Ogden and one in Provo. Even though Saints in other areas of the Church had to travel much greater distances to attend the temple, the Brethren decided that adding two temples in Utah would serve the largest number of people.[4]

Church members along the Wasatch corridor in northern Utah were elated to learn of the two new temples, the first to be constructed in Utah since the Salt Lake Temple had been completed in 1893. A site selection committee was formed to find an appropriate location in Ogden. The committee's original desire was to have the Ogden Utah Temple built on an elevation from which the temple could be seen anywhere in the valley. Various sites—one where the McKay-Dee Hospital now stands, another near Weber State University, and several others around the valley—were considered, but each was eliminated. The site finally chosen for the temple was in downtown Ogden on the ten-acre, Church-owned Ogden Tabernacle block. To make room for the temple, the historic pioneer tabernacle on the site had to be demolished. Knowing that removing this landmark might offend some in the community, Church leaders explained the decision at a press conference, emphasizing that although they loved the tabernacle and appreciated its significance in the community, the

Ogden Utah Temple

O Lord our God, unto thee we sing songs of praise and thanksgiving by day and by night! It pleases us that in this our day thou didst send Elijah the prophet, before the second coming of thy Son, to reveal that priesthood and confer those keys whereby thy children may be sealed up unto eternal life. We thank thee that the hearts of the children are now turning to their fathers, and that the ordinances of salvation and exaltation are now being performed in thy holy temples for both the living and the dead.

—FROM THE DEDICATORY PRAYER

Church was a growing organization that could not jeopardize the future in preserving the past.[5] The Church planned to replace the old tabernacle with a new one elsewhere on the same block.

Construction soon began on the Ogden Utah Temple. The design for both it and the Provo Utah Temple was created by Church architect Emil B. Fetzer to maximize efficiency and accommodate the largest possible number of patrons. In this new design, small ordinance rooms on the second floor surround and open into the celestial room at the center of the temple. With six ordinance rooms, this design would make it possible for a session to begin every twenty minutes, accommodating many more patrons each day than any other temple then in operation. And having the two temples nearly identical in design kept construction costs relatively low and made it possible to build them in a short time. Thus, while the Ogden and Provo temples can accommodate as many individuals in a day as the largest temples in the Church, they were built at a fraction of the cost.[6]

The cornerstone was put into place 7 September 1970, attracting one of the largest gatherings in Ogden's history. During the ceremonies President Joseph Fielding Smith commended all who had helped to construct the building. He used the occasion to call on parents to "prepare [their] children for temple marriage."[7] President N. Eldon Tanner echoed President Smith's sentiments and encouraged parents to teach their children the plan of salvation. He described the work that would take place in the completed temple as "the most unselfish work man can do."[8]

The open house took place in December 1971, one month

Rather than being hidden, the clear placement of a couple walking toward the doors of the temple reminds viewers of President Hunter's counsel to "let us truly be a temple-attending and temple-loving people."

before the dedication. Visitors were received in the new Ogden Tabernacle on the north side of the city block. They were then taken through a series of tents, which protected them from inclement weather as they waited to enter the temple. After touring the edifice, they gathered again in the tabernacle, where they could ask questions and talk about their feelings after having seen the temple's beautiful interior.[9]

Since its dedication on 18 through 20 January 1972 by President Smith, the Ogden Utah Temple has become one of the most productive temples in the Church. It has become an integral part of downtown Ogden's makeup and reminds passersby of eternal things. An *Ensign* article published soon after the temple was dedicated aptly describes the significance of this temple in northern Utah: "Centrally located in downtown Ogden amidst the businesses and institutions of man, the Ogden Temple effectively symbolizes the power of the gospel to reach down and out to the daily life of each of us, to bless, guide, and protect us as we walk and work and live in the real work-a-day world. The temple's modern design and materials focus our attention on the covenants made within rather than on monumentality or pioneer origins many think of with nineteenth-century temples. It testifies, architecturally, that a temple is more than a style or collection of symbols."[10]

Latter-day Saint philosopher and Brigham Young University professor Truman G. Madsen said: "The Temple is not just a union of heaven and earth. It is the key to our mastery of the earth. It is the Lord's graduate course in subduing the earth, which as only we understand ultimately will be heaven—this earth glorified."[11]

Provo Utah Temple

As the early Saints settled Utah Valley and began developing Provo City, they grew anxious for a temple in their midst. For years the area on the hill where Brigham Young University now stands was known as Temple Hill. President Brigham Young is credited with saying: "We have ascended to the summit of this beautiful Hill and now you are standing on Holy Ground. The day will come when a Magnificent Temple will be erected here to our God and I want you to look and behold the scenic beauty of this wonderful Valley."[1]

In the early 1960s stake presidents in Utah Valley and nearby areas were called to a meeting with the First Presidency, who spoke with them confidentially about building a temple in Provo. Ben E. Lewis, one of those stake presidents, was assigned to chair the site-selection committee and raise funds from local Church members for a temple. President Lewis spoke privately after the meeting with President N. Eldon Tanner about a site he knew was available.

Some years before, a German immigrant named Leathy, who owned several acres of land near Rock Canyon on Provo's east bench, had approached President Lewis after having a vivid dream in which a beautiful temple was erected on his property. He had been so moved by the dream that he offered the land to President Lewis for a temple site. President Lewis, involved in BYU and Church land acquisition in Provo, communicated the information to President Harold B. Lee, who declined the offer. Instead, the property was purchased for BYU so that it would be available for expansion or if circumstances changed, a temple site.

When President Tanner heard of the dream and the subsequent transaction, he was interested in the information but suggested considering other sites as well. After examining various sites around Provo, the committee recommended unanimously that the temple be placed on the Leathy property near Rock Canyon. But two concerns were soon raised. The Church Building Committee thought the temple should be located next to the Provo Tabernacle, just as the temple in Ogden would be situated next to the Ogden Tabernacle. Geologists pointed out that the proposed site was on the Wasatch fault line, and they feared a temple built there could be seriously damaged or destroyed during an earthquake. President Lewis and the committee, however, felt that the site on the hillside would be a more visible setting for the temple and that any temple site in Provo would be seriously affected if a major earthquake hit the area. Eventually the matter was referred to President Tanner. After due consideration, he decided that the temple should be built on the site on Provo's east bench.[2] The temple by Rock Canyon would become a spiritual beacon to all of Utah County.

When President McKay announced the new temple to the members of the Church, the response to fund-raising was immediate. An *Ensign* article reported on the Saints' enthusiasm for the temples in both Provo and Ogden: "One bishop discussed the quota for his ward in priesthood meeting, and by the time Sunday School was over, the total quota had been contributed in cash. One family had saved for a special vacation, but they voted in their family home evening to donate the total amount to the temple fund and save again for their postponed vacation. For Christmas of 1967 many families gave to the temple fund rather than to each other. Piggy banks were emptied, children's savings accounts were donated, and the widow's mite was contributed to make these beautiful buildings a reality."[3]

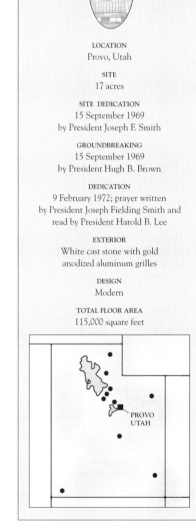

LOCATION
Provo, Utah

SITE
17 acres

SITE DEDICATION
15 September 1969
by President Joseph F. Smith

GROUNDBREAKING
15 September 1969
by President Hugh B. Brown

DEDICATION
9 February 1972; prayer written
by President Joseph Fielding Smith and
read by President Harold B. Lee

EXTERIOR
White cast stone with gold
anodized aluminum grilles

DESIGN
Modern

TOTAL FLOOR AREA
115,000 square feet

PROVO
UTAH

Provo Utah Temple

We turn our faces to this holy house, and we plead with thee to make us worthy to inherit the fullness of those blessings found only in thy holy temples, even those blessings which grow out of the continuation of the family unit forever. Thou knowest, O Father, that we seek these blessings, not only for ourselves and our descendants, but also for our forebears; for thou hast said that we, as saviors on Mount Zion, have power to save and redeem our worthy dead.

—FROM THE DEDICATORY PRAYER

PROVO TEMPLE
THE CHURCH OF JESUS CHRIST
OF LATTER-DAY SAINTS

Ground was broken for the temple in Provo on 15 September 1969 by President Hugh B. Brown, and construction soon began. Like the Ogden temple, the Provo temple is of a modern design and has a highly efficient layout that can accommodate a large number of patrons at one time. The exterior features white cast stone, bronze panels, and a single gold-anodized aluminum spire. Yet careful inspection of the exterior decoration shows differences in design. The temple in Provo has a bas-relief floral motif in its cast-stone walls and single tower; the walls and tower of the temple in Ogden have a fluted appearance. Both feature directional glass, so that during the daytime the windows reflect a golden luster when seen from the outside. At night, when the internal light exceeds the exterior light, the windows are draped and the temples are illuminated with floodlights. Their shining white walls and single golden spires are visible for miles.[4]

Almost a quarter of a million visitors toured the temple during the twenty days it was open to the public. The dedicatory prayer, written by President Joseph Fielding Smith, was read by President Harold B. Lee on 9 February 1972. Because members could view the dedication on closed-circuit television in many locations, including Brigham Young University's Marriott Center, which seated 23,000, only two dedicatory

Hidden in the mountains overlooking the temple is an image of Christ inviting all to come unto him. His arms can be seen in the mountain ridges with the shadows forming the folds in his robe.

sessions were required to accommodate all who wished to attend the services.

In October 1993 President Gordon B. Hinckley said that the Provo Utah Temple is the "busiest temple in the Church."[5] But even with the incredible number of ordinances performed every day in the Provo Utah Temple, patrons enjoy peace and tranquility within its walls. According to Arthur S. Anderson, a past president of the Provo Utah Temple, the amount of temple work performed and the reverent atmosphere maintained in the temple are largely due to the more than two thousand workers who regularly serve in the temple. President Anderson gave an example of one dedicated temple worker from Heber City. One wintry day the worker couldn't make the twenty-eight-mile drive through Provo Canyon because of a storm that had closed the canyon. Instead of missing his shift that day, he took the circuitous route north to Park City, west to Salt Lake City, and then south to Provo. He traveled one hundred miles, not twenty-eight, to perform his temple duties.[6]

Countless other examples of selfless dedication to temple work may be told of the Saints in the Provo temple district, who rejoiced to have a temple in their midst, in fulfillment of the words of a prophet of God.

Thou hast said that we, as saviors on Mount Zion, have power to save and redeem our worthy dead

Washington D.C. Temple

In a city famous for its monuments to freedom, the Washington D. C. Temple was designed as a monument to the Lord, the Source of that freedom. The sixteenth temple of the Church has become one of the most prominent landmarks in the vicinity of the District of Columbia. Sitting amid lush greenery atop one of the highest points in the area, the temple can be seen by millions every year who travel on the Capital Beltway (Interstate 495). The seven-story structure rises 288 feet, making it the tallest temple in the Church. It is thirty feet taller than the Washington Monument.[1] A woman visiting from Florida observed, "Your Temple preaches a profound sermon without saying a word."[2]

The site for the temple was secured in 1962 for $850,000. It is situated on a wooded hill overlooking beautiful Rock Creek Park. Only eleven of the fifty-two acres were cleared for construction, thus separating the temple from the distractions of the metropolitan area nearby. Ornately landscaped with numerous varieties of trees, flowers, and shrubs, the temple has received several prestigious landscaping awards.

In January 1969, a few weeks after the groundbreaking, a committee was formed to raise $4.5 million from the Saints living in the temple district. The remainder of the projected $15 million needed to build the temple would come from the general tithing funds of the Church. The Saints responded enthusiastically. Contributions poured in from people all over the eastern United States. An eleven-year-old girl from Mississippi gave her stake president a cloth bag that contained eighty dollars, which she had earned by baby-sitting. A large donation came from a wealthy Michigan banker in the form of stocks. Members eventually contributed more than $6 million to the temple fund.[3]

A team of four Utah architects was organized to create a

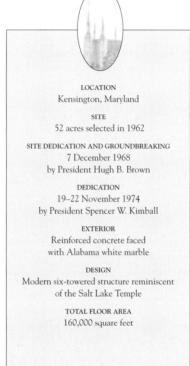

LOCATION
Kensington, Maryland

SITE
52 acres selected in 1962

SITE DEDICATION AND GROUNDBREAKING
7 December 1968
by President Hugh B. Brown

DEDICATION
19–22 November 1974
by President Spencer W. Kimball

EXTERIOR
Reinforced concrete faced
with Alabama white marble

DESIGN
Modern six-towered structure reminiscent
of the Salt Lake Temple

TOTAL FLOOR AREA
160,000 square feet

structure that would impress upon viewers the grandeur of the gospel plan and the strength of the growing Church. For the temple to stand prominently above the surrounding wooded area, it would need to be quite tall. Accordingly, they designed the body of the temple to a height of 120 feet. They later learned that local building ordinances set 120 feet as the maximum height for buildings in that area.[4]

Keith W. Wilcox described the architects' desires for the temple: "Our constant prayer was that the Washington Temple would 'glow with the spirit of enlightenment,' and that it would 'truly represent the majesty, dignity and vital message of the Church to all the world.'"[5] Elsewhere Brother Wilcox said, "I have a feeling of deep humility, realizing that we have been instruments in the Lord's hands in helping to give direction to the design of one of his temples."[6]

The Washington D. C. Temple is reminiscent of the Salt Lake Temple, with its six towers and similar shape. The towers on both temples symbolize the priesthood, the higher eastern towers representing the Melchizedek Priesthood and the western towers representing the Aaronic. The temple's vertical lines are a visual representation of our relationship to Deity.[7]

On the east and west ends of the temple are seven-foot-wide, W-shaped windows that run from the ground all the way to the top of the temple. Near the ground, the glass colored in rich and vibrant reds and oranges that give way to progressively lighter tones of blue, violet, and finally white. This succession of colors suggests the way the temple can shift visitors' minds from earthly concerns to thoughts of eternity. The windows rise unbroken to the top of the building, symbolizing the possibility of man's eternal growth.[8]

Washington D.C. Temple

We are so grateful, our Father, that thy Son has thrown wide open the doors of the prisons for the multitudes who are waiting in the spirit world. Wilt thou deign to make this temple thy house and let holy angels visit it to deliver thy messages, as the rushing of mighty winds with power and glory.

—FROM THE DEDICATORY PRAYER

Washington
D.C.

Avard Fairbanks's representation of the angel Moroni was chosen from nine different designs. Positioned atop the temple, the statue holds a trumpet to its lips with one arm; in the other are the gold plates. "I wanted the angel Moroni statue to conform to the spirit and architecture of the temple, that of aspiring upward," Fairbanks said. "I wanted the feeling of that upward reach, accomplished by the stress of vertical lines."[9] Fairbanks's three-foot model was enlarged in Italy and cast in bronze before a gold-leaf finish was added. When complete, the eighteen-foot statue weighed approximately two tons. A smaller bronze casting of this statue was used on the Seattle Washington, Jordan River Utah, and México City México Temples.[10]

During the construction process in early 1973, leaders became concerned with security at the site. On a Saturday about this time a stray German shepherd appeared near the temple gates. Residents in the area called animal control to pick up the dog, but when work began again the next Monday morning, the dog was still there. Taking pity on the hungry dog, workers fed him and decided to keep him on the site. Zacharias, as the workers named him, soon became an important part of the temple construction site's security. After sleeping during the day, the dog regularly woke at 4 P.M. to watch the workers depart. Then the dog made rounds on the property throughout the night. On one occasion, Zacharias led a security man to the temple president's office, where a fire was burning, apparently caused by a mishap with welding equipment. When the temple was completed, one of the workers took the trusted dog home with him. The construction foremen said they believed that the faithful German shepherd was sent by the Lord to help meet security needs at the temple site.[11]

The succession of colors in the windows represents the purity that comes as we leave behind earthly concerns to enter the temple. The Lord says, "Every soul who forsaketh his sins and cometh unto me . . . shall see my face and know that I am" (D&C 93:1). An image of Christ in the clouds symbolizes the promise of this verse.

As the structure of the temple began to rise above the trees, travelers on the Beltway became interested in this new and imposing building. A stream of visitors to the construction site encouraged Church leaders to finish a visitors' center on the grounds even before the temple itself was completed. The surplus from money raised by the Saints for the temple provided for two-thirds of the cost of the visitors' center. Church leaders dedicated the new center on 3 July 1976, one day before the United States bicentennial. During its first year of operation, the center welcomed more than 115,000 visitors, many of them not members of the Church.[12]

Because of the temple's proximity to the nation's capital, the first week of the open house was set aside for government officials from the United States and other countries. Betty Ford, wife of United States president Gerald R. Ford, participated in one of these tours and asked to have her photograph taken with President Spencer W. Kimball. Nearly three-quarters of a million people visited the temple during its seven-week open house.[13]

The Washington D. C. Temple was dedicated in ten sessions 19 to 22 November 1974, becoming the first modern temple in use east of the Mississippi River. For years the Washington D.C. Temple served all Church members living in the eastern United States and Canada and in all of South America. During its first twenty-five years of operation, some 38,520 marriages were performed in this temple.[14] To the public as well as to the Saints who participate in its sacred ordinances, the Washington D. C. Temple has become "a light unto the world."

. . . let holy angels visit it to deliver thy messages

São Paulo Brazil Temple

We thank thee that thou didst bring Father Lehi and his family to this land of promise and thou didst establish thy people, the Nephites and the Lamanites and their Book of Mormon. Lord, we regard with intense and indescribable feelings the completion of this holy temple. Please accept and bless it with holiness. We are jubilant and have hearts filled with praise to thee that thou hast permitted us to see this day for which we have hoped and toiled and prayed.

—FROM THE DEDICATORY PRAYER

"I have an important announcement," President Spencer W. Kimball said even before the opening hymn and prayer of the Brazil area conference in 1975. "A temple will be built in Brazil, it will be built [here] in São Paulo."[1]

The audience gasped, and many began to weep as he unveiled a painting of the planned temple. Elder L. Tom Perry called this "the greatest audience reaction I have ever seen."[2]

Twelve months later, Elder James E. Faust, then an Assistant to the Twelve and the South American area supervisor, broke ground for the temple as more than two thousand visitors looked on. Although the ceremony took place only a few hundred yards from some of the busiest traffic in bustling São Paulo, the Saints' enthusiastic singing of "We Thank Thee, O God, for a Prophet" and "The Spirit of God" overshadowed the noise and brought a peaceful spirit to the groundbreaking.[3]

To take part in the building of the first temple on their continent since the end of Book of Mormon times, Saints from all over South America made significant sacrifices to donate

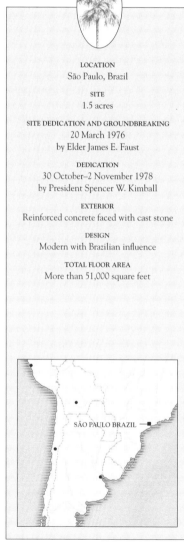

LOCATION
São Paulo, Brazil

SITE
1.5 acres

SITE DEDICATION AND GROUNDBREAKING
20 March 1976
by Elder James E. Faust

DEDICATION
30 October–2 November 1978
by President Spencer W. Kimball

EXTERIOR
Reinforced concrete faced with cast stone

DESIGN
Modern with Brazilian influence

TOTAL FLOOR AREA
More than 51,000 square feet

SÃO PAULO BRAZIL

to the temple fund. Elder James E. Faust noted that many followed the Lord's earlier counsel to the Saints in Kirtland: "Come . . . with all your gold, and your silver, and your precious stones . . . and build a house to my name" (D&C 124:26–27).

"They didn't have any money to contribute to the temple fund, or, the money that they managed to save wasn't worth much because of inflation," Elder Faust said. "So they started offering their wedding rings, bracelets, gold medals, diamond rings, graduation rings and many other personal objects of gold, silver and precious stones. One member of the Church in Argentina even offered his gold dental cap."[4] When the Saints in South America had reached 60 percent of their quota for donation, a member in São Paulo said: "A lot of [the members] already contributed everything they had. From now on they will have to start giving what they don't have. That is where the real sacrifice will begin."[5]

Evidence of that sacrifice shines forth from the temple's shimmering white exterior, the work of eight hundred members who, financially unable to import white stone, donated their time to produce on site fifty thousand blocks of cast stone composed of quartz, marble, and white concrete. The high quality of construction required by the Church for the temple set new building standards for the city. "I have never seen anything like it before," commented Josef Weinberger, the nonmember engineer of the project. "It is the most perfect building I have ever seen."[6]

Architects went to great lengths to make the temple sturdy (its foundation is said to be strong enough to sustain thirteen additional stories) and capable of withstanding a major earthquake with minimal damage. At the time, Brazil was considered an earthquake-free country, but during the construction a small earthquake shook downtown São Paulo. The following day newspapers were filled with articles by local scientists saying that more earthquakes of a greater magnitude were likely in the future.[7]

The marble cornerstone with gold lettering that reads "Erigido 1976–1978" was put into place on 9 March 1978 by President Marion G. Romney. He told the Saints who had gathered for the event that though this was the first temple in South America in modern times, temples had existed anciently in those lands. He also instructed the Saints about the temple's purpose. There, he said, "we inherit the potential to rise to Godhood. We covenant with God to obey all the laws of the gospel. . . . If we strictly obey the covenants we shall be saved in His kingdom and exalted in the heavens. In short we shall inherit eternal lives."[8]

When the temple was dedicated, President Spencer W. Kimball said, "I believe the Lord's Spirit is very close to us: He may be here in person. It would not be the first of the temples built to Him that He has occupied."[9]

Even with the temple in South America, many Saints have had to make great sacrifice to travel long distances to the temple. One memorable journey to the temple began on an early morning in November 1992 as a small passenger boat cast off from the pier at the Port of Manaus, a Brazilian city deep in the heart of the Amazon jungle. One hundred and two anxious Latter-day Saints were on board as the boat traveled down a network of rivers, finally reaching the powerful Amazon. Because these Saints' limited resources made air travel impossible, they had undertaken a nearly four-thousand-mile journey requiring six days and nights of continuous travel by boat and bus to reach the temple. The adults passed the time by reading the scriptures while the children played on the boat's small upper deck. On the third day, the passengers celebrated the eighth birthday of one of the children. The boat stopped at a port, and after checking to be sure the water was free of piranhas, the father of the young girl baptized and confirmed her a member of the Church. On the fourth day, the Saints left the boat and boarded a waiting bus. The ride was anything but comfortable as they traveled for another two days.

Arriving at the temple, they immediately got to the work that had brought them on their journey. Basking in the spirit of temple service almost constantly for four days, the group prepared to leave. Their hearts were overflowing with reverence and gratitude for the ordinances they had performed in that sacred edifice. At the end of another six days and nights of travel, these stalwart Saints arrived safely back in Manaus, forever changed by their journey.[10]

Temple president Athos Marques de Amorim related a story of a family from Paraguay who had exceptional faith and determination to obtain temple blessings. The poor family had spent all their resources to make the long bus trip. When the bus reached São Paulo, however, the family missed the appropriate stop and were taken to the central bus station some seventeen miles from their destination. Because they didn't have enough money to take a bus back to the temple, the family, most of whom were barefoot, walked the distance back to the temple. They were overjoyed when they finally reached their destination. Instead of asking for any relief from their exhausting journey, they said simply that they wanted to be sealed together as a family. While the family was in São Paulo, Church members there collected clothing and shoes to give them. When the family returned to Paraguay, they felt spiritually recompensed for their journey to the temple, which had cost them all that they had.[11]

These sacrifices represent the love that South American Saints feel for the Lord as he extends blessings to his children through the ordinances of the temple. The São Paulo Brazil Temple has become a great symbol both of the Lord's love for his people and of their commitment to him.

We regard with intense and indescribable feelings the completion of this holy temple

Tokyo Japan Temple

Kind Father, bless all those who come to this temple, that they may do so with humble hearts, in cleanliness, and honor, and integrity. We are grateful for these saints, for their devotion and their faith, for their worthiness and their determination to be pure and holy. . . . Bless this temple that it may be a house of prayer, a house of fasting, a house of faith, a house of glory, a house of eternal marriage, a house of sealings, and thy house, the house of God, wherein thy holy saving work may be done for the salvation of both the living and the dead.

—FROM THE DEDICATORY PRAYER

Soon after World War II ended, the Church reopened its mission in Japan with headquarters in the devastated city of Tokyo. In 1948 mission president Edward L. Clissold purchased an old building that had been hit by two bombs during the war. Though the building had to be completely reconstructed, the property was ideal for a mission home because of its proximity to several embassies and a beautiful park across the street. In 1949 Elder Matthew Cowley of the Quorum of the Twelve Apostles stood in the library of the newly completed mission headquarters and offered the dedicatory prayer. In his prayer he was inspired to prophesy, "There will some day be many Church buildings, and even temples in [Japan]."[1]

Considering the Church's condition in Japan at that time, this prediction was truly a wonder to those who heard it. Twenty-five years later at the Japan area conference in 1974, President Spencer W. Kimball announced: "We bring you a matter of grave importance to all the people of the Asian countries and the world. Brother Matthew Cowley, one of the Twelve Apostles,

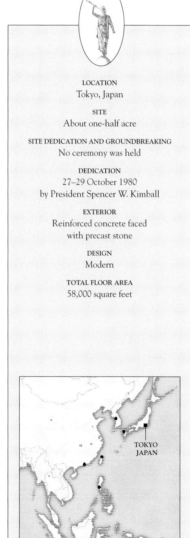

LOCATION
Tokyo, Japan

SITE
About one-half acre

SITE DEDICATION AND GROUNDBREAKING
No ceremony was held

DEDICATION
27–29 October 1980
by President Spencer W. Kimball

EXTERIOR
Reinforced concrete faced
with precast stone

DESIGN
Modern

TOTAL FLOOR AREA
58,000 square feet

TOKYO
JAPAN

made a prediction that there would be temples in Asia and in Japan. . . . And many of us have been almost holding our breath until the time could come when we could build a temple in this land. We, therefore, propose to you assembled here that we establish a temple in Tokyo, Japan, for all of Asia."[2] Although generally reserved in their outward reactions, the Japanese Saints spontaneously broke into applause and wept for joy.

Members all over Asia and the northern Pacific expressed their joy at the announcement. Baltazar G. Frederico, who was then serving as a branch president in the Philippines, declared: "Now I can work for the building of a temple. I have been saving every penny I could since December to save for a trip to the temple in Hawaii or New Zealand. But now I will work for the temple in Japan and take my family there." He noted that the announcement of a temple brought "warm brightness" to his life.[3] One Japanese Saint, a husband and the father of three teenage children, exclaimed, "I can't express in words what this means to us as a family. We will be able to be sealed together in two or three years when the temple is finished. I can't believe it yet."[4]

Work soon began at the temple site across from picturesque Arisugawa Park, just a few miles from downtown Tokyo, and on the very spot where Elder Cowley had made his prophecy of temples in Japan, a prophecy that was further fulfilled with the dedication of the Fukuoka Japan Temple on 11 June 2000. Materials for building the Tokyo Japan Temple were gathered from all over the world. The tower and the ornate entranceway were built from granite native to Japan and from onyx from Mexico. Black quartz from the Andes Mountains in South America was imported to use in the outer walls, and the stained glass windows were created in Seattle, Washington. The international flavor of the temple extends to the interior, which is furnished with carpets woven in the United States, decorative glass imported from Ohio and France, and chandeliers for the celestial room created in Czechoslovakia.[5]

Crowded living conditions and shortage of land in Tokyo prompted the Church to develop unique features for the building, including a parking garage and an apartment for the temple president. The temple, which cost ten million dollars to build, met the highest construction standards and was reported at the time to be the most earthquake-resistant building in the city.

Five years after announcing the Tokyo Japan Temple, President Kimball dedicated it on 27 October 1980. The ceremony was considered by the Saints to be the most important event in the history of Asia.[6] In the midst of a lengthy tour of the Far East, the eighty-five-year-old prophet was nonetheless able to stand at the pulpit for some fifty-three minutes to deliver the dedicatory address and prayer. In his address, he counseled the Japanese Saints:

"It would be foolish to come to the dedication of a temple and not make up our minds that we aren't just here for a visit; we are here to receive the word of the Lord. And from this hour," he continued, "to the end of our days, we pledge ourselves that we will live the commandments of the Lord and see that our children are properly taught so that they will also enjoy the great happiness that can come only through living the commandments."[7]

Attending the dedication was Elder Gordon B. Hinckley, who had long been responsible for the Saints in Asia. He predicted, "This nation will be blessed because this temple stands on its soil. This people will be blessed because of its presence."[8]

A year and a half later, eighty-nine-year-old Sakae Nagao's dreams were fulfilled when she was sealed to her husband, Yoshio Nagao. Sister Nagao had joined the Church in 1912, eleven years after the Japan Mission was opened by Elder Heber J. Grant in 1901. Her husband had not been a member and for years was indifferent to the Church.

"I never gave up," she said of her efforts to teach her husband the gospel. "It was my dream to be sealed to Yoshio for eternity. I knew I had to stay true to the gospel and to keep working on him."

Soon after the temple was dedicated, her efforts were rewarded, and Yoshio was baptized. Then, in March 1982, the couple was sealed in the temple. "I have waited for today," Sister Nagao said as she left the temple. "Now I can die happy. . . . This is the most wonderful thing that has ever happened to me."[9]

An editorial in the *Church News* discussed the significance of the Tokyo Japan Temple to the Saints in Asia:

"The construction and dedication of that sacred temple is both momentous and portentous. It portends a new day for the Orient, an extension of the light of Christ in that region such as never has been known before. . . .

"This is not just another temple. It is not just another dedication. It is the opening of an era, the extension of a dispensation, the dawning of a day when millions of Oriental people may have access to the Savior and His Atonement through the only ordinances that can save—those of His one and only true Church. . . .

"Now [members in the Orient] can enter their own sealing rooms and be married for all eternity. Now families may gather there and be bound together for eternity by their own priesthood brethren officiating in their own sealing rooms—a thing that has never been done before. . . .

" . . . They are entitled to salvation. They cannot achieve its fulness without a temple, and now they have their own. . . .

" . . . What a testimony to the love of God for all his children—everywhere."[10]

Seattle Washington Temple

Seattle, the most populous city in the state of Washington, is located between Puget Sound and Lake Washington. The temple was built in the suburb of Bellevue on more than twenty-three acres of pristine woodlands. With the exception of the area cleared for the temple and a stake center, the rest of the surrounding forest has been left undisturbed. Visitors to the temple walk on paths through the tall trees and native vegetation and enjoy the forest's beauty. To make the building harmonious with the surrounding trees, the architect used vertical lines throughout the exterior and interior of the temple.

A temple in the Pacific Northwest had initially been proposed to the First Presidency by a group of stake presidents in 1960 during the administration of President David O. McKay. But no action was taken until 1974, when the First Presidency assigned F. Arthur Kay, then a regional representative, to locate property suitable for a temple. The search for a site was a lengthy process and was at times very discouraging. In December 1974, as Brother Kay walked with his real estate agent to the agent's office, the property just behind the building caught his eye. In his journal he recorded:

"My eyes were drawn to it. I noticed immediately that it was situated higher than its surrounding property. It was heavily wooded with fir, hemlock, cedar, madronna, and alder trees. There were flowering cherry and numerous other species of trees and shrubs. I pointed to this beautiful hillside and I remarked to Mr. Cade [the real estate agent], 'You know, what we're really looking for is a piece of property just like this one above us, just behind your office!' I was impressed to say, 'Could this property possibly be for sale? Who owns it? What would it be worth?' Mr. Cade did not know but said he would

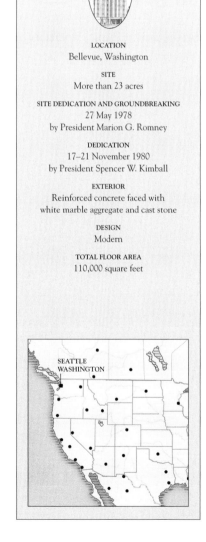

LOCATION
Bellevue, Washington

SITE
More than 23 acres

SITE DEDICATION AND GROUNDBREAKING
27 May 1978
by President Marion G. Romney

DEDICATION
17–21 November 1980
by President Spencer W. Kimball

EXTERIOR
Reinforced concrete faced with
white marble aggregate and cast stone

DESIGN
Modern

TOTAL FLOOR AREA
110,000 square feet

SEATTLE
WASHINGTON

find out. We drove around the property for the first time. Together we walked over and through and around the property. I knew plainly we had found the temple site."[1] When the owner of the property was contacted, he said that he had never considered selling the parcel. When the Church approached him about buying the property, however, he said that he would sell if the offering price seemed right to him.[2]

President Spencer W. Kimball's announcement on 15 November 1975 that a temple would be built in the Pacific Northwest was the third such announcement that year. Earlier he had announced temples for São Paulo, Brazil, and Tokyo, Japan. Saints in the temple district were excited by the news and eager to contribute to the building fund. One stake president said, "We have been looking forward to this for a long time. I can only describe the feeling of our members as one of elation. Some stakes in this area have had temple funds operative for some time. . . . After President Kimball's announcement there was a great rush of donations by the Saints."[3]

In addition to the general temple fund, several other fundraising projects were begun to pay for various elements of the temple project. One individual donated the money required to purchase the eighteen chandeliers that would be needed. Through individual contributions Relief Society sisters in the temple district donated sixty thousand dollars to purchase three life-size statues. Part of the *Monument to Women* series, the statues depict women fulfilling their role in the home and society.[4]

As the temple progressed, several details were added to beautify and give special symbolic meaning to the sacred edifice. On the exterior walls are high-relief sculptures of stalks of

Seattle Washington Temple

Bless, we pray thee, the presidency of this temple and the matron and all the officiators herein. Help them to create a sublime and holy atmosphere so that all ordinances may be performed with love and a sweet, spiritual tone that will cause the members to greatly desire to be here, and to return again and again.

—FROM THE DEDICATORY PRAYER

Seattle

wheat that appear to be growing out of the ground. These symbolize Christ, who is the "bread of life" (John 6:35).[5] In the foyer is an original oil painting by artist Greg Olsen entitled *The Transfiguration*. Also on display is a stone from the original Nauvoo Temple and a copy of the first edition of the Book of Mormon.

Various groups opposing the temple attempted to hinder construction throughout the entire planning and building process. Problems arose even before the Church had formally acquired the property. Initial concerns centered on the effect on trees and wildlife on the property. Another concern had to do with the height of the building. Because the temple was situated not far from a small airport, opponents argued that the spire would obstruct the flight path of airplanes approaching and leaving the airport. The Bellevue city planning department recommended that the temple be greatly reduced in height and built in a less prominent location on the property. The Church reduced the planned height of the single spire and proposed that a strobe light be placed at the base of the angel Moroni statue to make the tower visible to aircraft. In the end permission was granted for the Church to build the temple. When the city of Bellevue announced this decision, members of a nearby residential neighborhood filed a lawsuit against the city to reverse the approval. The lawsuit was dismissed.

Finally, on 13 August 1976, the Church closed on purchasing the property. F. Arthur Kay, who became the temple's first president, commented about these events, "I felt the influence of the adversary so strongly that it caused the very hairs on the back of my neck to stand straight up. But in time, the spirit of the Lord would prevail and assure me that in the end, all would be well."[6]

Among the trees and native vegetation of the Seattle Washington Temple grounds is an area affectionately referred to as "the grove." Linking this setting to the Sacred Grove, a representation of Joseph Smith's first vision is hidden in the grove of trees to the left of the temple.

Formal approval did not end the bitter opposition to the temple and the Church. Because of the Church's stance against the proposed Equal Rights Amendment, regular demonstrations were held outside the temple gates. When picketers attempted to block the entrance on the first day of the open house, some of them had to be physically removed. Despite the protest, well over half a million visitors toured the temple during the month-long open house. Later, on the first day of the temple's dedication, 17 November 1980, protesters attempted to chain themselves to the gates, but their efforts failed, and twenty-one were arrested.

While opposition raged outside, President Spencer W. Kimball counseled the Saints gathered within the temple's walls, saying, "Temples are a place of peace and holiness. Let us lay aside the cares and worries of the outside world. We can then center our minds on the things of the Spirit as the great mysteries of life are unfolded to us. Here we learn the answers to those important questions that puzzle all mankind. Where did we come from? Why are we here? Where do we go when this mortal life is finished and over? . . . We are here to receive the word of the Lord."[7]

The tremendous opposition only solidified the Saints' commitment to the temple and the ordinances performed in it. One hundred thousand endowments were performed in less than six months after the temple opened—double the number that had been expected by the temple committee.[8] This dedication to the temple and the sacred ordinances that are performed in it demonstrates both the faithfulness and the gratitude of the Saints in the Pacific Northwest for the Seattle Washington Temple.

. . . that all ordinances may be performed with love and a sweet spiritual tone

Jordan River Utah Temple

Even with the dedication of two more temples along the Wasatch Front in 1972, Church growth and an increase in temple attendance led to overcrowding in the Salt Lake and Provo Utah Temples. Of this circumstance, President Spencer W. Kimball said, "We are gratified that attendance at the Salt Lake, Ogden and Provo temples reached all-time highs during 1977, and the trend is still upward."[1] For that reason Church leaders in 1978 announced plans to build another temple in Utah, this one to be located in south Salt Lake County.

The Jordan River Utah Temple is situated on a fifteen-acre site atop a slight hill, making the temple easily seen from many parts of the valley. The property was donated to the Church by the family who had owned the land for nearly one hundred years. The temple is the first building ever to be constructed on the site.[2]

The location of the temple and its name have special symbolic meaning. The Jordan River, which connects Utah Lake and the Great Salt Lake, runs past the temple and was named after a similar river in the Holy Land, which connects the freshwater Sea of Galilee with the salty Dead Sea. When the pioneer Saints arrived in the Salt Lake Valley, they could not help but see the parallels between this land and the land where Christ had ministered and been baptized nearly two thousand years before. Naming the temple after the River Jordan recognizes these parallels and emphasizes the holy nature of the temple and temple work.

The temple, which faces east, was designed so that it would not appear to have a recognizable front or back. "All four facades of the temple will appear equally well," explained Emil B. Fetzer, Church architect and temple designer. The

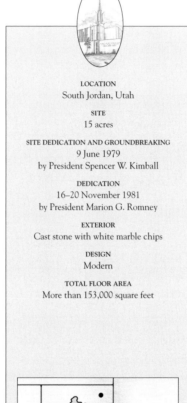

LOCATION
South Jordan, Utah

SITE
15 acres

SITE DEDICATION AND GROUNDBREAKING
9 June 1979
by President Spencer W. Kimball

DEDICATION
16–20 November 1981
by President Marion G. Romney

EXTERIOR
Cast stone with white marble chips

DESIGN
Modern

TOTAL FLOOR AREA
More than 153,000 square feet

JORDAN RIVER UTAH

153,000-square-foot building would be approximately 25 percent larger than the Provo and Ogden Utah Temples and would have the largest capacity of any temple in the Church up to that point.[3] The design called for vertical stained-glass panels adorning each of its four facades and the tower.[4] Architects also planned to place on the single spire of the Jordan River Utah Temple a larger version of the angel Moroni statue used on the Washington D. C. Temple.

After formally acquiring the property for the temple, the Church learned that the temple would straddle two areas with different zoning laws. It was fortunate that the part of the temple in the section with more restrictive regulations for height did not include the tallest parts of the building. There were no height restrictions in the zone where the two-hundred-foot-tall tower and twenty-foot-tall statue of the angel Moroni would be built. Because the temple met the respective zoning regulations, the architects were spared the difficulty of creating a new set of blueprints for the temple.[5]

Church leaders decided that the Jordan River Utah Temple, unlike other temples up to that point, would be funded entirely by contributions from members living in the area. A large fund-raising campaign was begun in all 122 stakes of the Salt Lake and Jordan River Utah Temple districts. When the fund-raising ended just over a year later, the members had contributed $14.5 million, 110 percent of the original goal.

This vast amount of money came from the sacrifices of thousands of members for their temple. A bishop recounted: "A woman with cataracts to the point that she cannot see eight inches from her face had been saving to have an

Jordan River Utah Temple

We are grateful for those who, in their generosity, donated this site for this purpose, and for all who have given so generously of their means, their time, their skills and their strength to make possible this sacred house.

—FROM THE DEDICATORY PRAYER

THE HOUSE OF THE LORD · HOLINESS TO THE LORD
THE CHURCH OF JESUS CHRIST OF LATTER-DAY SAINTS
JORDAN RIVER TEMPLE

operation to restore her sight. She took all the savings she had accumulated for this operation, emptied the entire account, and gave everything for the temple. As a bishop, what could I say? 'Don't do it?' No, I would never rob her of that blessing. I sat here and wept inside."[6]

One woman in the temple district had been struggling with many problems, including smoking. Accompanied by her daughter, she told her bishop in an interview that although she didn't have much she could contribute to the temple fund, she would donate as much as she was spending on her cigarettes. The bishop encouraged the sister in this idea but asked her to promise that she would give up her habit of smoking first and then give the money she would have spent on cigarettes to the temple fund. In that setting she found the courage to promise that she would quit. With great enthusiasm the three knelt in prayer to thank the Lord for his inspiration and help in this sister's life.[7]

Two young brothers, one eight years old and the other nearly ten, were excited to do their part in raising money for the temple. The two walked from door to door down the street, asking their neighbors if they would like to buy homemade bread. Before long they had requests for sixteen loaves. So they hurried home and told their unsuspecting mother that they needed her to bake sixteen loaves of bread right away. Their mother agreed to join in this fund-raising venture, and before long, sixteen hot loaves of bread were delivered. In all, the team sold about thirty loaves for the temple fund.[8]

One man put aside one dollar a day for the temple for the duration of the fund-raising campaign. To do this, the man,

Hidden in the clouds is a portrait of Christ watching over the Jordan River Utah Temple, reminding us of his baptism in the River Jordan.

who made less than a hundred dollars a week to support his wife and three children, went without lunch every day of the campaign.[9]

Ground was broken for the Jordan River Utah Temple on 9 June 1979. In a symbolic gesture, President Spencer W. Kimball departed from the traditional method of groundbreaking. President N. Eldon Tanner, who conducted the service, explained, "You will notice the large power scoop shovel which will be used instead of the traditional-type shovel for such programs. It will be operated by President Kimball in keeping with his oft-quoted counsel to 'lengthen our stride.'"[10] The powerful image energized members to make full use of the temple. Dedicated 16 November 1981, the Jordan River Utah Temple has been one of the most used temples since its completion.

In December 1981 President Gordon B. Hinckley, then a counselor to the First Presidency, spoke at a fireside in the Assembly Hall on Temple Square to many of the three thousand temple workers and their families. President Hinckley thanked them for their commitment, saying they were "shining examples of devotion and the spirit of consecration in the work of the Lord. I know that it isn't easy. Some of you arise very early in the morning, some travel very long distances, some of you leave work in order to go to the temple, and then have to make up for it." President Hinckley concluded by encouraging them to find joy in their temple labors. "When you go home so weary that you can scarcely put one foot ahead of the other, may you say to yourselves, 'This is the sweetest weariness I have ever known.'"[11]

We are grateful for those who, in their generosity, donated this site for this purpose

Atlanta Georgia Temple

The early history of the Church in Atlanta did not portend the great distinction that would come to the city more than one hundred years later when the first temple in the southern United States would be built there. Although missionaries in the Southern States Mission enjoyed some successes in the region, their gains were accompanied by great persecution. The opposition reached a peak in 1879, when Elder Joseph Standing was killed by a mob near Vernal, Georgia. By 1908, however, tensions in the region had eased considerably, and the Church had established a branch in Atlanta. In 1957 Elder LeGrand Richards organized Atlanta's first stake. The April 1980 announcement of a temple to be built in Sandy Springs, on the outskirts of Atlanta, was to Saints in the South the culmination of years of hard but steady growth.

The southern Saints' enthusiasm for the project was clearly evidenced on 7 March 1981, when nearly ten thousand members gathered on the temple site to witness the groundbreaking ceremonies. The crowd erupted into applause as President Spencer W. Kimball turned over the first shovelful of earth. President Kimball noted that the Church had "come a long, long way since the gospel was first taught in 1843 by one of our missionaries on a preaching tour through the South."[1] The Saints' enthusiasm was also seen in their willingness to make donations. By the end of 1981, nearly $1.4 million had been received from contributors worldwide, exceeding the goal of $1.2 million.[2]

Architects planned for the Atlanta Georgia Temple to be the first in a series of smaller temples built throughout the world. The smaller size of the building would keep costs relatively low, and the similar structure of several buildings would

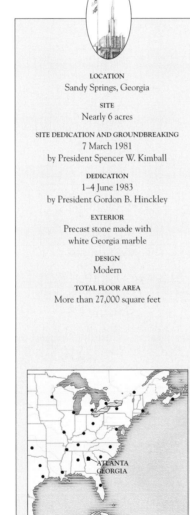

LOCATION
Sandy Springs, Georgia

SITE
Nearly 6 acres

SITE DEDICATION AND GROUNDBREAKING
7 March 1981
by President Spencer W. Kimball

DEDICATION
1–4 June 1983
by President Gordon B. Hinckley

EXTERIOR
Precast stone made with
white Georgia marble

DESIGN
Modern

TOTAL FLOOR AREA
More than 27,000 square feet

make it possible for the Church to produce them quickly. Even though these temples would be smaller than their predecessors, designers had learned much from their many years' experience in temple building and created a layout that was capable of accommodating a large number of patrons in a smaller amount of space.

Among the innovations first used in the Atlanta Georgia Temple was a system that allowed a temple session to be heard in five languages at one time. Using headphones, patrons who did not speak English would receive the words in their own language broadcast by an infrared beam. Another technological advancement was to link the temple's computer system to the family history library in Utah, allowing for the more efficient transmission of information between the temple and Church headquarters. The temple was also the first to include a video screen beside the temple's baptistry to aid in the reading of the names of those for whom the baptisms were performed. All of these advancements greatly facilitated temple work and were used in subsequent temples.

One aspect of the new temple plan was not well received by Church members in the Atlanta area, however. This temple and others of the same plan that would be built after it were designed without any steeple or spire. Two years after the original announcement of the temple, though, it was decided that the temple would have a spire and gold-leafed statue of the angel Moroni. President Kimball had reconsidered the design and determined that a steeple would beautify the building and make it a more prominent symbol of the Church in the community.

The statue of the angel Moroni that was eventually placed on the Atlanta Georgia Temple has an interesting history. In the early 1930s, Torlief Knaphus created a statue of the angel

Atlanta Georgia Temple

May all who enter these holy precincts feel of thy spirit and be bathed in this marvelous, sanctifying influence. May they come . . . in a spirit of love and dedication. May their minds be lifted above the mundane affairs of the world to a higher and more heavenly place.

—FROM THE DEDICATORY PRAYER

Moroni for the steeple of the Washington D. C. Ward chapel, which he based on the Cyrus Dallin statue atop the Salt Lake Temple. In 1976 the statue was removed from the Washington chapel, and LaVar Wallgren made two castings of it. One was placed on the spire of the Idaho Falls Idaho Temple, and the other was placed on the Atlanta Georgia Temple.[3]

The exterior of the temple consists of crushed white Georgia marble. Panels of faceted colored glass add beauty to the walls. The exquisite interior is decorated with walnut and red oak wood and large crystal chandeliers. Outside, the Church landscape architects used Atlanta's native shrubs, trees, and flowers to provide year-round symmetry and elegance to the grounds.

More than sixty thousand people visited the temple during the eighteen-day open house. The first day of the open house was reserved for local leaders in government, education, business, and the military. Among the visitors was Church member and baseball star Dale Murphy of the Atlanta Braves, who had scored the winning run in a game the night before. News coverage of both the open house and the temple was quite complimentary.[4] One radio editorial welcomed the temple to Atlanta by stating, "Our salute to Atlanta Temple President Robert Winston and his fellow Mormons in the eleven states of the Atlanta Temple District. You have chosen well in selecting Atlanta for your new temple. And you've given Atlanta one more thing for which it can be proud."[5]

Nearly fourteen thousand members of the Atlanta Georgia Temple district attended the eleven dedicatory sessions from 1 to 4 June 1983. The Atlanta Georgia Temple was the first of many temples to be dedicated by President Gordon B. Hinckley, then second counselor in the First Presidency. Although President Spencer W. Kimball was not well enough to attend the dedication, Church members who were there were frequently reminded of his love for the southern Saints, and his

The Atlanta Georgia Temple is surrounded by rows of brilliant flowers, bushes, trees, and colorful flowering vines. Hidden among the trees and landscaping to the right of the temple are images of the Savior's face and hands, directing us to his holy house.

enthusiasm for the building of their temple.[6] At the dedication of the temple, Elder Neal A. Maxwell of the Quorum of the Twelve Apostles said that the temple is "a needed sanctuary away from the world," where "the window of the soul is opened widely to the light of the heavens."[7]

Since its dedication, the Atlanta Georgia Temple has continued to be an important symbol of the Church in the South. This was true when the world's attention turned to Atlanta for the 1996 Summer Olympic Games. Church members willingly volunteered their services to the city to help make the games a success. One group of Latter-day Saint Boy Scouts stood among the crowds on the road alongside the temple to see the Olympic torch on its way to the opening ceremonies. The Scouts remained afterward to help clean up from the gathering.[8]

When President Gordon B. Hinckley dedicated the Atlanta Georgia Temple in June 1983, he promised that the temple's baptistry would someday be enlarged to accommodate more patrons. This promise was fulfilled 14 November 1997 when President Hinckley rededicated a reconstructed portion of the baptistry. Even though the temple district, which had included eleven states, had been significantly reduced in size with the dedication of the Orlando Florida and St. Louis Missouri Temples, the Atlanta Georgia Temple had remained busy, and the original baptistry was too small to accommodate all who wanted to attend. The effectiveness of the change quickly became evident. On the day after the baptistry's rededication, beginning at 6:30 A.M., groups performed baptisms for the dead throughout the entire day.[9]

The temple is an invitation to the southern Saints to dedicate themselves to temple work. President Hinckley prayed at the dedication: "May they come in ever-increasing numbers to partake of those blessings which are offered only in these holy houses. May they come with clean hands and pure hearts and a spirit of love and dedication."[10]

Apia Samoa Temple

Father, may this temple stand as a symbol of the faith and the integrity of thy people, and their knowledge, divinely given, of the immortality of the soul. May there emanate from it a spirit of peace and righteousness that will reach out into the homes of thy people that there may be love and harmony in those homes and that all evil may be kept therefrom. May even those who are not of the Church experience something of thy divine spirit radiated from this, thy holy house.

—FROM THE DEDICATORY PRAYER

The Church has a long history in the islands of Samoa. Since June 1888, when the first Latter-day Saint missionaries arrived in Samoa, the Church has enjoyed steady success among the open-minded islanders. Church-operated schools were soon built on the islands, giving the Latter-day Saints a center of strength in a place called Pesega, or "place of singing."

At the end of the nineteenth century, this plot of ground was occupied by a plantation and a large, wood-frame house. The home of Ah Mu, a Church member of Chinese descent, this structure was a center for Church activity in the area. Church leaders and members attended meetings and socials there. In 1898 Ah Mu generously offered to sell the land to the Church for the token price of one dollar. His offer was accepted, and the mission headquarters was moved to Pesega in 1902.[1] This complex later included such structures as the Church College of Western Samoa, the Pesega Elementary School, the Apia Samoa Mission headquarters, and a stake center.

Church growth has been rapid since then. Following a

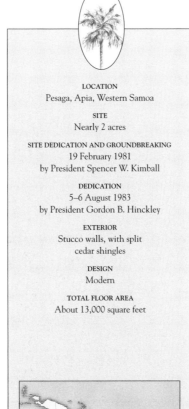

LOCATION
Pesaga, Apia, Western Samoa

SITE
Nearly 2 acres

SITE DEDICATION AND GROUNDBREAKING
19 February 1981
by President Spencer W. Kimball

DEDICATION
5–6 August 1983
by President Gordon B. Hinckley

EXTERIOR
Stucco walls, with split
cedar shingles

DESIGN
Modern

TOTAL FLOOR AREA
About 13,000 square feet

APIA SAMOA →

visit by President David O. McKay in 1921, Church membership increased dramatically with mass conversions of entire villages. In 1974 Samoa became the first country entirely covered by stakes. By the end of the twentieth century, Church members made up more than 25 percent of the population on the islands of Western Samoa and American Samoa.

On a visit to the islands in 1977, President Spencer W. Kimball complimented the Samoan Saints for their high proportion of temple marriages even though the nearest temples were in faraway New Zealand and Hawaii.[2] An example of the faith and dedication of these members to temple marriage is seen in the story of Kovana Pauga and Evelini Wesley. The two returned missionaries and fellow employees at the Church's Vaiola School had decided to be married in the Laie Hawaii Temple. To cover the cost of travel, they asked the superintendent of the school to withhold 80 percent of their income and set it aside to cover the airplane fares. They paid their tithing with 10 percent of their remaining income and lived on the other 10 percent. To save money during this time, the couple grew their food in a garden for nearly a year. By then they had saved enough money to make the trip to Hawaii, where they were sealed for time and eternity in the house of the Lord.[3] Like many families from Samoa, this young couple had made considerable sacrifice to receive the blessings of eternity in the temple.

To alleviate the great sacrifice of these members to attend the temple in Hawaii, the Church announced plans in 1977 to build a small temple in American Samoa to serve members from Samoa, French Polynesia, Tonga, and Fiji. The location for this temple seemed logical because of major air routes through Pago Pago. But in April 1980, after encountering difficulty in obtaining land, President Kimball announced a significant change in the original plans. Instead of one temple in American Samoa, the Church would build three temples—one each in Western Samoa, Tonga, and French Polynesia. Moving the location of the temple to Western Samoa put it closer to the majority of the members in the Samoan island chain. Members from American Samoa, who tended to be wealthier, would be able to travel more easily to the new temple location than Western Samoans would have been able to travel to the Pago Pago site. The temple was to be built on the Pesega complex. It was later noticed that the front doors of the temple were located where Ah Mu's house once stood.[4]

Ground was broken for the temple in 1981 by President Kimball, who was joined by head of state Malietioa Tunumafili II in turning the first shovelful of soil at the temple site. Temple construction proceeded with the help of members and missionaries who had come from all parts of the country to contribute their time and skills. As the appointed deadline approached, workers put in many extra hours to complete the temple in time for its open house.[5]

The workers used their ingenuity to overcome one obstacle that presented itself late in the construction process. They could not locate a crane tall enough to position the angel Moroni statue on the spire of the temple. The workers assembled scaffolding around the seventy-five-foot spire so that they could manually hoist the statue into place. The gold-leafed statue could not be touched by bare hands, so the workers wrapped the statue in flannel and wore white gloves as they moved it.[6]

Because of President Spencer W. Kimball's deteriorating health, President Gordon B. Hinckley, second counselor in the First Presidency, officiated at the temple dedication. In his remarks to those gathered for the dedication, President Hinckley said: "There has never been another day quite like this in the history of Samoa. There will never be another day like it again." He later spoke of the many individuals on both sides of the veil who rejoiced in this significant occasion. "I am confident the veil is thin and that on the other side there are many missionaries who served here in years past and many people of simple faith who accepted the message and endured much for it."[7] One member, Laiula Stehlin, who felt a similar impression at the dedication, said, "As I sat in the dedicatory session, I thought of my grandfather, who was the first in our family to join the Church. I know, on the other side of the veil, he is rejoicing. I know many on the other side are as happy as we are here."[8]

The building of the Apia Samoa Temple and the other two temples in the Pacific Islands provided more temples per capita in these areas than anywhere else in the world. And the Samoan Saints have shown their gratitude by making good use of their temple. The Apia Samoa Temple has consistently functioned beyond its projected capacity.

The temple has come to be treasured not only by the Samoan Saints but also by the larger community. In 1988 a postage stamp was issued in Samoa to commemorate one hundred years since the Church was officially established in the Samoan islands. The stamp features the Apia Samoa Temple, and the accompanying postal cancellation mark is a line drawing of the well-known angel Moroni statue. On the official first-day cover (9 June 1988) are two quotations from the Book of Mormon: "Great are the promises of the Lord unto them who are upon the isles of the sea" (2 Nephi 10:21) and "To him upon whom ye shall lay your hands, ye shall give the Holy Ghost" (Moroni 2:2).[9]

In 1991 Hurricane Val, one of the worst tropical storms in history, pummeled the islands of Western and American Samoa, killing at least seventeen people and damaging or destroying more than 65 percent of the homes on the two islands. When the storm ended, it was found that all sixty-nine of the Church meetinghouses in Western Samoa had sustained some damage, and most of the meetinghouses in American Samoa received considerable damage. Despite damage to most other structures in the area, the Apia Samoa Temple was protected from major destruction, receiving only minor damage from a water leak in the ceiling.[10]

The Apia Samoa Temple continues to extend God's blessings to his many faithful Saints of the islands of the South Pacific.

Nuku'alofa Tonga Temple

We thank thee for all of thy faithful Saints in these beautiful islands and invoke thy blessings upon them that they may be blessed with love and peace in their homes, that their lands shall be productive, that they shall be prospered in their righteous undertakings, that they shall be protected from the storms of nature and from the conflicts of men if they will walk in obedience to thy commandments.

— FROM THE DEDICATORY PRAYER

Missionary work in Tonga—where nearly one of every two persons is a member of The Church of Jesus Christ of Latter-day Saints—struggled during its early years. Although the first missionaries, who arrived in 1891, had some success in establishing schools and finding converts, the mission was closed just six years later, in 1897. Reopened a decade later, the mission began winning over hearts as more and more missionaries made their way to the islands. Soon the government became weary of these outsiders' influence on their people and limited the number of visas available to foreigners. Because of such restrictions, the Saints in Tonga were called as missionaries to their own land and given leadership responsibilities that helped them quickly mature in the gospel after their conversion to the Church. The faithfulness of these Saints in the "Friendly Islands" is manifested by their dedication to tithing, missionary work, and attendance at sacrament meetings.[1]

The devoted Tongan Saints have always looked forward to having in their islands a temple where they could worship and make supernal covenants with the Lord. This dream was bolstered in 1955 when President David O. McKay stopped in the

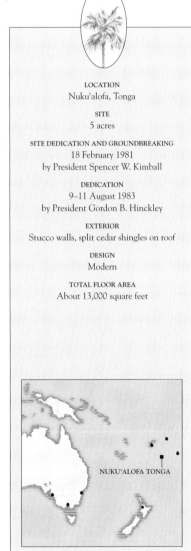

LOCATION
Nuku'alofa, Tonga

SITE
5 acres

SITE DEDICATION AND GROUNDBREAKING
18 February 1981
by President Spencer W. Kimball

DEDICATION
9–11 August 1983
by President Gordon B. Hinckley

EXTERIOR
Stucco walls, split cedar shingles on roof

DESIGN
Modern

TOTAL FLOOR AREA
About 13,000 square feet

NUKU'ALOFA TONGA

islands on his way to dedicate the ground for the Hamilton New Zealand Temple. The first Church president to visit Tonga, to the Saints there during his time with them, he announced, "Last night in vision I saw a temple in these islands."[2] For years members waited for the day when this prophecy would be fulfilled.

In the meantime the Tongan Saints had to travel great distances to obtain their temple blessings. The first opportunity for many of them came with the dedication of the Hamilton New Zealand Temple in 1958. Members soon began saving money for annual excursions to the temple in distant New Zealand. Many members sacrificed all they owned to go to the temple and receive the blessings of the holy house of the Lord.

When the Hamilton New Zealand Temple opened, Brother Viliami Kongaika and his wife, Lu'isa, desired to be part of the first group of Tongans to travel to the temple, but they did not have enough money for the entire family to go to the temple to be sealed for eternity. They therefore waited another year while they saved enough money for all family members to go to the temple. To cover the cost of travel, they sold nearly everything they owned, including their frame house, their roofing tin, their stove, Viliami's bicycle (their only means of transportation), Lu'isa's sewing machine, and the family's cows, horses, and pigs. The money garnered from these sales enabled the family to travel to the temple the following year, where they were sealed for eternity. The Kongaikas returned to face the reality of being without a home, job, or food. Soon after their return, a devastating hurricane destroyed almost everything on the island of Ha'pai, including the Kongaikas' newly built hut. Viliami then built from scraps and debris another shelter, in which the family

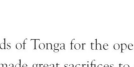

lived for quite some time. Yet the family recognized Lord's hand in their lives. Viliami said, "It was the Lord prompting me to get rid of my goods for a holy cause, because he was going to take them away from me anyway in the hurricane. I came back from the temple a poor man in terms of worldly goods. But after the hurricane, everyone else was just as poor as we were. The difference between us and them was that we were sealed as an eternal family in the Holy Temple of God."[3]

The Tongan Saints were thrilled to learn in 1980 that three temples planned for the Pacific islands would include one near Tonga's capital city, Nuku'alofa. It would be built concurrently with the Apia Samoa and Papeete Tahiti Temples and would closely resemble them in architectural style.

A five-acre site near the Church-operated Liahona College had been intended for a temple long before Church leaders decided it was time to build one in Tonga. The property owner, Brother Tevita Mahu'inga, had served faithfully in many Church capacities. Just before his death in 1973, he told his son: "There will be a temple built in Tonga someday; and our five-acre piece just next to Liahona I have reserved for a temple site. You give it to the Church at the appropriate time."[4] After several unsuccessful attempts at obtaining property on the island, Church officials approached Brother Mahu'inga's son and acquired the land for the temple. Thus Tevita Mahu'inga's dream was fulfilled seven years after his death.[5]

During its public open house, the temple was enthusiastically toured by more than half of the entire population of Tonga. The first of these visitors was King Taufa'ahau Tupou IV, who had participated in the groundbreaking ceremonies.[6]

Thousands of members journeyed to the capital from the scattered islands of Tonga for the open house and dedication of the temple. Most had made great sacrifices to afford the trip and participate in the dedication. In his address, President Gordon B. Hinckley noted that a group of prisoners accompanied by their guards had attended the temple open house. He compared them to the many good Tongans waiting in spirit prison for their ordinances so that they can progress. "I think I can hear in my mind their wardens cry out to the Tongan saints, 'won't you do something to help them?'" President Gordon B. Hinckley said. "They are your forebears. All you are and all you have came through them. The house is here; the keys are here. Unlock the door that these good Tongans may go forward into immortality and eternal life."[7] The Tongan Saints apparently took President Hinckley's admonition to heart, for they have consistently used the temple far beyond its projected capacity.[8]

Members from the island of Vava'u, some two hundred miles from the Nuku'alofa Tonga Temple, epitomize the enthusiasm of the Tongan Saints. Even though the cost of travel to the temple is high for members of the Vava'u Tonga Stake, many save enough money to make two excursions, lasting two to three weeks each, to the temple every year. The average trip includes ninety recommend holders and many children who will be sealed to their families. The stake, which encourages temple recommend holders to accomplish forty-eight endowments each year, performs an average of five thousand each year.[9]

The Nuku'alofa Tonga Temple, considered by many to be the most beautiful building in all of Tonga, has become a central point for the Saints of the numerous Tongan islands. For them, this place of refuge, symbol of righteousness, and fulfillment of prophecy represents God's love and compassion for his children scattered across the Pacific islands.

Santiago Chile Temple

We thank thee for the magnificent flowering of thy work in this part of the earth and for the stature to which it has grown. We thank thee for the faith and loyalty of thy saints here and throughout the world. . . . As we contemplate the marvelous blessings which will come through the exercise of the holy priesthood in this thy house, our hearts are filled with gratitude unto thee.

— FROM THE DEDICATORY PRAYER

In March 1977, at an area conference in Santiago, Chile, Elder Bruce R. McConkie told the seven thousand gathered there that the Church would eventually become the most powerful influence in Chile. This promise of future prosperity must have seemed miraculous to the Saints in Chile, where the Church had established a presence only twenty years earlier. Although Elder Parley P. Pratt traveled to Chile in 1850 to preach the gospel, he soon left because of difficulty learning the language. Not until 1956 did missionaries return to Chile. They found a people prepared to receive the gospel message. Soon the Chile Mission became one of the most productive missions of the Church. It was under these circumstances that Elder McConkie prophesied concerning a future temple: "The day will come when there will be a temple in Chile. I do not say when, but it surely will be."[1]

On 2 April 1980, President Spencer W. Kimball announced plans to build a temple in Santiago, fulfilling Elder McConkie's prophecy of three years earlier. It would be the first temple built in a Spanish-speaking country and the second in South America. The temple would be built in Santiago

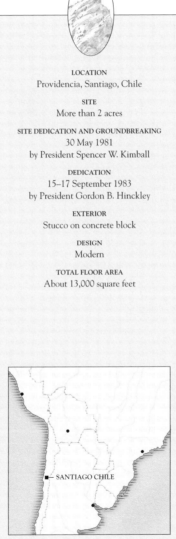

LOCATION
Providencia, Santiago, Chile

SITE
More than 2 acres

SITE DEDICATION AND GROUNDBREAKING
30 May 1981
by President Spencer W. Kimball

DEDICATION
15–17 September 1983
by President Gordon B. Hinckley

EXTERIOR
Stucco on concrete block

DESIGN
Modern

TOTAL FLOOR AREA
About 13,000 square feet

SANTIAGO CHILE

where the Church college building and the presiding bishopric area offices were then located.

In 1970 Gregory Billikopf attended a Catholic school. In religion class one day the priest announced that the school would shortly be sold to the Mormon Church. To help the children understand that many people held religious beliefs different from theirs, the priest assigned the students to write reports on The Church of Jesus Christ of Latter-day Saints. To fulfill the assignment, Gregory went the short distance to the mission home, where he received a copy of the Book of Mormon and other information about the Church. He read Moroni's promise, gained a witness that the book was true, and eventually joined the Church. He later wrote, "How was I to know, as a youth in that religion class, that one day, on that very property, I would attend the house of the Lord—the Santiago Chile Temple?"[2]

On 30 May 1981, President Kimball broke ground for the temple. Some six thousand Saints attended the ceremonies. Rodolfo Acevedo Acevedo, Chile area historian, described the importance of the day's events to Church members in Chile:

"A heavy rainstorm fell during the day when the ground was to be broken for the Santiago Chile Temple and the site dedicated.

"This occasion brought the hope of the years closer to being realized—a temple was to be constructed in our land. It was to be a house sacred and consecrated to the work of the Lord that transcended our mortal lives.

"The strength of the rain . . . proved the faith of the Saints, who ever since the announcement that a prophet would come and dedicate the temple site, had been preparing

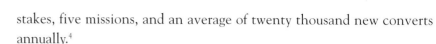

to take part in this once-in-a-lifetime experience. Upon arriving at the temple site, I was able to see the faith of my brothers and sisters, many of whom did not have hats or umbrellas. On this torrential May morning, thousands and thousands of them stood waiting for the sublime moment that the site would be dedicated for the temple.

"The rain continued to fall with force. All those present stoically waited for the ceremony to begin. As they waited, a choir sang beautiful hymns in the rainfall. Their clothing was soaked, but none moved from his place, even as the rain increased. We sang and we rejoiced in the experience.

"A great surprise was waiting for the Saints. As President Spencer W. Kimball arose from his seat to address the members, from among the dark clouds came a ray of sunshine, followed by others. Soon the clouds parted and bright sunshine warmed all those present. Two years later, the Santiago Temple, with the statue of the angel Moroni crowning its spire, was completed. Through all these years we remember the hope expressed beneath the rain; it was a true joy, something very special; we felt the presence of the Spirit of the Lord. All were inundated with warmth and happiness inside."[3]

On 24 August 1983, the completed temple was opened for public tours. Among the visitors during the open house was Ricardo Garcia, who had become the first Chilean convert when he was baptized in 1957. Brother Garcia stopped in the doorway when he saw the temple presidency in their white temple clothes standing in the temple. Overcome with emotion, he wept and said, "I never thought this could have happened. In the beginning we wondered if the Church would ever get started. Now we have a temple." Since Brother Garcia's conversion twenty-six years earlier, the Church had experienced exponential growth. At the time of the temple's dedication in 1983, the country had thirty-six

stakes, five missions, and an average of twenty thousand new converts annually.[4]

One remarkable experience that transpired during the temple's open house is recorded in the journal of Viviana Ayala, a young woman who assisted at the open house and dedication. On a Saturday during the open house, upwards of six thousand people from all over the country toured the temple. Sister Viviana wrote: "At first we could not contain our joy but soon it turned to worry. Because of the small size of the temple only so many people could go in at once. There was a long line of people waiting outside. . . . Suddenly the sky became dark and the wind started to pick up. We knew that soon there would be rain and that the people waiting outside would go home without having had a chance to look at the beautiful 'House of the Lord.' The local leaders and some visiting authorities . . . gathered in an office in the temple and decided to pray to ask Heavenly Father for His divine help. It was not until night had fallen and the Open House had finished for the day that the rain began to fall. All the people . . . had seen the temple. Only a few of us knew that they had also witnessed a miracle as the Lord stayed the rains from falling on them."[5]

At the first of the ten dedicatory services, President Gordon B. Hinckley stated: "I think I know why this temple is here. I think the Lord said, 'I have weighed the saints of Chile in the balance, and they have not been found wanting. I have determined that the richest blessings I can bestow should be made available to them—the preservation of the sweetest companionships of all human associations for time and all eternity.'"[6] He continued, "'This is a marvelous day for the Saints in Chile, a wonderful day, something that we've dreamed of for many years. . . . September 15, 1983, will be remembered by the Latter-day Saints in Chile' as the day a holy house of the Lord was dedicated."[7]

We thank thee for the faith and loyalty of thy Saints here

Papeete Tahiti Temple

There is now strength and maturity among the many thousands of the Saints of French Polynesia, for which we express gratitude unto thee. As a capstone to all of this effort we now have this beautiful and sacred house to present unto thee.

—FROM THE DEDICATORY PRAYER

The history of the Church in French Polynesia began in 1844 when Elder Addison Pratt arrived in Tubuai, an island about five hundred miles south of Tahiti, baptized many people, and established a branch. Called by the Prophet Joseph Smith, he and his companions found some success among the people, but government restrictions led to the mission's closure in 1852. Forty years later, in 1892, missionaries reopened the work in French Polynesia. They continued to face a myriad of difficulties, including natural disasters, economic problems, government restrictions, and international events. Still, the Church made steady progress in French Polynesia and eventually gained the respect of the local government.

Like other Saints living throughout Polynesia, faithful Tahitian members made great sacrifices to travel to New Zealand, Hawaii, or other locations to receive temple ordinances. The costs of attending the temple were high. Papeete Tahiti Stake president Victor Cave said that transportation to the Hamilton New Zealand Temple, the nearest temple, cost about eight hundred dollars for each person. But Tahitian families, who often have six or more children, generally make about five hundred dollars per month. Families who saved for years to travel to the temple made the very most of their experience. President Cave said that families who were able to attend the temple would stay a month "to get as much work done as they can."[1]

LOCATION
Pirae, Tahiti, near Papeete

SITE
5 acres

SITE DEDICATION AND GROUNDBREAKING
13 February 1981
by President Spencer W. Kimball

DEDICATION
27–29 October 1983
by President Gordon B. Hinckley

EXTERIOR
Stucco, using imported white sand

DESIGN
Combination of French and Polynesian architectural elements

TOTAL FLOOR AREA
More than 10,500 square feet

PAPEETE TAHITI

Countless stories tell of faithful Tahitian Saints who saved all they could from their meager incomes for long periods of time and made many sacrifices to travel to the temple. Eighty-four-year-old Tahauri Hutihuti had saved money for thirty years to be able to make one trip to the Hamilton New Zealand Temple. When he returned, he said he was eager to go again someday.[2]

The original plan to build a temple in Pago Pago, American Samoa, would not have significantly reduced the cost to Tahitian Saints of traveling to the temple because there were no direct airline connections between Tahiti and American Samoa. The Tahitian Saints rejoiced when they learned that the Church had decided to build three temples instead, with one in Papeete.[3]

The site chosen for the temple was on property where a Church-run elementary school had been located. Local leaders obtained permission from Francis Sanford, the head of the Tahitian government, to build the temple. Although the process was somewhat simplified because the Church already owned the land, the leaders worried that they might face opposition similar to what they had dealt with when the Church had built the school. But Sanford, who had visited the Laie Hawaii Temple, the Church College of Hawaii, and the Polynesian Cultural Center, had gained a favorable opinion of the Church and promised them that the government would not oppose the building of a Latter-day Saint Temple in Tahiti.[4] With this approval, President Spencer W. Kimball broke ground for the temple and dedicated the site on 13 February 1981, with two thousand people looking on.

Although somewhat smaller, the temple was similar in design and outward appearance to the temples in Samoa and

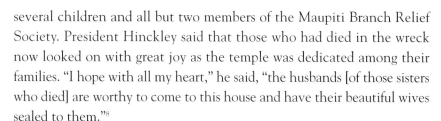

Tonga. Designers also incorporated both French and Polynesian influences into the plans. Because members in French Polynesia come from a variety of cultures, the temple was equipped to serve patrons speaking French, Tahitian, or English. As construction progressed, the building became something of a landmark and was widely admired for its stately entrance, white walls, and blue tile roof. Members and nonmembers alike responded with great excitement when the Church announced that a spire and a statue of the angel Moroni would be added to the structure.[5]

The open house attracted national attention. Some five hundred government, civic, and religious officials toured the temple on the first day. One official commented: "From the moment I entered, I felt a quietness and the sacredness of this building. I was particularly impressed with the ordinance rooms. However, the room that inspired me the most was the Celestial Room. Everything instills reverence and closeness to God. I have never felt that way before—it was difficult to leave the room."

During the ten-day open house, some 16,500 visitors, nearly 7.5 percent of the population of French Polynesia, toured the structure.[6] Many nonmembers expressed enthusiasm for the temple after touring it and encouraged friends and family to return with them. One member said, "My [nonmember] friends visited the temple four or five times." The open house resulted in a flood of missionary referrals and questions about temple work. Among the visitors requesting more information were the high commissioner and the head of the local government.[7]

President Gordon B. Hinckley dedicated the temple 27 October 1983. In his remarks he recalled a tragic shipwreck that had occurred twenty years earlier during his first visit to the Society Islands in French Polynesia. The accident had claimed the lives of fifteen people, including several children and all but two members of the Maupiti Branch Relief Society. President Hinckley said that those who had died in the wreck now looked on with great joy as the temple was dedicated among their families. "I hope with all my heart," he said, "the husbands [of those sisters who died] are worthy to come to this house and have their beautiful wives sealed to them."[8]

In the dedicatory prayer, President Hinckley expressed thanks for the miraculous progress of the Church among the islands: "While he [Joseph Smith] was yet alive and while the Saints were yet in Nauvoo, he was inspired to call the first missionaries to these beautiful Society Islands of the Pacific. From their dedicated labors in those early years there came a great harvest. Since that time there have been seasons of prosperity and seasons when problems were many and the harvest was lean. But through all of these years thy work has grown as with faith thy servants have labored among the Tahitian people. . . . There is now strength and maturity among the many thousands of the Saints in French Polynesia, for which we express gratitude unto thee. As a capstone of all of this effort we now have this beautiful and sacred house to present unto thee."[9]

In the years since its dedication, the Papeete Tahiti Temple has continued to have a great influence in the lives of Latter-day Saints in the islands. Temple president C. Jay Larson commented: "The temple has elevated the spirituality of the members. Since the temple was dedicated, we've had a 50 percent increase in the number of temple marriages. Now a lot of the young people qualify for temple marriage. They prepare for the temple."[10] The temple has become for the faithful Saints of French Polynesia both a goal to reach and a place to begin a new level of discipleship and consecration to the gospel.

There is now strength and maturity among the many thousands of the Saints in French Polynesia

México City México Temple

Bless thy Saints in this great land and those from other lands who will use this temple. Most have in their veins the blood of Father Lehi. Thou hast kept thine ancient promise. Many thousands "that walked in darkness have seen a great light" (Isaiah 9:2). May the harvest that we have witnessed here foreshadow greater things to come as thy work rolls on in power and majesty in this the dispensation of the fulness of times.

—FROM THE DEDICATORY PRAYER

The Mexico City Mexico Temple, the first Latter-day Saint temple to be built in that country, was announced 3 April 1976, a century after Mormon missionaries first arrived there. During a speech given at the Mexico City area conference in 1979, President Spencer W. Kimball told of an impression he had received on a trip to Mexico more than thirty years earlier: "I had great expectation for the Mexican people, and I had a dream about your progress and growth. . . . When I had my dream there was not a single stake or ward in all Mexico. I saw a temple, and I expect to see it full of young men and women."[1]

But many seemingly insurmountable obstacles stood in the way of plans to build the temple in the capital of the Republic of Mexico. Foreign missionaries were not formally recognized in Mexico, and laws required all buildings to be open to the public. Such stipulations would compromise the sacred nature of dedicated temples. Before long, however, laws regarding religion were changed in ways favorable to the Church, and the necessary building permits were approved in the latter part of 1979.[2]

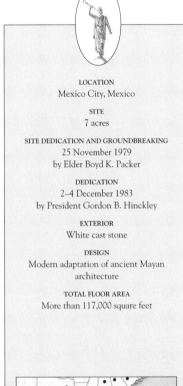

LOCATION
Mexico City, Mexico

SITE
7 acres

SITE DEDICATION AND GROUNDBREAKING
25 November 1979
by Elder Boyd K. Packer

DEDICATION
2–4 December 1983
by President Gordon B. Hinckley

EXTERIOR
White cast stone

DESIGN
Modern adaptation of ancient Mayan architecture

TOTAL FLOOR AREA
More than 117,000 square feet

MEXICO
CITY MEXICO

Another obstacle the Church faced was a federal law that prohibited importation into Mexico of building materials, furnishings, or furniture already available in the country. Because the Church desired to use only materials of the highest quality for the temple, leaders requested exemption from the importation law. They also asked that the government allow them to import those materials, worth some $2.6 million, without tax. In a spirit of fasting and prayer, Elder Richard G. Scott and other Church officials presented their request to government leaders. Miraculously, government leaders approved the request and signed the necessary documents, commenting that they could not understand why they had changed their mind and sided with the Church.[3]

Because the proposed site for the temple had once been covered by a lake, the ground was marshy, and local Saints feared it could not support the weight of a temple. Aware of this concern, President Kimball visited Mexico City before construction began and spent several hours alone on the property. He prayed for guidance regarding the site and received a confirmation that it was the will of the Lord for the temple to be built there.[4] Plans were modified to strengthen the foundation of the temple and make it resistant to the effects of earthquakes, which are prevalent in the area.

When Emil B. Fetzer, the architect, was assigned by President Spencer W. Kimball to design the temple, his thoughts turned to a book on Mayan architecture that Heber Grant Taylor, a grandson of Heber J. Grant, had given him more than ten years before. The book, which had come from President Grant's personal library, was an important heirloom to Brother Taylor, but he had felt that he should give it to Brother Fetzer. As Brother Fetzer prepared the design for the temple in Mexico City, he reread the book and produced a design in harmony with Mayan architecture. He also created four other potential styles for the temple, so that Church leaders would have several designs from which to choose. As the First Presidency examined each of the proposed designs, they felt that the one with the Mayan influences was the best.[5]

The result was equally approved by citizens of Mexico, both members and nonmembers. Considered by many to be one of the most beautiful buildings in the country, the Mexico City Mexico Temple is faced with white cast stone and white marble chips, in what Brother Fetzer called "a modern adaptation of ancient Mayan architecture."[6] The grounds are landscaped with traditional Mexican plants and feature a water fountain in front of the temple. Favorable reviews of the structure soon came in from citizens, the mayor of Mexico City, and from architecture students at the University of Mexico.[7]

When completed, the 117,133-square-foot temple was the fifth largest temple in the Church and the largest temple outside the United States. Each of the four ordinance rooms seats one hundred. The temple provides twelve sealing rooms and a three-hundred-seat chapel to serve hundreds of thousands of Saints from all over Mexico and Central America.

Enthusiasm for the temple was evidenced by the more than one hundred thousand people who toured the temple during its public open house. Many requested visits from missionaries to find out more about the Church. One visitor said he had decided to attend the open house not so much to see the interior as to feel the peace he had been told could be experienced there.[8]

On 2 December 1983, President Gordon B. Hinckley dedicated the temple, the sixth dedicated that year. In his remarks to the three thousand Saints gathered at the first session, he noted ways that the temple had already contributed to the growth of the Church in Mexico and to the members' spirituality: tithing donations had increased three-fold since construction had begun, and more than four times as many Saints now held temple recommends as had held them before work began.[9]

"We must recognize that this day in Mexico is one of the most important in the history of the nation," he said. In the dedicatory prayer, he asked, "Wilt thou accept it as the gift of thy thankful people, presented and dedicated unto thee as thy house. We pray that thou and thy Son may visit it according to thy will and that thy Holy Spirit may always dwell here."[10]

The change that takes place over Latter-day Saints when they partake of temple blessings and are sealed as families was described by Agricol Lozano Herrera, Mexico City Mexico Temple president: "The sealing of a husband and wife from the group of people often classified as 'field workers' is a particularly sweet, tender and beautiful experience. . . .

" . . . For cultural and social reasons, such couples have never been the center of attention, nor had such beautiful words spoken to them as they hear in the sealing.

"The wife perhaps in the past felt a tinge of envy as she saw a bride adorned for a formal wedding because life never gave her the opportunity to do more than dream of wearing such clothing. And now, though the comeliness of her youth has faded, she is actually experiencing that once-remote possibility.

"Within the beautiful sealing room, she and her husband are respected and are the subject of great tenderness. The husband, perhaps, feels excited for the prospects of the future. . . .

"In most cases, after the sealing, the couple stand and embrace, leaning their heads on each other's shoulders, weeping.

"They weep and rejoice at the culmination of the most sublime ordinances on earth. Their separate threads of life have been tied together, to form a union without beginning or end, an eternal union between the man and wife. And the binding of threads seems also to have been sealed by their love."[11]

Bless thy Saints in this great land and those from other lands who will use this temple

Boise Idaho Temple

Discussions about building a temple in Boise, Idaho, began decades before the actual announcement. In 1939, when Church leaders expressed interest in building a temple in Idaho, Boise Stake president Ezra Taft Benson invited President Heber J. Grant to visit the state's capital and largest city, to look at potential sites. During the visit some fifteen prominent businessmen from the area offered any available site for a temple in the Boise area. Despite the generosity of this offer, there were many more Saints in eastern Idaho at the time than in the western part of the state, so President Grant decided to build a temple in Idaho Falls. He did tell the businessmen, however, that when Church membership increased substantially a temple would be built. At the dedication of the Boise Idaho Temple in 1984, Elder Benson, then a member of the Quorum of the Twelve Apostles, testified, "Today, we are witnessing the fulfilling of that prophecy made forty-five years ago."[1]

Once the temple was announced, Church members from the Boise area offered land on which the structure could be built. The property eventually chosen, however, was a site owned by a nonmember. Because accessibility was the search committee's most important criterion for a temple site, this property, located near an exit from Interstate 84, was ideal.[2]

This location has made the temple a well-known landmark for travelers along the highway. And, located near the municipal airport, the temple provides a noticeable marker for pilots guiding their planes to the runway. The temple was originally designed with its entryway facing the busy street that runs beside the grounds, but President Spencer W. Kimball asked that the building be turned 180 degrees so the entrance would face west, toward the temple's parking lot.[3]

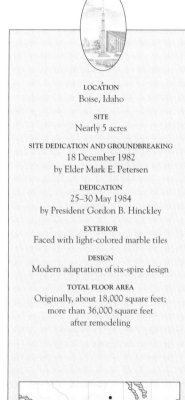

LOCATION
Boise, Idaho

SITE
Nearly 5 acres

SITE DEDICATION AND GROUNDBREAKING
18 December 1982
by Elder Mark E. Petersen

DEDICATION
25–30 May 1984
by President Gordon B. Hinckley

EXTERIOR
Faced with light-colored marble tiles

DESIGN
Modern adaptation of six-spire design

TOTAL FLOOR AREA
Originally, about 18,000 square feet;
more than 36,000 square feet
after remodeling

BOISE IDAHO

The Boise Idaho Temple was the first of a series of six-spired temples designed to maximize efficiency and space. These temples could be built at a lower cost in a shorter time, and they were easily adaptable for international construction. The original design did not include a statue of the angel Moroni, but as the plans were being finalized, President Kimball decided to have a statue of Moroni added to the eastern spire.[4] Between 1984 and 1989, fourteen temples around the world were built using adaptations of this original plan.

On a cold December day in 1982, approximately five thousand Saints gathered at the temple site to witness the groundbreaking. It was the eighth temple groundbreaking within four months. Elder Mark E. Petersen of the Quorum of the Twelve Apostles, who presided over the ceremony, taught the Saints that once they have received temple ordinances for themselves, they are "under solemn obligation to perform ordinances on behalf of our ancestors who have gone to the other side. There is an urgency to receive your own ordinances and an urgency to help the dead who have gone beyond. That is the reason we are here today."[5]

When construction was completed in the spring of 1984, seventy thousand visitors were expected to tour the temple during the nineteen-day open house. Instead, nearly twice that number attended. The open house proved to be a great missionary tool in the area. Two areas of the Idaho Boise Mission reported that thirty people joined the Church during the month following the open house, several of them responding to the feelings and impressions they had received while touring the temple.[6]

During the open house, Church officials worked to obtain

Boise Idaho Temple

May thy faithful Saints of this and future generations look to this beautiful structure as
a house to which they will be made welcome . . . as they serve unselfishly in assisting
thee in bringing to pass thine eternal purposes for the salvation and exaltation of thy sons
and daughters.

—FROM THE DEDICATORY PRAYER

BOISE IDAHO TEMPLE

an occupancy permit to accommodate the many Saints who wanted to attend dedicatory services because the number would exceed fire safety codes. Early one morning, architect Ronald W. Thurber called the city's fire chief and invited him to a personally guided tour of the entire temple. An appointment was made for 10 A.M. that day. Brother Thurber immediately notified Elder Hugh W. Pinnock of the First Quorum of the Seventy, the general authority assisting with the temple, who agreed to arrive at the temple half an hour early. As Brother Thurber, Elder Pinnock, and other Church officials gathered in the temple president's office, Elder Pinnock told the others that he had called the First Presidency that morning to make them aware of the challenge, and the First Presidency had put the item on the prayer roll that day and would pray for the situation during their meeting in the temple. Elder Pinnock explained that they would likely be praying while the tour was taking place.

At 10 A.M. the fire chief arrived and was given a private tour of the temple. Afterward, he agreed to grant the temple a permit for unlimited occupancy, as long as a few safety procedures were followed. As the fire chief drove away, Elder Pinnock said, "Brethren, I want you to know that we have just learned a great lesson. Come with me and I will show you." The men followed Elder Pinnock into the president's office. Asking them to kneel, he said, "We often forget to give thanks," and asked Brother Thurber to pray. Brother Thurber later said, "I was in such tears I could hardly pray. The First Presidency had taken a particular issue and solved it by imploring the assistance of Heavenly Father."[7]

In public remarks prior to the dedication, President Gordon B. Hinckley, second counselor in the First Presidency, explained the importance of temples: "Each temple stands as a witness to the faith of the Latter-day Saints that life is eternal, that death is not the end, that the soul of man lives on, and that we shall continue to live and function as individuals when we pass through the veil of death. Each of these buildings bears witness to our conviction that Jesus is the Christ, the living Son of the living God, and that all are beneficiaries of his redeeming sacrifice, that his resurrection was a reality, and that all may partake of the resurrection made possible through him."[8]

The temple was dedicated on 25 May 1984 by President Hinckley. Nearly twenty-eight thousand Saints participated, about three thousand more than had been expected. President Hinckley spoke at all twenty-four sessions, four sessions a day for six days, each time giving new insights and wisdom concerning the house of the Lord Jesus Christ. Not since the dedication of the Salt Lake Temple had so many dedicatory sessions been held for a temple.[9] During his addresses, President Hinckley spoke to the young people in attendance, many of whom had missed school to attend. "This temple has been built for you," he said. "School will be there next week and next year, but there will never be another occasion quite like this for you."[10]

Attendance at the temple over the first two years following the dedication was much higher than anticipated, so in October 1986 the temple was closed for significant renovations and additions. Completed in May 1987 were a new baptistry, a cafeteria, additional dressing rooms, and expanded office space.

The significance of the Boise Idaho Temple for the Saints in southwestern Idaho and for those who have died was highlighted in the dedicatory prayer. President Hinckley asked, "May the ordinances which will be performed herein be received with thankful and reverent hearts, and may those beyond the veil of death rejoice because of the work done here in their behalf."[11]

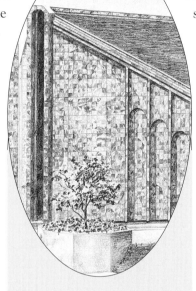

Carefully hidden in the marble surface of the temple wall is an image of the Savior's face, a symbol that this is his house.

. . . serve unselfishly in assisting thee in bringing to pass thine eternal purposes

Sydney Australia Temple

After years of growth and gaining experience in the gospel, the Saints in Australia were delighted when President Spencer W. Kimball announced in April 1980 that a temple would be built in Sydney, along with six others throughout the world. These new temples, smaller than previous temples, were to be built in the United States, South America, and several Pacific countries, including Australia.

The search for a suitable location commenced immediately. Within three weeks, five potential properties had been identified in the vicinity of Sydney. Several months were spent settling on a site, meeting legal requirements to begin building, and dealing with opposition from some members of the surrounding community. The location finally chosen and approved by the local government one year after the announcement was located in the Carlingford section of Sydney, about twelve miles north of the downtown area. The Church retained several school buildings on the site as offices. The beautiful site features eucalyptus trees with lush fields and the grand Blue Mountains in the distance.[1]

Soon after the temple was announced, regional representatives in the area organized a fund-raising project among the Australian Saints. The members responded to the task enthusiastically, achieving their goal of nearly 1 million dollars in just six months.[2] One contribution to the fund came as the result of an institute teacher's object lesson. The teacher had pretended to have received a letter from the stake president calling on his class to raise eight thousand dollars for the temple. His intention was to see how they would react to a difficult challenge, not for them to sacrifice to achieve it. But the class eagerly took on the challenge, deciding that each of the

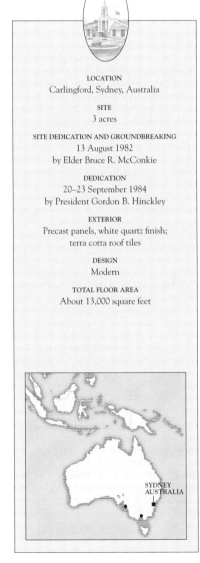

LOCATION
Carlingford, Sydney, Australia

SITE
3 acres

SITE DEDICATION AND GROUNDBREAKING
13 August 1982
by Elder Bruce R. McConkie

DEDICATION
20–23 September 1984
by President Gordon B. Hinckley

EXTERIOR
Precast panels, white quartz finish;
terra cotta roof tiles

DESIGN
Modern

TOTAL FLOOR AREA
About 13,000 square feet

SYDNEY
AUSTRALIA

forty students would need to raise two hundred dollars to meet the goal. For the rest of the semester, these young adult students found ways to earn the money, and by the end of the semester the class had earned forty dollars more than their goal.[3]

Elder Bruce R. McConkie, of the Quorum of the Twelve Apostles, broke ground for the temple 13 August 1982. Following the services he spoke at a fireside to an audience of more than fifteen hundred. "There could scarcely be a more memorable day in the entire history of this great nation," stated Elder McConkie. "I cannot use language that is too emphatic. There is no way to overemphasize what we are presenting—the fact that a House of the Lord is about to rise in Australia will be the crowning event for the Church here at this time, when the blessings and ordinances are made available."

Elder McConkie went on to say that this was only the beginning of temple work in Australia. "There is no reason why we can't have temples in Adelaide, Melbourne, Brisbane, Perth, or wherever the number of saints justifies it."[4] Elder McConkie's statement proved prophetic when, eighteen years later, temples were dedicated in Adelaide and Melbourne (both in 2000), and temples were under construction in Brisbane and Perth.

The design of the Sydney Australia Temple is similar to that which had been used in other temples built recently in the South Pacific. Local designers decided to use blue tile for the roof, as had been done with the Papeete Tahiti Temple. A striking azure blue color, dubbed "Mormon blue," was developed for the temple. More than twenty-five thousand terra cotta tiles were manufactured specifically for it.[5]

Sydney Australia Temple

May thy Saints here covenant with thee to walk in thy ways and follow after thy pattern. At the time of marriage may they kneel at the altars of this thy house, pledging their love and loyalty before thee, angels and witnesses, and here, under the authority of thine everlasting priesthood, may they be sealed for time and eternity according to thy great plan.

—FROM THE DEDICATORY PRAYER

Sydney

The beauty and spirit of the temple touched many lives during the public open house. People wanted to know more about the Church and the feelings they had experienced during the tour. At the end of one tour, a young couple asked where they could sign up to become members. A member of another faith seemed very interested in what he was told about temples and asked many questions. One minister, a genealogy enthusiast, asked the guide if the Church would be interested in having access to the three thousand names he had collected.[6]

The temple was dedicated on 20 September 1984. In the first of fourteen dedicatory sessions, President Gordon B. Hinckley, second counselor in the First Presidency, said, "There will be other temples here as the Church grows in this vast land. . . . As we assemble here, a large audience of unseen eyes is witnessing. I believe the God of Heaven smiles on us this day. This temple is part of his plan. I am satisfied that the Prophet Joseph smiles on us."

In the dedicatory prayer, President Hinckley petitioned: "Father, bless the land and the citizens of Australia. May this choice nation remain free from bondage, and may its people enjoy liberty and prosperity, now and in the generations to come."[7] Because President Spencer W. Kimball was not well enough to attend, President Hinckley conveyed the prophet's love and a special request of the youth of Australia: to prepare to serve a mission, get a good education, and marry in the temple.[8]

Since the dedication of the temple, the Latter-day Saints have performed faithful service in the Sydney Australia Temple. In 1994, more than forty Australian aboriginal Saints attended a weeklong temple trip during which they performed ordinances for the entire Larrakee Tribe in the Northern Territory. "The aboriginal people have always been a deeply spiritual people," said Donna Ballangarry of the Sydney Australia Parramatta Stake, "and the Church provides an opportunity for us to express that spiritu-ality. Our dreamtime legend says that the aboriginal people came to Australia from the waters the same way Lehi sailed to the promised land, and that's one reason why we find it so easy to accept the Book of Mormon."[9]

The dedication of the Australian Saints and their love for the temple are clearly evident in their desire to attend, even if that means traveling great distances under difficult circumstances. In the Busselton Branch, nine of the eleven active adults determined in June 1997 to make the nearly three-thousand-mile trip to the temple the following year.

"Within a month of making that commitment, things happened that might have prevented us from going," said Marilyn Domroe, branch Relief Society president. "In July, one of the sisters in the branch in her mid-seventies suffered a stroke. Later, another sister came down with a serious bout of pneumonia. Then our branch president, Charles Roper, broke his back while surfing, and another sister was stricken with a serious gall bladder condition. Every one of us experienced setbacks that reduced our savings for our intended trip."

Then she noted how blessings came to the branch members as they sought to keep their commitment despite the setbacks. Through medical help, prayers, and healing blessings, those with physical problems, including President Roper, recovered sufficiently to make the trip. In March 1998 the group set out on its journey across the entire continent of Australia. During their four-day visit to the temple, the group participated in three endowment sessions each day as well as in baptisms, initiatory ordinances, and sealings. "It was difficult to leave the temple," Sister Domroe said. "But we will return, and with Heavenly Father's guidance, we will overcome any obstacle that Satan puts in our path to prevent us from honoring our commitment."[10]

The Savior's image has been hidden in the tall tree to the right of the temple. The familiar shape of Australia is found among the shadows in the foreground of the full picture.

May thy Saints here covenant with thee to walk in thy ways and follow after thy pattern

Manila Philippines Temple

We are thankful for this day when we dedicate this sacred building. Its completion brings to full fruition the marvelous and wonderful work of establishing thine eternal ordinances in this nation. Now thy sons and daughters of the Philippines have available every gift and blessing, every act and ordinance pertaining to the dispensation of the fulness of times.

—FROM THE DEDICATORY PRAYER

Although the first official missionaries did not arrive in the Philippines until 1961, the archipelago of more than seven thousand islands off the southeast coast of Asia has seen some of the most dynamic growth in the Church. By 1969 the Philippine Mission was the highest-baptizing mission in the Church. As the Church grew in numbers, so the members grew in experience and understanding of the gospel plan. Just twenty years after the Church first became established in the islands President Spencer W. Kimball announced plans to build the Manila Philippines Temple.

Approximately seventy thousand Saints in the Philippines were overjoyed to hear the news. The expense of traveling to the nearest temple, in Tokyo, Japan, was prohibitively high for most. Not only would a temple in the Philippines make temple blessings available to a quickly growing area of the Church, but it also represented an era of stability and maturity in the country. This maturity was reflected in the creation of nine new stakes in the Philippines in 1981 and three more in 1982.

In January 1981 the Church purchased some land in Quezon City, in the metro Manila area, on a street called

LOCATION
Quezon City, Philippines

SITE
More than 3 acres

SITE DEDICATION AND GROUNDBREAKING
25 August 1982
by President Gordon B. Hinckley

DEDICATION
25–27 September 1984
by President Gordon B. Hinckley

EXTERIOR
Ceramic tile

DESIGN
Modern adaptation of six-spire design

TOTAL FLOOR AREA
More than 19,000 square feet

MANILA PHILIPPINES

Zebra Drive, which was later changed to Temple Drive. The site, which overlooks the Marikina Valley, was chosen in part because of its relative accessibility to members throughout the temple district.[1]

A fund-raising campaign for the temple was quickly set up among Church members in the Philippines. The Saints sacrificed greatly but nine months later, they had reached only 65 percent of their goal. Church leaders again encouraged members to give all they could to the fund, and the devoted Filipino Saints responded once again, reaching and exceeding the goal in three months' time.[2]

President Gordon B. Hinckley, second counselor in the First Presidency, and Elder Marion D. Hanks of the Seventy arrived in August 1982 to break ground for the temple. It was then typhoon season in the Philippines, so there had been a daily downpour of rain for some time. At a meeting with missionaries of the Philippines Manila Mission on the morning of the groundbreaking, President Hinckley asked the missionary assigned to offer the benediction to pray that God would temper the elements for the duration of the ceremony. The elder expressed this plea, and almost immediately the sky began to clear. That afternoon some twenty-five hundred people attended the groundbreaking. Though the skies were still ominous and the winds still blew, no rain fell on the spectators. As soon as the ceremony ended, however, the rains returned and continued falling well into the next day.[3]

Several events in the Philippines during the construction of the temple hampered its progress. In 1983 the assassination of a senator led to riots and demonstrations throughout the nation. And in 1984 the already-weak economy slipped again when the Philippine peso was devalued for the third time in nine months. In addition, the unemployment rate was high. Because of these problems, most people were struggling to get by, and crime increased throughout the country. During these trials the Church established ways to help members become more self-reliant and encouraged them to stay close to the Lord. Church leaders later said that these difficulties served as a "refiner's fire" for the Saints, strengthening those who endured the challenges.[4]

Another challenge faced by Church leaders during the construction was that of making temple garments available to the many members who would soon attend the temple for the first time. Because of the Philippine government's strict rules concerning the importing of any clothing, the Church commissioned a local clothing manufacturer to make 28,000 sets of garments. After the garments were manufactured, twenty endowed sisters volunteered to complete the sewing, mark the sizes, and package the garments. Because of these sisters' sacrifice, the process was completed in less than three months.[5]

Two powerful typhoons hit the Philippines in the days preceding the temple open house. The second, named Nitang, led to the deaths of more than nineteen hundred people and caused an estimated $111 million worth of damage. Because of this natural disaster many who had planned to attend the VIP day of the open house were unable to travel to the temple. Midway through the open house, a volcano on the island of Luzon erupted, sending ash high into the air. And two days before the dedication, a strong earthquake shook the island but did no damage to the temple.

Despite these powerful displays of nature, some twenty-seven thousand people toured the 13,800-square-foot temple during the open house. Many expressed to their guides the impressions they had received while touring the sacred structure. Celson Carunungan, a writer, spoke of "a feeling of holiness, that when you get inside you are going to confront your Creator."[6] Colonel Bienvenido Castillo, the chief chaplain of the Philippine constabulary, said the temple was "a place where you can contemplate heavenly things because you are in such an environment."[7]

On 25 September 1984, President Hinckley dedicated the Manila Philippines Temple. In his remarks to the audience, he spoke of the Philippines as a "nation of heroes." He described the young men and women who participate in baptisms for their kindred dead as heroes, saving their ancestors from spiritual bondage.[8]

Expressing gratitude for the temple in the dedicatory prayer, President Hinckley said: "Its completion brings to full fruition the marvelous and wonderful work of establishing thine eternal ordinances in this nation. Now thy sons and daughters of the Philippines have available every gift and blessing, every act and ordinance pertaining to the dispensation of the fulness of times."[9]

Since its dedication, the Manila Philippines Temple has been a great blessing for the Saints in the Philippines, Indonesia, Malaysia, Thailand, and Singapore. Temple president Myron F. Francom described the dedication of these members and the love they have for the temple:

"These beautiful people come from far, far distances to be sealed as an eternal family in the House of the Lord. They come by boat and by land, by bus, by 'Jeepney' and by tricycle, often traveling two or three days and nights to come to the temple.

"They come with great faith and a longing desire to become an eternal family. Because many are very poor, it becomes a once-in-a-lifetime experience for some of them to come to the temple. They will give all they have for this wonderful opportunity. They never seem to complain about the trials and hardships they may endure.

"Some come with seven or eight or more children and little babies in their arms. Some come with only a few of their children, hoping that in the future they will have enough money to bring the rest of their children to be sealed.

"I will never forget the experience I had when I sealed ten children, all dressed in white, to their parents. As they all looked at me with such childlike faith, I could feel their joy and happiness. We felt very close to our Father in Heaven and the tears filled our eyes.

"Yes, the temple is an experience of love: our love for our Father in Heaven and His children and His great love for us."[10]

Dallas Texas Temple

On 1 April 1981, President Spencer W. Kimball announced plans to build nine temples in various parts of the world. These temples were designed to be small, efficient, and more economical to build than earlier temples. One of them, the Dallas Texas Temple, would serve nearly 120,000 members in most of Texas, all of Oklahoma, and parts of Arkansas, Louisiana, and Missouri.[1]

A fund-raising committee was promptly formed after the announcement. Almost immediately individual members' contributions and money from ward and stake projects began coming in. By collecting and selling aluminum cans, children in one stake raised seven hundred dollars. In another stake the children raised money through a program they called "Nickels for Nails."[2] Even members with limited means responded generously. A bishop encouraged one widow, who had a very limited income, to pledge twenty dollars to the fund. Instead she gave him one hundred dollars, saying, "This is money I've been saving to go to the temple in Salt Lake City, but I'll contribute it to the building fund and go to the temple here."[3] The Saints made generous contributions, and by the time ground was broken to begin construction of the temple, they had raised 140 percent of their assessment.[4]

Not all contributions were monetary, however. Relief Society sisters in the area were asked to crochet cloths that would cover the altars. To have money to buy the needed thread, one sister and her sick husband went without several meals until they had saved enough. When offered assistance, she refused, saying, "I have never been able to do anything for my Father in Heaven until now. Don't deny this blessing to my ill husband or me."[5]

After considering a variety of sites, the Church chose one

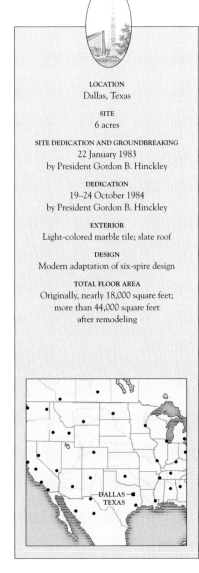

LOCATION
Dallas, Texas

SITE
6 acres

SITE DEDICATION AND GROUNDBREAKING
22 January 1983
by President Gordon B. Hinckley

DEDICATION
19–24 October 1984
by President Gordon B. Hinckley

EXTERIOR
Light-colored marble tile; slate roof

DESIGN
Modern adaptation of six-spire design

TOTAL FLOOR AREA
Originally, nearly 18,000 square feet;
more than 44,000 square feet
after remodeling

DALLAS
TEXAS

in a quiet residential neighborhood twelve miles north of downtown Dallas. The property included an orchard of pecan trees. During a visit to examine the site, Elder Mark E. Petersen, of the Quorum of the Twelve Apostles, described the location as peaceful and serene and expressed his opinion that this was indeed an appropriate location for a temple.[6]

Before the announcement of the Dallas Texas Temple, the Church had been largely unnoticed by the area's media. But with the announcement, some groups voiced strong opposition to the Church and its teachings. One headline in a major local newspaper read, "Southern Baptists Brace for Invasion of Mormons," and a story stated, "Southern Baptists, alarmed by a potential influx of Mormons into the South, are putting on their gospel armor and mounting their defenses against an invasion."

Opposition was also voiced in magazine articles and radio and television programs devoted to warning the Christian community of the dangers of Mormonism. Church members had never experienced such an intense opposition from other people in the community. A group opposed to the temple went as far as writing down the license plate numbers in the parking lot during a Latter-day Saint Sunday meeting so they could find out their addresses and encourage them to leave the Church. But such efforts were largely ineffective, and the Saints were strengthened in their beliefs as they renewed their conviction of the truth of the gospel.[7]

During this time, Bishop H. Burke Peterson, of the presiding bishopric, and Elder Ivan L. Hobson, a regional representative, visited the temple site to discuss these problems. While they were speaking, a man approached them and introduced

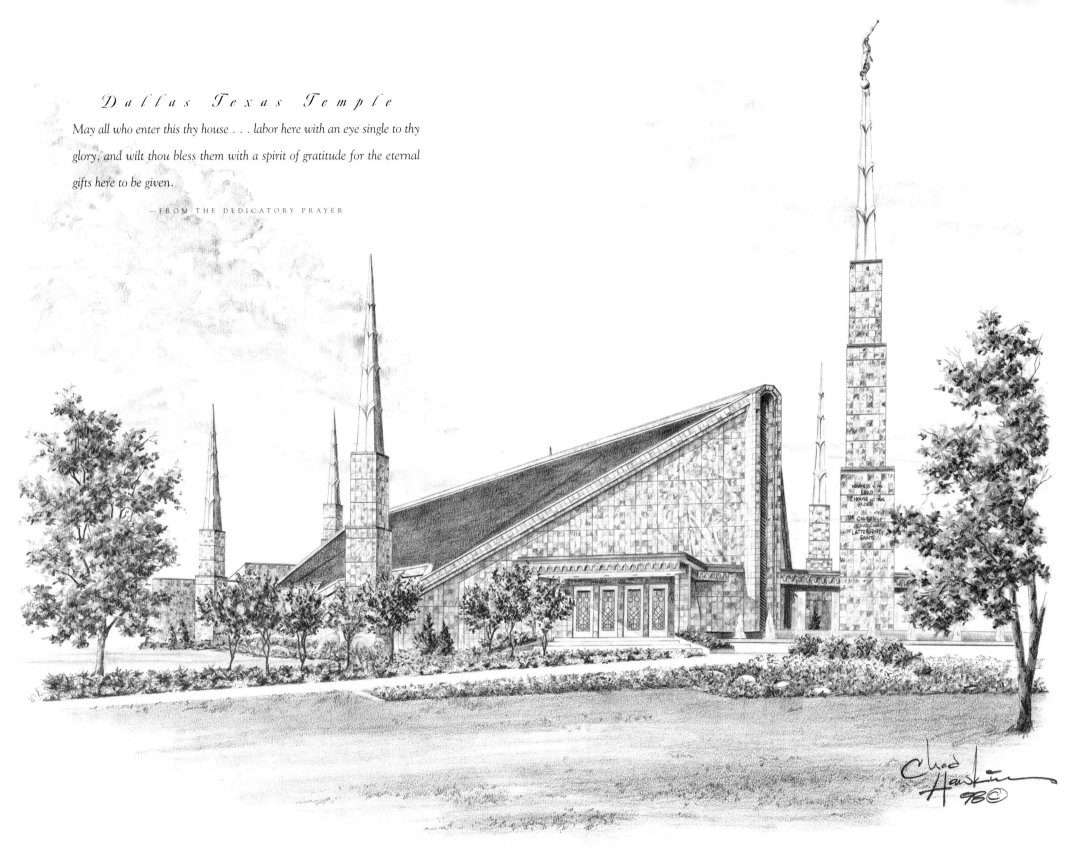

Dallas Texas Temple

May all who enter this thy house . . . labor here with an eye single to thy glory, and wilt thou bless them with a spirit of gratitude for the eternal gifts here to be given.

—FROM THE DEDICATORY PRAYER

himself as Reverend Pryor. Bishop Peterson asked the reverend what he thought of their plan to build the temple and about the community's reaction. Reverend Pryor explained that although he had been pressured to speak against the temple, he had decided not to take a stand for or against it. He noted that years earlier, when his church had been building the facility he preached in, his church had received similar opposition. But, he said, once the building was completed, opposition had ceased, and they had not had any further problems.[8]

At the groundbreaking ceremony on 22 January 1983, a prayer was offered, asking the Lord to ease animosity toward the temple and help the local people come to appreciate the temple as a beautiful addition to the community. President Gordon B. Hinckley, second counselor in the First Presidency, emphasized that "this is the Lord's work; it cannot be stopped, it will not be stopped, it will roll forth. We'll build this temple here, we will build all the others presently scheduled, and there are others yet to come which have been tentatively designated."[9]

Much was done was done in answer to this prayer when the temple opened its doors in September 1984 for a twenty-day open house. Some eighty thousand visitors, more than half of whom were nonmembers, came to visit the edifice. Many of them expressed interest in the Church, and some were baptized in the weeks following the dedication.[10]

On 19 October 1984, the temple was dedicated by President Gordon B. Hinckley before an audience of eleven hundred people. He noted, "Texas is filled with other buildings that are larger and far more expensive than this temple. But this is the most significant of all in the Lone Star State.

Hidden on the wall of the temple is an image of Jesus Christ, the Good Shepherd, cradling one of his sheep. His flock can be found in the clouds and in the landscaped grounds, reminding us that we should know our Shepherd's voice and follow him.

Nowhere else can the power and authority of reaching beyond the veil of death be exercised." He encouraged the Saints to use this power "to do for others what they are powerless to do for themselves."[11]

Like the Boise Idaho Temple, which was built according to a similar plan, this temple was remodeled in 1987 to increase its size and make it more functional and efficient. The addition gave the temple 22,749 new square feet of space, an additional ordinance room, a cafeteria, and expanded laundry facilities. It also relocated the baptistry.[12]

Over the years the Dallas Texas Temple has been used by patrons to receive ordinances for themselves and for the dead. In addition to thousands of family members for whom patrons have acted as proxies, ordinances have been performed for individuals of historical significance in the temple district. For instance, in 1986 work was completed for the men who perished at the Alamo on 6 March 1836, and their families.[13] Work was also performed for the fifteen hundred Choctaws who were forced to relocate more than five hundred miles in the middle of winter. Many of them died in zero-degree temperatures. The route they took has since come to be known as the "Trail of Tears."[14]

In dedicating the Dallas Texas Temple, President Hinckley prayed, "Prosper thy work in this part of thy vineyard. May the dedication of this temple mark the beginning of a new and glorious day for thy Church in this area."[15] With the stability and respect the temple has brought to the Church in Texas, its creation truly has marked the beginning of a new and glorious day for the Saints.

May all who enter this thy house . . . labor here with an eye single to thy glory

Taipei Taiwan Temple

May peace and prosperity reign in the land. May thy work spread from here to the vast numbers of thy sons and daughters wherever they may be found. Touch the hearts of those who govern that they may open the doors of their nations to thy messengers of eternal truth. May thy work grow in beauty and in strength in the great Chinese realm.

— FROM THE DEDICATORY PRAYER

The people of Taiwan, whose island was once called *Formosa,* meaning "beautiful," were first introduced to the Church when American servicemen were stationed there in the mid 1950s. The servicemen gathered to hold meetings and were organized into a branch in 1956, the same year that missionaries from the Southern Far East mission arrived in Taiwan.[1] One of the missionaries described his first glimpse of the island as they approached: "The mountains shot abruptly out of the blue waters with their peaks reaching up as though they wanted to puncture the blue sky overhead. Despite the steepness of the peaks, dry earth was not to be seen, but only the dark green vegetation which mantles the island."[2]

These missionaries and those that followed soon organized branches among the Taiwanese converts. The printing of the Book of Mormon in Chinese in 1965 was a great boon to the local members, who had waited for years to have the book available in their own language. It is the building of the Taipei Taiwan Temple, however, that the Taiwanese Saints see as the greatest development in the history of the Church in their land.

The Saints talked for many years about making an

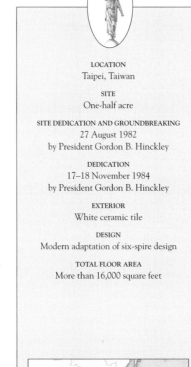

LOCATION
Taipei, Taiwan

SITE
One-half acre

SITE DEDICATION AND GROUNDBREAKING
27 August 1982
by President Gordon B. Hinckley

DEDICATION
17–18 November 1984
by President Gordon B. Hinckley

EXTERIOR
White ceramic tile

DESIGN
Modern adaptation of six-spire design

TOTAL FLOOR AREA
More than 16,000 square feet

TAIPEI TAIWAN

excursion to the Laie Hawaii Temple; but because of the high cost of travel, the trip never took place, and the members could not receive their temple blessings. As Church membership grew in Taiwan, the Saints began to hope that temple blessings would some day be brought to them. In 1971, President Harold B. Lee, first counselor in the First Presidency, told members during a trip to the island that they should "prepare themselves, that they might be able to receive the greater blessings of the Lord."[3] Four years later, during the first area conference in Taiwan, President Spencer W. Kimball explained the purpose of building a temple in Japan, adding, "You, too, can have one."[4] He explained the necessity of growing in the gospel and preparing for such developments.

After the announcement of the temple in 1981, Church leaders decided to build on the site of the mission home in the center of Taipei. Although not on a hilltop or in a wooded area, and therefore different from those of many other temples throughout the world, the location is easily accessible to members. Church leaders hoped the beauty of the temple would attract the attention of passersby who would notice the contrast between it and the surrounding secular buildings.

Materials used on the building were scheduled to arrive on site early to facilitate an uninterrupted flow in the construction process. But it was often difficult to find room to store supplies on the limited space at the site. In one instance, additional storage space was provided in an unusual way. When crates containing the baptismal font and its large oxen, as well as the statue of the angel Moroni, arrived in the country, customs authorities declined to release them. LaVar Wallgren, who sculpted the statue and the oxen, described the situation:

"The Church authorities were not concerned at all, and they did not push the matter because they did not have any place to put them. When the construction officials finally needed them for the temple, they called up [customs authorities] and said, 'We have some containers that have been on your dock for a long period of time—a month or two.' The person managing the dock was surprised and, after going through his papers, said, 'Get these things off the dock!' The whole thing was a blessing in disguise."[5]

The temple was completed in 1984, and more than twenty thousand visitors toured it during the open house. Awed viewers were reported to have said it was the most beautiful building they had ever seen. Among those who attended the open house were government officials, influential businesspeople, and leaders of area churches. One professor of architecture from a Taipei university took his students to the open house several times so they could study the structure and its workmanship. The structure was later nominated as one of the most beautiful buildings in all of Taiwan.[6]

The Taipei Taiwan Temple was dedicated 17 November 1984 by President Gordon B. Hinckley, second counselor in the First Presidency. Although a typhoon was reportedly headed toward Taiwan on the second day of the dedication, members were undaunted as they stood in line to participate. Five dedicatory sessions were held, four in Mandarin (the language spoken in Taiwan and much of China) and one in Cantonese (the language spoken in Hong Kong, which was part of the temple district). President Hinckley pointed out that the ordinances of the temple were available not only to the living members of the Church but also to the millions of their ancestors who had preceded them in life.[7]

In his dedicatory prayer, he expressed gratitude for "the firm foundation on which thy Church is now established in this part of the earth. We thank thee for this day when those who will use this temple may turn their hearts to their fathers, participating in thy holy house in those ordinances which will make it possible for their deceased forebears to move forward on the way that leads to eternal life."[8]

Part of the Church's favorable reception in Taiwan stems from Taiwanese interest in their ancestors and family history. David C. H. Liu, who served as recorder for the Taipei Taiwan Temple, said that he believed the Lord had been preparing the Taiwanese for centuries for the coming of the gospel and temple work to their island. "They love their families and have a good tradition of keeping the family genealogy," he said. Some families in Taiwan have family records dating back two thousand years. Even before the dedication of the temple, some twelve thousand names had been submitted for temple work.[9]

Since the dedication of the Taipei Taiwan Temple, the Saints in Taiwan and Hong Kong have made good use of it. Records show that average monthly attendance exceeds the number of recommend holders in the temple district. Part of the reason for the high rate of attendance is the proximity of the temple to Church members. Even the Saints in Hong Kong were greatly blessed by the nearness of the temple, travel to it costing just one-third of what it cost to travel to the Tokyo Japan Temple.

But the high attendance is even more attributable to the members' love for their ancestors and their gratitude for the blessing of having a house of the Lord among them. President Pan Kuang I, first counselor in the Taipei West Stake presidency at the time of the temple's dedication, commented that the temple reminds the Saints in Taiwan that Heavenly Father and the Church leadership are aware of them and love them. "That is really encouraging to the people."[10]

May thy work grow in beauty and strength in the great Chinese realm

Guatemala City Guatemala Temple

Thou kind and gracious Father, our hearts swell with gratitude for thy remembrance of the sons and daughters of Lehi, the many generations of our fathers and mothers who suffered so greatly and who walked for so long in darkness. Thou hast heard their cries and seen their tears. Now there will be opened to them the gates of salvation and eternal life.

— FROM THE DEDICATORY PRAYER

The stately Guatemala City Guatemala Temple is a worthy addition to its location on Vista Hermosa, which means "beautiful view." Faced with white Guatemala marble and flanked by six elegant spires, the temple stands at the foot of rolling hills in southeastern Guatemala City.

The interior of the temple is equally beautiful, featuring authentic Mayan articles. Those assigned to select materials for the temple's interior believe they were guided by the Spirit to local marketplaces, where they purchased two beautiful *guipiles* (handwoven, embroidered blouses) that were framed and hung in the temple's foyer.[1]

Guatemala City always struggles with water shortages, so prior to construction, the temple's first president, John Forres O'Donnal, suggested drilling a well to supply the needs of the new building. After grinding through two hundred feet of solid rock, the drillers found an abundant supply of pure water.[2]

During the open house, some twenty-four thousand people visited the temple, requiring 179 missionaries from the Guatemala City Mission to work in six-hour shifts with twenty missionaries per shift. About thirty-seven hundred copies of

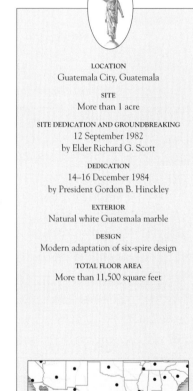

LOCATION
Guatemala City, Guatemala

SITE
More than 1 acre

SITE DEDICATION AND GROUNDBREAKING
12 September 1982
by Elder Richard G. Scott

DEDICATION
14–16 December 1984
by President Gordon B. Hinckley

EXTERIOR
Natural white Guatemala marble

DESIGN
Modern adaptation of six-spire design

TOTAL FLOOR AREA
More than 11,500 square feet

GUATEMALA CITY
GUATEMALA

the Book of Mormon were distributed. Of these, thirty-five hundred had been donated by Guatemalan Saints, who included their testimonies. A university student who toured the temple described it as a "beautiful pearl" overlooking the capital city.[3]

During the first dedicatory session, President Gordon B. Hinckley noted that the temple was a blessing "for which many generations have prayed behind the veil, descendants of Father Lehi, who have been taught the gospel . . . so they may continue with their journey to eternal life." In the dedicatory prayer, he expressed gratitude that the temple would open "the gates of salvation and eternal life" for "the many generations of our fathers and mothers who suffered so greatly and who walked for so long in darkness."[4] Each session was filled to capacity with about nine hundred Saints, who came not only from Guatemala City but also from remote rural areas in Guatemala and from neighboring Honduras, El Salvador, and Costa Rica.

The temple's matron, Sister Carmen O'Donnal, the first Guatemalan baptized in modern times, said that having a temple in her native land was the culmination of thirty-six years of work and growth. "It will be a blessing not just for the members," she said, "but for the whole nation, as the people come to know Jesus Christ through this holy and sanctified place."[5]

Adjacent to the temple is the Guatemala Missionary Training Center, evidence of the Church's growth in Central America. At the center's groundbreaking ceremony, Udine Fallabella, a regional representative and the first stake president in Central America, noted, "The Church is growing faster than our steps keep up with it. We must follow the admonition of President Spencer W. Kimball to lengthen our stride."[6]

During his service as the temple president, Owen Dean Call wrote: "Since its dedication in 1984, the Guatemala City Temple has blessed the lives of thousands of faithful members. Indeed, the impact and influence of the temple in the lives of the members can be measured in the increasing number of stakes and missions. In 1984 there were eight stakes and two missions in Guatemala. At the end of 1993, there were 24 stakes and four missions in this country.

"We have seen the influence and spiritual impact of the temple as the many indigenous groups come for their sacred ordinances: Mam, Kekchi, Quiche, Pocoman, Cakchiqel, Sutuil, and others who are direct descendants of the ancient Lamanites. One of the most beautiful sights one can enjoy in the temple is to watch these pure Lamanites, indigenous to the country, come to claim the blessings that by royal birthright belong to them. All the temple workers know that they are special; they have such a strong spirit that the temple's atmosphere changes when they walk in. We have never seen people as reverent, humble, and with such spirituality as these 'true Lamanites.' To see them arrive, a little nervous and full of expectations, and after a few hours to see them leave with the brightness of eternity shining in their eyes is the most rewarding feeling one can have working in the temple.

"Two responses demonstrate the impact of these ordinances: 'After being in this holy building, I have been able to better understand the order of things pertaining to eternal life,' said one indigenous brother. 'I have understood that if we desire we can be instruments in the hands of God to bless the lives of others on this or the other side of the veil.' Another patron commented, 'As I ponder the privilege we have, as part of the children of God, to receive through correct channels and from authorized servants the saving ordinances, I cannot go forward without thanking Heavenly Father for the opportunity to partake of them.'

"We are also touched by the great sacrifices made by many of the Saints who come. Saints from Honduras and Nicaragua spend from fourteen to thirty-two hours on a bus to get to the temple. A sister ordinance worker spends two hours or more by bus to get to the temple and takes in washing on other days so she will have the money needed for her bus fare. She seldom misses a day and is always on time."[7]

*Our hearts swell with gratitude for thy remembrance
of the sons and daughters of Lehi*

Freiberg Germany Temple

Thou knowest we have long prayed that we might have a temple in our midst. Thou knowest that we love thee, and that we love the ordinances and blessings of thy house. We thank thee that we are able to worship thee in spirit and in truth. We thank thee that we may now come to this sanctuary and feel of the hallowed influence here to be found.

—FROM THE DEDICATORY PRAYER

The Freiberg Germany Temple stands on a beautiful site in Freiberg, a city about 120 miles south of Berlin. Cut off from the West from the end of World War II until 1989, the German Saints remained faithful during their years behind the Iron Curtain, despite their isolation. "The war cost us everything," one said, "but there was something they couldn't take—our testimonies."[1]

On a Sunday morning in 1975, Elder Thomas S. Monson and a group of local Church leaders stood on a hill between Meissen and Dresden. Looking down onto the Elbe River, President Monson offered a dedicatory prayer for the land and its people. In his journal he later recorded, "I remember offering these words in the extemporaneous prayer: 'May today mark the dawning of a new beginning of thy work in this land.' I mentioned that at this juncture, far below in the valley through which flowed the Elbe River, a bell in a church steeple began to chime and the shrill crow of a rooster shattered the Sabbath silence, each event heralding the beginning of a new day. I felt warmth of sunshine upon my face and hands, even though my eyes were closed and an incessant rain had been

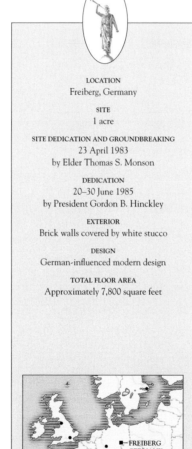

LOCATION
Freiberg, Germany

SITE
1 acre

SITE DEDICATION AND GROUNDBREAKING
23 April 1983
by Elder Thomas S. Monson

DEDICATION
20–30 June 1985
by President Gordon B. Hinckley

EXTERIOR
Brick walls covered by white stucco

DESIGN
German-influenced modern design

TOTAL FLOOR AREA
Approximately 7,800 square feet

FREIBERG
GERMANY

falling all morning. At the conclusion of the prayer, I gazed heavenward and discovered that a ray of sunshine had penetrated the thick cloud cover, encompassing the small area where our group stood. It was evidence to me that Divine help was at hand and that our prayer had been heard by a loving Heavenly Father."[2] Within fifteen years, two new stakes and a mission had been formed, and the magnificent temple had been dedicated. In 1989 the Berlin Wall fell, leading to the reunification of Germany.

After the groundbreaking ceremony in 1983, Elder Monson recorded: "This is a miracle of miracles! I think it all began when we made a final effort with the government to get permission for our faithful couples to go to the Swiss Temple. The [German] minister in their government then said, 'Why not build a temple in your country?' We took him up on his offer, and the building is now under way."[3]

There were other miracles, too. Henry Burkhardt, president of the Freiberg Germany Temple, explained that private ownership of property was not permitted in East Germany, and yet the Church was granted private ownership. The building of a temple had never before been permitted in a Communist nation, but in this case, government officials themselves suggested the building of a temple as an alternative to considering the request that Church members be permitted to visit the temple in Switzerland. Allowing the temple to be built was a totally incredible, unprecedented move for Communist leaders. A third miracle was that land for the temple was purchased with German Democratic Republic marks rather than with currency from the West. "All in all, the event [was] miraculous," said President Burkhardt.[4]

Only four thousand Church members lived in the German

Democratic Republic at the time, but nearly ninety thousand people went through the open house. President Monson considered that attendance to be an answer to his prayer in 1975, when he had asked Heavenly Father to "instill within the citizenry a curiosity concerning the Church and a desire to learn more of our teachings."[5]

A few months after the temple was dedicated, President Burkhardt discovered early one morning that baptisms had not been performed for 108 males scheduled for ordinance work that day. He felt that the work should not be interrupted, even though the heating system was off and the water in the baptismal font was icy cold. He called Andreas Kleinert, a faithful fourteen-year-old Latter-day Saint who lived nearby, and thirty minutes later they both entered the freezing water.

"When I was immersed for the first time, it felt like I was rolling in snow," said Andreas. "I just could not get used to the cold water."

They were determined not to stop, however, and they continued until the 108 baptisms had been performed.

Andreas commented, "Never had I shivered like this before. But neither President Burkhardt nor I even caught a cold. I was happy that I was once again able to do work in the temple."[6]

In 1992 a group of Ukrainian Saints attended the temple. Their week-long journey was described by government authorities as "the Mormon pilgrimage." After months of red tape to secure necessary approvals, they traveled by bus thousands of miles through the nations of the Communist Bloc. The expense was enormous—the equivalent of a year's tithing for most of those making the trip. Unable to convert their currency, the travelers had to carry with them their own food, sleeping bags, and other provisions. They described being in the temple as a "wonderful feeling of heaven" and the "presence of the Savior." There, in the house of the Lord, the Ukrainian couples and families were sealed for eternity.[7]

Elder Monson wrote in his journal: "Frequently people will ask, 'How has it been possible for the Church to obtain permission to build a temple behind the Iron Curtain?' My feeling is simply that the faith and devotion of our Latter-day Saints in that area brought forth the help of Almighty God and provided for them the eternal blessings which they so richly deserve."[8]

We thank thee that we may now come to this sanctuary and feel of the hallowed influence here to be found

Stockholm Sweden Temple

Bless this nation where is found thy temple, and its sister nations, that these may be lands of freedom and peace, and may their people walk in righteousness that they may be deserving of thine overseeing power.

—FROM THE DEDICATORY PRAYER

The Stockholm Sweden Temple, reflecting traditional architecture of the "Land of the North," is located in Vasterhaninge, a suburb of Haninge, about thirteen miles southeast of Stockholm. Its six spires rise above the pines in the nearby forest, and a cobblestone path leads to its doors. Near the temple is a Church-owned guesthouse with 120 beds for patrons who have traveled long distances to attend the house of the Lord.

After President Spencer W. Kimball announced that a temple would be built near Stockholm, Sweden, a site-selection committee was formed to consider twenty-eight possible sites. Two were presented to the First Presidency for consideration. The First Presidency chose the community of Haninge because of its large concentration of Latter-day Saints.[1] City officials and merchants welcomed the temple project, and later the city showed further support by changing the name of the street on which the temple is located to Temple Drive. City officials also renamed the three blocks of the temple site as Temple, Genealogist, and Chapel.[2]

When the local Environmental Party raised concerns, temple president Bo G. Wennerlund, then a regional representative, attended a community meeting to discuss the issues. At first the people seemed hostile, but as the meeting pro-

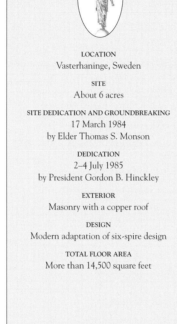

LOCATION
Vasterhaninge, Sweden

SITE
About 6 acres

SITE DEDICATION AND GROUNDBREAKING
17 March 1984
by Elder Thomas S. Monson

DEDICATION
2–4 July 1985
by President Gordon B. Hinckley

EXTERIOR
Masonry with a copper roof

DESIGN
Modern adaptation of six-spire design

TOTAL FLOOR AREA
More than 14,500 square feet

gressed, their feelings changed, and matters were resolved amicably. When the temple architect asked Elder Wennerlund later how he turned the crowd around, Elder Wennerlund told him, "I didn't do it. It was the Lord."[3]

On 17 March 1984, more than four hundred people braved frigid weather to attend the groundbreaking for the first temple in Scandinavia. Heaters had to be used to thaw the ground. President Thomas S. Monson, who was presiding, said, "On this cold morning you have warm smiles on your faces and warm feelings in your hearts, for it is a day of thanksgiving."[4] Many Church members described the occasion as a new day in Sweden, a phrase Elder Monson had used on 8 July 1977 in a prayer dedicating and rededicating the country.

During his first visit to Temple Square in Salt Lake City, Elder Wennerlund thought, "Here I would like to live and die." He later remembered, "I loved going to the temple. I was so impressed with everything I saw. I looked and looked, trying to commit everything to memory. I couldn't believe I was actually there; I didn't want to think about leaving such a wonderful place. I dreaded the thought of returning home."

Later, however, he had a strong desire to go back to Sweden. "I am a Swede," he told himself. "Sweden, not Utah, is my place. I am going to return home and help build the Church in Sweden. Someday, members of the Church will come to a place in Sweden and feel about it the way I felt when I saw Temple Square the first time." After he was called as president of the Stockholm Sweden Temple, he counseled visitors, "Go home and be a blessing to your nation." Welcoming them to the temple with one hand, he turned them back home with the other.[5]

In the Stockholm Sweden Temple, sessions are routinely conducted in nine languages, with sessions in other languages as needed. Here people from many nations put aside their traditional differences—Estonians, Finns, Russians, Germans, Danes, Swedes, and Norwegians—working together in love. An ordinance worker who fled the second Russian invasion of Estonia at the end of World War II is now glad to see the Russians—coming to the temple.[6]

That in itself is a miracle. In 1973 President Spencer W. Kimball asked the Saints to pray that the doors of all nations—including those behind the Iron Curtain—would be opened to missionary work.[7] The Saints responded, praying for years that it might be so. In 1989 the Iron Curtain began to fall. Church members in Russia, Hungary, Poland, and the Baltic States began preparing to go to the temple in Sweden.

On 10 December 1991, the first Russian family was sealed in the Stockholm Sweden Temple. Their trip cost more than most Russians earn in a year. Temple president Reid Johnson described their visit: "They have immersed themselves in the ordinances of the temple. All have been 'anxiously engaged' in performing ordinances, receiving the covenants of the endowment, striving to absorb and understand the almost unfathomable depths of the eternal marriage covenant and sealing power. They were more literally immersed in the baptismal font, leaving tears in the water as the names of parents, grandparents and other loved ones were read."[8]

Since then many other patrons have traveled to the temple from Russia and the Baltic states. Eventually, however, they must return home, a journey of four to six days. "They wave good-bye," said one temple worker. "Some look up at the statue of the angel Moroni and say, 'Good-bye, Moroni, we may never see you again.'"[9]

Bless this nation where is found thy temple,

and its sister nations, that these may

be lands of freedom and peace

Chicago Illinois Temple

The Chicago Illinois Temple, dedicated in 1985, was the first temple to be built in the Midwestern United States since the Nauvoo Temple, which was begun during the life of Joseph Smith and afterward was destroyed by mobs. The land on which the Chicago Illinois Temple sits is known as "The Grove" and is famous for its wildflowers, birds, and grasslands. This site, in Glenview, Illinois, about twenty miles north of Chicago, was selected after two years of searching and two more years of seeking governmental approvals amid intense opposition by groups concerned about the visual effect the temple would have on the area.

When ground was finally broken and construction of the temple commenced, President Gordon B. Hinckley sought to allay the fears of local residents. At the groundbreaking ceremony he said, "We promise that what we do here will be beautiful and will enhance rather than diminish the charm of this lovely area."[1] The Church was true to these words, taking measures to preserve the native landscape on the temple grounds and allowing for a one-hundred-foot buffer zone along the southern border of the site. The southern side of the temple roof remains unlighted so as not to disrupt bird migration flyways.[2] Large trees and beautiful lawns surrounded by an ornate brick-and-iron fence beautify the grounds. The site has proven to be a perfect, peaceful setting for a house of the Lord. Elder Robert L. Simpson, a member of the Seventy, commented that the selection of this site was heaven directed.[3]

The temple adds to the natural beauty of its setting. Because of contributions from faithful Saints in the area, both the outside and the inside of the building reflect the love the members have for the temple and the sacrifices they made to beautify it. The landscaping in part was funded with "temple

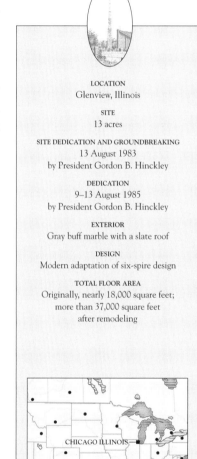

LOCATION
Glenview, Illinois

SITE
13 acres

SITE DEDICATION AND GROUNDBREAKING
13 August 1983
by President Gordon B. Hinckley

DEDICATION
9–13 August 1985
by President Gordon B. Hinckley

EXTERIOR
Gray buff marble with a slate roof

DESIGN
Modern adaptation of six-spire design

TOTAL FLOOR AREA
Originally, nearly 18,000 square feet;
more than 37,000 square feet
after remodeling

CHICAGO ILLINOIS

pennies" donated by Primary children in the temple district. Members gave of their time, talents, and money to provide furnishings for the temple. A group of young women made dolls for the temple nursery. Women crocheted and tatted altar cloths for the ordinance and sealing rooms. One of them, a seventy-eight-year-old sister from Indiana, wrote that although her infirmities kept her from attending the temple, she felt blessed to be able to participate by creating something beautiful for the temple. Another sister sent her finished cloth and a note offering to make another one if needed. She wept with gratitude after a phone call came accepting her offer.[4]

In addition to preparing the temple for its open house, dedication, and subsequent use for the performing of ordinances, members began preparing themselves to serve in the temple regularly. Home teachers in the Naperville Illinois Stake asked the families they taught to consider the question, "Are you really spiritually prepared to go to the temple?" Members who took this assignment seriously felt a change occur. Robert Ensign of the Woodridge Ward, Naperville Stake, said, "People's lives are changing, and we're finding that the closer we draw to the dedication, the more that momentum is building."[5]

Many members volunteered to help with the open house of the temple. During the time it was open to the public, more than one hundred thousand people walked through the halls of the sacred building, marveling at its beauty, learning of its purpose, and feeling the peaceful spirit that is only found in a temple. Visitors made such comments as "an obvious place of devotion," "everyone should feel closer to God in this special place," and "I felt the hand of God."[6]

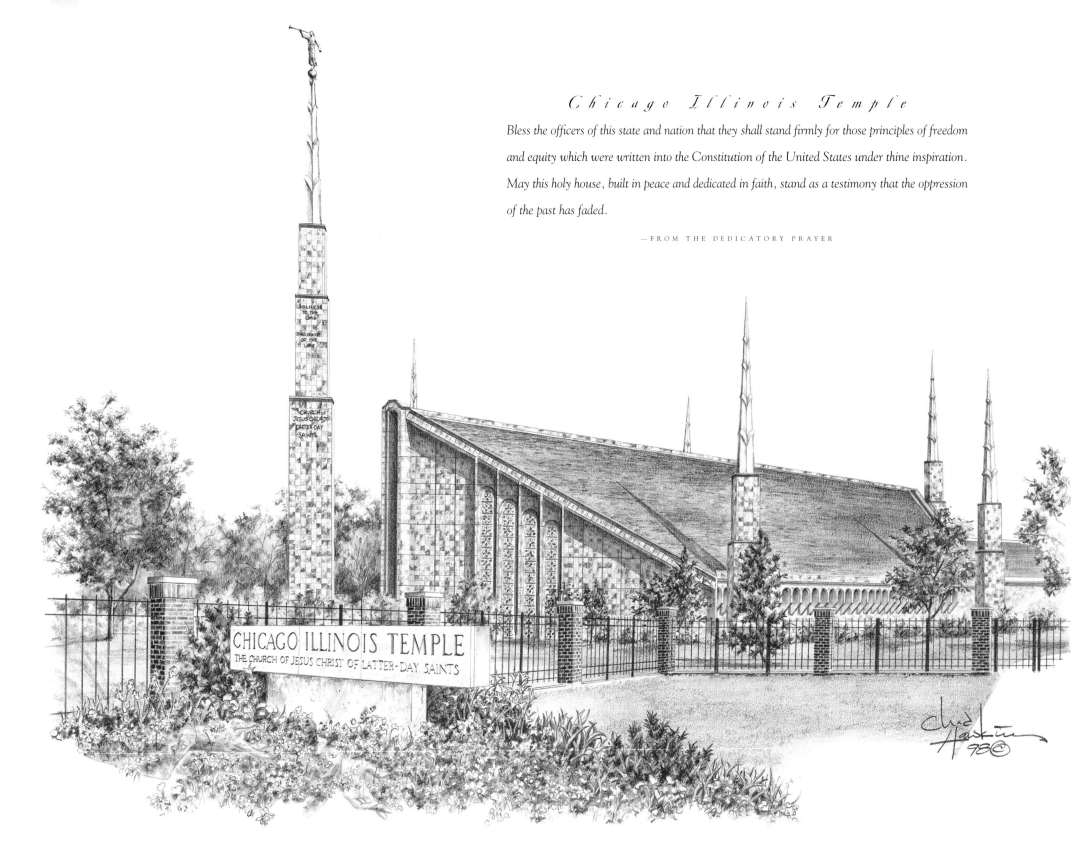

Chicago Illinois Temple

Bless the officers of this state and nation that they shall stand firmly for those principles of freedom and equity which were written into the Constitution of the United States under thine inspiration. May this holy house, built in peace and dedicated in faith, stand as a testimony that the oppression of the past has faded.

—FROM THE DEDICATORY PRAYER

CHICAGO ILLINOIS TEMPLE
THE CHURCH OF JESUS CHRIST OF LATTER-DAY SAINTS

The dedication of the Chicago Illinois Temple took place nearly 140 years after the dedication of the Nauvoo Temple. "We of this generation remember Nauvoo," remarked President Gordon B. Hinckley, second counselor in the First Presidency. "We think of the sacred edifice which stood high on its hill. We remember with appreciation and gratitude those who built it. We recall their sacrifice when they were driven from it. Knowing they soon would be banished, and with many of their number already gone, they yet chose to complete it."[7]

"I have a feeling that the erection and dedication of this House of the Lord carries something of a redemption of what happened in the past. It brings together the tradition of Nauvoo and the blessings of today," President Hinckley said before the dedication.[8]

"I think there is an unseen audience today. I cannot escape the feeling that God, our Eternal Father, and the Risen Lord today are looking down on us. I am confident Joseph and Hyrum, who gave their lives in testimony of this work—who gave their lives and were buried in the soil of Illinois—are looking down upon us. I am confident that John Taylor looks down upon us.

"I'm grateful for this day when another temple now stands in Illinois, built in an environment of peace, goodwill, appreciation, and respect."[9]

President Hinckley offered the dedicatory prayer, which referred to the faithful Saints of the past as well as those in the present: "O God, we thank thee for the inheritance of faith that has come down from that generation. We thank thee for a new and better day when our people have returned to this area

Hidden among the beautiful trees to the left of the temple is an image of Jesus Christ with his hands among the flowers, guiding us to his house.

and large numbers have been added to thy Church in this part of the nation."

Referring to the Prophet Joseph Smith's prayer at the dedication of the Kirtland Temple, when the Prophet prayed that the Church would be "adorned as a bride for that day when thou shalt unveil the heavens, . . . that thy glory may fill the earth," President Hinckley continued, "Heavenly Father, we see the dawning of that glorious day. Thy people, once few in number, have become a great multitude, living in many lands and speaking many tongues. Their numbers are constantly increasing. The virtue of their lives is widely acclaimed. We are profoundly grateful for thy blessings upon thy work and upon thy faithful Saints throughout the earth." He prayed, further, that temple workers and patrons would have an increase of faith by serving in the temple. "May gratitude well up in the hearts of thy faithful Saints throughout the earth, and may the dead beyond the veil rejoice over what will here be accomplished to their eternal blessing."[10]

Twenty-four thousand Church members attended the nineteen dedication ceremonies. Speaking in one of the sessions, stake president Willard B. Barton reminded the Saints: "It is now our opportunity and our great blessing to do our genealogical work, to accept the great blessing and opportunity to work in the temple as temple workers, and also to donate and devote our time as patrons of this great temple. The challenge is ours."[11] Members have accepted that challenge and have consequently experienced the spiritual blessings that come from attending the temple to participate in the work of the Lord.

Bless the officers of this state and nation

Johannesburg South Africa Temple

We thank thee for the dimensions of thy Church in this nation of South Africa. We thank thee for men and women of great strength who constitute its membership, for the goodness of their lives, for the manner in which thou hast enlightened their minds and quickened their understanding of thy ways and thy purposes. Many of them, dear Father, sacrificed much in years past to travel afar to partake of those blessings which are available only in the Lord's house. Now there is a temple in our midst. It is beautiful and much appreciated.

—FROM THE DEDICATORY PRAYER

The Johannesburg South Africa Temple is a sparkling jewel in a land noted for its diamonds. Located two miles north of Johannesburg, the temple is visible from many parts of the city, its six spires gleaming in the sunlight. At the northeast corner of the one acre temple site is an area of grass, trees, and massive rock outcroppings that provides a panoramic view of the Johannesburg suburbs. A prominent landmark, the temple attracts thousands of curious visitors.

Once the site of estates built by nineteenth-century mining magnates and financiers, the area around the temple now features hospitals, office buildings, and schools, many of which are housed in mansions from the Victorian era. In an effort to preserve the area's historical value, planners selected indigenous quartzite for the temple's perimeter walls and entrance archways. The gray brick and slate on the temple's exterior are harmonious with the historic buildings nearby.[1]

LOCATION
Parktown, Johannesburg, South Africa

SITE
1 acre

SITE DEDICATION AND GROUNDBREAKING
27 November 1982
by Elder Marvin J. Ashton

DEDICATION
24–25 August 1985
by President Gordon B. Hinckley

EXTERIOR
Gray brick and slate

DESIGN
Modern adaptation of six-spire design

TOTAL FLOOR AREA
More than 13,000 square feet

JOHANNESBURG—
SOUTH AFRICA

The temple is a refuge of peace in this land of political strife. Afrikaners and Zulus greet each other warmly; the clicks of Zulu, Sotho, and other African languages mingle with the sounds of Saints whose ancestors came from England, Ireland, Holland, Germany, Portugal, and India. Church members come not only from South Africa but also from Zimbabwe, Lesotho, Swaziland, and Botswana. Temple sessions are conducted in six languages, including English, Afrikaans, French, and Portuguese, to meet the needs of the patrons.

Before the Johannesburg South Africa Temple was erected, Church members in Africa had to travel to London—eight thousand miles—to visit the house of the Lord. One family ate next to nothing for some time so they could save money to go to the temple. Another family gave them one hundred dollars, enabling them to travel to London, where they spent three weeks doing temple work. When they returned home, they saved another one hundred dollars, which they gave to still another family who wanted to go to the temple. That family in turn gave to yet another family. And so the tradition continued.[2]

At the laying of the temple's cornerstone, President Gordon B. Hinckley commended the members: "Our witness to you about the temple is that the Lord wanted it built because of the faith of the Saints of South Africa and Zimbabwe. Treasure the blessings of the temple! It houses all of the facilities to do the work required for salvation. God placed you in this land."[3] Elder Neal A. Maxwell observed, "Families sealed in this temple in South Africa will still be sealed when the pyramids in northern Africa have become nothing but shifting sands."[4]

During the dedication service, President Hinckley noted that the Church now has a temple on every continent but Antarctica. Even so, reaching the temple is no easy matter for many African Saints. Travel costs are high, and air travel can be confusing. Many still find it easier to fly to London than to Johannesburg. Land travel, too, is difficult because few roads are paved, and bridges are often washed out.[5]

One family, Joseph and Gladys Sitati and their five children, traveled two thousand miles from Nairobi, Kenya, to keep their promise to Heavenly Father that they would be sealed to each other in the Johannesburg South Africa Temple. Elder J. Ballard Washburn, first counselor in the Africa Area presidency, performed the ordinance. "It was one of the sweetest experiences," Elder Washburn said. "The father and mother had worked hard, and planned a long time. As they knelt at the altar in fulfillment of their dream, the Spirit of the Lord was there with power." Brother Sitati said, "With what has happened this one week in the temple and receiving our patriarchal blessings, I would say that our family will never be the same again. The light has been lit and we have something to follow. There is a guide."[6]

We thank thee for the dimensions of thy Church in this nation of South Africa . . . for men and women of great strength who constitute its membership

Seoul South Korea Temple

Located in west central Seoul, the Seoul South Korea Temple was dedicated in 1985 in the "Land of the Morning Calm." Following Oriental tradition, the meticulous temple grounds are groomed as a natural garden. The temple walls feature Korean granite reminiscent of the Salt Lake Temple, its six white pillars drawing the viewer's eyes toward heaven. A traditional, tiled "hundred-year roof" gives the temple a uniquely Korean appearance. Inside, the temple is decorated with delicate brush paintings, intricate wooden molding, silk wall coverings, gold leaf, dome chandeliers, and white lacquer furniture inlaid with mother of pearl.

The first member of the Church in Korea was baptized in 1951, at a time when Korea was in the midst of a civil war with Communist armies from the north. Latter-day Saint servicemen from America taught the gospel through the way they lived. As one convert noted, "Many of these men had come fresh from the front line . . . yet even that did not deter [them] from meeting to honor the Sabbath and to share their testimonies."[1]

In October 1980 Korean Church leaders attended the dedication of the Tokyo Japan Temple. President Spencer W. Kimball encouraged those in the temple district, which included Korea, to attend the temple often. A Korean stake president commented, "I wondered how I could deliver the

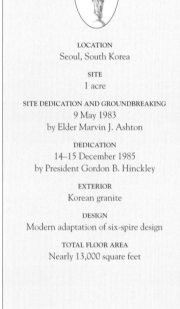

LOCATION
Seoul, South Korea

SITE
1 acre

SITE DEDICATION AND GROUNDBREAKING
9 May 1983
by Elder Marvin J. Ashton

DEDICATION
14–15 December 1985
by President Gordon B. Hinckley

EXTERIOR
Korean granite

DESIGN
Modern adaptation of six-spire design

TOTAL FLOOR AREA
Nearly 13,000 square feet

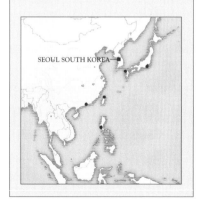

SEOUL SOUTH KOREA

prophet's message to my people when we had no temple and they were not allowed to leave the country, to be sealed as man and wife."[2] Legal restrictions prevented Korean husbands and wives from leaving the country together or with their children. But during President Kimball's visit to Korea the next week, the government promised to review the restriction. On 26 October 1980, President Kimball paused during his opening address to the Seoul area conference to say, "Before long we hope there will be a temple in Korea."[3] At the time only a hundred Korean members had received their endowments, and only twenty couples had been sealed.

The next year, the Church announced that a temple would be built in Seoul. A local priesthood leader recalled, "I was born in North Korea. I escaped when I was young. My mother died after we crossed the border. I will be able to do her temple work now. Think of all the people whose work can be done now!"[4] When stake patriarch Lee Bum-tae heard the news, tears streamed down his face. He had always promised Church members the blessings of the temple. He declared, "The sounds of [Moroni's trumpet] will now reach my country. From the Paekdu Mountains in the North to Cheju in the South. And because of this, my country, which we love, will be blessed."[5]

The temple is built upon property that the Church had purchased almost two decades earlier. During excavation before the construction began, a large supply of spring water was discovered under the temple site. A 165-ton storage tank was installed to hold the large amount of water the spring produced. The water, which is pure and does not need to be boiled, is used in the temple as drinking water.[6]

The eagerly anticipated temple would not be completed without opposition. The thirteen thousand visitors at the open house were heckled by protesters from as far away as Hawaii. Referring to the opposition, President Gordon B. Hinckley said, "We have been strengthened and we have moved forward under the promise of the Lord, who said 'I will not suffer that they (the enemy) shall destroy my work: yea I shall show unto them that my wisdom is greater than the cunning of the devil.' (D&C 10:43.)"[7]

After the dedication, entire sessions were composed of members receiving their own endowments. Ken Jennings, a temple worker from the military servicemen's district, noted, "The unity of our human family was . . . made manifest as we assisted our Korean brothers and sisters to receive these holy ordinances. The differences in appearance, language, and culture vanished, and our common heritage as children of an Eternal Father with an eternal future ahead of us was manifest."[8]

Respect for one's ancestors and the importance of families have long been traditions in Korea. Some families have kept records for hundreds, even thousands, of years. Kim Jung Shik, whose family had kept extensive records, said, "As we learned about the Church family history program, I became even more interested in my personal family records." After the temple's dedication, he submitted his direct line back to his first known ancestor, representing more than fifty generations.[9]

In 1954 Elder Harold B. Lee had said, "I feel the Spirit of the Almighty brooding amongst the Korean people and the unfolding of a great work is yet to come."[10] That work is now being fulfilled.

Now, crowning all, is this beautiful edifice in which we meet and which we dedicate unto thee

Lima Peru Temple

We are particularly mindful this day of the sons and daughters of Lehi. They have known so much of suffering and sorrow in their many generations. They have walked in darkness and in servitude. Now thou hast touched them by the light of the everlasting gospel. The shackles of darkness are falling from their eyes as they embrace the truths of thy great work. Surely father Lehi has wept with sorrow over his posterity. Surely he weeps today with gladness, for in this holy house there will be exercised the fullness of the priesthood to the blessing, not only of those of this and future generations, but also to the blessing of those of previous generations.

—FROM THE DEDICATORY PRAYER

Religious structures are nothing new to Peruvians. Their country, whose geographical features range from tropical jungles to the towering Andes and whose temperatures span the thermometer, also has numerous cathedrals and the ruins of ancient Incan temples with a history that spans the centuries. Since 1986 the capital city, Lima, has been home to a true house of the Lord, the Lima Peru Temple, which serves one hundred thousand Peruvian Saints.

Members of the South America North Area presidency discussed the Lima Peru Temple during a 1997 meeting, noting the profound influence the temple has had on their communities and nation. The temple was constructed in an undeveloped area, but today beautiful homes and streets surround it. "Wonderful things also happen inside people's hearts as the influence of the temple reaches them," the presidency

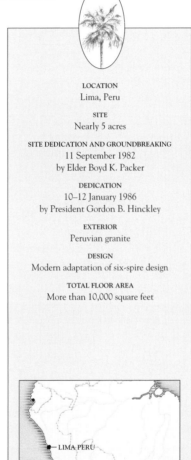

LOCATION
Lima, Peru

SITE
Nearly 5 acres

SITE DEDICATION AND GROUNDBREAKING
11 September 1982
by Elder Boyd K. Packer

DEDICATION
10–12 January 1986
by President Gordon B. Hinckley

EXTERIOR
Peruvian granite

DESIGN
Modern adaptation of six-spire design

TOTAL FLOOR AREA
More than 10,000 square feet

LIMA PERU

said. "Building a new temple is like throwing a stone into a lake: the resulting ripples radiate out and lift everything they touch."[1]

The growth of the Church in Peru has been tremendous since the dedication of the temple in 1986. For example, two years later, in 1988, Elder M. Russell Ballard organized seven new stakes in Lima in a single twenty-eight-hour period.[2] Despite serious economic and political problems in Peru, temple attendance has also increased, tripling from 1988 to 1990. The temple has added additional sessions to accommodate the faithful members. On Saturdays and holidays, when the temple is heavily attended, extra chairs are placed in sessions. The temple has no chapel, so patrons often wait in sealing rooms until an ordinance room is available.[3]

For some members, attending the temple is difficult and costly. Saints from Iquitos, in the heart of Peru's jungle, must come to the temple by air because there are no roads from this area to Lima. A single plane ticket costs three months' worth of an average worker's salary, making transportation for large families extremely expensive. Still, the six thousand members in Iquitos are finding ways to make the trip—mostly through personal sacrifice and financial help from members of the Church in more prosperous areas.

A Church member from another outlying area told temple president Isidoro Villanueva: "My family and I met in family home evening and made the commitment to travel to the temple. We found a box in which to save the necessary money for my wife, my two youngest sons and me to receive our ordinances and be sealed to each other and our deceased ancestors. After the passing of several months we had collected by a united effort, [Peruvian] *sole* by *sole*, the amount of 150 *soles* (about $55 U.S.). We considered this to be sufficient to purchase our tickets for passage. Then my married daughter visited with the pleasant surprise of a gift to us of 100 *soles* to use for buying our food and temple clothing. We estimated now that we would have enough for food. We were very pleased to receive this help and were excited and ready to begin. However, the trip would be long and difficult, and my health had been deteriorating. As we prepared to buy these tickets, you can imagine our great surprise when our oldest married son told us that such a trip would not be good for my health. He unselfishly went to a travel agency and bought four round-trip airplane tickets for us. This was a blessing of an indescribable nature for us. I feel that the money we have left should be given to our stake president to help the others who are not as fortunate as we."[4]

The temple's workers, missionaries, and employees often work more than their scheduled hours at the temple, and operational challenges must be met almost daily. Commercial power outages, for instance, are common, requiring the use of a backup generator. During a power outage on one of the busiest days of the year, the generator stopped, halting work in the temple. Numerous prayers and the quick work of temple engineers soon had it going again. The temple's engineers are often required to repair and even manufacture components for mechanical, electrical, and electronic systems. Yet the temple has never had to close because of mechanical problems. Temple president Glen V. Holley credits the ordinance workers, temple missionaries, office staff, security force, and maintenance crew, who keep the temple going.[5]

The dedicatory prayer for the Lima Peru Temple, offered by President Gordon B. Hinckley, included these words: "Surely father Lehi has wept with sorrow over his posterity. Surely he weeps today with gladness." During the service President Hinckley also said, "The day has arrived. Lehi, Sariah, Nephi, and others in that other sphere are rejoicing. This is the day of salvation for generations." Pedro Chinchay, financial clerk for the Lima Peru Limatambo Stake, commented, "As it says in the scriptures, the Lamanites will blossom as a rose (see D&C 49:24). For me, the temple is an indication that that day is coming."[6]

This is the day of salvation for generations

Buenos Aires Argentina Temple

May all who enter this, thy house, be privileged to say, as did the psalmist of old, "We took sweet counsel together, and walked unto the house of God in company" (Psalm 55:14). We express to thee our abiding love. We desire to honor thee and thy Son each day of our lives. May our posterity follow the example of thy Son and "increase in wisdom and stature, and in favour with God and man" (Luke 2:52). We pray thou wilt accept of our offering and hallow this house which we have built.

— FROM THE DEDICATORY PRAYER

When traveling to downtown Buenos Aires, many visitors are struck by the beauty of the Buenos Aires Argentina Temple, which stands near the busy thoroughfare from the airport. This house of the Lord was dedicated in 1986, the second temple to be built in Spanish-speaking South America (the Lima Peru Temple was the first). Twelve million people—more than a third of Argentina's inhabitants—live in greater Buenos Aires. The cosmopolitan city is the political, economic, and cultural capital of Argentina. With the dedication of the temple, the city has become a focal point for Latter-day Saints as well.

In the early 1920s, Latter-day Saints who had emigrated from Germany to Argentina asked the First Presidency to send missionaries to their new country. On Christmas Day 1925, Elder Melvin J. Ballard dedicated South America for the preaching of the gospel. Since that time the Church has grown rapidly in Argentina, the high point coming with construction of the Buenos Aires Argentina Temple.

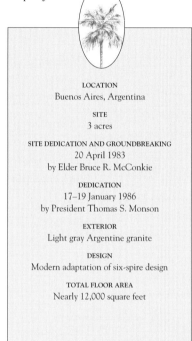

LOCATION
Buenos Aires, Argentina

SITE
3 acres

SITE DEDICATION AND GROUNDBREAKING
20 April 1983
by Elder Bruce R. McConkie

DEDICATION
17–19 January 1986
by President Thomas S. Monson

EXTERIOR
Light gray Argentine granite

DESIGN
Modern adaptation of six-spire design

TOTAL FLOOR AREA
Nearly 12,000 square feet

BUENOS AIRES
ARGENTINA

Ramon B. Paez, a counselor in the bishopric of the Centro Ward, Mar del Plata Argentina Stake, was chosen as the Argentine architect for the temple. Church leaders asked him to remember that he was working for a "very special client"—the Lord. Brother Paez later said that his work on the temple brought great changes in both his professional and spiritual life.[1]

Although Argentine Saints were generally unable to contribute much money toward building the temple, they contributed in other ways. A group of sisters, for example, crocheted sixty-four altar cloths, although only seven had been requested.[2]

During the temple's eight-day open house in December 1985, more than twenty-nine thousand visitors toured the building, some waiting as long as two and a half hours to get in. The temple's influence on these people was profound. One member noted in the guest book, "I have become a bit removed from the Church, and this visit makes me think about many things I could come to lose." Another person wrote, "Very pretty, and I need to know more. It interests me." A third visitor, perhaps an investigator, prayed: "Lord, guide me and help me to be baptized. Today I did not deserve this reward of knowing thy temple."[3]

Alfredo Goyeneche, a member of the high council in the Buenos Aires Banfield Stake, and his wife, Marina, now take advantage of the temple's proximity by attending regularly. "I tell Marina," Brother Goyeneche said, "that going to the temple weekly will be like vaccinating ourselves against the illnesses of the world."[4]

Near the temple are a Missionary Training Center and a patron housing facility, dedicated in 1994 by Elder Joseph B.

Wirthlin. "We see here an example of the Church," Elder Wirthlin said. "It is compacted in these three buildings. The Missionary Training Center is where we train and send out these wonderful missionaries in order to bring many people to the gospel of Jesus Christ. And then, later, as the converts proceed and improve themselves, they will be able to come to the patron housing and then go to the temple."[5]

In 1993, Primary children all over the world learned about temples, and groups of Primary children visited the Buenos Aires Temple every Saturday. Rodolfo Mortensen and Joanne Mortensen, the temple president and matron, described such an occasion: "One Saturday, we had a visit that touched the lives of those in the temple that day. Two large tour buses pulled up at the curb. We could see children aligning and forming rows, with three in a row, holding hands and slowly moving toward the temple gates.

"There were nearly 100 of them, and they were singing, 'We love to see the temple.' All were dressed in white, the girls in long dresses with white ribbons in their hair, and the boys in white trousers and white shirts. The leaders accompanying them were also dressed in white. As the children entered the temple annex, they stopped singing and moved with great reverence toward the annex room where they were to assemble. We noticed the details of their preparation. Each child was also wearing white shoes or had white terrycloth shoe covers. Each was carrying a booklet that he or she had made that had a picture of the temple on the front, and special things inside, such as a copy of the dedicatory prayer offered by President Thomas S. Monson, second counselor in the First Presidency; the history of the temple and the site; teachings about the temple; and his or her own impressions of the temple. Not a word was spoken. During a short service, the children, ages three to twelve, gave the prayers, testimonies and sang. As we invited them to return to the temple to be sealed with their families and receive their own ordinances, the love in the room was overflowing. As each child left, still completely reverent, each one gave me and my wife, Joanne, a kiss on the cheek. These children returned home and bore their testimonies in their wards. We have since heard reports of several of the testimonies. In addition, several of the children have returned with their families to be sealed in the temple."[6]

Youth groups often visit the temple to do baptisms, even though some who live in the city find it difficult to get there—the distances are great in the huge metropolis. Those living closest to the temple perform baptisms once a month. One young woman, Vanesa Ray, commented, "Coming to the temple is wonderful, because I can be baptized in the name of people who have died. They can receive the blessings of the gospel because of me. I can feel the Spirit because I know I am doing something good for the work, and I know my Father in Heaven is going to be happy about it."[7]

May all who enter this, thy house, be privileged to say, as did the psalmist of old, "We took sweet counsel together, and walked unto the house of God in company"

Denver Colorado Temple

The tops of the mountains have long been a place of communion with God. It is fitting, then, that in the Rocky Mountain state of Colorado stands a house of the Lord, located on seven acres in Littleton, about twenty miles south of Denver.

The Church faced intense public opposition while selecting a site for the temple. Two locations were rejected in a four-month period. Joseph H. Barton, chairman of the Denver Temple Committee, recorded: "We didn't realize the forces Satan can muster when he really puts his mind to stopping a project. Literally all hell broke loose when we announced the first two sites to the public. We weren't welcome at those locations. . . . We obtained the third site, the right site, with very little opposition. Had we gone ahead with the site we're at now without knowing what kind of blockades Satan was setting up for us, we would have failed. I bear testimony we have the right site and the Lord helped us to get it by diverting our attention elsewhere until we learned the proper procedures to get approval."[1]

This third and eventually providential site was a hilltop that had once featured a nine-hole golf course and country club. President Barton described his first impressions of the place: "I'd never set foot on the land until that time, but as I stood for the first time on the spot where the clubhouse used to be, and where the temple is now, I was awed by the gorgeous, unobstructed view. I had the strongest feeling that this was the right site."[2]

The temple's construction helped one local Church member fulfill his longtime dream to help build a house of the Lord. John Wheeler, an expert welder, offered to work once or twice a week for one of the subcontractors, donating his labor.

LOCATION
Littleton, Colorado

SITE
More than 7 acres

SITE DEDICATION AND GROUNDBREAKING
19 May 1984
by President Gordon B. Hinckley

DEDICATION
24–28 October 1986
by President Ezra Taft Benson

EXTERIOR
Precast stone walls

DESIGN
Modern

TOTAL FLOOR AREA
Nearly 30,000 square feet

Not understanding, the foreman asked, "Why would you want to do that?" Working on the temple while maintaining his regular job often required Brother Wheeler to labor thirty hours straight. The entire family sacrificed for this effort. For Brother Wheeler, however, it was an effort filled with blessings worth more than any sacrifice.[3]

"The First Presidency feels temples should reflect the highest expression of man's talents. . . . What is used in the temple must be of the highest quality and appropriate to the building and its purposes," explained Lawrence Wyss, the temple's interior designer.[4] Attention to detail is a hallmark of this beautiful building. Hundreds of feet of hand-carved woodwork adorn the interior, along with hand-painted designs on the walls and ceilings. The temple also features more than six hundred square feet of specially designed stained glass windows. The fountain near the entrance has moldings patterned after designs on the temple.

Several times during the construction of the temple, three white doves were noticed circling it. They appeared again when the statue of the angel Moroni was set in place. Temple architect Bobby Thomas wrote in his journal, "The ceremony was complete and most of the spectators had dispersed. Then, just above Moroni, President Joseph Barton saw three white birds circling above the angel and pointed them out to me. I then related the seeming approval or blessing that was in process and the three previous [dove sightings] which I had witnessed."[5]

A year later, when the temple open house began, dozens of seagulls circled the angel Moroni statue. Media representatives caught the birds on videotape, and one of the seagulls

Denver Colorado Temple

May all who come within these walls do so in cleanliness before thee.

May their hearts be lifted and their minds be elevated to consideration of

things divine.

—FROM THE DEDICATORY PRAYER

was featured in a photo that appeared in the *Denver Post*. A woman who was investigating the Church called the stake missionaries to say, "Every seagull in Colorado must have been there. Surely there must be some spiritual significance. I want to know more."[6]

Thousands of members in the Denver Colorado Temple district contributed to building and beautifying the Lord's house. Nineteen sisters spent hours and hours tatting altar cloths. Primary children earned and donated nearly ten thousand dollars for three stone "bride's benches" at the rear of the building. Young men and women spent a thousand hours building an ornate dollhouse for the temple's youth center. More than six hundred members volunteered to clean the temple before the open house. During the open house, missionaries received fourteen thousand referrals, resulting in at least fifty baptisms within a few months.[7]

In 1997, eleven years after the dedication of the temple, twenty-two thousand people gathered to celebrate the one-hundredth anniversary of the establishment of the first permanent branch of the Church in Denver. President Gordon B. Hinckley was the featured speaker, and during the celebration he and Sister Hinckley were presented with two Colorado blue spruce trees. Commenting that he loved Colorado blue spruce but didn't have a way to get the trees home, President Hinckley gave them to temple president

Hidden among the trees and landscaping is an image of the Savior beckoning a couple to the temple with his left hand and gently offering support with his right. Three white doves are depicted in the clouds circling the statue of the angel Moroni.

Russell C. Taylor and said, "If you want to call them the Hinckley trees, it's all right with me." The trees now stand on the grounds of the Denver Colorado Temple.[8]

For several years after the temple was completed, Roy V. Sneddon, president of the Lincoln Nebraska Stake, organized trips there. On one such trip, in the fall of 1988, a man noticed the people getting off the bus and asked who they were. When he learned they had come from Nebraska to attend the temple, he contacted the motel where they were staying and told the clerk to put their bill on his credit card.

"We've taken that money saved from the motel bill," President Sneddon explained, "and are going to use it to help the people from a branch in southeastern Iowa attend the temple. That branch is located in one of the poorest areas in the United States because of the struggling agriculture economy. . . . I told them that they would be able to go and have all of their costs paid. All they would have to do is qualify themselves for a temple recommend." The branch members immediately began preparing for their trip to the temple.[9]

Described by President Ezra Taft Benson as "a refuge from the evil and turmoil of the world," the Denver Colorado Temple stands as a haven to the Saints of the Rocky Mountains.[10]

May their hearts be lifted and their minds be elevated to consideration of things divine

Frankfurt Germany Temple

In the center of the old Huguenot city of Friedrichsdorf, Germany, nine miles north of Frankfurt, stands the Frankfurt Germany Temple. The town lies in a mountainous region removed from cities and major industry. The temple site was originally occupied by two five-story noodle factories and a one-hundred-foot brick chimney, which hid the area's natural beauty. Nevertheless, Church leaders chose the site because of its accessible location in the city's center. The home of the temple president and lodgings for visiting patrons are nearby.

The proposal to build a temple in Friedrichsdorf brought intense opposition from local religious leaders, who fought the idea in town meetings and newspapers, which characterized the battle as a "religious war." A letter in one paper claimed that the Church would "turn [the] town into a Mormon city." A minister warned the city council, "They will attempt to win the citizenry over to their sect."[1] Latter-day Saint leaders tried to overcome misconceptions and stereotypes by providing correct information about the Church. They also offered to provide beautifully landscaped temple grounds that the public could enjoy.[2]

Unconvinced, three city councilmen traveled to Zollikofen, Switzerland, to gather information about problems they thought the temple in that city must have caused. They returned to Friedrichsdorf disappointed. At a later town meeting, one of the councilmen tried to argue that building offices, an apartment complex, and a shopping center would be better than allowing the Latter-day Saints to build a temple on the site, but his idea failed to gain support. Church representative Immo Luschin spoke briefly and then asked attendees if they would like to see a film about the Mormons. The group

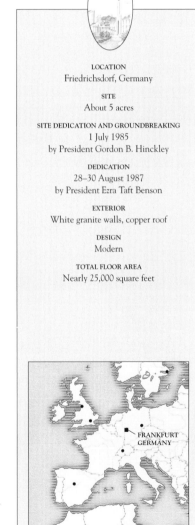

LOCATION
Friedrichsdorf, Germany

SITE
About 5 acres

SITE DEDICATION AND GROUNDBREAKING
1 July 1985
by President Gordon B. Hinckley

DEDICATION
28–30 August 1987
by President Ezra Taft Benson

EXTERIOR
White granite walls, copper roof

DESIGN
Modern

TOTAL FLOOR AREA
Nearly 25,000 square feet

FRANKFURT
GERMANY

overwhelmingly voted to watch the film, which clarified misunderstandings and increased public support of the project.[3]

After the temple was approved, Friedrichsdorf officials placed restrictions on the temple's appearance, insisting that their skyline not be "stamped with a Mormon symbol." They ruled that the temple's spire could not be higher than the tower on the nearby Protestant church.[4] Brother Peter Mourik, who played a key role in securing approval for the temple, wrote about the process: "Looking back over the last two years, it is a miracle that the project finalized against so much opposition of the Prince of Darkness. But the Prince of Peace won the victory—a major one. Many people said that a temple never would be built in Friedrichsdorf."[5]

During the construction of the temple, Friedrichsdorf celebrated the anniversary of its founding three hundred years before when settlers had come from France seeking refuge from religious persecution. Known as Huguenots by their persecutors, they were threatened, "Change your beliefs or you will be driven out." Living true to their ideal "to obey God more than man," thousands of these people were granted sanctuary in Germany on 13 March 1687 by Count Friedrich II. The town was named for him as an expression of gratitude. The people built a chapel, which they called a temple, hoping for greater fulfillment in their quest for truth.[6] The old white church neighboring the temple site features inscriptions on its walls, in German and in French, written in the spirit of Moroni's Title of Liberty: "For our liberty, our wives, our children" (see Alma 46:11–13).[7] During the temple's open house, Friedrichsdorf mayor Schmidt characterized the temple as "a modern version of religious tolerance that should prevail among mankind."[8]

Frankfurt Germany Temple

We are grateful for the consecrations of thy faithful Saints throughout the world who, with their tithes, have made [this temple] possible. We thank thee particularly for the offerings of thy Saints in Europe who, with testimony and faith, have imparted of their substance with generous hearts and with love for thee. Bless them, Father, and open the windows of heaven and shower down upon them every needful gift. Prosper them in their labors and magnify them for good before their associates. May the example of their lives lead others to seek thine everlasting truth.

—FROM THE DEDICATORY PRAYER

Frankfurt

Chad Hawkins
© 2000

In 1987 Rudi W. B. Mueller was set apart as a counselor in the temple presidency, and his wife, Erika F. Mueller, was set apart as assistant matron. Researching the town's history, Sister Mueller pondered the similarities between the Huguenots and the Mormon pioneers. She developed a love for the Huguenots and began searching for their records. Eventually she met a man who gave her a book about Friedrichsdorf's founders. The book was organized by families and contained names, dates, and locations for all of the town's births, marriages, and deaths from 1687 to 1900! She said that as she held the book, "the Spirit bore witness . . . that many of these men and women, now on the other side of the veil, had prayed that their names would be found and that their temple work would be performed." Three hundred years after they had established their city of refuge, the Huguenots' prayers were answered. In all, 1,666 family group sheets were completed, 5,002 endowments performed, and 1,651 marriages sealed.[9]

These essential temple ordinances continue to be performed in the Frankfurt Germany Temple, sealing families together both for this life and for eternity. One family desiring the blessings of the temple had to travel quite a distance to make their dream a reality. The Marreos, a family of eight, live in the Canary Islands, about fifty miles off the coast of Morocco. To reach their goal of being sealed in the temple in

The image hidden in this drawing is that of the Savior, with his arms outstretched in invitation to attend the temple.

Frankfurt, they had to take a five-hundred-mile ferry trip to Spain. Then they had to drive for many hours through Spain, France, and Germany, stopping to sleep under the stars at night. One of the daughters said of their adventure: "The trip was a lot like life, really. You go through some tough times, and you work really hard, but it is worth it when you make it to the celestial kingdom. We made a lot of sacrifices so that everyone could arrive together."[10]

Visitors to the Frankfurt Germany Temple come from many lands. During French Week, patrons and workers come from the stakes in France. Many other visitors come during German Week and Dutch Week. Church members mark their calendars months and even years in advance, arranging for vacation time to serve for a week in the temple. E. Lionel Brady, who served in the Frankfurt Germany Temple presidency, described a typical prayer meeting on the last day of one of these temple weeks: "Tears come to the eyes of temple workers and patrons as we sing 'God Be with You Till We Meet Again.' Each one sings in his own language, but the same message comes to all through the Spirit. As we say Auf Wiedersehen, or Au Revoir, or Tot ziens, or Good-bye, we know that we really will see one another again, if not in the Frankfurt temple, then in another place where friends who are united in the gospel will meet and continue to work together as participants in the great plan of eternal salvation and exaltation."[11]

We thank thee particularly for the offerings of thy saints in Europe

Portland Oregon Temple

In the 1960s the Church purchased land in Oregon for a junior college, but two decades later the property became the site for the Portland Oregon Temple. Elder James H. Bean, vice chairman of the temple committee, said, "I've watched the things that have happened on this property for 20 years. I have felt the whisperings of the Spirit, that it was intended to be preserved for special purposes, and I've seen the Lord soften the hearts of people . . . to the point that the work is going forward uninhibited."[1]

This does not mean, however, that the process of building the temple began without opposition. "Whenever temples are built," commented Elder Bean, "there are challenges that come. The Saints are tested; it is almost as though the Lord wants the members to know how much they want a temple. It really isn't easy."[2] The process of getting the property approved for the temple included at least twenty-seven public hearings, eight lawsuits, and four petition drives intended to stop development.[3] Local feelings seemed to change, however, when the initial opposition subsided and plans for a temple became a reality. When the temple was completed, one of the architects observed, "There's been a change of attitude in the community. People appreciate the quality of the building. They pull over on the highway to look at it."[4]

The Portland Oregon Temple is indeed a striking sight, with six white spires contrasted against a backdrop of deep green in the daylight and interior lights glowing through walls of translucent marble at night. The white marble exterior is accented with green marble trim and topped with a green slate roof. The temple is equally stunning on the inside, where trees and flowers fill a skylit atrium in the foyer and Honduras

LOCATION
Lake Oswego, Oregon

SITE
7.3 acres

SITE DEDICATION AND GROUNDBREAKING
20 September 1986
by President Gordon B. Hinckley

DEDICATION
19–21 August 1989
by President Gordon B. Hinckley

EXTERIOR
White marble walls; slate roof

DESIGN
Modern design with six spires

TOTAL FLOOR AREA
65,000 square feet

PORTLAND
OREGON

mahogany woodwork runs through all the rooms. No windows are visible on the outside, but sunlight enters many parts of the building through white marble. The beauty of the Portland Oregon Temple impressed President Thomas S. Monson, who said, "You won't find a better example of beautiful craftsmanship combined with the beautiful craftsmanship of the Lord—the lovely trees and vegetation—than here at the Portland temple. . . . I've seen none more beautiful."[5]

The appearance of the Portland Oregon Temple has more to offer than visual appeal, however. As with all temples, certain features both inside and out are symbolic of the higher meaning the temple holds. The spires are symbolic of priesthood authority on earth; the east spires represent the Melchezidek Priesthood and the west spires represent the Aaronic Priesthood. The celestial bodies depicted on the temple—sun, moon, and earth—represent the varying kingdoms of glory.[6] The celestial room features different levels, with the highest tier opening to a hallway where the sealing rooms are located. This arrangement shows that celestial marriage is essential to exaltation in the highest heaven. Symbols such as these add deeper meaning to the solemn beauty of the building.

When the Portland Oregon Temple was opened to the public during its twenty-three-day open house, a total of well over three hundred thousand people walked through its halls and entered its rooms. More than 240 pictures of the Savior displayed in the temple emphasized to those on the tour that Christ is the center of Latter-day Saint worship. Those in charge of the open house estimated that more than half of the visitors were not Latter-day Saints, and many of the Church members who attended were less active. Hearts were softened

Portland Oregon Temple

May a spirit of solemnity rest upon all who enter herein. Open to their vision a glimpse of thy great and everlasting designs. Bless all who shall preside and serve in this house, now and in the years to come. Give them strength according to their need. Give them faith to accomplish thy work. Give them that love which is the essence of the gospel of Christ. Bless thy work in all the earth. Look down upon thy people everywhere, and open the windows of heaven and shower blessings upon the faithful.

—FROM THE DEDICATORY PRAYER

Portland
OREGON

as visitors felt the influence of the temple. One member commented, "I've been away from the Church for several years now. I haven't felt the Spirit in all that time. This experience today has convinced me that I must come back—I'll see you in church tomorrow."[7] A man who was handing out anti-Mormon literature decided to tour the temple before continuing his task. When he came out of the temple, he chose to stop distributing the materials and destroy them.[8]

Following the successful open house was the dedication of the Portland Oregon Temple on 19 August 1989. It was pronounced "a place of peace and holiness, a refuge from storms of life."[9] President Ezra Taft Benson, who had recently celebrated his ninetieth birthday, presided over three of the eleven dedicatory sessions. The prophet's voice was strong as he gave his testimony. "I thank the Lord for temples. God bless you who will join in the great temple work of the Lord. . . . Bless you as you go forward in this great work. It is true and I know it." President Benson added, "I thank the Lord for you, and for all that you do. This is your temple. . . . This temple is going to have a great mission, and some day you will find it."[10] The dedicatory sessions ended and the temple work began, bringing with it an abundance of blessings and unforgettable spiritual experiences for Saints who attended.

One of these experiences occurred on a stormy day in February 1996. The temple had recently been closed several times because of bad weather and icy roads, and on this day the patrons and workers had been sent home because of a freezing rain storm. A couple from Washington arrived to receive their temple blessings and be sealed for eternity. In the

Hidden among the Douglas firs to the left of the temple is a full-length image of the Savior, Jesus Christ. The image represents the harmony between the temple and its forest setting.

year since their baptism, they had visited the temple once a month to sit together in the lobby and experience the spirit felt there. Despite the terrible weather and the shortage of staff workers, these two new members were allowed to stay and receive their long-awaited blessings. They were sealed by Don Lind, a former astronaut who now serves as a temple sealer.[11] For one couple, that day of freezing tempests outside was one of deep peace and contentment within.

Elder W. Craig Zwick of the First Quorum of the Seventy, who worked twenty years in the construction industry, served as general contractor on the Portland Oregon Temple. Speaking on the act of building as a metaphor of life, he has referred to a scripture found in the Book of Mormon: "And now, my sons, remember, remember that it is upon the rock of our Redeemer, who is Christ, the Son of God, that ye must build your foundation; that when the devil shall send forth his mighty winds, yea, his shafts in the whirlwind, yea, when all his hail and his mighty storm shall beat upon you, it shall have no power over you to drag you down to the gulf of misery and endless wo, because of the rock upon which ye are built, which is a sure foundation, a foundation whereon if men build they cannot fall" (Helaman 5:12).

According to Elder Zwick, "No matter how architecturally beautiful the building, unless it has a solid foundation, it cannot withstand destructive elements. Likewise, our lives must be firmly built upon faith in the Lord Jesus Christ in order to withstand the inevitable challenges of life."[12] The Portland Oregon Temple, standing firm in the face of both opposition and mighty storms, is a beautiful symbol of the faith needed to withstand adversity and build a foundation on Jesus Christ.

Open to their vision a glimpse of thy great and everlasting designs

Las Vegas Nevada Temple

Although Las Vegas has a reputation as a tourist mecca dedicated solely to entertainment and escape, there is another side to this growing metropolis. It is a community of committed citizens, including numerous devoted Latter-day Saints striving to live their lives in the service of the Lord. In fact, before the neon signs and busy streets, before the casinos and high-rise hotels, and before the sprawling suburbs, Las Vegas was a little fort founded by Mormon pioneers in 1855. When the railroad arrived, a city was started, and a few years later a small branch of the Church was formed. As the city of Las Vegas grew into a booming tourist attraction, local membership of the Church also grew.[1]

In 1987, two years before the Las Vegas Nevada Temple was completed, fifteen thousand Latter-day Saints gathered for the first multiregional conference ever held in Nevada. President Gordon B. Hinckley, first counselor in the First Presidency, spoke of the temple and made a challenge and a promise to the Saints: "As the years pass, you will never miss a dollar you have contributed to the construction of the temple. And, as the years pass, there will grow in your heart a sense of gratitude you were able to do so."[2] The members in the area accepted his challenge and contributed $11 million,[3] and the Las Vegas Nevada Temple now stands as "the crowning jewel overlooking the city,"[4] a highly visible reminder that there is more to Las Vegas than its reputation suggests.

Located near the mountains in the outskirts of a residential area on the east side of the city, the temple overlooks downtown and can be seen at night from almost every part of the Las Vegas Valley. The statue of the angel Moroni stands on the central eastern spire, facing the eastern mountains. The copper roof and white, cast stone towers have made the temple

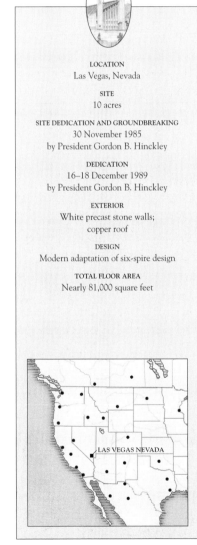

LOCATION
Las Vegas, Nevada

SITE
10 acres

SITE DEDICATION AND GROUNDBREAKING
30 November 1985
by President Gordon B. Hinckley

DEDICATION
16–18 December 1989
by President Gordon B. Hinckley

EXTERIOR
White precast stone walls;
copper roof

DESIGN
Modern adaptation of six-spire design

TOTAL FLOOR AREA
Nearly 81,000 square feet

LAS VEGAS NEVADA

a recognizable landmark in the city's scenery. Commenting on the presence of the temple, James K. Seastrand, vice chairman of the temple committee, said, "The Lord has not overlooked our valley. There are many great LDS people here as well as many God-loving people who live apart from the lifestyle that many tourists engage in when they come here for entertainment. They accept the temple here as a strong religious testimony of God." He also said that the temple proclaims that the "Church of Jesus Christ is vibrant and alive, and is making a statement for good."[5]

The temple attracted almost three hundred thousand visitors during its twenty-three-day public open house, exceeding the expectations of local leaders. "Before the temple opened, we felt that if we had two hundred thousand visitors, we would be very successful," reported Brother Seastrand.[6]

The response of visitors was overwhelmingly positive. Following the tour, one member wrote: "I have been inactive for such a long time. The spirit I felt today testifies that which I have been taught in my youth is true. As of today, I commit myself to living the gospel, and relearning what perhaps I have forgotten. I will be back and will enter the temple as a worthy and devoted member."[7] A man visiting from Minnesota said, "This is one of the most beautiful houses of worship I have ever visited. It is the highlight of our visit to Nevada."[8]

Peace is almost tangible in the interior of the temple, which is decorated in soft colors such as rust and dusty rose to reflect the Southwest's desert landscape. The open courtyard, with trees and a fountain, lets natural light into the entranceway. One interior designer who worked on the temple explained that the design helps temple patrons enter the proper frame of mind for worship. "We have tried to use not

We pray that thy Spirit may fill this sacred structure and that thy influence may hover over it by day and by night. We pray that thou might hallow it by thy presence.

—FROM THE DEDICATORY PRAYER

LAS VEGAS TEMPLE
THE CHURCH OF JESUS CHRIST OF LATTER-DAY SAINTS

only the depth of colors but the light and dark values and the intensity of light and its warmth," he said. "We have used a little brass, silver, polished marble, and soft fabric. All of this creates a wonderfully human interior that becomes restful, serene, and peaceful."[9]

The highlight of the temple is the celestial room, with prism-cut glass in the windows casting small rainbows on the soft curve of the walls. This kaleidoscope of colors rotates slowly, following the rotation of the earth. Two large, elegant chandliers with thousands of pieces of cut crystal hang from the ceiling. The narrow windows at the sides of the celestial room each contain a transparent cut star. All of these elements combine to create an interior unique to this temple and a peaceful atmosphere that harmonizes perfectly with the spirit felt in every temple.

Architects and workers paid great attention to every detail of the temple during construction. Before the windows were installed, one section of glass was sent back to California to be reworked. While the glass was in the shop, a large earthquake shook the San Francisco area, destroying much of the delicate glasswork in the building. The glass for the temple window was spared, however, as it swayed in the sling where it had been suspended to be worked on. The glass was finished and returned safely to the temple, where it now takes its place in the flawless design.[10]

As the temple's architect and later a stake president, stake patriarch, and temple sealer in Las Vegas, President George

Hidden in the clouds and representing the sealing of a husband and wife for time and all eternity is the image of a husband's hand sliding a ring onto the finger of his bride.

Tate developed a unique appreciation for the Las Vegas Nevada Temple. He said, "As I am within the temple and my eyes look around and I notice certain details, I remember the picture of some craftsman working on that specific area. Those pictures keep coming back to me because those scenes are lost now, and the members who use the temple today maybe do not have that appreciation of the skill, precision, time, and effort that went into every detail on the temple. I notice the small details that are overlooked by many. Eleven years after its completion, I am still amazed at the quality that went into the temple."[11]

That quality is seen in every detail of the structure, including a symbol unique to the Las Vegas Nevada Temple—a stylized desert lily. It is found on the edges of all six spires and in various locations within the temple. President Tate explained why he found that flower a particularly appropriate symbol of what the temple represents:

"When our children were small, we used to explore the desert. One thing that I remember noticing is that in the valleys along the sides of the roads there were dark green leafy plants with a beautiful large white lily flower. I was impressed that even in such an arid climate, the plant was able to produce a beautiful blossom. We used the desert lily on the temple because just as the beautiful lily stood out amidst the barren desert, the temple stands out with great contrast from the world."[12]

. . . that thy influence may hover over it by day and by night

Toronto Ontario Temple

At the time of the dedication of the Toronto Ontario Temple, which is located in a suburb twenty miles west of downtown Toronto and just north of Lake Ontario, the temple district included Latter-day Saints living in an enormous geographic area that has been called "the cradle of Mormonism." Covering six Canadian provinces and parts of five American states, this district included such Church history sites as Sharon, Vermont, where the Prophet Joseph Smith was born; the Sacred Grove and the Hill Cumorah near Palmyra, New York; and Kirtland, Ohio, where the Church was located in the early and mid-1830s. The district also covered an area in Canada where the Church sent the first missionaries outside of the United States. Early converts baptized in Toronto included John Taylor, the third president of the Church. Everett S. Pallin, who collected histories and artifacts for the cornerstone box of the temple, described the significance of the site with these words: "From the location of the statue of Moroni on the temple, I assume we could see Cumorah—the birthplace of the Restoration. . . . And Moroni looks east toward home, Cumorah."[1]

President Thomas S. Monson and Elder M. Russell Ballard, each of whom had served as mission president in Toronto, officiated at the groundbreaking for the Toronto Ontario Temple in 1987. During the ceremony, President Monson told the congregation of the question President Gordon B. Hinckley had asked during a discussion about building a temple in Toronto. Turning to President Monson and Elder Ballard, President Hinckley had asked, "Can you guarantee we'll have enough members in Ontario to keep a temple busy?"

President Monson replied, "Brother Hinckley, we'll have more than enough members in the city of Toronto, without considering Ontario. I'll guarantee it, and Brother Ballard will second the matter."[2]

Members in the area followed through on President Monson's guarantee from the very beginning. As the final touches were being put on the temple construction a labor strike was called that involved workers at the temple site. Church leaders were concerned that the work would not be completed in time for the scheduled open house, but union leaders allowed a few union members to do finishing work inside the temple on a voluntary basis. The project manager, Jerry D. Sears, was "working night and day" to finish the work.[3]

During the thirteen-day open house, more than twenty-six hundred members from across the temple district volunteered to help in such activities as hosting and cleaning, donating more than sixty-four thousand hours of service. Members also volunteered to clean the temple between dedicatory sessions. After the last session, they completed in just two and one-half hours the cleaning and furniture moving that had been scheduled to last through the night.[4]

The interior reflects the great care that goes into designing, building, and generally maintaining a temple. The walls are decorated with off-white and pastel colors and accented with fine woodwork and wall coverings. Beautiful stained glass windows and paintings of the Savior are found throughout. The celestial room features white tones with crystal candelabra and gold accents adorning the walls. An elegant chandelier hangs from the center of the vaulted ceiling. These details all contribute to the tranquil feeling inside the temple.

As visitors walked through the building during the open house, they were awed by what they saw and felt. A Welsh visitor

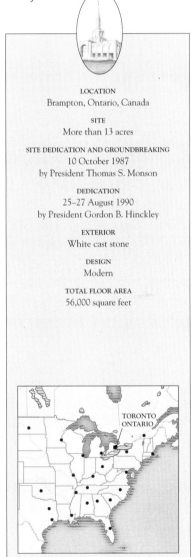

LOCATION
Brampton, Ontario, Canada

SITE
More than 13 acres

SITE DEDICATION AND GROUNDBREAKING
10 October 1987
by President Thomas S. Monson

DEDICATION
25–27 August 1990
by President Gordon B. Hinckley

EXTERIOR
White cast stone

DESIGN
Modern

TOTAL FLOOR AREA
56,000 square feet

TORONTO
ONTARIO

Toronto Ontario Temple

Our Beloved Father in Heaven, on this day of dedication, and in this solemn assembly in thy sacred house, we pledge to thee our love, our strength, our means, our faith, and bear witness to the world that thou art our living God, the God of all the universe, the extent of whose kingdom no man knoweth; and that thine Only Begotten Son is the Savior of mankind, the Spotless Lamb who was sacrificed for the sins of the world, the Holy One of Israel, "the only name under heaven given among men whereby we must be saved" (Acts 4:12).

—FROM THE DEDICATORY PRAYER

of another faith described the temple as "the most impressive place of worship I've ever seen." Another visitor wrote, "An excellent presentation of the Christian faith."[5] A neighbor of the temple said, "We are so pleased to have such a beautiful structure right close to where we live." An usher was surprised to hear one woman's request: "I have been so impressed with what I have seen—how do I join your Church?"[6] More than sixty-one thousand people came to the open house, and the response was overwhelmingly positive.

As evidence of the community's admiration of the temple, the city of Brampton gave the temple an award of excellence. The award is given every two years to honor a quality development that enhances the city. Of thirty-six submissions, the temple won one of only two awards given.[7]

More than seventeen thousand members of the temple district—from two countries and a number of different cultures—attended the dedicatory sessions of the Toronto Ontario Temple. The dedicatory prayer, which was read in each session, mentioned the cultural diversity of the temple district: "This nation has become a gathering place for people from scores of other lands. In their veins flows the blood of Israel."[8] The dedication was translated into French, one of the official languages of Canada, as well as Spanish, Portuguese, Mandarin, Cantonese, and Korean. The inscription on the outside of the temple—Holiness to the Lord, The House of the Lord—is etched in both English and French, hinting at the diversity of the members served by this particular temple.

Either President Hinckley or President Monson presided at each of the dedicatory sessions. Members of the Quorum of the Twelve Apostles also spoke. Elder Richard G. Scott taught, "We learn in the temple the three ways we learn everything—by what we hear, what we see and especially what we feel." Elder Joseph B. Wirthlin said, "Every stone that is laid in every temple lessens the power of Satan on the earth and increases the power of God." Elder L. Tom Perry spoke on foundations: "The cornerstone is the center or principal part of the foundation of a

Temple attendance and ordinance work symbolize our commitment to "press forward with a steadfastness in Christ" (2 Nephi 31:20). In the trees to the right of the temple is a full-length image of the Savior, reminding us that temple work is the Lord's work.

building. . . . Jesus Christ is the anchor of our foundation, the fundamental part of our belief and hope. Let us remember where our foundation is, where we should place our trust, our hope in the eternities to come."[9] Each session of the dedication was an uplifting, spiritual experience that, to the members in attendance, was well worth the sacrifice it took to get there.

One Latter-day Saint family, the Davidsons of St. John's, Newfoundland, traveled four days by car and ferry to attend the dedication. They felt it a privilege to make the trip because of the opportunity it gave their family to "experience the Spirit. It was everything we hoped it would be for them," Brother Davidson said.

Nine hundred members of the Bloomfield Hills Michigan Stake also attended the dedication. Stake president David H. Olsen remarked afterward, "There was a tremendous outpouring of the Spirit there that will certainly encourage our people to attend often."[10]

The members of the Toronto Ontario Temple district do more than just attend often. They have continued to show their appreciation by sacrificing time and means to keep the temple clean and beautiful. Ten years after the dedication, a group of nearly two hundred young single adults gathered to paint the fence surrounding the temple grounds. They purchased paint and brushes, coveralls and paint trays, and went to work, demonstrating their love for the temple and their understanding of the importance of the work that takes place inside.[11]

At the dedication of the Toronto Ontario Temple, Elder Marvin J. Ashton reflected: "The temple is not a destination. I prefer to refer to the temple as a starting point where we not only prepare ourselves but we help prepare others, even those who have gone ahead, for the important events and occasions that are available and so necessary for all of us."[12] The temple in Toronto has made it possible for local members to take this teaching to heart and return many times, bringing blessings upon themselves and countless others.

San Diego California Temple

Twin spires rising majestically into the warm blue air of Southern California, the breathtaking San Diego California Temple shines in white splendor for those living nearby or traveling on the freeway near the temple. Ground was broken for the temple in February 1988, and construction took nearly five years to complete.

The visual marvel of the San Diego California Temple was achieved by design architect William S. Lewis Jr. and architect Kenneth Moeller. The exterior is matched by a stunning interior design. Dennis and Shelly Hyndman, also members of the design team who collaborated on the temple, said they "wanted to create a vertical scheme to symbolize an ascension toward heaven." They accomplished this in part by using "darker colors on the lower levels and lighten[ing] the wall and carpet colors on the higher levels."[1] Dennis added that the design for the temple was inspired by the Salt Lake and Washington D. C. Temples. Although the Hyndmans, who are Roman Catholics, were unable to visit the interior of those temples, they toured the Las Vegas Nevada Temple before its dedication.[2]

Rabbi Wayne Dosick, who viewed the San Diego California Temple during the open house, commented on the beauty of the building: "We have argued that what is important is not the building but what goes on in the building. . . . God, we say, doesn't live in a building, but in us." Then he added, "But the Mormons are right, too: the building we construct in which to worship God should be special, a place to come in awe and reverence, a place that invokes God's presence, a place of transcendence, lifting us beyond and above."[3]

As are other temples, the San Diego California Temple is surrounded by beautiful landscaping and gardens that help to create a reverent and appropriate setting for the house of the

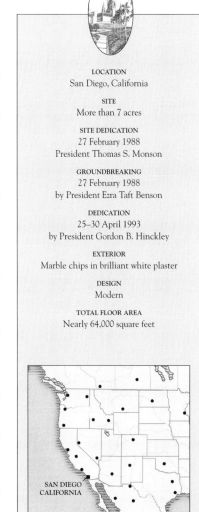

LOCATION
San Diego, California

SITE
More than 7 acres

SITE DEDICATION
27 February 1988
President Thomas S. Monson

GROUNDBREAKING
27 February 1988
by President Ezra Taft Benson

DEDICATION
25–30 April 1993
by President Gordon B. Hinckley

EXTERIOR
Marble chips in brilliant white plaster

DESIGN
Modern

TOTAL FLOOR AREA
Nearly 64,000 square feet

SAN DIEGO
CALIFORNIA

Lord. As plans were made for the temple's construction and surrounding grounds, many members sought ways to give of their time and talent to its completion. Primary children were even able to contribute, as youngsters from 180 different wards and branches in the temple district were given charge to water and care for some of the flowers that would be used to decorate for the dedication. After the dedication, the potted flowers were planted in the beds around the flagpole.[4]

Children in northern Mexico also wanted to participate but had to come up with a different idea because border restrictions would not allow them to bring plants across. Instead they designed and made a handcrafted rug for the First Presidency to stand on as they laid the cornerstone for the temple. A microfiche with the names of the Primary children in the temple district was later placed in the cornerstone along with other significant items.[5]

Before the dedication, an open house was held to allow the public to walk through and tour the temple. Thousands of volunteers helped beautify and prepare the grounds for the open house. While the children's flowers were being set around the entrance down below, Ron Andersen was hoisted above the temple to work on the angel Moroni perched atop the two-hundred-foot spire. On 18 January 1993, the spire had been struck by lightning and some of the gold leaf on the statue had been damaged. So Andersen, who did the original gold leafing on the statue, was lifted by crane to clean and repair the statue in time for the open house.[6]

Almost two thousand volunteers pitched in to help clean the temple for the open house and dedication in March and April 1993. Sister Jo Ann Autenrieb, who coordinated the

San Diego
California Temple

We are living in the greatest era in the history of the
world in the construction of these sacred houses. Open
the way before us, provide the necessary means, and
hedge up the way of the adversary that he shall not have
power to frustrate or delay this work.

—FROM THE DEDICATORY PRAYER

San Diego

cleaning efforts, noted that while the work was hard, "the volunteers worked with a sweet spirit and harmony, with patience and consideration. Sometimes the work was especially dusty and dirty, and sometimes the workers had to wait for equipment or there was a shortage of supplies, yet I have received many letters from volunteers saying that this was one of the best experiences of their lives."[7]

Even the Saints who lived in Mexico were able to be involved, many of them traveling great distances to participate. Sister Autenrieb was touched at their sacrifice and dedication. "Some came through the floods to clean the temple. . . . About 20 members came from Colorado del Rios, driving 4 hours in the night to arrive in time to clean one morning."[8]

Sister Autenrieb also shared a story about a group of sisters who traveled from Ensanada. They wore white clothes and carried with them white cloths they had bought especially to clean with. When told that there were rags already available for cleaning, the sisters answered that they would like to use the ones they had brought, because they were planning to take them home and wash them and then embroider and frame them as decorations in their homes.[9]

The dedication of the San Diego California Temple brought a renewed bonding and sense of unity to members of the Church on both sides of the United States-Mexico border. Elmer Monroy, second counselor in the Tijuana LaMesa Third Ward bishopric, expressed the feelings of many Saints as he talked about how members from both sides of the border worked "shoulder to shoulder": "The temple is for every member of the Church, for all people."[10]

The dedication of the San Diego California Temple was held from 25 through 30 April 1993. Fifty thousand people attended

The Savior and his atoning sacrifice are constant reminders of the saving work performed in temples. Hidden in the shadows of the palm trees is an image of Christ kneeling in prayer.

the twenty-three sessions, which were conducted by either President Gordon B. Hinckley, first counselor in the First Presidency, or President Thomas S. Monson, second counselor in the First Presidency.

In one of the sessions, President Hinckley cautioned the members of the Church never to lose sight of the purpose of temples: "The whole purpose is to provide a place where we can worship God according to the dictates of our own conscience, exercise the priesthood that has been restored in its fullness and receive the blessings that are administered only in these holy houses."[11]

President Hinckley also addressed the issue of craftsmanship in the building of temples. "We have been criticized," he said, "for spending so much on the building of temples and asked why not spend the money taking care of the poor. Nothing is too good for the Lord. Temples don't have to be ostentatious, but they do have to be of high quality. We wouldn't want to give a shabby kind of building to the Lord, whom we love."[12] President Hinckley then pointed out that the Church also does much to help the poor and needy. "The Church has done generous and marvelous things to take care of the poor. The Church has spent millions and millions of dollars to help those across the world who are not members of the Church."[13]

President Monson, during one session, admonished members to "come to the temple and place your burdens before the Lord and you'll be filled with a new spirit and confidence in the future. Trust in the Lord, and if you do He'll hold you and cradle you and lead you step by step along the pathway that leads to the celestial kingdom of God.

"Make the temple part of your lives. The temple can bring you the supreme feeling of peace."[14]

Orlando Florida Temple

Before the dedication of the Orlando Florida Temple in 1994, Saints in Florida had to travel as far as Salt Lake City and Mesa Arizona to attend the temple. These distances shortened with the building of the Washington D. C. and Atlanta Georgia Temples, but Floridian Saints had long looked forward to a time when they would have a temple in their own area. President Spencer W. Kimball is said to have told an Orlando stake president, "Do your temple work and you'll get a temple." Thereafter, this president's stake led all others in the Washington D. C. and Atlanta Georgia Temple districts in temple work performed.[1]

The search for a temple site began in 1982, and the city of Orlando was selected for a temple because of its central location in Florida and its popularity as a tourist destination. The temple site, just south of Orlando, is located on a knoll a few miles north of Universal Studios. The location, described as one of Florida's most beautiful areas, was chosen by President Gordon B. Hinckley, first counselor in the First Presidency. When he first saw it, he exclaimed, "That's it!"[2] Of the site, which sits on the highest elevation in Orange County, President Ezra Taft Benson said, "A more beautiful site could not have been chosen."[3]

Because the site is in an environmentally sensitive area, many neighboring citizens opposed the building of the temple. In response to these community voices, local Church members organized a petition drive, going door to door to collect signatures in support of having the temple built. After two weeks, the members delivered to the county commission nearly eleven thousand signatures in favor of the temple; more than two-thirds of them were from nonmembers. With this evidence of community support, the tide eventually turned in favor of the Church. The commissioners voted six to one to allow the temple to be built. The Saints felt that the Lord had intervened to make their dream become a reality.[4]

On 20 June 1992, Elder James E. Faust, of the Quorum of the Twelve Apostles, broke ground for the Orlando Florida Temple. In his remarks he recalled the many temples that had been built in ancient times. He noted that the temple of Herod in Jerusalem had been built so meticulously that each stone was marked with a signature. Of this grand temple in the meridian of time, he said, "This is the temple to which the Savior went. Now, when the Savior comes to Florida, surely He will come to this house that will be at this spot."[5]

Evan D. Porter Jr., president of the Orlando Florida Stake, handled most of the negotiations and legal procedures for the temple. During the groundbreaking ceremony, he told of the many struggles he had faced over ten years as he had tried to locate and purchase land and receive permission to build the temple. "On several occasions I found it was impossible to move forward without the Lord's intervention," he said. "I came to realize that He does not want this to move forward without His intervention. This is His will."[6]

The temple's brilliant white exterior, beautiful stained glass windows, and carefully tended grounds make the building at once imposing and beautiful to observers. The structure, with walls twelve inches thick, is capable of withstanding a major hurricane or earthquake. Inside, the temple's most impressive room is the celestial room, with its contemporary style furniture and a stained glass dome in the ceiling.[7]

During the temple's three-week open house, ninety thousand people witnessed the beauty of the structure's interior.

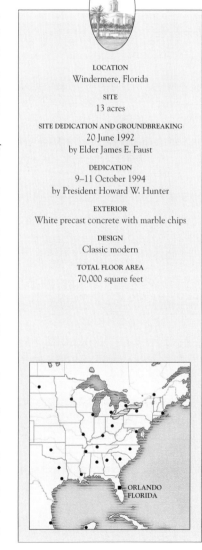

LOCATION
Windermere, Florida

SITE
13 acres

SITE DEDICATION AND GROUNDBREAKING
20 June 1992
by Elder James E. Faust

DEDICATION
9–11 October 1994
by President Howard W. Hunter

EXTERIOR
White precast concrete with marble chips

DESIGN
Classic modern

TOTAL FLOOR AREA
70,000 square feet

ORLANDO
FLORIDA

Orlando Florida Temple

May the generations of the families of thy sons and daughters be joined in unbroken linkage that thy divine purposes may be brought to pass concerning the immortality and eternal life of thy children. . . . May the spirit of the prophet Elijah rest upon thy people that the hearts of the children may turn to their fathers that the earth shall not be wasted, and that thy divine will may be brought to pass for the blessing of thy sons and daughters of all generations.

—FROM THE DEDICATORY PRAYER

Local news media reporting on the open house soon began calling the site "Temple Hill."[8] Ten thousand Church members volunteered their time to either lead tours or serve in some other way at the open house.

Many of those who had toured the structure were impressed by its simple beauty and significance. One member led his blind father-in-law through the temple. Feeling the delicate molding and woodwork throughout the temple, the father-in-law, who had been a carpenter by trade, was deeply impressed by the quality of the workmanship. A Catholic clergyman who toured the temple later said publicly, "It is very impressive. The structure is magnificent, and the people were very hospitable and welcoming. It is obvious the temple was built for the Lord."[9]

When the sun rose Sunday, 9 October 1994, more than a thousand people had already lined up to take part in the cornerstone ceremony. The occasion was made particularly memorable by the presence of all three members of the First Presidency. It had been six years since the entire First Presidency had officiated together at a temple dedication.[10]

Local Saints placed inside the cornerstone various objects and statements of their faith and commitment to the temple. Among the items were pledges signed by the young men, young women, and single adults from the temple district, all of whom planned to be married in the temple someday. A letter stated: "We feel that this pledge will encourage our young people to be more involved in the temple and look forward to the day when they will be married for time and all eternity. It will increase their faith. Each time they come to the temple to perform baptisms or simply to visit, they will know that their names and promises are inside their temple."[11]

Hidden in the clouds to the left of the temple is an image of the Savior, motioning Saints to take joy in the beauty of tropical flowers and Canary Island date palms before entering his holy house.

After the cornerstone ceremony, President Hunter dedicated the Orlando Florida Temple. In his remarks he expressed his joy in being in the house of the Lord: "What a beautiful occasion this is for us to step out of the busy, noisy world into the peace and quiet of the temple, where our thoughts can turn to things of the Spirit and we truly feel ourselves in the presence of God our Eternal Father."[12]

The talks given in the second dedicatory session were either given in or translated into Spanish. Talks were also translated into Haitian, Creole, Portuguese, Cambodian, and American Sign Language.

Cathy Payne, a Church member in Florida, had greatly desired to attend the temple dedication. But having recently received a liver transplant, she was unable to go on October 9, the day she had planned to attend with her husband and two daughters. Determined nonetheless to be part of this historic occasion, she and her husband took a shuttle from the hospital in Miami to the temple two days later, and she sat through a dedicatory session in a wheelchair. Sister Payne later said, "I have known since they mentioned that a temple would be in Orlando that I had to be here for its dedication. I don't know why, but I just know beyond reason that I, personally, needed to be here. Coming here has been my fondest wish. I'm incredibly happy to be here."[13]

Concerning the dedication ceremonies, the *Church News* reported, "As the last group exited the temple in twilight each evening, tears glistened on many smiling faces. Again and again, there was evidence of the blending of gratitude and humility, exuberance and joy that scarcely could be contained."[14]

May the spirit of the prophet Elijah rest upon thy people

Bountiful Utah Temple

Plans to build the Bountiful Utah Temple, the eighth temple constructed in Utah, were first announced in May 1988. Earlier that month the Church had purchased a nine-acre site on Bountiful's east bench. The site, high above Davis County, offers a stunning view of the Great Salt Lake and the bustling communities that lie along the Wasatch Front.

The known history of the temple site began in 1897, when John Haven Barlow Sr. purchased from the United States government a forty-acre plot that included the future temple site. Because of a lack of water and the steep terrain, little could be done with the land. In 1947 portions of the north acreage were cleared, and an orchard of four hundred apricot trees was planted. In the spring of 1983, flash flooding from Holbrook Canyon caused a great deal of damage in Bountiful, resulting in the decision to build an earthen dam across the canyon to limit the flow of water during heavy rainstorms. The city requested use of the soil from the future temple site. Construction crews removed some two hundred thousand cubic yards of soil from the site, leaving an ideal plateau on which the temple would later be built.[1]

The Church had considered several sites before making a final decision about the temple's location. But on 3 April 1988, after conference meetings, the entire First Presidency traveled to the site, and President Ezra Taft Benson said, "This will be a beautiful site for the House of the Lord." President Thomas S. Monson later recalled the spiritual affirmation he felt as President Benson spoke these words. Upon their decision, the site earned the distinction of being the only temple site chosen with the entire First Presidency present.[2] It is also the only temple site personally chosen by President Ezra Taft Benson.[3]

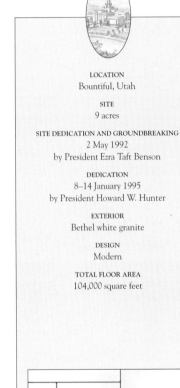

LOCATION
Bountiful, Utah

SITE
9 acres

SITE DEDICATION AND GROUNDBREAKING
2 May 1992
by President Ezra Taft Benson

DEDICATION
8–14 January 1995
by President Howard W. Hunter

EXTERIOR
Bethel white granite

DESIGN
Modern

TOTAL FLOOR AREA
104,000 square feet

BOUNTIFUL UTAH

Approximately four years later, President Benson, at age ninety-two, turned the first shovelful of soil at the groundbreaking ceremony of the Bountiful Utah Temple on 2 May 1992. More than eight thousand people attended the ceremony. Many in the large group, who were there for several hours, had brought food to eat while they waited. Concerned about possible litter on the site, the temple committee arranged to have volunteers clean up after the event. "To our surprise, we removed less than half a sackful of refuse from the nine-acre site," said Blaine P. Jensen, who was then serving as a regional representative in the area. "It was an indication of the great sanctity of the event, as well as the people's attitude toward it."[4]

The Bountiful Utah Temple was intended to be both figuratively and actually a light on a hill. Architectural plans called for the structure to stand prominently on the hill, where it could be seen from many miles away. At night, under bright floodlights, the temple is the most visible landmark in the entire valley.

Symbols traditional to temple architecture are featured in the design of the Bountiful Utah Temple. These include a statue of the angel Moroni, the keystone symbol (representing Christ), earth stones, and design elements representing the sun, moon, and stars. The temple also features twelve round windows, six in the celestial room and six in the chapel, which represent the Quorum of the Twelve Apostles.

Equally important is the symbolism in the temple's interior. As patrons progress through the ordinances of the temple, they ascend toward the sealing rooms, which, representing the highest degree of the celestial kingdom, are one step higher than the celestial room. Light also plays an important role in

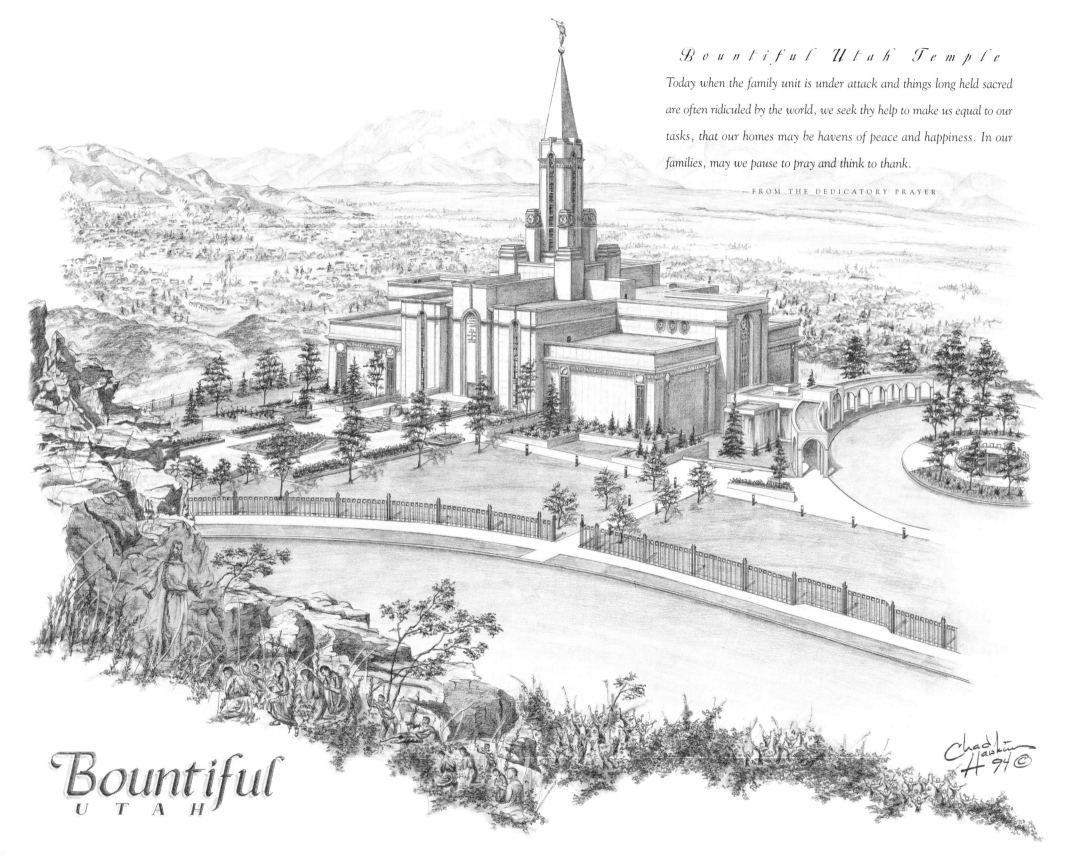

Bountiful Utah Temple

Today when the family unit is under attack and things long held sacred are often ridiculed by the world, we seek thy help to make us equal to our tasks, that our homes may be havens of peace and happiness. In our families, may we pause to pray and think to thank.

—FROM THE DEDICATORY PRAYER

Bountiful
UTAH

the interior design of the temple, with the light increasing as one progresses upward. The brightest rooms in the temple are the eight sealing rooms.[5]

Another feature of the building that adds both beauty and symbolic significance is the art glass windows. The temple features forty windows totaling approximately four thousand square feet of art glass. "There is an ascending feel to the glass," said Allen B. Erekson, projects administrator for the Church's temples and special projects. Brother Erekson explained: "It is more open as you go up . . . , with more clear glass higher that allows more light to come in and still gives privacy to the building."[6] The windows follow a motif of Jacob's ladder, as recorded in the book Genesis, and increase in detail as they rise, representing man's progression toward heaven.

Of the design, Brother Erekson said, "What we are trying to accomplish in the Bountiful Utah Temple is to have a level of elegance that doesn't distract from the Spirit."[7] Perhaps this is best achieved in the celestial room, which, with its thirty-four-foot ceiling and its spectacular chandelier, with twenty-five hundred pieces of crystal, represents the glory and sublimity of heaven. The fifteen-foot-tall chandelier, created in the Czech Republic, is one of the artistic highlights of the entire building.[8]

When the temple was opened for public tours from 5 November through 17 December 1994, eight hundred and seventy thousand people toured the edifice. "The open house was almost miraculous," said Elder John E. Fowler, a member of the Seventy who chaired the temple committee. "In spite of the record snowfall in November and the difficult environmental concerns, we had a tremendous experience. Lives were touched and changed as a result of visiting the temple."[9]

More than fifty thousand volunteers worked to prepare the temple for the open house and dedication. Before winter arrived, youth groups laid sod and planted trees. During the open house, Church members led tours through the temple, and priesthood brethren removed snow from the walkways.

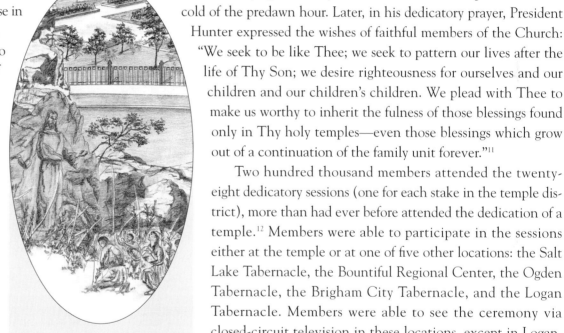

In the rock is hidden an image of the Savior, our Rock and our Salvation. Surrounding him are multitudes of Nephites, representative of those in the land Bountiful at the time of the Savior's appearance recorded in 3 Nephi.

Blaine P. Jensen, who also served on the temple committee, mentioned a poignant service provided by the youth: "One of the most humbling experiences of the open house was when the beautiful young people, dressed in their Sunday best and often sitting in the cold, reached down and put clean white footlets on the visitors' feet," he said. "Many people were moved to tears by that simple act of service."[10]

The Bountiful Utah Temple was dedicated by President Howard W. Hunter on 8 January 1995. Before the dedicatory service, a brief cornerstone-laying ceremony was held outside the temple in the bitter cold of the predawn hour. Later, in his dedicatory prayer, President Hunter expressed the wishes of faithful members of the Church: "We seek to be like Thee; we seek to pattern our lives after the life of Thy Son; we desire righteousness for ourselves and our children and our children's children. We plead with Thee to make us worthy to inherit the fulness of those blessings found only in Thy holy temples—even those blessings which grow out of a continuation of the family unit forever."[11]

Two hundred thousand members attended the twenty-eight dedicatory sessions (one for each stake in the temple district), more than had ever before attended the dedication of a temple.[12] Members were able to participate in the sessions either at the temple or at one of five other locations: the Salt Lake Tabernacle, the Bountiful Regional Center, the Ogden Tabernacle, the Brigham City Tabernacle, and the Logan Tabernacle. Members were able to see the ceremony via closed-circuit television in these locations, except in Logan, where they viewed a videorecording of it.

Members were grateful for the new temple and quickly began using it following the dedication. Twelve weddings were held the day after the dedication. Some nine hundred temple workers were called to fill the great demand, and the temple became the first to operate for a full day on Saturdays.

Hong Kong China Temple

May the blessings of freedom continue to be enjoyed by those who live here and, in a particular way, we pray that future events may be conducive to the growth and strengthening of thy work, that rich and marvelous blessings may come into the lives of thy sons and daughters. Inspire thy Saints in all of their decisions, that they shall know much of happiness and peace.

— FROM THE DEDICATORY PRAYER

In 1992, President Gordon B. Hinckley, first counselor in the First Presidency, announced plans to build the Hong Kong China Temple. President Hinckley, who visited Asia in 1960 to oversee the Church's activities there, later said to a group of missionaries the day before the temple dedication in Hong Kong, "This temple represents one of the great dreams of my life."[1]

The Church has had many years of experience in Hong Kong—the first missionaries being sent to that land in 1853, nearly 140 years before President Hinckley's announcement of a temple. Missionary efforts in the 1850s were generally unfruitful, however, and the Church made little progress. In 1921, Elder David O. McKay of the Quorum of the Twelve Apostles, on his worldwide tour, blessed the entire land of China for the preaching of the gospel. An additional apostolic blessing was pronounced in 1949 when Elder Matthew Cowley climbed the highest peak overlooking Hong Kong and blessed the land for the preaching of the gospel. Subsequent missionary work progressed slowly but steadily among the Chinese in Hong Kong.

Beginning in the 1840s, Hong Kong was ruled by the British. In 1898, England signed a ninety-nine-year lease of

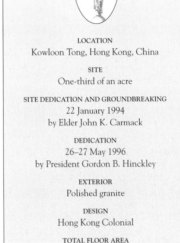

LOCATION
Kowloon Tong, Hong Kong, China

SITE
One-third of an acre

SITE DEDICATION AND GROUNDBREAKING
22 January 1994
by Elder John K. Carmack

DEDICATION
26–27 May 1996
by President Gordon B. Hinckley

EXTERIOR
Polished granite

DESIGN
Hong Kong Colonial

TOTAL FLOOR AREA
22,600 square feet

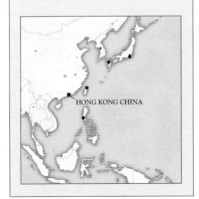

HONG KONG CHINA

Hong Kong that was to expire on 1 July 1997. At that time, Hong Kong would revert to the control of the government of mainland China. President Hinckley commented in a 1996 interview: "This is a time of uncertainty in this land, but it is going to come, everyone faces it, and we face it with faith," he said in a 1996 interview. "We do not know what will happen. No one knows, but we have faith that everything will work out and go forward."[2]

Showing faith that the government of communist China would allow the Church to function after the government of Hong Kong was reunited with that of the mainland, Church leaders were determined to find a location where the temple could be built and dedicated before July 1997.

When President Hinckley traveled to Hong Kong in 1992 to consider several potential temple sites, he felt unsatisfied with all of them. "We looked at one after another after another. I became very discouraged," he later said. "The sites were so tiny in some respects and the cost of real estate is so high, many millions of dollars for a little piece of ground." One night, he retired with no clear understanding of how he should proceed on his assignment to find a location for the temple, but in the middle of the night, he awoke with an impression to have the temple built on the site of the mission home and chapel at No. 2 Cornwall Street. "To me it was inspiration," he said. "I drew [the temple] out, and I still have the little drawing that I made . . . in my journal. [This drawing] is essentially the plan which we had for this temple."[3]

President Hinckley's drawing called for a temple plan unlike any other. Of the temple Elder Rulon G. Craven of the Seventy said, "The cost of land in Hong Kong is very expensive, and therefore, instead of spreading out to build, we had to build up."[4] The six-story building was designed to house not only a temple but also a chapel, mission offices, and living quarters for the temple president, mission president, and several missionaries. The ordinance rooms, celestial room, and sealing rooms are in the top three floors of the building, and the baptistry is in the basement. The other purposes of the building are carried out on the three floors in between. The building has two separate main entrances, one for the temple and the other for the mission offices and chapel.

When construction of the building was finished in May 1996, the temple was opened for public tours, which were attended by more than thirteen thousand people. Guests were impressed that amid the traffic and confusion of Hong Kong, quiet, peace, and tranquility were so easily felt inside the temple. A minister from another religion wrote a letter to Elder Jerry D. Wheat, who as a public affairs missionary was heavily involved in the open house, saying, "There is something different about your temple. Hong Kong lacks what you have in your temple—it is reverence."[5] Visitors also expressed feeling something special while touring the building.

At the time of the temple's dedication, President Hinckley described the events that had lead to a temple being built in Hong Kong as a miracle: "It is a miracle that we have reached this point of maturity here in Hong Kong. . . . I look upon it as a miracle because of what I have known in the past, the growth I have seen, the stabilization of the work, and the strength of it today, it is a miracle."[6] He noted during his meetings prior to the dedication that when he first came to Asia in 1960 the Church owned only one piece of property in the entire region—a small meetinghouse in Japan. At the time of the dedication of the temple, there were some twenty thousand members in five stakes in Hong Kong alone. In his dedicatory prayer, President Hinckley said that the Church in the area "now comes to full maturity with the dedication of this sacred temple."[7]

The first temple president and matron of the Hong Kong China Temple were President Ng Kat Hing and Sister Ng Pang Lai-Har. This brother was one of the early converts in the city of Hong Kong and had served the Church in a variety of callings. He was able to provide a great service for the temple in the time of political change that followed the dedication, for he presided over the Church's largest temple district—one-quarter of the world's population lives in China.

Among the five thousand Latter-day Saints who attended the dedication were about two hundred who had traveled from Singapore, more than three hundred from Taiwan, about one hundred from Thailand, and several expatriates from China. Also attending were three hundred returned missionaries and several mission presidents. The members expressed their deep gratitude for the blessing of having a temple in their midst. Sister Susanna Leung said: "This is the house of the Lord, and this is so important to my life. Most Hong Kong members are converts, so this will be our first time in a temple. I am so very excited."[8] Sister Ersia Kwan shared her enthusiasm: "It is very important for me, because it is the way that I can prepare myself for the celestial kingdom."[9]

President Thomas S. Monson, first counselor in the First Presidency, expressed his zeal both for the outcome of the building and the prospect of temple work in Hong Kong's future:

"We were absolutely thrilled with the beauty of the Hong Kong Temple. . . . The colors and furnishings have been so carefully coordinated to reflect the atmosphere of this temple that it astounded all of us. The workmanship of the temple is superb. . . .

"The spirit of the Saints there in the temple was a marvel to behold. They love the temple, and have waited a long time for it. They are very anxious for it to open. With all the great numbers of Chinese people who have gone on in the years past—this being one of the ancient civilizations—surely there is no dearth of names for whom the current Chinese members can officiate."[10]

Elder Kwok Yuen Tai, a member of the Seventy and a native of Hong Kong, saw the dedication of the Hong Kong China Temple as an important step forward for the Church in the region: "This has been a very special occasion; we've witnessed the dedication of a holy edifice. It has been a time of celebration, a time of thanksgiving, a time of happiness, a time to rededicate ourselves. It's a spiritual boost."[11]

Mount Timpanogos Utah Temple

In an address at general conference on 4 April 1993, President Gordon B. Hinckley announced that the ninth temple in Utah would be built in American Fork. The site chosen was already owned by the Church and had once been part of a Church welfare farm.[1] It sits on the top of a rise overlooking the city of American Fork as well as Utah Lake; the majesty of Mount Timpanogos and the Wasatch Mountains rise behind it. At night the brilliant glow of the temple can be seen from Orem to Lehi.

At the groundbreaking ceremony on 9 October 1993, President Hinckley answered questions about the decision to build the temple in American Fork. "People across the Church are asking why build another temple in Utah, when there are so many people without temples. . . . The answer lies in the pressure on the Provo Temple and the Jordan River Temple. The Provo Temple is the busiest temple in the Church." President Hinckley then commended the members of the Church in Utah County for their faithful temple attendance, which essentially created the need for another holy edifice.[2]

President Thomas S. Monson's address at the groundbreaking ceremony was quite memorable. He directed his remarks to a young man named Samuel Barnes, age nine. Samuel, who suffers from a chronic condition of the digestive system known as Crohn's disease, had written President Monson a letter asking how he might help contribute to the temple's construction. President Monson had suggested that Samuel hang a picture of the temple in his room, where he could look at it as he knelt to pray. He also said that if he were Samuel, "I would have within my heart a desire to attend the dedication of the temple, and attend the temple and do vicarious baptism work as a boy. And then later to have my

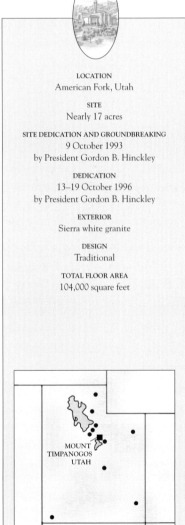

LOCATION
American Fork, Utah

SITE
Nearly 17 acres

SITE DEDICATION AND GROUNDBREAKING
9 October 1993
by President Gordon B. Hinckley

DEDICATION
13–19 October 1996
by President Gordon B. Hinckley

EXTERIOR
Sierra white granite

DESIGN
Traditional

TOTAL FLOOR AREA
104,000 square feet

MOUNT
TIMPANOGOS
UTAH

endowment prior to my mission and then kneel at a sacred altar with a sweet daughter of our Heavenly Father, an eternal companion, and hear those words, 'I pronounce you husband and wife for time and all eternity.' "[3]

President Monson made sure that Samuel received a shovel from the groundbreaking ceremony; the two of them continued to correspond during the three years of construction. In October 1996, during a dedicatory session in which Samuel was present, President Monson invited him to stand by the podium, presented him with a piece of granite from the temple, and asked him if he wanted to say anything. Samuel expressed gratitude for having a temple nearby and then, looking at President Monson, expressed his thanks for having a wonderful friend to help him when times were hard.[4]

Counsel by President Monson for the Saints to sacrifice to build the temple brought many touching experiences and created enduring memories for those who gave of their time and substance to complete the Mount Timpanogos Utah Temple. Howard Ault decided that he and his family could contribute to the temple by donating the sod for the temple grounds from his family's sod farm. In addition to giving the care and time required to grow the sod, the Ault family, including five children, twenty-eight grandchildren, and one great-grandchild, all volunteered to help lay the sod as well. Brother Ault observed that "most of the family have been here every night helping, along with many other volunteers. I think it's a great tie for the children with the temple. This temple will always have a special place in their hearts, since they helped work on it."[5]

Students of the American Fork High School seminary

Mount Timpanogos
Utah Temple

May this in very deed be "*a house of prayer, a house of fasting, a house of faith, a house of learning, a house of glory, a house of order, a house of God*" (D&C 88:119). May its beauty never be marred by evil hands. May it stand strong against the winds and storms that will beat upon it. May it be a beacon of peace and a refuge to the troubled. May it be a holy sanctuary to those whose burdens are heavy and who seek thy consoling comfort.

—FROM THE DEDICATORY PRAYER

Mount Timpanogos

decided that they could use the construction of the temple as motivation to help them improve spiritually. They built a ten-foot model of the temple out of Popsicle sticks; students who memorized ten scriptures could put their name on a stick and add it to the model.[6]

The temple's exterior is covered in a beautiful granite facing that represents the solidness of the mountains behind it. Numerous stained glass windows fill the interior of the temple with a radiant display of light and color. The art glass for the windows was created using a patented technique that seals together several matched layers of glass. Not only does this new technique allow for larger windows with better insulation but it also creates windows that maintain their beauty and integrity when viewed under reflected light. This means that the full color and splendor of the windows is visible from the exterior during the day and from the inside at night—an effect not wholly possible with traditional leaded glass.[7]

An interesting event occurred during the construction of the temple on a particularly sunny summer day. In the middle of a committee meeting that was being held in the chapel, a sister sitting on a bench suddenly exclaimed, "My purse is smoking!" About the same time the man sitting in front of her felt his hair and added, "My hair is singed!" The large round window that is a prominent feature of the chapel was focusing sunlight into the room like a giant magnifying glass. Special thermometers were used to measure the temperature of the beam of light, which registered at 165 degrees Fahrenheit. Where the light hit an object, the temperature was as high as 500 degrees Fahrenheit! The glass in the window was immediately sandblasted to help diffuse the light, and all present were grateful that the problem had been discovered before the temple was opened.[8]

Nearly twenty thousand people crowded the streets around

Hidden on the mountainside is an image of the Good Shepherd cradling a lamb in his arms. His flock is hidden among the clouds and snowcapped mountains.

the temple on 17 July 1995 to watch a crane lift the statue of the angel Moroni atop its resting place on the 190-foot spire of the temple. The statue, which was made of fiberglass and covered in gold leaf, weighed about two hundred pounds and measured thirteen feet, three inches tall. As the statue was fitted into its place, the crowd spontaneously began singing "The Spirit of God." The number in attendance at this event was almost equal to the number of people who had attended the groundbreaking ceremony.[9]

The Mount Timpanogos Utah Temple was dedicated on 13 October 1996 after an open house of several weeks, which permitted nearly seven hundred thousand people to tour the temple. When completed, it was the forty-ninth operating temple of The Church of Jesus Christ of Latter-day Saints. The twenty-seven dedicatory sessions included Church members in the temple and at local stake centers via satellite broadcast, permitting almost one hundred sixty thousand worthy Church members to attend.

Stephen M. Studdert, who served as vice chairman of the temple committee, commented on the spiritual outpouring during the dedication ceremonies: "It has been a spiritual feast for all who have prepared themselves and come in the spirit of worship and reverence. Each day has been a day of joyous grandeur."[10] Then, adding a personal note, he remarked, "My heart is full of very tender feelings. I think they can be mostly described as feelings of profound gratitude, coupled with feelings of a witness of the divinity of the work of the Master. I have been deeply moved by the outpouring of the Spirit and by the faith and faithfulness of the thousands of Saints who helped prepare this temple. It is clear that the Spirit of the Lord surrounds all that goes on with temples. From the preparation of a temple to the work for kindred dead, the Lord directs it all."[11]

. . . a house of learning, a house of glory, a house of order, a house of God

St. Louis Missouri Temple

During the time the Church was centered in Missouri in the early days of the Restoration, the Saints there experienced wonderful spiritual manifestations as well as intense persecution. As settlement increased in western Missouri, so did distrust and persecution from their neighbors. Although the Saints had planned for temples in Independence and Far West, mob activities prevented them from finishing them. Eventually Lilburn Boggs, the governor of the state, issued his infamous extermination order, the Prophet Joseph and other leaders were jailed, and the Saints were forced from that region at gunpoint in the middle of winter.

But not all parts of Missouri were hostile to the Saints. In eastern Missouri, in the city of St. Louis, newspapers and officials decried the injustices to the Saints on the other side of the state. After the exodus from Missouri and during the later general westward migration of the Saints, St. Louis provided refuge in a climate of tolerance. In St. Louis, where the Saints established a stake, thousands of immigrants earned money and were outfitted for their long trek to Utah.

In part because of the Church's strong history in the region and the long distances required for members in the area to attend the temple, Missouri Saints were overjoyed in 1990 at the announcement of the St. Louis Missouri Temple, which would be the fiftieth operating temple in the Church. When members of the First Presidency separately considered the handful of potential sites for the temple, all agreed that the temple should be located on a beautiful site in Town and Country, a community approximately twenty miles west of St. Louis. The site is located atop a prominent hill that overlooks the surrounding region. A wooded area provides a barrier between the temple and a busy highway.

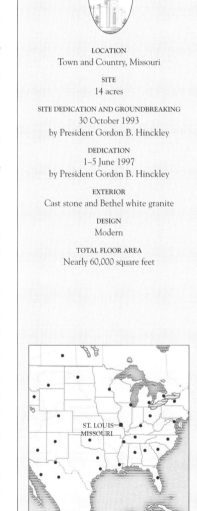

LOCATION
Town and Country, Missouri

SITE
14 acres

SITE DEDICATION AND GROUNDBREAKING
30 October 1993
by President Gordon B. Hinckley

DEDICATION
1–5 June 1997
by President Gordon B. Hinckley

EXTERIOR
Cast stone and Bethel white granite

DESIGN
Modern

TOTAL FLOOR AREA
Nearly 60,000 square feet

ST. LOUIS
MISSOURI

The welcoming spirit of friendship that citizens of St. Louis had extended to the early Saints in Missouri was clearly seen again when the temple committee sought city approval for the building. One example of local enthusiasm for the project came at an aldermen's meeting, at which approval for the temple would either be granted or denied. During the course of the meeting, an architect's rendering of the proposed temple was unveiled. Several moments of silence followed as the aldermen and others in the crowded hall gazed at the beautiful rendering. One leader rose and said, "I am not going to move approval of this project!" After a long pause, he continued, "I move unanimous and enthusiastic approval of this project." The aldermen then cast a unanimous vote in favor of approving the temple, causing the audience to erupt in applause.[1] These actions and others in the process of building the temple all happened without any opposition to the project.

On an unseasonably cold day, 30 October 1993, Church leaders and some five thousand members from the area gathered for the St. Louis Missouri Temple groundbreaking ceremony. Despite the uncomfortable temperatures, members began flocking to the site two hours before the ceremonies began.

In his remarks, President Gordon B. Hinckley reminisced about the Saints' past in the area. "This may sound strange, but I am rather glad it is cold," he said. "I think it brings us to a greater appreciation for the Saints who left the state of Missouri in 1838 under the orders of the then governor; a tragic episode in the history of our people, and I think that it must be so for Missouri."[2] He later added, "I am satisfied that the Prophet Joseph smiles on us today. And I am satisfied that

St. Louis Missouri Temple

We are reminded that this temple stands on the soil of the state of Missouri, where the Prophet and his associates suffered so much and were finally banished by a cruel and illegal order of extermination. Terrible were their losses, terrible their suffering. We are grateful that the extermination order has been revoked and the persecution is long since gone. Today thy Church basks in the sunlight of good will.

—FROM THE DEDICATORY PRAYER

those who were with him on that long trek across Missouri in the winter of 1838 smile upon us as they see what we begin here today."[3]

President Thomas S. Monson, in his address, noted that Charles A. Lindbergh made his famous flight in *The Spirit of St. Louis* in 1927, the year President Monson was born. He said, "I love the name—'The Spirit of St. Louis.' It reflects a pioneer spirit. Those who helped establish the Church in this area and continue to help it grow are real pioneers. I simply say, 'Thanks be to God for a temple, a temple of the Lord, to be erected here.' That will be the true spirit of St. Louis."[4]

Work began immediately on the temple, which was to be completed in three and a half years. The temple, based on the general design of the Nauvoo Temple, included white granite facing and a single, one-hundred-fifty-foot spire with a gold-leafed statue of the angel Moroni. Beautiful vertical art glass windows add elegance to the spire and the temple walls. In designing the structure, the architects had set out to create a structure that would communicate the wholeness and solidarity of the Church and be both recognizable and dignified.

When the doors of the completed temple were opened for public tours at the end of April 1997, the community response was overwhelming. Along with many prominent government officials from across the state, some two hundred sixty thousand people visited the new temple. Because of the great interest that was shown, the open house was extended for an extra week. Missouri St. Louis Mission president Stuart R. Preece reported that the mission received some two thousand referrals from the publicity that the temple garnered during the open house and dedication. "The missionaries are teaching a lot of discussions," he said. "People around the temple have

Hidden in the distant trees is the image of a pioneer mounted on a horse and leading a team of oxen pulling a covered wagon. In the clouds is the world-famous Gateway Arch, commemorating the role of St. Louis as a gateway to the West.

been watching it and wanted to come see it. One person came into the mission home to tell us how happy he is that St. Louis has its very own Mormon temple now, just like San Diego and other cities."[5] Missionaries and members of the temple committee speakers bureau gave some two hundred presentations about the temple to area schools, clubs, and churches.[6]

On June 1 President Gordon B. Hinckley dedicated the St. Louis Missouri Temple. Twenty-three thousand members from throughout the temple district—which included Missouri and parts of Nebraska, Kansas, Illinois, Indiana, Kentucky, and Tennessee—participated in the dedication services despite rain during some of the sessions. Members of the First Presidency participated in the nineteen sessions.

Members commented on how having a temple nearby had encouraged them to increase their spirituality. Stephanie Daher, a local Relief Society president, said, "Our lives have changed because of the temple. There are a lot of people who, because of the temple coming and their being challenged to prepare to attend the dedication, have put their lives in order. A Relief Society sister came up to me one Sunday and whispered, 'I'm worthy to go to the dedication.' She had been having a problem with the Word of Wisdom, but stopped smoking so she would be ready."[7]

In a city that provided early Latter-day Saints with a haven from raging persecution, it is fitting to have a temple dedicated to the Lord. The St. Louis Missouri Temple is a tribute to those who endured the hardships of the past and to the community that gave them refuge. And it is a promise of life everlasting to those who enter its doors in the years to come.

We are grateful that . . . today thy Church basks in the sunlight of good will

Vernal Utah Temple

In August 1907 President Joseph F. Smith dedicated the recently completed Uintah Stake Tabernacle, one of Ashley Valley's most outstanding landmarks, which was used through the years for such gatherings as quarterly conferences, concerts, baptisms, weddings, and funerals. The faithful Saints in that area donated seven years of toil and sacrifice to complete the structure. At the dedication, President Smith said he "would not be surprised if a temple were built here some day."[1] His prophecy was fulfilled ninety years later when the beloved old tabernacle was converted into the beautiful new Vernal Utah Temple.

Although for decades the Uintah Stake Tabernacle had served and unified the Vernal community, by the 1970s its practical uses had become limited. The building was old and could no longer be used for Church gatherings. Many in the community feared that it would be condemned and torn down. One group of citizens formed a "Save the Tabernacle Committee" to raise money, write petitions, and do whatever they could to save the tabernacle that their ancestors had labored on and sacrificed to build.

The First Presidency knew of the concerns and the deteriorating state of the tabernacle. President Gordon B. Hinckley and President Thomas S. Monson traveled to Vernal to tour the building. Laird M. Hartman, the stake president who accompanied them on their tour, recorded: "They arrived at 10 in the morning. We spent approximately two hours touring the tabernacle. Their purpose was to look at its condition and see if they could feel what the Lord wanted them to do with that beautiful old building. . . . As they left, President Hinckley said, 'I don't know what the Lord wants us to do with the building. We will find out.'"[2] Not long after this visit, the First Presidency

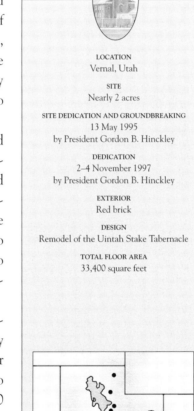

LOCATION
Vernal, Utah

SITE
Nearly 2 acres

SITE DEDICATION AND GROUNDBREAKING
13 May 1995
by President Gordon B. Hinckley

DEDICATION
2–4 November 1997
by President Gordon B. Hinckley

EXTERIOR
Red brick

DESIGN
Remodel of the Uintah Stake Tabernacle

TOTAL FLOOR AREA
33,400 square feet

VERNAL
UTAH

invited all the stake presidents from the Vernal area to meet with them in Salt Lake City. There the stake presidents received news that the Brethren felt impressed to convert the tabernacle into a temple.[3] Later an official letter was read to the members, who rejoiced at the news that their tabernacle would be saved. That it would become a holy temple was even more of a wonder and cause for greater rejoicing.

Before construction began, the Church opened the tabernacle for public viewing. In the spring of 1994, more than eighteen thousand people attended the open house, which featured missionary displays, guided tours, music provided by volunteers, and a thirty-minute documentary video about the building. After the open house, such original tabernacle furnishings as heaters, the organ, the piano, and light fixtures, were sold at public auction.[4]

On 13 May 1995, approximately ten thousand members attended the construction commencement ceremony. President Hinckley admonished them, "Let's clean up our lives, reach heavenward a little more, be faithful Latter-day Saints. Let us choose the right in all of our decisions. Let us walk more faithfully before the Lord." President James E. Faust also spoke, emphasizing that the Vernal Utah Temple would be a monument to the early settlers of the Uintah Basin, who had the faith and determination necessary to sacrifice in order to build the Uintah Stake Tabernacle.[5]

With the beginning of construction in the summer of 1995 came a search throughout the area for high-quality period brick to match the brick on the tabernacle walls. This brick would be used to replace damaged bricks and to construct a gateway. Satisfactory brick was found on only one house,

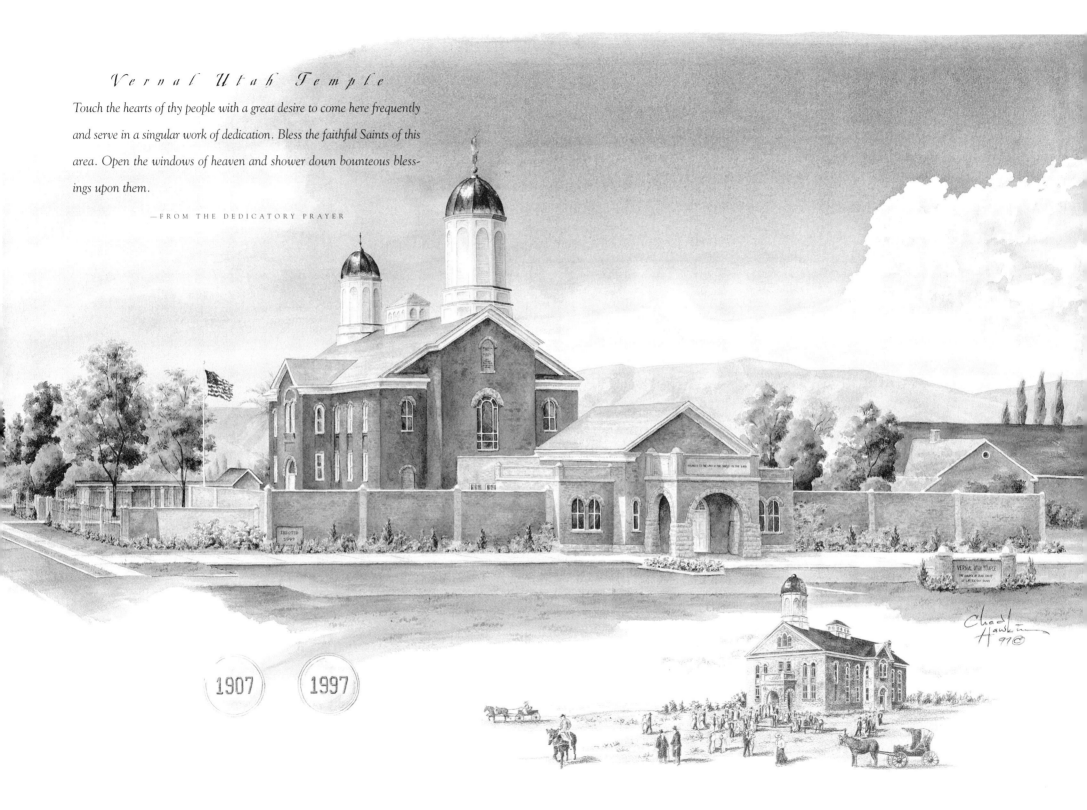

Vernal Utah Temple

Touch the hearts of thy people with a great desire to come here frequently and serve in a singular work of dedication. Bless the faithful Saints of this area. Open the windows of heaven and shower down bounteous blessings upon them.

—FROM THE DEDICATORY PRAYER

1907   1997

owned by Nick J. Meagher. He had planned to raze the home but instead agreed to donate it to the Church. The bricks on the old home had the same markings as those used in the tabernacle, suggesting that they came from the same clay pit and kiln as the tabernacle bricks.[6]

More than a thousand volunteers helped dismantle the home, brick by brick. The job took nearly two months of evenings and Saturdays to be completed. Members of all ages throughout the temple district donated their time and service. Small children stacked bricks while adults removed and cleaned them. Even a ninety-year-old man in a wheelchair helped clean bricks. When the project was over, about sixteen thousand bricks had been salvaged and prepared to become a part of the temple.[7]

Making a temple out of the existing tabernacle was no easy feat for the architects and builders. They had to remove the interior of the building and excavate the ground below. Elder Ben B. Banks of the Seventy commented, "The building literally was just four walls by the time construction started."[8] Roger Jackson, the project's chief architect, explained the process: "The walls are four bricks thick. We actually took off the inside layer of brick and did some reinforcing to the entire building and left just the four walls and part of the roof. The original roof was made of hand-sawn, thick, huge, timber trusses. We thought we could save them, so the roof trusses stayed, but the rest of the roof came down, and then we built on to the roof trusses. So basically, we kept the outside and built a new building inside."[9]

In addition to the original walls and roof trusses, the temple features many historically significant items. The stained glass window displayed on the temple's east side was originally made for the Mt. Olivet Methodist Episcopal Church of Hollywood.

The drawing of the Uintah Stake Tabernacle within the depiction of the Vernal Utah Temple is based on a photograph taken after the tabernacle's dedicatory service. Hidden in the clouds is a picture of the Savior with his arm outstretched, inviting all to partake of temple blessings.

The Church purchased that building in 1937 and held meetings in it for many years. When the building was demolished, the stained glass window was saved for future use and was later found to be ideal for the Vernal Utah Temple. The oxen under the baptismal font also have a unique history—they were on public display for more than twenty years in the South Visitors' Center on Temple Square in Salt Lake City. Eighteen original pews from the tabernacle were refinished for use in the temple. The newel cap at the bottom of the grand stairway is the original cap from the tabernacle, set aside when renovations began.[10] From the woodwork to the furniture, the interior of the temple was designed to be reminiscent of the early nineteenth-century style found inside the original tabernacle.

When construction was completed, the building was again opened to the public for tours but this time as a temple of the Lord. One young woman at the temple's open house commented to me that her great-grandfather had been told in a blessing that he would help construct a temple for the Lord. Motivated by that blessing, he traveled to Salt Lake City to receive instruction. He was told to go and use his talents on the Ashley Uintah Stake tabernacle, where he stayed and worked until its completion. Not having built any other building for the Church, he died believing his blessing had been unfulfilled. The dedication of the Vernal Utah Temple on 2 November 1997 marked the fulfillment of her great-grandfather's blessing.

The dedication of the temple was a spiritual feast for the thousands who attended and participated in the Hosanna Shout. Talks were given, prayers were offered, and hearts were filled with rejoicing as members silently celebrated the conversion of their beloved tabernacle into a temple of the Lord.

Touch the hearts of thy people with a great desire to come here frequently

Preston England Temple

In July 1837 Heber C. Kimball, Orson Hyde, and five other elders arrived in Liverpool as the first missionaries of the restored gospel to serve in England. They began their work in Preston, where the first English converts were baptized in the River Ribble. Fifty people were baptized within the week, and despite opposition from local preachers and the press, nearly two thousand people were baptized in the next nine months.[1] The work continued to progress, and thousands of converts gathered to America to join the Saints, but many other faithful members stayed in the British Isles, where there are now seventh-generation Latter-day Saints. The Preston Ward is the world's longest-functioning unit of the Church.[2]

This area rich in Church history became the site for England's second temple. President Gordon B. Hinckley announced the Preston, Lancashire, vicinity as the chosen site on 19 October 1992, during the second day of the rededication of the London England Temple.[3] Almost two years later, a large group of Church members gathered for the groundbreaking of the Preston England Temple. President Hinckley, who had served as a missionary in Preston sixty-one years earlier, presided at the ceremony.

Before the meeting began, President Hinckley shook hands and mingled with the members. He was reunited with Robert Pickles, his member-missionary companion from decades earlier, in a tearful embrace. "This is an emotional experience for me," said President Hinckley, addressing the congregation.

"Never, all those years ago, would I have dreamed that a temple would be built here. This will become our ensign upon the mountain. A temple is a unique structure: a monument to

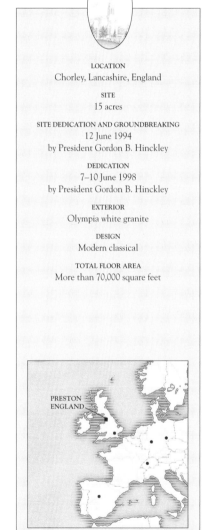

LOCATION
Chorley, Lancashire, England

SITE
15 acres

SITE DEDICATION AND GROUNDBREAKING
12 June 1994
by President Gordon B. Hinckley

DEDICATION
7–10 June 1998
by President Gordon B. Hinckley

EXTERIOR
Olympia white granite

DESIGN
Modern classical

TOTAL FLOOR AREA
More than 70,000 square feet

PRESTON
ENGLAND

our convictions, belief and knowledge that life is eternal; that we go on living after death."[4]

More than seventy thousand people learned about the beliefs of the Latter-day Saints during the temple's two-week open house. Tour guides led group after group through the rooms and hallways, and missionaries received referrals from many people interested in learning more about the Church.

Individual responses to the open house were positive. Bryan J. Grant, the Church's director of public affairs for the Europe North Area, told of a particular couple who toured the temple. "[They] own a Georgian mansion," said Brother Grant, "so they're used to very elegant living. When they came out, they walked around the temple about three times to come up with a word that described how they felt about it. And they said the word they came up with was 'exquisite.'"[5]

Another visitor, who drove to the open house on a motorcycle, toured the temple on behalf of his local motorcycle club. After the tour he remarked to a security guard, "I wish my life had the peace and tranquility you have in the temple."[6]

Local members seized the opportunity to share the gospel with their neighbors by talking with them about the temple. Bishop Bernard Walsh was one of those members. "[He] went personally to every door along the Preston Road that borders the site and extended a personal invitation to every family there to come and visit the temple," Brother Grant said. "Every single person along that road was delighted at what they now have, as it were, in their back garden. One lady even said that 'you ought to know I was the person who organized the group against the temple.' She said, 'I think it's a lovely building.' And so they've all been won over."[7]

Preston England Temple

We dedicate unto thee and unto thy Son this the Preston England Temple. . . . We pray that thou wilt accept it as the sacred offering of thy thankful people. This is thy house and we ask that thou wilt sanctify it with thy presence. From this day forth may thy Holy Spirit dwell within these walls and touch the hearts of all who enter herein.

—FROM THE DEDICATORY PRAYER

Neighbors of the temple continue to enjoy the beauty of the building and grounds. During the open house, an elderly man who had been quite opposed to the temple told Elder Cecil O. Samuelson of the Seventy that his negative opinion had changed. He asked permission to stroll around the grounds in the evenings. Local Church member John Phillipson said, "Quite a few people have mentioned the same thing: that even though they could not go in the temple [after it was dedicated], they were glad to be allowed to visit the grounds."[8]

That the neighbors were pleased with the appearance of the temple and grounds is not surprising. The beautiful grounds, with seven hundred trees and more than one hundred thousand other plants, earned the landscapers a prestigious industry award three years in a row. The temple itself, with its exterior of white granite and zinc roof, has been described as "reminiscent to the old churches built in this land many years ago."[9]

The temple is located at the junction of the M61 motorway, making it highly visible to all who pass by. Ian D. Swanney, president of the temple, said of its location, "I love the vision that all motorways seem to lead to the temple."[10] This beautiful building is the perfect addition to the surrounding countryside as well as to the lives of Church members in Scotland, Ireland, and the northern part of England.

When the Preston England Temple was dedicated, President Hinckley returned to his former mission area to preside over thirteen of the fifteen dedication ceremonies. He addressed the members in attendance, speaking of his memories and his love for England. "I feel as if I've come home," he said. "This is an emotional day. . . . It has been a treasured experience for me to come back to this area of Lancashire

Just as farmers tend the sheep dotting the green hillsides of England, so the Good Shepherd lovingly cares for each of his sheep. Hidden among the clouds is an image of Jesus Christ with a lamb cradled in his arms.

where I served as a missionary 65 years ago." He continued, "I never dreamed there would come a time when there would be 45 stakes, two houses of the Lord, family history research centers, all these things. God has had His hand on this place through the centuries, I believe, and more recently, in terms of His cause and kingdom."[11] After four days of dedicatory sessions, the Saints gratefully began serving in their temple.

Ian D. Swanney spoke of his experience as president of the Preston England Temple: "We never lose the lovely feeling of seeing the temple as we drive toward it every day. When we arrive early in the morning, it's still dark. The temple is lit up. It looks beautiful in all kinds of weather, but on stormy days, it seems to have such a strength about it. . . . The thrill of seeing the temple on that hillside never goes away. . . .

"The temple is a great symbol of our message to the world. It's sort of silently displayed, yet it's noticed by everybody. It's a beacon to all. . . .

"We are so blessed to have two temples in England, the one in London and now this one in Preston. It means so much to members here who have had to travel such distances to the temple. The members in the Shetland Islands, for example, had to travel 14 hours on an overnight ferry to the mainland in Scotland, and then had an 11-hour drive to London. Now, the drive portion of their trip is just five hours. That's still a long journey, but the members love having the temple so much closer."[12] The members of the Preston England Temple district take advantage of the proximity of the temple, returning again and again. "When people leave," explained President Swanney, "they express reluctance of having to go back into the world after having been in the temple."[13]

Monticello Utah Temple

The beautiful Monticello Utah Temple, nestled at the foot of the Abajo Mountains, was the first of a new series of smaller temples announced by President Gordon B. Hinckley in general conference in October 1997. Although smaller than earlier temples, it is in every way as beautiful, with elegant chandeliers, high-quality marble from Turkey, and stained glass from Germany.

The Monticello Utah Temple district is rich in pioneer history. In the summer of 1879, an expedition from Cedar City settled Bluff, near the San Juan River. The trek that was meant to last six weeks became a journey of almost six months as the pioneers fought their way through tortuous conditions and a country unfamiliar to those who had planned the expedition.

To cross the Colorado River, they had to make an eighteen-hundred-foot descent at now-famous Hole-in-the-Rock. Women and children walked and slid down the steep incline and men steered the wagons, which they had prepared for the descent by wrapping heavy chains around the wheels and attaching ropes and chains to the back. As many as twenty men were needed to hold onto the chains to prevent the wagons from plunging into the river below. The company of two hundred fifty people and twenty-six wagons successfully reached their destination that day.[1] Many who live in the Monticello Utah Temple district are descendants of those heroic pioneers.

The land for the temple is in the northwest part of town, next to a chapel, and was donated to the Church by a father and his son. The groundbreaking ceremony took place just six weeks after President Hinckley introduced in general conference the idea of small temples. About twenty-six hundred

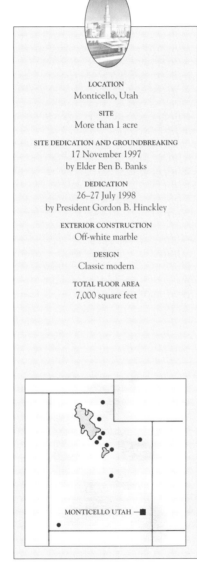

LOCATION
Monticello, Utah

SITE
More than 1 acre

SITE DEDICATION AND GROUNDBREAKING
17 November 1997
by Elder Ben B. Banks

DEDICATION
26–27 July 1998
by President Gordon B. Hinckley

EXTERIOR CONSTRUCTION
Off-white marble

DESIGN
Classic modern

TOTAL FLOOR AREA
7,000 square feet

MONTICELLO UTAH ■

people attended the event, and some had to stand on construction equipment and truck beds to see the proceedings.[2]

Elder Neil L. Andersen of the Seventy spoke to the congregation. "Isn't it wonderful," he said, "to know that the Lord knows and loves you, the people of Monticello? . . . He knows you, He knows your heart, He knows of your testimonies and your goodness. And He has directed His prophet to build for you and for your children a house unto Him, here on this spot."[3]

Construction began quickly following the groundbreaking ceremony. Much care was taken to ensure that the Monticello Utah Temple was as well built and as beautiful as any other temple in the Church. The exterior is finished in a marble called Noah's Creme, which was chosen for its color, range of shades, and availability. The hue of the temple seems to change with the weather conditions and time of day. Members in the area agree that the color of the marble perfectly complements the color of the local landscape. Some thirteen thousand tiles used on the temple were evaluated carefully to make sure they blended with each other for a uniform effect. The marble on the exterior of the temple is the ideal material for weathering severe sandstorms, which are common in the Four Corners area.[4]

The statue of the angel Moroni originally placed on the spire of the Monticello Utah Temple was six feet tall and made of white fiberglass. It was a new model created especially for use on smaller temples. The statue served its purpose well until the first overcast day, when it seemed to disappear against the cloudy sky. It was also difficult to light properly at night because it was not as bright as the gold-leafed statues. The Brethren

Monticello Utah Temple

Since the beginning of thy work in this dispensation, thy people have been commanded to build temples. Even in seasons of great poverty, they have struggled to erect these sacred houses. Now, thou hast made thy will known and blessed us with the means to erect many more temples, smaller in size, but complete in their necessary appointments. These will be convenient to thy faithful Saints and will meet the needs of thy growing Church throughout the world. This is the first of a new generation of such structures.

—FROM THE DEDICATORY PRAYER

considered these observations and decided to use a different style of statue—one covered with 23-karat gold—on the small temples. When the new statue arrived from Salt Lake City, workers discovered that it was two feet taller than the fiberglass statue, which was transported to Salt Lake City for display in the Church Office Building.[5]

The temple was soon finished and opened for public viewing before the dedication. One morning a member of the temple committee arrived just before the open house to find thousands of moths covering the grounds and walls of the temple. After some unsuccessful attempts to remove the moths, maintenance workers began to scatter them with air blowers. As they did so, starlings that had been building nests on the nearby meetinghouse swooped down and caught the moths in mid-air, ridding the temple of most of the insects in about twenty minutes.

"It was just like the crickets and the seagulls in Salt Lake," mused Brother Cooper Jones, referring to the 1848 incident when seagulls devoured the crickets that threatened to destroy the pioneers' crops.[6]

More than eight thousand members attended the eight dedicatory sessions of the Monticello Utah Temple. President Hinckley told the story of a San Juan Stake conference in

Hidden in the mountain is an image of a horse head, reminiscent of a natural feature that folklore says protects the people of the valley. Also hidden nearby is an image of two men lowering a driver and his team, a tribute to the Hole-in-the-Rock pioneers.

1894 during which Brigham Young Jr., a member of the Quorum of the Twelve Apostles, spoke on vicarious work for the dead and declared, "In the near future a temple will be built in this country."

President Hinckley said, "It's taken a long time to fulfill Brigham Young Jr.'s prophetic statement. I'm glad to be in harmony with Brigham Young Jr. The inspiration of the Spirit is strong, clear and certain that this is where the House of the Lord should be built. . . . No one could be happier than I am."[7]

In speaking of Monticello as the site of the first smaller temple, President Hinckley said, "We wanted to build one that we could get to, that we could observe. This is somewhat new ground we were treading, and we wanted to be able to examine it and see how things fit together. We knew of this part of the state, which is isolated and a long ways from a temple. These people had to travel all the way to Manti in the past, more than a four-hour drive each way, so we concluded to put one here in San Juan County. And the determination was made to put it in Monticello."[8]

In the first three months following the temple's dedication, faithful members showed their gratitude by performing nearly fifty-seven thousand ordinances—no small work for a "smaller" temple.

Thou hast . . . blessed us with the means to erect many more temples, smaller in size. . . . This is the first of a new generation of such structures

Autumn at Temple Square

Autumn is a time of transition, and as the leaves change, vibrant colors adorn all the trees—the historic elms as well as the honeysuckle, crab apple, and catalpa trees. Colorful autumn foliage against the monochromatic grounds of the Salt Lake Temple emphasizes the beauty of the season, a busy time for the gardeners who must finish planting spring bulbs before the first snow arrives. This is one of only a few of my works that do not include a hidden image.

Lights at Temple Square

Images of the wise men are in the western sky, as they follow the star in the east that "went before them, till it came and stood over where the young child was" (Matthew 2:9). The temple stands beneath the new star because that is where wise men today find the Savior—within the temple. This painting captures the joyful spirit of Temple Square in celebrating the Savior's birth, reminding us of cherished moments shared with our loved ones.

Logan—The Morning Breaks

The hymn "The Morning Breaks," in which lyricist Parley P. Pratt boldly declares the restored gospel of Jesus Christ, was the inspiration for this work. Just as glorious dawn dispels the shadows of darkness, the restored gospel brings light to a world waiting in spiritual darkness. Hidden in this painting is an image of the young Prophet Joseph Smith shielding his eyes from the sun's rays shining through the trees as he looks into the light of the First Vision. Closing the doors of the Apostasy, this event commenced the Restoration—truly the dawning of a brighter day.

This rendering is dedicated to my parents, Spencer and Janet, who were sealed in the Logan Temple in March 1960. I am grateful for their example of a temple marriage and for their continual encouragement of my art.

Manti—The Morning Breaks

This painting, based on the hymn "The Morning Breaks," depicts the day's first light shining through dense trees, illuminating the upper portions of the temple as it conveys serenity and peace to the beholder. Hidden in the evergreens below the temple is the figure of Moroni, who is raising his right hand toward the temple and carrying the gold plates with his left. Moroni's connection with the Manti Utah Temple was identified by Brigham Young, who is recorded as saying that the prophet Moroni had anciently dedicated the ground upon which the temple now stands.

Cardston Alberta Temple

A magnificent sculpture located in the main entryway to the temple depicts the story of Jesus and the Samaritan woman at the well. Hidden within the trees and flowers to the right of the temple, in commemoration of that sculpture, are images of the Savior and the woman with her water vessel. Another hidden image is that of Old Chief Mountain, a mountain legendary to those living in southern Alberta, which can be seen from the temple grounds. Its famous silhouette is hidden in the shadows on the grass in the lower left-hand corner.

Vernal Utah Temple

The Vernal Utah Temple is the first temple constructed from an already-existing structure, the Uintah Stake Tabernacle. Marking the transformation from tabernacle to temple, the historical tabernacle is portrayed in black and white as it appears in photographs taken at its dedication in 1907; the modern-day temple is painted in full color as it appeared at its dedication ninety years later. The two circles with the respective dedicatory years are located on the west end of the temple. In the clouds to the right of the temple is hidden an image of the Savior with his arm outstretched, inviting us to partake of the blessings of the temple. Created using a transparent watercolor technique and graphite, the original was selected to be on permanent display inside the Vernal Utah Temple.

1907   1997

Nauvoo—The Beautiful

Inspired by President Gordon B. Hinckley's announcement that the Nauvoo Temple would be rebuilt to "stand as a memorial to those who built the first such structure there on the banks of the Mississippi," this painting is a tribute to those faithful Saints. An image of the Prophet Joseph Smith, who helped to quarry the stone for the temple walls, is hidden to the right of the temple. He is holding a copy of the Book of Mormon in his hands. The trees, landscaping, and flowers appear as they would in June, the month of the Martyrdom; the time of day on the temple's clocks is 5:16 P.M., the hour of the Prophet's death.

Chad Hawkins

Anchorage Alaska Temple

The Anchorage Alaska temple was the second of the Church's smaller temples to be completed and is the smallest of the first one hundred temples. It is also the northernmost temple in the world. Before the announcement that a temple would be built in Anchorage, the eighteen thousand Saints in Alaska had watched and prayed for the day they would have a temple nearby; they had previously had to travel well over a thousand miles to attend the Seattle Washington or Cardston Alberta Temples.

The Church had already purchased five acres of land on which to build a stake center to accommodate the growth of Church membership in Anchorage. The land, however, was triangular in shape and was not large enough for a stake center. Though at first the Saints thought a new site would have to be found, the Church was able to buy some of the adjoining land, making the entire tract rectangular shaped. Today, the chapel and the temple fit perfectly on the property, leaving adequate space for landscaping and parking.[1]

Although Church leaders originally intended the Anchorage Alaska Temple to be the first of the smaller temples, architect Doug Green suggested that the first small temple be built somewhere closer to Salt Lake City, where Church officials could monitor construction more closely and discover any potential problems that might arise in the building of other small temples. President Gordon B. Hinckley agreed with this idea and decided to have the prototype for small temples built in Monticello, Utah.

During the process of building that first small temple, architects and designers learned many valuable things. Accordingly, Brother Green made nearly three hundred changes to improve plans for the Anchorage Alaska Temple. Design elements that

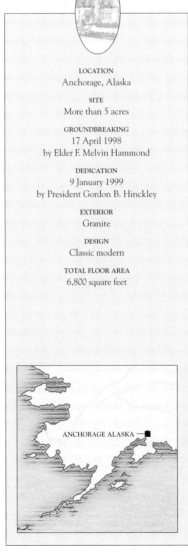

LOCATION
Anchorage, Alaska

SITE
More than 5 acres

GROUNDBREAKING
17 April 1998
by Elder F. Melvin Hammond

DEDICATION
9 January 1999
by President Gordon B. Hinckley

EXTERIOR
Granite

DESIGN
Classic modern

TOTAL FLOOR AREA
6,800 square feet

ANCHORAGE ALASKA

he added to the Anchorage Alaska Temple include such features as a canopy over the entrance and heated stairs to help keep walkways clear of snow and ice.[2]

Speaking of his job as a temple architect, Brother Green said, "You hit your knees and pray. You do have to pray. To me, if you're going to build something for the Lord, you have to ask for his help and inspiration." One challenge Brother Green faced was finding ways to make the temple uniquely Alaskan. He prayed for inspiration, and on a trip to Salt Lake City he noticed something on the Salt Lake Temple that he hadn't seen before: the seven stars of the Big Dipper pointing to the North Star. That symbol is found on the Alaskan flag, and is now depicted on the west side of the Anchorage Alaska Temple.[3] The Big Dipper and the North Star, which have been used for thousands of years as navigation aids, are appropriate symbols for a temple, which, as Hugh Nibley said, is where we take our "bearings on the universe and in the eternities, both in time and space."[4]

Brother Green also found other ways to make the temple look and feel like it belongs in Alaska. The stained glass is reminiscent of water, and stylized evergreens with patterns resembling native designs are used to adorn interior furnishings. Forget-me-nots, the official flower of Alaska, adorn the walls and carpeting in the sealing room.[5] These elements combine with other features—such as the celestial room chandelier, which is made of exquisite Hungarian crystal and weighs seven hundred pounds—to create the peaceful, elegant atmosphere that prevails in the temple.

The Anchorage Alaska Temple is covered with Sierra white granite that was quarried near Fresno, California. This

Anchorage Alaska Temple

We are grateful for the inspiration which has come to build it, and pray that thy faithful people in this part of thy vineyard may treasure it and use it for the purposes for which it is designed. Increase their faith, deepen their understanding of things divine, acquaint them with thy holy and everlasting purposes. Bless them as they walk in righteousness before thee, contributing their tithes and offerings, working with faith to build thy cause and kingdom. Open the windows of heaven and shower down blessings upon them.

—FROM THE DEDICATORY PRAYER

same granite was also used on the exteriors of the temples in Oakland and Fresno, California. Surrounded by tall trees, the temple is located just off a main freeway. The statue of the angel Moroni faces the Chugach mountain range to the east. During the dark hours of the day, the steeple is lit, but in consideration of nearby neighbors, the lights are turned off before midnight. This lighting schedule means that in the winter months the steeple is lit most of the day.

The Church made every effort to be considerate of local residents during all phases of construction. Builders went to great expense to save as much forest as possible during landscaping so neighbors could continue to use the surrounding land for recreation. After requests from people living nearby, designers changed the roof and spire so it wouldn't cast an overwhelming shadow. "We lowered the thing as much as we could so it wouldn't loom," Brother Green said.[6]

Finally construction was complete, and the dedication of the Anchorage Alaska Temple began early on a freezing January morning. More than six thousand members braved the weather and traveled to the temple to hear the prophet speak. Some came from as far away as the Yukon, a journey of fourteen hours by bus. Outside, the temperature was eighteen degrees with a freezing wind. Snowdrifts were three feet high, and eight-foot-long icicles hung from the nearby chapel roof. An enclosed heated walkway sheltered members as they walked from the chapel to the temple.[7]

The *Church News* commented: "No matter how strong the

The Big Dipper and the North Star are hidden among the distant mountains and trees in this rendering of the Anchorage Alaska Temple. An image of Christ kneeling in prayer is hidden in the tall trees and grass to the right of the temple.

cold winds of winter blast against our lives—and surely the winds of adversity will come—we must keep the gospel flame in our hearts warm and bright. If we do that, then we will be as those whom the Savior spoke of as He concluded the Sermon on the Mount: 'Therefore whosoever heareth these sayings of mine, and doeth them I will liken him unto a wise man, which built his house upon a rock: And the rain descended, and the floods came, and the winds blew, and beat upon that house; and it fell not: for it was founded upon a rock.' (Matt. 7:24–25.)"[8]

Elder F. Melvin Hammond of the Seventy later shared his feelings about the dedication: "I have been in many, many meetings and some dedicatory sessions of temples, but I have never felt a greater spirit of love and warmth and the Holy Ghost pouring out on the people than I did in those dedicatory sessions. The people were so excited and so touched. There were tears in every session. They were so happy to have a temple."[9]

Members continue to attend and serve in the Anchorage Alaska Temple, seeking and finding the same spiritual warmth they felt there on that cold day of the dedication. Supervisors in the temple's baptistry say that every session is a "journal experience" for them. One day two young men brought eighty-five names to the temple. They were all names of Inupiat Eskimos from St. Lawrence and King Island. The supervisor commented, "It was an incredible experience to watch the baptisms and confirmations performed for these true Alaskans in the first Alaska temple."[10]

Increase their faith, deepen their understanding of things divine

Colonia Juárez Chihuahua México Temple

We remember before thee those who, more than a century ago, came here and established these and other communities. How hard they worked, how heavy was their labor. They established a Zion in this part of the earth. . . . Bless thy Saints that they may continue to live here without molestation. May they live in peace and security. . . . Open the windows of heaven and shower down blessings upon them. . . . Bless their posterity that they may go over the earth as teachers of eternal truth.

—FROM THE TEMPLE DEDICATORY PRAYER

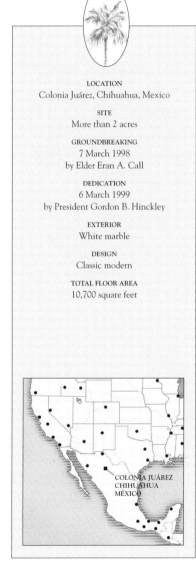

LOCATION
Colonia Juárez, Chihuahua, Mexico

SITE
More than 2 acres

GROUNDBREAKING
7 March 1998
by Elder Eran A. Call

DEDICATION
6 March 1999
by President Gordon B. Hinckley

EXTERIOR
White marble

DESIGN
Classic modern

TOTAL FLOOR AREA
10,700 square feet

COLONIA JUÁREZ
CHIHUAHUA
MÉXICO

The tiny community of Colonia Juárez, Chihuahua, Mexico, is about two hundred miles southwest of El Paso, Texas. On a hill west of town, at the very end of the paved road and overlooking the little valley, sits the first of the smaller temples to be completed outside of the United States. The temple is the answer to the hopes and prayers of this little group of faithful, deserving Latter-day Saints who have sacrificed much through the years and contributed greatly to the growth of the worldwide Church.

The Mormon colonies of northern Mexico are an important part of the Church's history. Pioneers arrived there in the mid-1880s and settled the region. They suffered many hardships during the Mexican revolutions of 1912 and 1914, but they built an enduring legacy of faithfulness and Church service that has been passed down to their children and grandchildren. Today those descendants are found in leadership positions in many Spanish-speaking areas throughout the world, passing on the values of endurance and faith that they learned growing up in a close-knit Mormon colony.

President Gordon B. Hinckley visited the Saints in Colonia Juárez in June 1997 as the guest of honor at the graduation ceremony of Juárez Academy, a highly rated Latter-day Saint preparatory school. During the three-and-a-half-hour drive back to the airport in El Paso, Texas, President Hinckley thought about the situation of the members he had just met. He later explained, "As we were riding to El Paso, I reflected on what we could do to help these people in the Church colonies in Mexico." He continued, "I thought of these things and what could be done. The concept of these smaller temples came into my mind. I concluded we didn't need the laundry. We didn't need to rent temple clothing. We didn't need eating facilities. These have been added for the convenience of the people, but are not necessary [for the temple ordinances]." When he was on the airplane, he continued to refine the idea. "I took a piece of paper," he said, "and sketched out the [floor] plan, and turned it over to the architects to refine it."[1] This inspiration was the beginning of the small temples that have come to bless the lives of so many Saints in remote areas of the world.

The groundbreaking ceremony for the temple in Colonia Juárez took place in March 1998. A congregation of about eight hundred people endured the sleet, wind, rain, and snow to participate in the ceremony. President Meredith I. Romney of the Colonia Juárez Stake remembered: "It was cold and snowy all during the prayers and during the singing of the choir. As soon as Elder [Eran A.] Call got up to speak and give the dedicatory prayer, the sun came out and all the time he was speaking it was just like another day. As soon as he sat down, it clouded up and started snowing."[2] Another member in attendance said, "It was such a special occasion that no one will forget it for years to come. In spite of the weather and maybe because of the weather, thoughts were on our ancestors and the many trials that they had in coming to Mexico to settle the colonies."[3]

Just as their ancestors had worked together and sacrificed to establish the colonies, members in Colonia Juárez collectively donated their time, goods, and services to make the temple a reality. Sister Nellie Romney and her children donated the land, giving up part of their apple orchard to make room for the temple. As soon as the temple was announced, one member designated a plot on his farm, planted grass, and watered and fertilized it for almost a year. Then he rigged up a sod cutter and took all the sod from his farm and laid it on the temple grounds. The Church members in the area helped with the landscaping. At times nearly four hundred people with their equipment were at the temple, working on the grounds.

In this small town of only one store, one hamburger restaurant, one school, and many farms, the building of a temple was the center of activity. Often the Church-owned academy let students out early so they could help on the temple. Local Saints even helped to position the spire and statue of the angel Moroni. It was done without a crane, just lots of rope and people working together. When the temple was completed, an estimated eighty-two thousand work hours had been donated. Elder Richard Skidmore and Sister Bon Adell Skidmore, the temple construction missionaries who served among these Saints and witnessed their contributions, concluded, "This could not have happened anywhere else. It was a community project. It was a huge project for everyone that unified the community in purpose. Their rendered service really has made the temple theirs."[4]

Temple construction unified not only one small community but also Saints from two different cultures as they worked together to build the temple. For a time, the stakes in El Paso, Texas, belonged to the Colonia Juárez Temple district, and bonds of friendship were formed that reached across the border. After the temple was dedicated, a member's home in Colonia Juárez was destroyed by fire. The Saints in El Paso quickly gathered clothing, food, and money and traveled two hundred miles to rebuild the home. Within twenty-four hours, they had prepared a temporary house for the family to stay in. The house was newly painted, the laundry was done, the beds were made, and they had all they needed to feel comfortable. This service was a direct result of the friendships made during the temple's construction.[5]

The dedication of the Colonia Juárez Chihuahua México Temple was a joyous occasion for the nearly five thousand Saints who attended. President Hinckley and Elder Boyd K. Packer spoke, along with Elder Eran A. Call of the Seventy. Knowing that the Mexican Saints had been experiencing a drought, President Hinckley petitioned the Lord for moisture as part of the dedicatory prayer: "Open the windows of heaven and shower down blessings upon them. Cause rain to fall upon their thirsty fields." After the final dedicatory session on Sunday, the first raindrops began to fall.[6] The dedication was over, but the blessings were just beginning.

The road leading to Colonia Juárez drops down a hill and allows a beautiful view of the peaceful little valley. The white marble temple, the "crowning glory to this community," as President Hinckley described it,[7] rests upon a knoll, overlooking the rest of the town and standing as a symbol of the same faith and beliefs of those Saints that founded the colony more than a century ago.

"This temple is the result of the work of those who went before," explained Elder Packer, "and while it is a fulfillment and a fruition, it is also certainly a great beginning in this beautiful valley where the Saints have been so faithful, and have sent mission president after mission president. Ninety mission presidents from these two stakes have gone out to preach the gospel, and innumerable missionaries. They have undergone sacrifice for generations, and now the Lord has blessed them with a House of the Lord."[8]

Open the windows of heaven and shower down blessings upon them

Madrid Spain Temple

As histories go, the Church's experience in Spain has not been particularly long, but it has been challenging. In 1955, when President Gordon B. Hinckley first passed through the country, the Church had essentially no presence there, officially or otherwise. In 1967 Spain passed a religious liberty law, allowing for official recognition of The Church of Jesus Christ of Latter-day Saints. The first branch was organized in Madrid one year later, and in May 1969, the first four full-time missionaries entered the country.

The temple is part of a larger building complex that has become known as the Temple Square of Spain. Other buildings on the square include an eight-story building and a shorter building, which combine to offer a family history center; accommodations for temple administrators and visitors; a missionary training center; a distribution center; and a stake center. The square is surrounded by red brick apartment buildings.

The design of the temple is rich in symbolism and Spanish culture. Designs throughout the temple are patterned after Charles IV's royal palace in Madrid, and much of the interior furnishings are Mediterranean in appearance. Temple architect Carlos Langdon said, "I am not a member of the Church but I am very proud of the result. I think it combines very well what the Church wanted with the very honorable traditions in this country."[1]

When he arrived in Spain to break ground for the new temple in June 1996, Gordon B. Hinckley became the first president of the Church to visit this land. During the groundbreaking ceremony, President Hinckley said, "This is a happy day for me. I came here in 1992 to find a site where this temple

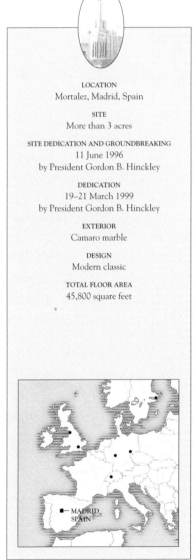

LOCATION
Mortalez, Madrid, Spain

SITE
More than 3 acres

SITE DEDICATION AND GROUNDBREAKING
11 June 1996
by President Gordon B. Hinckley

DEDICATION
19–21 March 1999
by President Gordon B. Hinckley

EXTERIOR
Camaro marble

DESIGN
Modern classic

TOTAL FLOOR AREA
45,800 square feet

MADRID,
SPAIN

may be built. After looking at many areas we felt that this would be an appropriate place.

"I hope we will be good neighbors to those who live around here. I promise you and the officials of Madrid that what is built here will be beautiful. . . . The structure will be beautiful and the grounds will be beautiful. This will be a hallowed and sacred place."[2] At the end of the ceremonies, the prophet waved farewell and began to move toward his car, but then he stopped and returned again to the congregation to repeatedly wave to them. Feeling of his love for them, many wept when he at last left them.

From its groundbreaking to its dedication, the temple has been a means of bringing nonmembers to a greater awareness of the Church. Although 97 percent of Spain's population is Catholic, the people welcomed the Church. Government representatives visited the temple during its open house and seemed to agree with Madrid's mayor, who stated that the holy edifice "has enriched the tradition of Spanish architecture."[3]

Spain Madrid Mission president Steven R. Shallenberger knew of a man whose interest in the temple was piqued after reading an article about the temple in a newspaper and then viewing a newscast about it on television the next morning. President Shallenberger said that the man commented, "'Something made me want to see that temple.' The man and his wife invited two neighbors to drive with them . . . to attend the open house. After they toured the temple, his wife asked how she could be baptized for her ancestors. The couple made an appointment for missionaries to teach the discussions."[4]

While President Hinckley was in Spain to dedicate the temple, he visited King Juan Carlos and Queen Sofia at the

Madrid Spain Temple

We thank thee for this great kingdom of Spain which has been hospitable to thy Saints. Bless this land. We are mindful that it was from these shores that Columbus sailed to discover America as foretold in the Book of Mormon. . . . Bless those who govern in any capacity in this nation and in other nations from which thy people will come to this house. May they be friendly and generous toward thy cause and kingdom. Bless this thy work that it shall flourish and grow in wondrous splendor, touching for everlasting good the hearts of people everywhere.

— FROM THE DEDICATORY PRAYER

TEMPLO DE MADRID
LA IGLESIA DE JESUCRISTO DE LOS SANTOS DE LOS ULTIMOS DIAS

royal palace, making this his third visit with the royal couple. Following up on his 1992 visit, in which he had presented them with a leather-bound Book of Mormon, he gave them a special gift created by well-known Spanish artists: a Lladro figurine of the *Christus*, modeled after the original by Bertel Thorvaldsen and "created in commemoration of the opening of the very first temple in Spain pertaining to The Church of Jesus Christ of Latter-day Saints."[5] Jose Lladro, president of the Lladro company, had personally delivered the first five issues of the figurine to President Hinckley at the Madrid Spain Temple site. One of the five figurines is now on permanent display in the temple's foyer.

Faustino Lopez, an early convert in Spain, shared his feelings about the temple: "When we think about the temple we feel as if it were a dream. Something impossible. It is a miracle of the Lord he has given us. We will try to be faithful to it and be worthy for this wonderful blessing. A temple in Spain means the Lord and the prophet have faith in us."[6]

Elder Jeffrey R. Holland, who participated in the dedicatory services, commented: "To have a beautiful temple—an exquisitely beautiful temple—in this country with such a Christian tradition and historic influence has been truly inspirational." He continued: "I have been so deeply touched by the love, devotion and emotion of the members here, such as the sisters who served in the cafeteria and volunteers who

Hidden in this drawing is a sketch of the Lladro Christus, *which Lladro artists based on Bertel Thorvaldsen's* Christus *and presented to President Gordon B. Hinckley.*

have cleaned every aspect of the temple grounds, to say nothing of the temple itself. A sweet sister, in the dark on her hands and knees, washed the marble trim at the base of the fountains of the garden plaza. They are all so grateful for this temple and so moved to realize that this magnificent edifice is for them."[7]

President Hinckley was confident that the new temple would be very busy: "We're not building any temples where there is not a need for them," he told local reporters.[8] Indeed, before the construction had even risen above ground level, President Carlos Jesus Somoza Diaz of the Madrid Spain Stake said, "The stake is holding meetings and activities that will motivate members to prepare themselves to attend and serve in the temple. We also have three functioning family history centers, and will soon open a fourth. We are preparing for a great work to be done in Madrid." He explained that the family history centers were so busy there was hardly ever free time.[9]

Before the dedication of the temple, President Hinckley was asked, "If you could say any one thing to the members of the Church here in Spain, what would it be?" The prophet responded, "Live worthy to go to the temple. Then you will be worthy of every other blessing this Church has to offer."[10] That promise is the hope not only of the prophet but also of every faithful member served by this landmark temple on the Iberian Peninsula.

We thank thee for this great kingdom of Spain

Bogotá Colombia Temple

We are grateful for those who have gone before us in establishing and strengthening thy kingdom in this part of the earth. Now stands this beautiful temple as a witness and testimony of the truth of all that they taught and did. It offers the crowning blessing of the gospel to everyone who accepts the ordinances to be given herein. It extends thy holy work from mortal life to the eternities that lie beyond. It gives greater understanding of the atonement wrought by the Savior of all mankind.

—FROM THE DEDICATORY PRAYER

In the Niza section of Bogota, about ten miles from downtown, stands an incredible structure. It is surrounded by high-rise buildings and a busy freeway, yet it is considered by many to be the most beautiful building in Bogota, perhaps the most beautiful in all of Colombia. That building is the Bogota Colombia Temple.

The temple is a masterful edifice that combines local architectural themes and building materials with beautiful grounds to occupy an entire city block. The temple itself is faced with a silver-gray Brazilian granite that portrays a subtle elegance and reverence on both rainy and sunny days. The placement of windows enhances the amount of natural light that brightens the interior of the temple. Some of that light enters through tall, stained glass windows, designed both functionally and aesthetically to enhance local Colombian craftsmanship.

On the inside, local motifs continue, as evidenced by fixtures that bear a distinct likeness to ancient Incan designs.

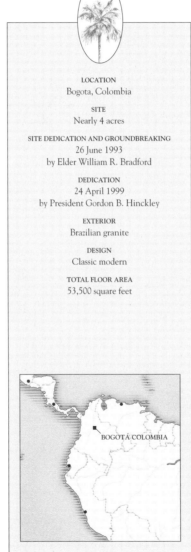

LOCATION
Bogota, Colombia

SITE
Nearly 4 acres

SITE DEDICATION AND GROUNDBREAKING
26 June 1993
by Elder William R. Bradford

DEDICATION
24 April 1999
by President Gordon B. Hinckley

EXTERIOR
Brazilian granite

DESIGN
Classic modern

TOTAL FLOOR AREA
53,500 square feet

BOGOTÁ COLOMBIA

Marble finishes tastefully preserve the light, whether natural or otherwise, creating an atmosphere conducive to spiritual warmth, enlightenment, and peace, each shade and vein of color within each piece of marble adding interest and natural beauty. In the celestial room, a rose-colored marble promotes a graceful peace. The baptismal font is sheathed in the strength of a darker marble. One feature of the celestial room is the room's arches, which are made of hollow marble blocks. This preserves the marble's inherent beauty while substantially reducing its weight.

The temple grounds are landscaped with plants indigenous to Colombia, such as flowering eucalyptus trees with beautiful red flowers. Other buildings on the temple grounds include housing to accommodate Saints in the temple district who must travel long distances.

Among those who rejoiced at the temple's beauty was President Gordon B. Hinckley. He said, "What a beautiful building it is—the workmanship is superb. I have never seen any (stonework) finer, anywhere. It is beautiful, a fitting monument to the good people of Colombia."[1]

Rain, which promotes the area's lush, natural vegetation, is a regular feature in Colombia's climate. During one three-month stretch of temple construction, rain fell every single day. The workers got used to the rain and continued their labors without stopping.

The workers laboring on the temple gave special care to their craft. As the temple's construction progressed, even those workers who were not members of the Church began to develop great reverence and respect for the building they were constructing. Temple project manager, Jim Aulesita, later explained: "There came a time that one particular contractor,

who was a Catholic, would not talk aloud to me in the celestial room—he would whisper. All of the workers who entered the celestial room would not talk aloud. Although the temple was not completed, it produced a reverence that was felt by many of the workers."[2]

One electrician showed great faith and determination to complete his responsibilities on the temple. While working on the wiring, he was electrocuted so severely that he received third degree burns on his arms. Brother Aulesita described his thoughts regarding the accident: "I thought that I would never see the man again. Monday morning he was there and I asked him, 'Why are you here?' He responded by saying, 'Because we have not finished our work in the temple.' I was very touched. He is a nonmember and he feels that he needs to complete the job and needs to do it well. I watched him as he went to work with his arms burned, covered with bandages, and in a great deal of pain. I then made the comment that because of his faithfulness that he would not have any problems recovering. A couple of months later his bandages were off and he barely had any scars. He worked to the last minute. Why didn't he just quit? I think it is because he felt the spirit of the temple."[3] Brother Aulesita believed there were many such unsung heroes who made the temple beautiful.

Early one morning during the construction, a man was noticed walking around the grounds recording various measurements. Not until they read a local newspaper article did the project managers learn the identity of this man. The article mentioned that a city inspector had visited many construction sites throughout the city, and the Mormon temple was the only project that complied with local building codes in every way.

The Colombian Saints waited fifteen long years between the announcement of the temple and its eventual dedication in April 1999. They were not idle during this time, however. Many members, for example, took advantage of the waiting period to do family history work so they would have names ready to take to the temple for vicarious ordinance work when the temple was completed. Under the direction of the area presidency, local leaders prepared their members spiritually by encouraging them to live worthy lives and obtain temple recommends, even though they might not

have the resources to go to a temple. During the decade and a half of waiting, stakes continued to contract with buses to make the five- or six-day trip each way to the nearest temple—in Lima, Peru. Family history centers were also established where members could do research on their family lines.

Elder Jay E. Jensen of the Seventy served as president of the South America North Area during many of the significant events required to take the temple from announcement to actual construction. He later commented on the spiritual support the Saints gave: "The progress on the Bogota temple is a fulfillment of members' faith and fasting." Members would have countrywide fasts whenever critical moments were reached in the approval process. "In each instance when a particular obstacle was faced, a special focus in fasting and prayer would produce miracles."[4]

Elder Francisco J. Viñas, who served as chair of the temple committee, explained that both the members and the community prepared for the completion of the temple, as evidenced by the fact that approximately ten thousand missionary referrals were received during the days of the temple open house. Missionaries could hardly keep up with the need to follow through on the abundance of referrals, skipping preparation days and working long hours in an attempt to do so. But more than just referrals came from the open house—each day an average of twenty people expressed a desire to join the Church!

Church members from throughout Colombia rejoiced at the dedication, grateful that the temple would provide for them a place of refuge in their troubled land. Indeed, as Elder Jensen stated, "Frankly, I think that temples, in their completions and dedications, have a ripple effect starting from the temple and going out into the entire nation; the peace and the power of the temple and its blessings will help change the destiny of a nation."[5]

This beautiful temple contrasts the peace it brings within its walls with the daily difficulties faced by Latter-day Saints in the region. Given the challenges faced by the country of Colombia, this house of the Lord will indeed be a great blessing.

Guayaquil Ecuador Temple

Wilt thou accept of [this temple] as the offering of thy sons and daughters who love thee and who seek to accomplish thy purposes. Our hearts reach to thee in gratitude for thy wonderful blessings upon us. With the completion of this house thou hast given to the Saints of Ecuador every blessing of the restored gospel of Jesus Christ.

—FROM THE DEDICATORY PRAYER

Ecuador is rich in natural resources, but they are largely underdeveloped. Its spiritual resources, however, are quietly increasing day by day. Named for the equator, which passes through it, the country itself is rugged and filled with a variety of beauties. Its lands range from the Pacific coastline, with the fascinating Galapagos Islands lying offshore, to the semi-desert lands and plains in the east. In the middle are two ranges of glacial Andes.

The Church's fifty-eighth operating temple stands prominently on a hill in a quiet section of northern Guayaquil, Ecuador's largest city. Fertile volcanic soil and bounteous rain create a perfect setting for the temple's well-designed landscape. Shrubs, a variety of large palm trees, and colorful native plants enhance the temple's outward appearance.

The Guayaquil Ecuador Temple has four ordinance rooms, three sealing rooms, and a celestial room. Its floor plan is identical to that of the Bogota Colombia Temple, and its exterior is adorned with the same Brazilian granite. Despite similarities between the two temples, however, the interior decor of the Guayaquil Ecuador Temple has unique qualities. Local wood

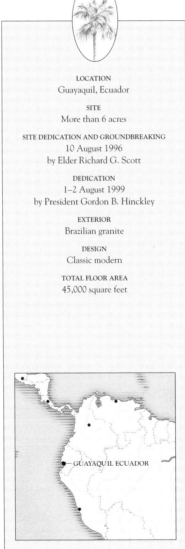

LOCATION
Guayaquil, Ecuador

SITE
More than 6 acres

SITE DEDICATION AND GROUNDBREAKING
10 August 1996
by Elder Richard G. Scott

DEDICATION
1–2 August 1999
by President Gordon B. Hinckley

EXTERIOR
Brazilian granite

DESIGN
Classic modern

TOTAL FLOOR AREA
45,000 square feet

GUAYAQUIL ECUADOR

with a cherry finish accents the flawless quality of workmanship throughout the building. No nails can be seen, joints come together flawlessly, and the grain patterns in the wood match consistently.[1] The temple has been described by members, nonmembers, and the press as "the most beautiful building in Ecuador."[2]

President Spencer W. Kimball announced the temple in 1982, but it took fourteen years to secure the necessary government authorizations. Meanwhile, the Saints in Ecuador continued to travel by bus, often at great sacrifice, to attend the Lima Peru Temple. In 1994, Elder Jay E. Jensen, president of the South America North Area, explained, "Many stakes, if not all, continue to have their excursions to Lima, which take three days one way, and then they spend one day or two in the temple. Then they come back, another three days on the bus. We just marvel at their faith. It almost makes you weep when you see the sacrifices they make in order to go to the temple for their one time. Some will return during their lifetime, but not many."[3]

The announcement of a temple in Ecuador was received with rejoicing by Saints in Ecuador, who now would be able to attend more often and at less expense. Couples such as Santiago León and Raquel Plúas de León exemplify how Latter-day Saints prepared for the Guayaquil Ecuador Temple. Santiago and Raquel were married in the Lima Peru Temple, despite economic difficulties and family problems. "Just seeing the temple from outside made me happy," recalls Santiago. "But to be able to go inside and participate in the ordinances there—that was a real blessing." On the wall in the front room of their small home is a photograph of the Washington D. C. Temple. Under it hangs a hand-lettered sign: "Ecuador: Prepare Yourself for Your Temple."[4]

The temple's open house was a resounding success by all accounts. More than one hundred thousand people toured the sacred edifice, demonstrating the support that member and nonmember alike gave to the arrival of a house of the Lord in their country. After waiting seventeen years, faithful Saints would have done nearly anything to show their love of the temple. Some, for example, walked six miles at night so they could arrive at the temple by 5 A.M. to begin their volunteer work of cleaning the temple. That evening, they walked back to their homes. These same members attended the dedication with similar enthusiasm.[5]

President Gordon B. Hinckley dedicated the Church's fifty-eighth temple before thousands of grateful Saints who had waited for the temple since President Kimball's announcement seventeen years earlier.

In an interview with the *Church News*, President Hinckley commented on the appreciation of the Church members in Equador for the new temple. "I sense a great spirit of gratitude for this new temple in Guayaquil," he said. "The Saints have waited a very, very long time. They contributed generously toward its construction, but for one reason or another, it has been delayed until now at this late date. It is finished and completed and dedicated and they are grateful for this and indicate their gratitude." He noted: "It has been a very interesting thing to see the descendants of Father Lehi in the congregations that have gathered in the temple. So very many of these people have the blood of Lehi in their veins and it is just an intriguing thing to see their tremendous response and their tremendous interest."[6]

Members came from stakes throughout the nation by bus, some traveling for three or four hours. Among those who attended the dedication were the colorful natives of Otavalo, adorned with gold necklaces and wearing long braided hair. Following the ceremonies, the first ordinance sessions were held for the Saints from Otavalo, who are among the most faithful members in the country.

After the dedication, Elder Russell M. Nelson commented: "The presence of a temple here and the establishment of a people worthy of entrance to the temple will make a great difference to the future of this country and for the nations round about. It is really a very important hinge point in the history of this nation."[7]

President Hinckley echoed that sentiment when he said: "This is a day of history. This is a day to be remembered by Latter-day Saints for many years to come, when for the first time in all of Ecuadorian history a temple will be dedicated to carry forward His eternal purposes. We are blessed, so richly blessed, for this opportunity. And this evening, I want to make a plea to all the Latter-day Saints who are gathered here to make up your minds, to determine within yourselves that you will be worthy to go to the House of the Lord and there partake of the wonderful blessings which are available only in this place."[8]

The Guayaquil Ecuador Temple is a symbol that the Lord has heard the supplications of the many Latter-day Saints for a temple in their country. Gustavo Maruri, a longtime member of the Church, shared his feelings about the temple: "I like this temple. It is the best in the world because it is in my city. . . . I see the temple every day. I look up early in the morning and see the statue of the Angel Moroni standing way up there, the fulfillment of our faith, our work, our efforts."[9] After the temple's dedication, Guillermo Granja Garcia, vice chairman of the temple committee, summed up the feelings of many: "All Ecuador is blessed today."[10]

Our hearts reach to thee in gratitude for thy wonderful blessings upon us

Spokane Washington Temple

The Spokane Washington Temple was the fourth small temple built by the Church. Its walls covered with speckled, light gray granite, the temple is situated in the Spokane suburb of Opportunity, in a beautiful eastern Washington valley among farmhouses, wheat fields, and pine trees. Alongside the temple is the Spokane Washington East Stake center, with which it shares a common parking lot and an LDS recreational complex. In the 1980s shade trees were planted on the field and now form a pleasant border between the temple and the recreational complex.

In the year 2000, Church membership in eastern Washington and northern Idaho numbered eighty thousand. Recent growth is a result of two nearly equal factors: Latter-day Saint families moving in and new convert baptisms.[1]

As Church leaders worked to bring a temple to eastern Washington, many people came to recognize the sacred feeling present at the site. For example, when looking for property on which to build, Dick Waide, a Church physical facilities representative, visited the location that was eventually chosen and received the feeling that it was holy ground. Elder Don McGary, a building missionary, walked across the site and "felt that he should take his shoes off" because it was sacred ground.[2]

The morning of 10 October 1998 was rainy and cloudy, but by the time a thousand people had witnessed the temple's groundbreaking, the sun was shining. President Steven N. Holdaway, whose local stake had coordinated the groundbreaking ceremony, later reported: "We had the groundbreaking in the sunshine. By the time the groundbreaking was over, it clouded up again. So the sunshine was just for the period of time of the groundbreaking." Speaking of the joy of having a

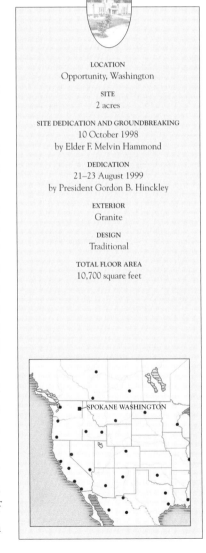

LOCATION
Opportunity, Washington

SITE
2 acres

SITE DEDICATION AND GROUNDBREAKING
10 October 1998
by Elder F. Melvin Hammond

DEDICATION
21–23 August 1999
by President Gordon B. Hinckley

EXTERIOR
Granite

DESIGN
Traditional

TOTAL FLOOR AREA
10,700 square feet

SPOKANE WASHINGTON

temple in the area, he added, "The members, of course, are delighted we'll have this. I don't think anyone thought we'd have a temple this soon, but they are very appreciative and thankful for it."[3]

A number of other, smaller temples were being constructed during the same period of time as the Spokane Washington Temple. The First Presidency subsequently chose to avoid the logistical challenges that would come from dedicating several temples simultaneously and thus moved forward the Spokane temple completion date by two months. Great faith was combined with hard work on the part of the construction workers to meet this tight deadline. One worker observed, "The completion date was made possible due to favorable weather conditions and efficient contractors."[4]

Professional construction workers were not the only ones to manifest their faith by hard work. On 22 May 1999, approximately forty Aaronic Priesthood young men from the Spokane Washington East Stake carried the oxen to the baptismal font area and carefully placed them in position.[5] Even young children helped to the extent that they were able. For example, over the holiday weekend of July 4, little ones brought their toy wheelbarrows and hauled small unwanted rocks from the areas to be landscaped.[6]

Rush Hashie, a truck driver and Latter-day Saint from Albuquerque, New Mexico, delivered a load of cargo to the Spokane Washington Temple. Only after his arrival at the site did he learn that he had just transported the statue of the angel Moroni, the oxen for the baptismal font, and the font itself. Temple historian Mark Bickley records: "Brother Hashie was so overcome with emotion when he learned what his cargo was that he went to the grove of trees just east of the temple and cried."[7]

Spokane Washington Temple

May those who go forth as missionaries to the nations here be empowered from on high to bear witness that thou hast moved for the last time to bless all who come unto thee and keep thy commandments, thereby becoming worthy to receive those ordinances which will save and bless them in both time and all eternity.

—FROM THE DEDICATORY PRAYER

Spokane

Another man involved with the temple was Dale Reese of the Spokane Washington East Stake, who served as the building's project manager. For months he worked fourteen- to sixteen-hour days at the temple site. He remembered laying sod in early August before the open house. "The landscaping company that was supposed to do it failed to get the job done sooner," he related. "I and some other members started rolling the grass out and it looked bad. It was basically dead. Look at that grass now. . . . It's gorgeous. All we did was water it and pray. That grass looks like it's been there for five years. You don't even see any seam lines in it. It was all done by members."[8]

The statue of the angel Moroni was placed atop the temple spire on 21 April 1999. Handlers were required to wear white cotton gloves whenever they touched the statue. Although this event was not publicized, approximately two thousand people attended, some waiting for several hours to see the statue raised and placed. Cars filled the parking lot, found places on adjoining streets, and lined the highway for almost a mile. When the statue was put into position, facing east toward the hills, the afternoon sun broke through the clouds, gleaming on the golden figure.

When the time for the dedication arrived, from 21 through 23 August 1999, President Hinckley spoke to approximately twelve thousand young people and their families in a hockey arena near downtown Spokane. Some of his counsel included encouragement to follow the six "B's": be grateful, be smart, be clean, be true, be humble, and be prayerful.

"I love you," President Hinckley told his listeners. "I believe in you. I have every confidence that you're going to do the right thing, that you're going to make a good life. That

The Spokane Washington Temple is located on a beautiful plot of land typical of the Evergreen State of Washington. Hidden in the tall evergreens to the left of the temple is a full-length image of the Savior, Jesus Christ, who offers everlasting love to all.

you're going to make a contribution to society. That you're going to live the kind of lives that are productive and produce wonderful results. I have every reason to regard you as the greatest generation we've ever had in this Church—notwithstanding all of the temptations which you face. . . . Don't you ever do anything which will weaken that family chain. You come with a great inheritance of courage and faith. Pass it on to those who come after you and pray that they will magnify it and live worthy of it."[9]

More than sixteen thousand members attended the eleven dedicatory sessions, watching the proceedings from within the temple or in the stake center by means of closed-circuit television. Another two hundred huddled together in unseasonably cold morning temperatures at the southeast corner of the temple to view the 8 A.M. ceremonial sealing of the cornerstone. The morning greeted them with dark clouds, light rain, thunder, and chilling winds, but as President Hinckley exited the temple doors for the cornerstone ceremony, the sun broke through the clouds.

Before the dedication, members living in northeastern Washington had to travel nearly three hundred miles to attend the Seattle Washington Temple. Their attendance was often limited in the winter months because they had to travel over a mountain pass that is frequently treacherous in the winter.

The Spokane Washington Temple opened for ordinance work 24 August 1999 and was filled to capacity. Having the temple filled to capacity aptly portrays the joy of the Saints here in having their own temple—a temple in which they serve with the same relentless faith and dedication exhibited during its construction.

Thou hast moved for the last time to bless all who come unto thee and keep thy commandments

Columbus Ohio Temple

The Columbus Ohio Temple is located approximately 150 miles south of Kirtland, where the first temple of this dispensation was dedicated in 1836. Adjacent to the temple is the building that houses the Hilliard and Riverside Ohio Wards. When that ward house was dedicated in 1991, Keith L. Smith, then president of the Columbus Ohio Stake, mentioned a temple being built nearby, even at the "doorsteps" of the building in which they stood. "Bless those who come to worship here," he prayed, "that they will be moved to attend the temple. All the roads of righteousness lead to the temple. This concept needs to be taught in this thy house. Help us to realize that as we attend more regularly, the temple could move closer, even to our doorsteps. He that hath ears to hear let him hear."[1]

On 25 April 1998, nearly seven thousand Ohio Saints assembled to hear President Gordon B. Hinckley speak. Not only did they have occasion that day to hear the words of a prophet but they were given hope that a temple would soon be in their midst. The following account was taken from the book *The Columbus Ohio Temple,* which was prepared for placement in the temple's cornerstone:

"'What does the Lord expect from us?' asked the prophet, 'To be Latter-day Saints.' He expounded on the great expectations required of members and thanked the Ohio Saints for being faithful in temple attendance. He then asked the question the Saints had long hoped for, 'Do you need a temple here?' A soft but excited 'Yes' was echoed. 'Are you worthy of a temple here?' Again, a little louder and with more determination, the congregation said in unison, 'Yes!' . . .

"The prophet then uttered the most beautiful words: 'I feel impressed to say that when we leave here, we are going to take

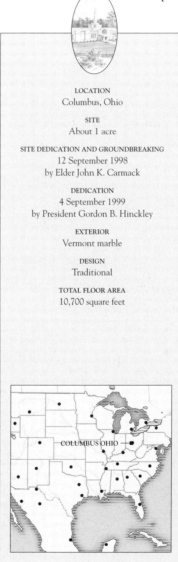

LOCATION
Columbus, Ohio

SITE
About 1 acre

SITE DEDICATION AND GROUNDBREAKING
12 September 1998
by Elder John K. Carmack

DEDICATION
4 September 1999
by President Gordon B. Hinckley

EXTERIOR
Vermont marble

DESIGN
Traditional

TOTAL FLOOR AREA
10,700 square feet

COLUMBUS OHIO

an hour or so . . . to look around for a place where we might build a small temple in Columbus or in the nearby community, where you will have a temple of your own. . . .'

"As the prophet stood to leave, the congregation arose and brought out their white handkerchiefs, which they waved high in the air. President Hinckley stood and admired the Saints, then gently removed his [handkerchief] and returned the gesture."[2]

The entire congregation turned into a sea of white as members waved in response, marveling at the thought of a temple of their own.

David W. Martin, who researched the property rights of the land on which the temple stands, observed, "As far as we can tell, good and honest people have always owned the land."[3] Interestingly, the land has historic ties to early Church history through Julia Clapp Murdock, a devoted member of the Church who lived in Kirtland at the time of Joseph Smith. Her uncle Abner Clapp held the first recorded deed to the land. Julia died after giving birth to twins on 30 April 1831, the same day that Emma Smith's twins were born and died. Julia's husband, John Murdock, who was among the first to join the Church in Kirtland, felt unable to rear the twins and asked the Prophet and Emma to care for them. The request somewhat softened Emma's sorrow.

Architecturally, the Columbus Ohio Temple also has ties to Kirtland and the Church's first temple there. Perhaps most noticeable is the Window Beautiful, a window designed by early Church architect Truman O. Angell for the east side of the upper court in the Kirtland Temple. This distinctive window is characterized by a delicate, running vine, a hand-carved flower keystone, distinctive moldings, and 23-karat gold

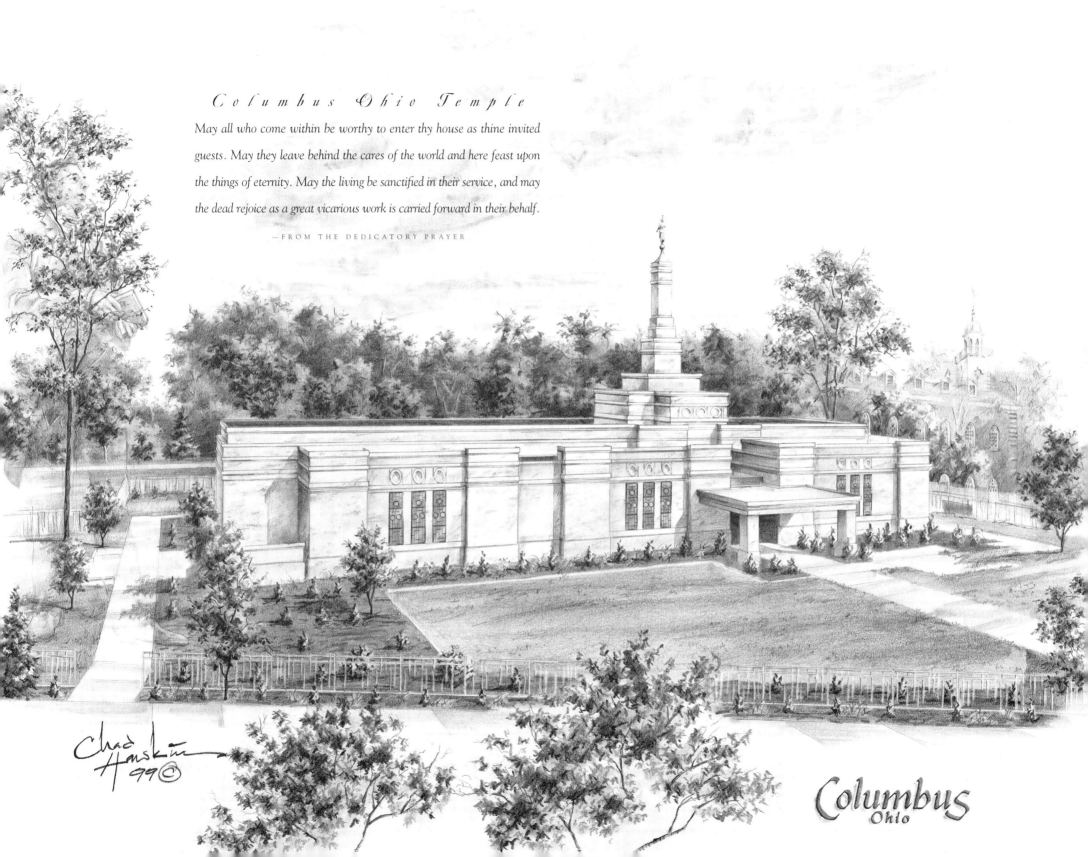

Columbus Ohio Temple

May all who come within be worthy to enter thy house as thine invited guests. May they leave behind the cares of the world and here feast upon the things of eternity. May the living be sanctified in their service, and may the dead rejoice as a great vicarious work is carried forward in their behalf.

—FROM THE DEDICATORY PRAYER

Columbus
Ohio

leafing. When Rich Christensen, a member of the temple construction committee, proposed including elements of the Kirtland Temple, Brent Harris, a member of the Cambridge Branch and a skilled wood craftsman, volunteered to build a replica of the Window Beautiful for the Columbus Ohio Temple.[4]

The Columbus Ohio Temple was built to meet high standards. The foundation is engineered to withstand quakes two seismic zones higher than required by local building standards, and the parking lot is made of material durable enough to land an airplane on. This is an edifice truly built to last.

The temple's exterior is covered completely with glistening white "sugar marble" quarried in Danby, Vermont, about forty miles south of the Prophet Joseph's birthplace. This high-quality marble is covered with small round granules, which look like sugar crystals, thus the name "sugar marble." Installing the marble was tedious work, requiring careful attention to detail. Elder Clyde Stewart, a temple construction missionary, examined and organized each piece of marble according to its different shade and pattern, placing the slabs into stacks that would result in the uniform appearance of the exterior walls.[5]

Great attention was also given to the grounds that surround the temple and are adorned by eighteen varieties of trees, shrubs, perennials, and ground cover, totaling more than thirty-five hundred plants. A noteworthy flower on the grounds is a special species of lilies donated by the family of Donald Werling, who suffered a nearly fatal heart attack during the temple's construction. He had previously propagated a beautiful hybrid lily that his family affectionately referred to as "Dad's Millennium Day Lily." After the heart attack left him permanently disabled, his family honored him by supplying the temple with his special

At the right of the Columbus Ohio Temple is hidden an image of the Kirtland Temple; at the left, a hidden image of the Prophet Joseph Smith holds the Book of Mormon and looks at both Ohio temples.

lilies. "One of Dad's greatest desires is to have his day lilies beautify the temple grounds," said Brother Werling's daughter Julie Hausfeld, who spoke of her conversation with David McBride, the temple's landscape architect: "As I told him about my dad and the quality of the lilies, McBride said, 'This is your father's legacy. We would love to have his lilies, and we would like you to help plant them.'" A few weeks before the open house, five hundred clusters of "Dad's Millennium Day Lilies" were planted on the sacred temple grounds.[6]

Other members living within the Columbus Ohio Temple district eagerly took part in a variety of special projects. "I could tell countless stories of young people helping," said Neil C. Farr, second counselor in the temple presidency. "One evening, during the open house, we had some young women cleaning the celestial room after tours that day. Gradually, all the young women left except one. When she came out, tears were streaming down her cheeks. She simply said, 'I can't wait to attend the temple.'"[7]

Ed Hammond, who assisted with the operational details of preparing the temple, commented, "This has been a Zion-like project. People would come to the door and say with excitement, 'I'm here to clean. What can I do?' All the way down the line, we had the right people willing to help—like Erik and Lois Mars, who are landscapers. They worked late at night landscaping the grounds while their baby slept in the carriage."[8]

Some eleven thousand members from eleven stakes attended six dedicatory sessions for the Columbus Ohio Temple. More than 150 years after the first Saints gathered to dedicate their temple in Ohio, another generation of Church members met together in this great state to welcome the Lord to his house and dedicate their lives in service to him.

May all who come within be worthy to enter thy house as thine invited guests

Bismarck North Dakota Temple

Bismarck, the capital of North Dakota, is located in the south central part of the state and is a port on the Missouri River. The state's flat prairies yield the largest crop of spring and durum wheat in the nation. Built in a residential neighborhood on a double lot adjacent to the local stake center, the Bismarck North Dakota Temple is the first operating temple in the upper Midwest of the United States.

The temple serves about five thousand members scattered throughout a vast district that stretches from northern Nebraska to northwestern Minnesota. North Dakota's first stake—organized in Fargo in 1977—is not quite twenty-five years old. One year before the stake was organized, Church officials began searching for a site on which to construct a chapel for the Bismarck Branch and accommodate future expansion. Reed E. Barker, branch president at the time, stated, "We selected a site on the open prairie where we knew there would be expansion in the future. There was only one house in the area at that time." The dimensions of the site were somewhat odd, forming the shape of the letter L. Although the Church acquired the property, some Saints in the area wondered what to do with one leg of the property, which seemed useless. President Barker explained that others, however, including himself, "felt differently about it, without ever having a confirmation of what it was to be used for." Each time they considered selling the land, the district presidency received strong impressions that the land should not be sold, but they did not know why.[1]

When the Bismarck North Dakota Temple was announced, the purpose for preserving this extra piece of land became clear. Unlike the seemingly endless delays and struggles that

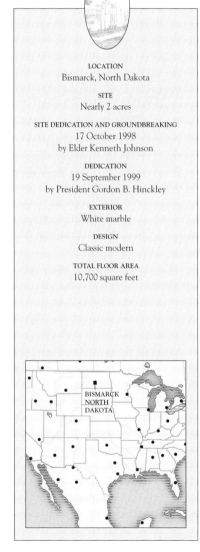

LOCATION
Bismarck, North Dakota

SITE
Nearly 2 acres

SITE DEDICATION AND GROUNDBREAKING
17 October 1998
by Elder Kenneth Johnson

DEDICATION
19 September 1999
by President Gordon B. Hinckley

EXTERIOR
White marble

DESIGN
Classic modern

TOTAL FLOOR AREA
10,700 square feet

had been experienced with other temples throughout the world, very little effort was required for this temple to receive approval from the city. When the building permit request was submitted, the city employee simply asked, "You own the property, don't you?" The answer was affirmative. "Then we don't see a problem."[2]

Lowell L. Cheney, a counselor in the stake presidency, shared his thoughts on these events: "Though individually each of these events may not have seemed exceptionally significant, an overview of what has transpired gives profound assurance of the Lord's awareness of His children in this part of His vineyard and the desire for them to receive His choicest blessings. If we will but follow as directed by the Spirit, even though we may not see the whole picture, we can be confident that the work will go forth, for the Lord surely directs His work to completion."[3]

Close to a thousand people attended the groundbreaking ceremony on 17 October 1998. Bishop Keith B. McMullin of the presiding bishopric observed, "Many of Lehi's descendants are here in the Dakotas. We have a sacred obligation to them."[4] There are eleven Native American reservations in the Dakotas, and many children of Lehi live in Canada, directly to the north. Bishop McMullin challenged every Anglo-American visiting the temple to invite two children of Lehi. Elder Thomas A. Holt, an area authority seventy, explained that CTR to a Church member younger than twelve years of age means Choose the Right, but "CTR to [someone] 12 and older should also mean have a 'Current Temple Recommend.'"[5]

Church member Dr. Tyson Williams of Minot, North Dakota, created an acrylic painting of a local landscape that is

Bismarck North Dakota Temple

May [Church members] come here frequently. Wilt thou bless them for their efforts and reward them for their faith. Watch over them and keep them from harm and trouble in the long distances many will still travel. This sacred edifice has been made possible by tithe payers of the Church throughout the world. Wilt thou pour out thy blessings upon them and prosper them in their labors.

—FROM THE DEDICATORY PRAYER

displayed in the temple. "I consider this as a gift to the Savior and his holy house," Williams said. "I've made this donation as a token of the gratitude of the members of the Church in this region." After working long hours, he completed the painting half an hour before his deadline. "I don't take full credit for the painting," he said. "I thank the Lord for giving me the talent and blessing me with the ability to complete the painting on time."[6]

Another member, Brother Robert Colvin of the Sioux Falls South Dakota Stake, participated in the choir that sang during the dedicatory services. He wrote: "Yesterday I had the incredible opportunity to sing in a thirteen-voice choir for the dedication of the temple in Bismarck, North Dakota. The spirit of God truly was burning like a fire in that beautiful celestial room. The prophet Gordon B. Hinckley pronounced some wonderful blessings upon the people and workers of the temple.

"One of the most memorable points of the dedicatory prayer was asking the blessing of safe travel upon those coming to this temple. Living in the Dakotas, winter travel is often dangerous and that should bring peace of mind to Saints traveling to do work in the temple during those months."[7]

President Gordon B. Hinckley, whose travels have taken him far and wide since becoming president of the Church— approximately three hundred thousand miles—had never been

An image of the Savior is hidden in the sky and across the marble walls of the temple. Stalks of wheat in the foreground symbolize that Christ is the bread of life.

to North Dakota until the dedication of the temple in Bismark. With a touch of humor, the prophet told the Saints gathered for the dedication that if he were governor of the state, he would move the cities closer together.

President Hinckley said, "I love these smaller temples; I am very grateful for them. They are very efficient and exceedingly well built with the best materials."[8] The Bismarck North Dakota Temple is constructed of materials gathered from throughout the world. The marble for the exterior came from Quebec, other marble from Italy, the stained glass windows from Germany, and the chandeliers in the celestial room and sealing rooms from the Czech Republic.

At the dedication, President Hinckley explained that "even with the temple here, some will still have to travel a very long distance, but it will be much shorter than it was before. There is so much faith on the part of the people in these areas. They're willing to go anywhere to accomplish the temple work."[9]

Bismarck North Dakota Temple president Robert B. Dahlgren spoke of one such willing couple who had retired and were living in an area some distance from Bismarck. He asked them, "Would you be willing to move to Bismarck and work in the temple full time?" The couple agreed and promptly made the arrangements.[10]

Will thou pour out thy blessings upon them and prosper them in their labors

Columbia South Carolina Temple

Nestled among native loblolly pine and tall, green oak trees is the beautiful Columbia South Carolina Temple. Immaculate homes, quaint churches, and dense woods surround the temple site. The grounds themselves are lanscaped with a variety of plant species, including crape myrtle (a summer-blooming shrub), large holly, mums, dogwood trees, maples, and oak—all combining to increase the natural beauty of the temple's setting. And though the temple itself is similar in design to many of the new, smaller temples, its furnishings, grounds, and décor reflect the flavor of the Carolinas and surrounding areas.[1]

Ground was broken for the temple on 5 December 1998, with more than thirty-five hundred people in attendance. Record-breaking temperatures—eighty degrees Fahrenheit during the first week of December!—made the ceremony particularly memorable. Many of the thousands of Church members in attendance used umbrellas to shade themselves from the hot afternoon sun. Elder Gordon T. Watts, first counselor in the North America Southeast Area, presided over the ceremony and called on members to begin their own spiritual construction. "As the contractors and building people prepare and begin construction, let us also begin a program of personal construction that we will be as exemplary as this beautiful temple when it is completed," he said. "If changes are required in your life to gain entrance into the temple, let them begin now."[2] Elder Watts invited a few Primary children and young men and women to step forward to "represent the young people whose lives [would] be benefited now and in the future as a result of the temple."[3]

Throughout the building process, the Saints living in the

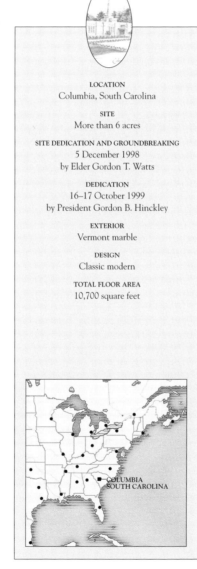

LOCATION
Columbia, South Carolina

SITE
More than 6 acres

SITE DEDICATION AND GROUNDBREAKING
5 December 1998
by Elder Gordon T. Watts

DEDICATION
16–17 October 1999
by President Gordon B. Hinckley

EXTERIOR
Vermont marble

DESIGN
Classic modern

TOTAL FLOOR AREA
10,700 square feet

COLUMBIA
SOUTH CAROLINA

area were willing to assist in any way. For example, one stake held a youth conference at the park across from the temple. Youth and their leaders beautified the temple property by spreading mulch, building steps, and repairing retaining walls. Groups of members and missionaries planted bushes, flowers, and trees and laid sod around the temple. Both the adults and youth cleaned the temple during construction. Priests from one ward cleaned the baptismal font and oxen. Young women from the area strung crystals on the chandeliers. Sister Janie Smith, a member of the Caughman Park Ward, described her memory of the event. "They lowered the celestial room chandelier and the girls were sitting in a circle with it almost in their laps. The girls were covered with the strings of lights and sparkling crystal. It was a beautiful sight."[4]

When the temple was ready to be opened to the public, citizens from throughout the community eagerly toured the building. One of them, Rabbi Philip Silverstein, was impressed to find so many references in the temple to the Old Testament. "You are the only Church that cares about the spirit of Elijah," he said. Following a tour for residents in the neighborhood, another citizen, the president of the homeowners association, said, "Call us day or night and we will help with the landscaping or anything else."[5]

After a public open house, the temple was dedicated in six sessions over the weekend of 16 and 17 October 1999. Hurricane Irene, which was assaulting the Florida coast, threatened the proceedings. The heavy rain predicted for both days of the dedicatory services did not materialize, and the moderate rainfall did not detract from the historic event. President Gordon B. Hinckley conducted all six sessions. "The

Columbia South Carolina Temple

We pray that all who cross the threshold of this structure will be worthy to do so, that they will be Latter-day Saints in very deed, living the gospel, and fully qualified to come here to serve in thy work. . . .We pray that the very presence of this thy house will have a sanctifying influence upon the people of this area, and particularly upon those who enter its portals.

—FROM THE DEDICATORY PRAYER

Columbia

gospel was first preached here 160 years ago," said President Hinckley. "In the generations that have followed, hundreds and thousands of people have joined the Church. We have placed a temple here in Columbia because it's the capital of the state and somewhat in the center of the state."[6]

As President and Sister Hinckley left the temple after the final session, a large group of Church members lined the parking lot and sang "We Thank Thee, O God, for a Prophet." President Hinckley waved to them and then rolled down his window and waved again as the car drove away. Regarding her experience at the dedication, Sister Sigg, a member of the Charlotte North Carolina Stake, said: "I will never for the rest of my life forget the feeling in the celestial room. I will never ever forget that feeling that confirms everything I've been taught since I joined the Church. There is no doubt!"[7]

Over the years, members in the area have seen their proximity to a temple gradually shrink, first with the construction of the Washington D. C. Temple in 1976 and then by the completion of the Atlanta Georgia Temple in 1983. Now, with the temple in Columbia no more than an hour or two away from most areas in the district, members feel particularly blessed. Faithful members who had been serving as temple workers in Atlanta were pleased to transfer their service to a temple closer to home. Such circumstances allowed the temple

Hidden in the foreground is a baptismal scene, representing the importance of the ordinance of baptism. In the foliage is hidden an image of the Savior with outstretched hands, inviting us to receive the blessings found in temple service.

to function at near capacity immediately following the dedication. During the temple's first year of service, more sessions were added to the schedule to better serve those wishing to attend.[8]

The temple has been a source of strength and courage for John and Patty Cline, members of the Beaufort South Carolina Ward, who served as ushers for the Columbia South Carolina Temple dedication. "I was overwhelmed with the cornerstone ceremony," Sister Cline said. "Just to be in the presence of the prophet—the Spirit was overwhelming."

The experience was particularly poignant for Brother Cline, who had been diagnosed with terminal cancer just a week before the dedication. "I've got some time, one and a half, two, maybe three years. But I'm still happy," he smiled. "I still feel good, and I've got some good times left."

There is yet a 20 percent chance that the cancer could go into remission. Brother and Sister Cline cling to that hope, but they are prepared to accept the will of their Father in Heaven. "I'm the only one in my family who is a member of the Church," he said. "I told my brother, 'If you knew in your heart what I know in mine, you would know that I have absolutely no fear of crossing over. None.'"

He said colleagues at work express amazement that he is so positive. "I tell them it's because I know what I know. It's because of the things that we learn in the temple."[9]

Thy house will have a sanctifying influence upon the people of this area

Detroit Michigan Temple

Fifty tons of glistening white Vermont marble form the façade of the Detroit Michigan Temple, which is nestled at the foot of gently rolling hills twenty miles north of Detroit. This beautiful landmark is well suited for the area. While it is simple in design and thus unobtrusive, it is also easy to access from one of Detroit's major thoroughfares. For the Michigan Saints, the temple is a ready respite from the hustle and bustle of daily life.

The history of the Church in the Detroit area began with Lucy Mack Smith, mother of the Prophet Joseph Smith. In 1831 Lucy traveled to Michigan to visit the family of her brother Colonel Stephen Mack, founder of Pontiac, Michigan. Stephen Mack, the proprietor of a large mercantile establishment in Detroit, built a turnpike from Detroit to his farm in Pontiac at his own expense. That same road now runs in front of the temple and is known today as Woodward Avenue. The Prophet Joseph himself may have stood on the grounds of the temple site during his 1834 visit to Detroit, when he likely traveled this road to his uncle's home.[1]

In 1956 the Church bought nearly eight acres of land for construction of the area's first stake center. The stake center stands on part of this land, and many individuals felt that the Church should sell the remaining acreage. George Romney, the first stake president in Michigan and future governor of the state, felt strongly that the land should not be sold. Decades later, President Thomas C. Bithell, who was in charge of finding a site for the temple, said he looked at the property in question—which was just north of the stake center—but did not pursue the possibility because it was assumed the lot was too small. But then, after reviewing several properties near other chapels, President Bithell looked again at the lot outside

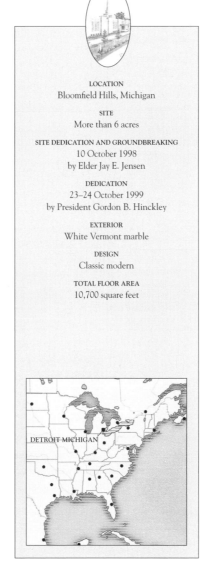

LOCATION
Bloomfield Hills, Michigan

SITE
More than 6 acres

SITE DEDICATION AND GROUNDBREAKING
10 October 1998
by Elder Jay E. Jensen

DEDICATION
23–24 October 1999
by President Gordon B. Hinckley

EXTERIOR
White Vermont marble

DESIGN
Classic modern

TOTAL FLOOR AREA
10,700 square feet

DETROIT MICHIGAN

his office window in the Bloomfield Hills Stake Center and wondered about the property. It was measured, "and it was just perfect," he said.[2] "The more I looked and contemplated, the more this seemed to be the right location."[3]

Over the years, the property where the temple now stands had been landscaped with grass and a variety of trees. Members had always kept the grounds free of weeds and litter. Many remember holding various outdoor activities on the property. Sister Bonnie Shurtz reminisced about being a Primary president in the Bloomfield Hills Ward: "We used to have Primary activities right where the temple is, under the trees, and we never realized there was enough land there to build a temple."[4]

On 10 October 1998, more than a thousand people attended the groundbreaking for the Detroit Michigan Temple. During the ceremony, President Bithell observed, "To the best of my knowledge, nothing has ever been built on this property. It is sacred ground, preserved for this very purpose."[5] With emotion, one member said, "We have prayed to have a temple in Michigan. Today, we are looking at a tangible reply to prayers."[6]

As construction on the temple progressed, the Saints prayed that Michigan's winter weather would be moderated and thus facilitate the work. Workers began pouring concrete for the temple's foundation in January and continued to do so through the cold and snowy months that followed. To allow the concrete to set up properly, it had to be covered and heated for several days until it had properly cured. Temple construction missionary Elder Keith Brown said, "As cold as it was, I do not think that we ever had weather severe enough to

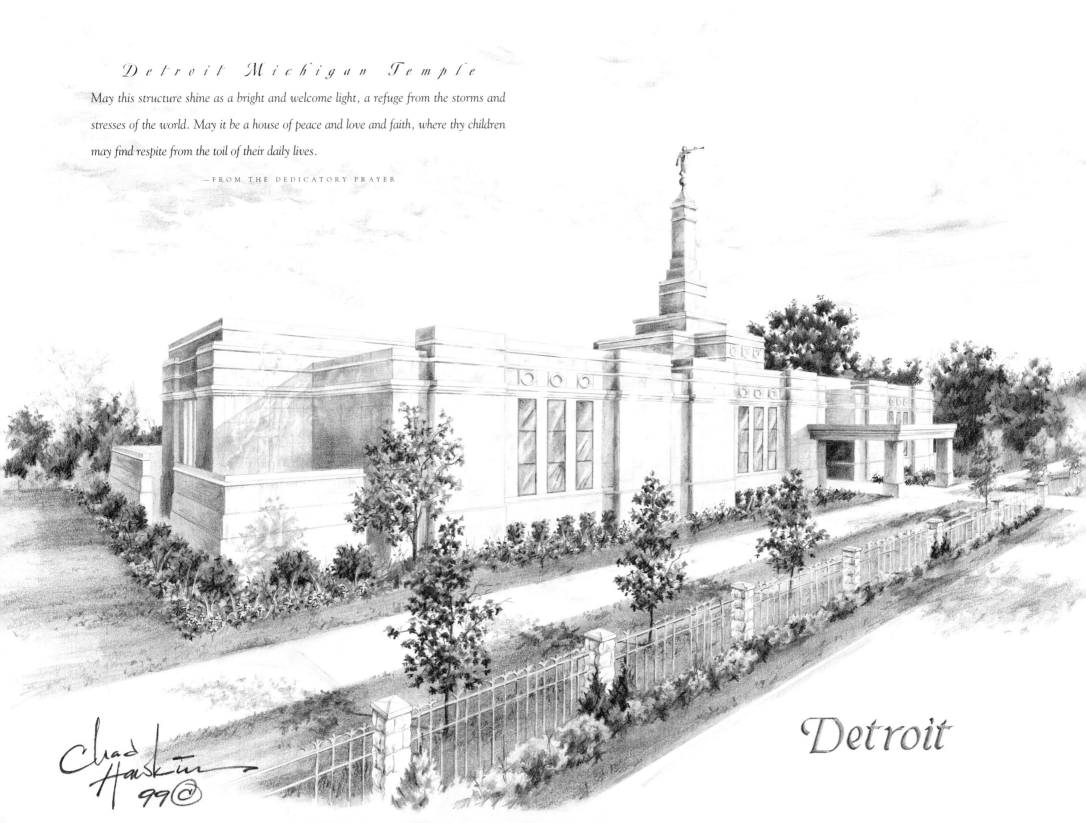

Detroit Michigan Temple

May this structure shine as a bright and welcome light, a refuge from the storms and stresses of the world. May it be a house of peace and love and faith, where thy children may find respite from the toil of their daily lives.

—FROM THE DEDICATORY PRAYER

Detroit

interrupt construction." The weather was also tempered on the day that the temple walls were put in place. The walls were assembled flat on the ground and then hoisted by a crane into position. Elder Brown described the experience: "The day the crane arrived the area was experiencing thirty-mile-an-hour wind. But on the building site, it was never too windy to set the walls. Can you imagine a forty-foot wall, twenty feet high in a thirty-mile-an hour wind? On the site it was not that windy and we set all of the walls in one day."[7]

The temple quickly became an important feature in the lives of area Saints, including the Primary children. The Primary room in the meetinghouse nearby has windows that face the temple. During all phases of the construction, the children would look toward the temple and sing "I Love to See the Temple." In addition to remembering the temple in their prayers, the children saved their pennies so they could put them into a bank—a hollow wooden replica of the temple. In the end, nearly two hundred dollars were collected.[8]

Thirty thousand visitors toured the sacred edifice, set against the backdrop of vibrant fall colors, in October 1999. During a special tour prior to the public open house, two local

A full-length image of the Savior is hidden on the temple wall beside the celestial room, symbolizing that Christ is the focal point of all that happens inside.

government officials, referring to the statue of the angel Moroni, said, "We are glad to have an angel watching over our city." The open house attracted many visitors of other faiths from Michigan and Canada. Television, radio, and daily and weekly newspapers throughout the state covered the event. One front-page headline read, "Close to God, Closer to Home."[9]

Cyrus J. Webber Jr. and his wife were called to serve as the first temple president and matron of the Detroit Michigan Temple. President Webber commented, "I cannot tell you in words the feelings I had when the Lord's prophet laid his hands on my head and set me apart for this position, nor when Elder Eyring set apart my wife as the temple matron. The blessings that came from their lips enlarged my soul and quieted the fears I had about this calling."[10]

In President and Sister Webber's first month of service, more than ten thousand ordinances were performed. With loving words of encouragement to Church members living in the temple district, President Webber said, "My prayer is that all members will qualify themselves to take full advantage of this beautiful temple. May we bring to pass the promises of pleasing the Lord and receiving all the blessings promised to the 'faithful and their generations after them.'"[11]

May this structure shine as a bright and welcome light

Halifax Nova Scotia Temple

We thank thee for the ordinances to be performed herein. Thou hast revealed these in this the dispensation of the fulness of times for the blessing of thy sons and daughters of all generations. All of these ordinances bespeak our testimony of the eternity of life and of thy grand and sacred plan for thy children that they might move forward on the way of immortality and eternal life made possible through the atoning sacrifice of thy Beloved Son.

— FROM THE DEDICATORY PRAYER

Halifax, the capital of Nova Scotia, Canada, and the largest city in the Canadian Maritime Provinces, is a busy port in a harbor inlet of the Atlantic Ocean. In this land known for its lighthouses that protect seafarers from the treacherous shores, a new beacon of spiritual light has been erected. That beacon is the Halifax Nova Scotia Temple, located in the Cole Harbour area of the city of Dartmouth, across the harbor from Halifax. The temple serves Church members in a temple district roughly the size of the western United States.

The Church was first organized in Halifax in 1843. Thanks to the commitment and sacrifice of the early Latter-day Saints in the area, Halifax and Dartmouth stand as the hub of Church activity in the region a century and a half later. And now the temple has become a benchmark of beauty in the area as well as a symbol of spirituality and family togetherness. People are aware of the architectural distinction and religious commitment the temple adds to the community, which, in turn, has brought new respect for the Church. Even

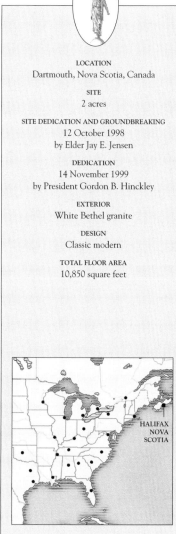

LOCATION
Dartmouth, Nova Scotia, Canada

SITE
2 acres

SITE DEDICATION AND GROUNDBREAKING
12 October 1998
by Elder Jay E. Jensen

DEDICATION
14 November 1999
by President Gordon B. Hinckley

EXTERIOR
White Bethel granite

DESIGN
Classic modern

TOTAL FLOOR AREA
10,850 square feet

HALIFAX
NOVA
SCOTIA

some nonmembers have hung distinctive pictures of the temple on the walls of their homes.

President Gordon B. Hinckley said in the October 1997 general conference: "There are many areas of the Church that are remote, where the membership is small and not likely to grow very much in the near future. Are those who live in these places to be denied forever the blessings of temple ordinances? . . . We will construct small temples in some of these areas, buildings with all of the facilities to administer all of the ordinances."[1] For Latter-day Saints living in such areas as the Maritime Provinces of Canada, President Hinckley's announcement brought much happiness and gratitude.

For Church members in Maritime Canada, attending the temple had been a major effort. Stephen Maxwell, president of the Dartmouth Nova Scotia Stake, said, "From my home to either the Washington D. C. Temple or the Toronto Temple requires a twenty-four-hour drive—which is about the same as someone in Salt Lake City driving to St. Paul, Minnesota—to attend the temple."[2]

David and Carol Ray, like many Saints living in New Brunswick, also had been driving to the Washington D. C. Temple or Toronto Ontario Temple to attend the house of the Lord. "It's eighteen hours either way," Sister Ray, an institute and seminary teacher in the St. John's New Brunswick Stake, observed. "For other people in Nova Scotia, Newfoundland, and Prince Edward Island, it's even farther by another four or five hours. It's a big deal [to go to the temple] and very expensive for the people here. [The new temple] will be less than five hours away."[3]

She continued, "Isn't this fabulous? We are very, very

excited." Now they would be able to go to the temple much more often, she observed, adding with enthusiasm, "We can go spontaneously."[4]

Approximately seven hundred Church members in Maritime Canada spent their Thanksgiving Day, 12 October 1998, participating in the groundbreaking ceremony. Unfortunately, heavy rains forced the groundbreaking ceremony indoors to the nearby Dartmouth stake center. Later, Elder Jay E. Jensen, a member of the Seventy and president of the North America Northeast Area, led a small group of local leaders outdoors to turn over shovelfuls of mud. "Thanksgiving Day in Canada, and what a happy day it is," said Elder Jensen. "Whoever thought that during your mortal life we would really be here doing this? If everything goes well, we could be back here in about a year."[5]

Many Saints drove six to seven hours one way just to attend the groundbreaking. All expressed gratitude to Heavenly Father for the blessing of the temple. James Bailey, branch president in the New Glasgow District, said, "I never thought it would happen in my day. I have driven this road many times, but today was a different feeling." Elder Jensen, quoting President Gordon B. Hinckley, admonished, "Don't think of it as a small temple; make it big in your hearts."[6]

The open house for the Halifax Nova Scotia Temple lasted four days, which brought heightened emotion and increased interest in the Church for many of the approximately eight thousand people who attended. Church officials were pleased with the attendance and with the responses of those who came. One elderly man, after completing a tour, tapped the shoulder of a member and said, "I'm so emotional I can hardly speak. God bless you and your people. Please tell your leaders that."[7] And after the last session of the open house, one newspaper reporter said there was no way he could write what he felt in the small space he would be given for the article.[8]

The dedications of the Halifax Nova Scotia Temple and the Regina Saskatchewan Temple on 14 November 1999 marked the first time in Church history that two temples were dedicated on the same day. They are the sixty-fourth and sixty-fifth operating temples, respectively.

The Halifax Nova Scotia Temple was dedicated in three sessions by President Gordon B. Hinckley. Richard Moses, second counselor in the Dartmouth Nova Scotia Stake presidency and chairman of the local temple committee, said, "It is impossible—there are not words—to adequately express our gratitude for this temple."[9]

We thank thee for the ordinances to be performed herein

Regina Saskatchewan Temple

Pour out thy blessings upon thy people in the great expanse of this temple district. Prosper them as they serve thee in righteousness.

— FROM THE DEDICATORY PRAYER

In the heart of the Canadian prairie, Regina, the provincial capital of Saskatchewan, is home to the legendary Royal Canadian Mounted Police, or "Mounties." It is also the site of the Regina Saskatchewan Temple, which is built in Wascana View, a suburb of Regina. In addition to the temple itself, the site provides ample parking and room for a future meetinghouse to be built. The temple district covers a 252,000-square-mile area in central Canada that has a population of one million people, about forty-five hundred of whom are Church members.

Part of a residential subdivision, the temple is surrounded by beautiful homes with well-maintained and landscaped yards. Near the temple is a community park that contributes to the neighborhood's peaceful and comfortable atmosphere. Although the property itself is quite flat, the landscape architect ingeniously created a setting suitable for wedding photographs. Part of the site east of the temple was hollowed out, and then landscaped with trees and vegetation. Temple visitors may enjoy the serenity of the area while resting on benches or walking along its paths.

As president of the North America Central Area, Elder Hugh W. Pinnock of the Seventy presided over the groundbreaking service on 14 November 1998. Nearly five hundred people gathered in a meetinghouse nearby for a ninety-minute

LOCATION
Regina, Saskatchewan, Canada

SITE
1 acre

SITE DEDICATION AND GROUNDBREAKING
14 November 1998
by Elder Hugh W. Pinnock

DEDICATION
14 November 1999
by President Boyd K. Packer

EXTERIOR
Light gray Canadian granite

DESIGN
Classic modern

TOTAL FLOOR AREA
10,700 square feet

REGINA SASKATCHEWAN

service before attending the ceremony outside in the cold. In his talk before the ceremony, Elder Pinnock urged the Saints to make the temple the center of their personal lives. He reminded them that it is in the temple where covenants are made and ordinances performed "so we may be with our Heavenly parents . . . and also with our earthly mother and father."[1] He said he had recently talked with a mother who lost a little girl through disease. "Through tear-stained eyes, the mother communicated profound grief but looked to me and said, 'I could not endure the pain of not being able to talk and laugh and tease my daughter except I know we will be together again. We are sealed together!'"[2]

The two-toned granite that adorns the temple's exterior comes from a quarry in Quebec. When it was being placed on the temple, many young people were given a unique opportunity they will never forget. After a stake youth conference, the young men and women gathered at the park across from the temple. Having received permission from Church officials and the temple contractor, they signed their names with the date on the back of the granite pieces, which were then placed on the temple. Construction missionary Sterling L. Burch assisted in the process and told them exactly where each stone was going to be placed. They walked away knowing that their names were going to become a permanent part of the temple.[3]

Elder Burch initiated another project involving the young men and women. Stake leaders offered them the opportunity to record their testimonies and commitments to temple worthiness on paper. These treasured documents were then placed in a capsule crafted by Elder Burch. A young man and a young woman were then selected to help place the capsule in the temple's spire, directly beneath the statue of the angel Moroni. Elder Burch described the event:

"Right after the angel Moroni was placed into position, I took two of the youth up the scaffolding and I had them fasten the capsule right under his [Moroni's] feet. I could have easily done this but I thought, 'No, this is for the youth; I want them to do it.' All of the stone was not yet attached to the spire so all of the youth could look up and see where the box containing their precious feelings, goals, and commitments was permanently placed." This choice experience serves as a constant reminder for the youth to be true to their testimonies and commitments that are now a part of the temple.[4]

During the week between the conclusion of the open house and the official dedication, crews worked around the clock to finish the temple exterior and landscape the grounds. A truckers' strike had delayed necessary materials until a few days before the deadline. Granite facing was being set twenty-four hours a day—right up to the night before the dedication. A group of more than one hundred Latter-day Saints—missionaries, youth, and adults—laid eighteen thousand square feet of sod, planted trees, and raised the granite sign in front of the temple just hours before the temple dedication.[5] Two thousand members attended the three dedicatory sessions.

Dedication plans originally called for the Regina Saskatchewan Temple to be dedicated one day after the dedication of the Halifax Nova Scotia Temple. But plans were altered at the last minute when technicians were unable to repair the airplane that was to carry President Gordon B. Hinckley from Salt Lake City to Nova Scotia, causing a one-day delay to the dedication in Halifax. At that point, Church officials decided to hold both on the same day: President Hinckley would dedicate the Halifax Nova Scotia Temple, and President Boyd K. Packer, acting president of the Quorum of the Twelve Apostles, would dedicate the Regina Saskatchewan Temple.

"The only last-minute change we're having to make is getting used to not having President Hinckley here," said Lorin J. Mendenhall, president of the Regina Saskatchewan Temple. "We're looking forward to being here with President Packer. We're definitely excited about the temple being here. We're thrilled to share this day with Halifax. It's kind of a historic event in that respect, having two temples dedicated on the same day."[6]

Pour out thy blessings upon thy people in the great expanse of this temple district

Billings Montana Temple

Late in August 1996, the First Presidency announced plans to build a temple in Montana's largest city, Billings. The ninth western state to become home to a house of the Lord, Montana is known for its breathtaking scenery and wide-open spaces. Before this temple was completed, Latter-day Saints in the area performed sacred ordinances at the Idaho Falls Idaho and Cardston Alberta Temples.

President Gordon B. Hinckley personally chose the Billings Montana Temple site, visiting the location where the temple now stands and later returning to see it again. Edward E. Jorden, president of the Billings Montana Stake, who accompanied President Hinckley during the search, recalled: "I may have been a little overzealous as I told him how beautiful this spot would be in the evenings and mornings with the sun and shadows on the Rims [nearby cliffs]. . . . The afternoon was the most memorable and awesome of my life."[1]

Once President Hinckley had chosen the site, the next phase was to secure local approvals for building the temple in that location. To gain access to such services as water, sewer, electric power, and natural gas, it was necessary to ask the Billings city council to make the proposed temple site part of the city. The Billings city council denied the request, surprising the thousand people attending the council meeting.

Church members quickly organized a petition drive to persuade the city council to reconsider the annexation request. Sister Susan Smith, who was given responsibility to organize the drive, recorded: "I sought direction by means of prayer in the work that was about to begin, and the Spirit testified to me how this work was to be done. . . . More than four hundred members of the Church—men, women, teenagers and

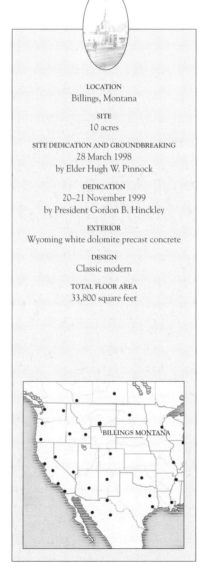

LOCATION
Billings, Montana

SITE
10 acres

SITE DEDICATION AND GROUNDBREAKING
28 March 1998
by Elder Hugh W. Pinnock

DEDICATION
20–21 November 1999
by President Gordon B. Hinckley

EXTERIOR
Wyoming white dolomite precast concrete

DESIGN
Classic modern

TOTAL FLOOR AREA
33,800 square feet

BILLINGS MONTANA

children—labored with love as they gathered signatures of support from the community. The drive was successful beyond merely gathering thousands of signatures in that it gave Church members a chance to talk with hundreds of people about concerns related to the temple and misconceptions about the LDS Church. . . .

"As more petition signatures came in, cheers of joy erupted and tears were shed. Church members had gathered nearly ten thousand signatures over the weekend. Exhausted, many labored all night and into the morning to complete the recording and get copies of the signatures run off to present to each member of the City Council the next day. We made a presentation and explained our labor of love to many of the City Council members. Some accepted with appreciation and others with doubt, but in our hearts we knew we had accomplished the wishes of our Heavenly Father."[2]

At last, with approvals in place, the groundbreaking was scheduled for 28 March 1998. Despite a spring snowstorm, forty-eight hundred Church members from twelve states and two Canadian provinces attended the event. The day started off cool and cloudy, and by noon snowflakes had started to fall. Although some tents had been assembled, the seven-hundred-member youth choir and all spectators remained exposed to the elements. Workers even turned metal music stands upside down to push away the snow and ice.

One faithful sister in her sixties had arrived two hours early to ensure she would have a front-row seat. Huddled under a blanket and umbrella, she sat on a lawn chair for more than four hours during the snowstorm. When she moved indoors at the conclusion of the ceremony, the perfectly dry ground beneath her chair was ringed by snow five inches deep.

Billings Montana Temple

We pray for all who will use this beautiful edifice in the accomplishment of thine eternal purposes. May they not weary in their sacred service. May they know that they are the means of opening the prison doors beyond the veil, all of which is made possible through the great atoning sacrifice of thy beloved Son, the Lord Jesus Christ.

—FROM THE DEDICATORY PRAYER

BILLINGS MONTANA TEMPLE
THE CHURCH OF JESUS CHRIST OF LATTER-DAY SAINTS
3100 RIM POINT DRIVE

Later, Church members learned that a large anti-Mormon organization from northern Wyoming had planned to disrupt the groundbreaking ceremonies. Not one protester was able to reach the temple site because of the hazardous weather and traveling conditions.[3]

Construction began soon after the groundbreaking ceremony. The temple site is north and east of the city, near the sandstone cliffs that form a landmark border three to five hundred feet high. Known as the Rimrocks, these cliffs provide a dramatic setting for morning and evening shadows. Temple project leaders located the temple near the base of the cliffs, preserving the Rimrocks' integrity and natural beauty. Throughout the ten-acre temple site are stone-like retaining walls and fence columns made of formed concrete painted to match the Rimrocks. On some Saturdays as many as three hundred volunteers painted the stones by hand. Many of the Primary children who participated will always remember which stone was "their" stone.[4]

The Rimrocks are not the only Montana beauty the temple reflects. To amplify the sunsets at the Rimrocks, glassmaker Mark Walton and his wife, Susan, designed the windows in the celestial room with cream and amber tones, geometric patterns, and beveled glass. As the sun sets in the west, the sunlight refracts, providing a splendid display of color and brightness. The temple interior also reflects

An image of Jesus Christ, the Good Shepherd, is hidden in the famous Rimrocks, his flock of sheep in the cliff tops and among the clouds.

the Montana landscape. The Montana state flower, the bitterroot, is skillfully detailed in the carpet and gold leafing in one of the sealing rooms.

Local Latter-day Saints donated their time and talents to beautify the temple's interior. A group of young women assembled the imported Czechoslovakian crystals for the chandelier in the brides' room. In the celestial room, young women teamed up with their mothers to assemble the crystals on the chandelier. Local youth also donated handmade quilts for the cribs in the temple's youth center.

After the temple was completed, it was ready for the public open house. Despite all the signatures collected early in the approval process, it still faced opposition at the open house. During the open house, one of the temple's major opponents visited the temple, hoping to cause problems. His wife later said that when he entered the temple's lobby and looked through the skylight to the statue of the angel Moroni on the steeple, he was so overwhelmed that he decided not to say one word throughout the tour. When he exited the temple, he said that he had never felt like that before.[5]

At the dedication of the Billings Montana Temple, the Saints' immense gratitude for a temple in their midst matched the magnificence of the big sky country of Montana.

May they know that they are the means of opening the prison doors beyond the veil

Edmonton Alberta Temple

Edmonton, the capital of Alberta, is on the North Saskatchewan River in the central part of the Canadian province. Edmonton is also the largest metropolitan area in the province and is known as the "Gateway to the North." The Edmonton Alberta Temple, with its gold-leafed statue of the angel Moroni rising eighty feet above the ground, is Canada's fifth and Alberta's second temple. This temple in Alberta eliminates the need for Church members to drive hundreds of miles south to Cardston to attend the temple.

Marjorie H. Scully of the Edmonton Bonnie Doon Stake shared her feelings on having a temple in Edmonton: "During President Hinckley's Canadian tour last August, he talked to us about the temple but he didn't announce that we were going to get a temple here. Then the official word came. It was so wonderful to know that Edmonton was going to get a temple. We had waited and hoped and prayed for years for this, and now the dream had come true. Having a temple twenty-two minutes away will change things dramatically.

"To go to the [Cardston] Alberta Temple has been a six-hour trip," Sister Scully continued. "Some of us have to arrange for time off from work as well as for babysitters. Most people don't drive there and back in one day, so sleeping arrangements have to be made as well. Now I can go at least once a month and hopefully more often and increase the number of family names that I can do proxy work for in the temple. What a joy that will be! My heart fills with such love for my Father in Heaven and my Savior Jesus Christ for sending this great blessing to us at this time. I'm also grateful to our beloved

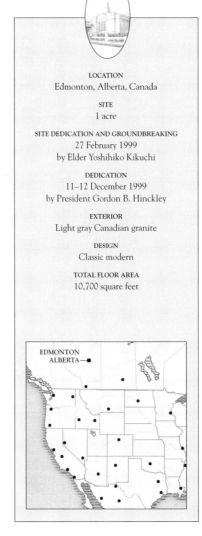

LOCATION
Edmonton, Alberta, Canada

SITE
1 acre

SITE DEDICATION AND GROUNDBREAKING
27 February 1999
by Elder Yoshihiko Kikuchi

DEDICATION
11–12 December 1999
by President Gordon B. Hinckley

EXTERIOR
Light gray Canadian granite

DESIGN
Classic modern

TOTAL FLOOR AREA
10,700 square feet

EDMONTON
ALBERTA →

president who saw the need for temples to be nearer the people. I am truly thankful for a prophet to lead us in these latter days."[1]

"To have a temple located here is going to bless lives in ways we really don't even understand yet," said Elder Blair S. Bennett, an area authority seventy. "This has literally been a fulfillment of the hopes and dreams and aspirations of a generation that has lived and served in Edmonton."[2]

Elder Yoshihiko Kikuchi of the Seventy presided over the groundbreaking for the Edmonton Alberta Temple on 27 February 1999 in a crowded stake center. The proceedings were carried by audio feed to nineteen other locations in northern Alberta and part of British Columbia. "This is a monument of your faith, and Heavenly Father truly has answered your prayers," declared Elder Kikuchi regarding the temple, constructed to the west of the Edmonton Alberta Riverbend Stake Center. An estimated thirty-five hundred people witnessed the service.[3]

After the groundbreaking, construction began. Temple construction missionaries Leo C. Udy and Rhea Udy were two of the workers. "Achieving the highest quality of work was not difficult because the workers wanted to do it right the first time," Elder Udy said. "They understood that if they didn't do it right the first time that they would be back doing it over again. They read the specifications required and did it right the first time."[4]

Elder Udy also remembered a time when the contractors were gathered to discuss an important decision. "We were discussing a few ways that we could solve a problem. One option was to slip by and do it poorly, and the other way would have

Edmonton Alberta Temple

All that we have and are we place in thy hands, dear Father. Accept of our labors. Accept of our love. May the covenants we have made with thee remain ever bright in our memories, that we may walk the straight and narrow path that leads to thy divine presence.

—FROM THE DEDICATORY PRAYER

Edmonton

been the right way. To do it the right way would take a little longer and cost a little more money. Those gathered could not quite come to a decision, so I took my ring off and said, 'See that? What is on there? It says 'CTR' and that means 'Choose the Right. . . .' ' That was the end of the discussion and we did it the right way."[5]

The native granite exterior of the temple is supported by laminated lumber, one of the few materials able to support the heavy stone facing. Although the sheer weight of the stone would seem to guarantee the stability of the temple, Robert Bennett, the architect, said he was required to design the building two earthquake-zone categories higher than the usual Edmonton code.[6]

Yet the heavy clay soil of the area would not support the weight of the temple. To support the building and provide enhanced earthquake protection, holes forty-five feet deep and twenty-four inches in diameter were lined with steel cages and filled with noncorroding concrete. The actual temple floor was built six feet above the concrete foundation, leaving a crawl space under the temple floor so that the building rests above the ground.[7]

The massive stonework is offset by the use of wild rose

Images of four oxen are hidden in the landscaping near the baptistry, exactly where the baptismal font is placed.

patterns throughout the architecture and landscaping. This prominent symbol of Alberta adds a finishing touch to the immovable structure.

As the completion date approached, the president of the Red Deer Stake encouraged members of the stake to prepare for the temple by gathering names to be submitted for ordinance work. They set the goal of preparing seventy-five hundred names by the time of the temple's dedication. When that time arrived, they had prepared information for forty thousand individuals, more than five times their goal.[8]

The temple was dedicated by President Gordon B. Hinckley in seven sessions held 11 and 12 December 1999. "Let Thy providence be felt in this great nation of Canada, that it shall continue to be a land where Thy sons and daughters enjoy the precious boon of freedom of assembly and worship," President Hinckley said in the dedicatory prayer.[9]

After the dedication, when the temple was open to the Saints for ordinances, Elder and Sister Udy watched the members walking in. As they reminisced about their tireless service rendered while building the temple, they thought, "Our work is over here, but their work is just beginning."[10]

. . . that we may walk the straight and narrow path that leads to thy divine presence

Raleigh North Carolina Temple

The Raleigh North Carolina Temple is located on a twelve-acre site about ten miles southwest of metropolitan Raleigh in the small railroad town of Apex.

Throughout much of the Church's history in North Carolina, the nearest temples were in Utah. Couples traveling to the temple to be married needed a chaperone to make the long journey to Utah. Often the trip could be made only after a period of saving money, and generally family members could not afford to travel with them. With the building of the Washington D. C. Temple in 1974 and then the Atlanta Georgia Temple in 1983, many more of the Saints in the South have been able to take part in the blessings of the temple.[1]

As with other temples, volunteerism was a hallmark of construction on the Raleigh North Carolina Temple and its grounds. For example, early in the morning of 23 January 1999, about twelve hundred young Latter-day Saints began to arrive at the building site to clear it of underbrush and small trees and render it suitable for the groundbreaking ceremony. The young men and young women worked very hard in a cooperative effort and enjoyed serving the Lord in this way. Although all the weather services predicted a 100 percent chance of heavy rain throughout the day, not until five minutes after the last group prepared to leave did the rain begin to fall.[2]

Another weather miracle occurred near the end of May when workers were preparing to pour the concrete floor slabs of the temple. When the air temperature is too high, concrete can dry too rapidly, causing it to cure improperly and then crack. Although everything was ready for the pouring and the cement trucks were coming, the weather was still much too hot.

Temple construction missionary Alaire Johnson, who kept a history of the project, recorded, "Suddenly, out of a clear blue sky came a dark cloud that hovered over the area, bringing the temperature down about ten degrees."[3]

Sister Johnson said that the workers proceeded, and the concrete set up perfectly.

A highlight of the temple construction was placing the statue of the angel Moroni atop the temple. On 1 September 1999, nearly fifteen hundred spectators gathered to witness the placement of both the tower and the statue.

Before the statue was lifted from ground level, a blind woman and two young children were escorted to the box holding the statue of Moroni. Wearing soft cotton gloves, the woman slowly reached out, tenderly caressing the form and the trumpet he was holding. She would never see this marvelous golden statue, but she would always remember how large and how smooth it felt. The two children were also permitted to touch it.[4]

The Raleigh North Carolina Temple committee assigned a number of women in the local stakes to make altar cloths for the temple's four altars and provided them with specific guidelines for the size, thread, pattern, and durability of the cloths.

Sister Chloe Hodge commented: "I spend twelve to fourteen hours a day on them. It's a tremendous amount of work. It's a great labor of love. It's such an honor and privilege to be able to make something to be used for the Lord's house."[5]

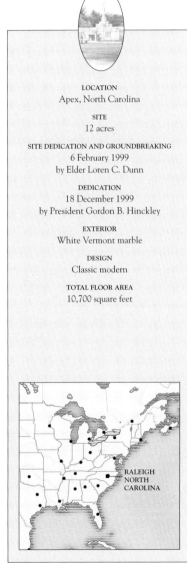

LOCATION
Apex, North Carolina

SITE
12 acres

SITE DEDICATION AND GROUNDBREAKING
6 February 1999
by Elder Loren C. Dunn

DEDICATION
18 December 1999
by President Gordon B. Hinckley

EXTERIOR
White Vermont marble

DESIGN
Classic modern

TOTAL FLOOR AREA
10,700 square feet

RALEIGH
NORTH
CAROLINA

Raleigh North Carolina Temple

May all who come as patrons to this temple know that they are dealing with the things of eternity, and that the relationships here entered into are everlasting. Bless all who are here sealed in the bonds of eternal marriage that they may live together with love and respect for one another. Bless the fathers and mothers that they may rear their children as thy children, in a spirit of kindness and encouragement, that the encircling hand of love may bind together the relationships of the family.

—FROM THE DEDICATORY PRAYER

Raleigh

Each cloth required about two hundred hours of work. Sister Hodge took four weeks to make one of the large altar cloths.

Primary children in the Raleigh area used the Articles of Faith to contribute financially to the temple. Family members pledged a dime for every one of the thirteen Articles of Faith their children could learn. The children were honored during a special ceremony held in front of the nearly completed temple. They had exceeded their goal of two hundred dollars, raising two hundred and fifty dollars to help pay for stained glass windows. As a result of their efforts, the names of the Primary children and the youth in the temple district were recorded and sealed in the temple's cornerstone.[6]

When Gary Stansbury was confirmed a member of the Church, Bishop Bruce Nay of the Apex Ward commented, "Most people come to the temple by way of the gospel; Gary came to the gospel by way of the temple."[7]

Brother Stansbury, whose expertise is in building such huge projects as shopping complexes costing $65 million, had planned to spend a year doing that kind of project in St. Louis, Missouri. He was disappointed when the project was delayed and he was asked to build the $5 million temple instead.

"This wasn't what I did. I hadn't built a $5 million job in

The beam of the Cape Hatteras Lighthouse focuses on the Savior, the Light of the world. His image is hidden on the right side of the full picture.

years," he said. "But I knew I couldn't leave. I didn't want to leave. I do not think it's chance that I'm here," Brother Stansbury said, adding that while studying the Book of Mormon, he had gained a testimony of "building only that which is worth building. I'm doing that. That's what I want to do."[8]

He concluded, "I needed to be here. And thinking back now, it almost seems that I've kind of been led to learn for forty-four years, and now, this [joining the Church] is what I'm supposed to do."[9]

Brother Stansbury was taught the gospel and baptized by temple missionary Elder Gaylen Johnson. A year after his baptism, Brother Stansbury and his wife were sealed in the temple.

On 18 December 1999, hundreds of faithful members braved the bitter cold morning to hear President Gordon B. Hinckley petition in the dedicatory prayer:

"Bless all whose tithes have made possible this Holy house. Open the windows of heaven and shower blessings upon them. Bless them in their basket and in their store. Bless them in their faith and give strength to their testimonies. Nurture their children and their children's children with a love for the gospel of thy divine Son."[10]

Bless the fathers and mothers that they may rear their children as thy children

St. Paul Minnesota Temple

St. Paul is Minnesota's capital city and the state's second largest city after neighboring Minneapolis; together the two cities form the Twin Cities metropolitan area. The temple itself is actually in Oakdale City, an eastern suburb of St. Paul on the Mississippi River. The eighteen acres that include the temple site and that of the St. Paul stake center are heavily wooded and have several marshy areas.

The Oakdale City fathers gave the proposed temple a warm reception, and the St. Paul community offered remarkable support to the Church in its efforts to build it. Long-time neighbors living near the stake center voluntarily attended town meetings to speak in support of the temple proposal. They commented that Latter-day Saints are wonderful to have as neighbors. Through the years the stake center had been so well maintained that the community welcomed the idea of another building of a similar nature. In fact, around the time of the temple's announcement, the chapel won an award from the city of Oakdale as the city's most attractive building. Not a single known negative comment originated from the neighbors or community during the construction of the temple.[1]

The first stake in Minnesota was organized in 1960. Through the years, Church membership in the state grew. When Elder Thomas A. Holt, area authority seventy and long-time resident of the area, was assigned to find a site for the state's second stake center, he "looked at several sites and felt nothing" until he visited "this beautiful site heavily wooded with oak trees." The Spirit bore witness to him and he insisted that they purchase additional property beyond what was needed for the stake center. He said "that . . . was to be the

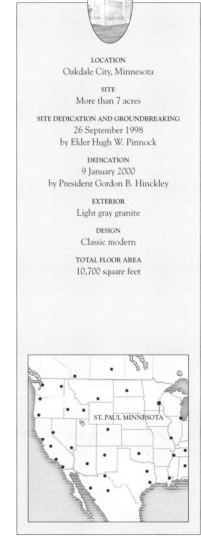

LOCATION
Oakdale City, Minnesota

SITE
More than 7 acres

SITE DEDICATION AND GROUNDBREAKING
26 September 1998
by Elder Hugh W. Pinnock

DEDICATION
9 January 2000
by President Gordon B. Hinckley

EXTERIOR
Light gray granite

DESIGN
Classic modern

TOTAL FLOOR AREA
10,700 square feet

ST. PAUL MINNESOTA

place for the St. Paul stake center—and now the site for our Minnesota Temple. The Lord chose this place."[2] The temple is built on the highest portion of the ground purchased by Elder Holt.

The dedication of the stake center was presided over by Elder Jacob de Jager of the Seventy. During his comments before the dedicatory prayer, he referred to a temple being built nearby. Years later, when the St. Paul Minnesota Temple was announced, members remembered Elder de Jager's talk and felt that his comments were inspired.[3]

For decades, Minnesota Saints had had to drive for two days to Salt Lake City, Utah, to attend the temple. They were subsequently assigned to the Chicago Illinois Temple district, a seven- to fourteen-hour drive for most. It was even farther for Church members living in the Canadian part of the temple district. According to Mel Hiscock, president of the Ft. Francis Ontario District, Canadian Latter-day Saints paid an average of two hundred dollars in Canadian funds to travel two days each way to the Chicago Illinois Temple. President Hiscock said, "That $200 is a tremendous amount of money to most of these people who have very limited incomes." He said when they get to the temple they serve nonstop, because they know it will be a long time before they can return. These Church members are now in the St. Paul Minnesota Temple district, and the distance is half what it was to Chicago.[4]

One of these faithful members who had to travel to Cardston, Alberta, Canada, to receive his endowment promised himself he would create a painting to decorate a temple some day. When the St. Paul Minnesota Temple was announced, the Temple Department chose this artist, Wayne M. Howell, to have two of his paintings on display in the temple.

*St. Paul
Minnesota Temple*

*We pray for all who shall come as patrons that they may
ever look upon this service as a labor of love performed in
the spirit of the Redeemer who gave his life for all
mankind. May the wonder and the majesty of that great
act of atonement enter the minds and hearts of all who
serve here in behalf of those beyond the veil of death.*

—FROM THE DEDICATORY PRAYER

SAINT PAUL MINNESOTA TEMPLE
THE CHURCH OF JESUS CHRIST OF LATTER-DAY SAINTS

The two paintings, *Temperance River* and *Silver Creek*, reflect the beauty of northeastern Minnesota. Brother Howell said the sites in his paintings have a peaceful, temple-like feeling for him. In fact, he said, he felt he was in a temple-like setting while he was painting *Temperance River:*

"I needed a sunny morning [to paint the river] so I prayed for one. At 5:30 A.M. I was in a clearing noticing a long slender opening in a very cloudy sky. I said another prayer, loaded the painting and equipment in the car and made the forty-five-minute journey to the Temperance River. As I hiked up the half mile to the top of the cascades the sun shone brightly against the trees on the far side of the river, exactly the effect I wanted. For the rest of the morning the area was surrounded by clouds, but where I painted it remained sunny until I finished at 11:30 A.M. When I arrived at the car, clouds had closed over me, and it had started raining. During the time I painted I had no visitors or disturbances on a Wednesday morning in a state park. The prayers, the sun, and the serenity gave me a peace that I have often felt in the temple."[5]

The placement of the statue of the angel Moroni is a much-celebrated milestone in temple construction, so the organizing committee chose a day with additional significance. When the crane hoisted the seven-foot statue into position, it was 21 September 1999, the 176th anniversary of the day that the angel Moroni first appeared to the Prophet Joseph Smith.[6]

Members of the St. Paul Minnesota Temple committee were key figures in developing an advertising campaign for the

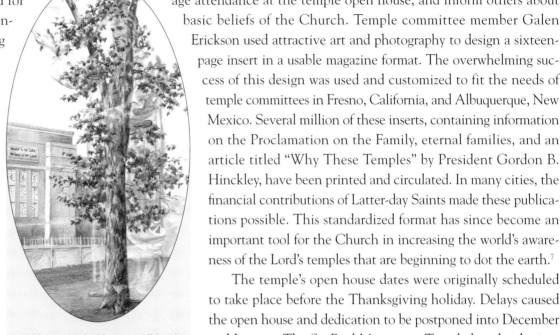

Hidden among the foliage is a full-length image of the Savior, inviting us to return to the temple often.

Church that had an enormous effect on other temples that followed. They refined a newspaper insert that was first used in conjunction with the Billings Montana Temple. The goal of the insert was to increase public awareness of the new temple, provide local history of the Church, encourage attendance at the temple open house, and inform others about basic beliefs of the Church. Temple committee member Galen Erickson used attractive art and photography to design a sixteen-page insert in a usable magazine format. The overwhelming success of this design was used and customized to fit the needs of temple committees in Fresno, California, and Albuquerque, New Mexico. Several million of these inserts, containing information on the Proclamation on the Family, eternal families, and an article titled "Why These Temples" by President Gordon B. Hinckley, have been printed and circulated. In many cities, the financial contributions of Latter-day Saints made these publications possible. This standardized format has since become an important tool for the Church in increasing the world's awareness of the Lord's temples that are beginning to dot the earth.[7]

The temple's open house dates were originally scheduled to take place before the Thanksgiving holiday. Delays caused the open house and dedication to be postponed into December and January. The St. Paul Minnesota Temple has the distinction of being the last temple to have an open house in 1999 and the first to be dedicated in the year 2000. Thus, the panel on the cornerstone of the temple is engraved "ERECTED 1999–DEDICATED JANUARY 2000."

. . . that they may ever look upon this service as a labor
of love performed in the spirit of the Redeemer

Kona Hawaii Temple

The temple in Kailua-Kona is on Hawaii, the state's largest and southernmost island. White marble walls and orderly rows of royal palms contrast with the island's green hills. The temple itself rests on a hillside flanked by Mount Hualalai to the east and overlooking the Pacific Ocean to the west.

As president of the Kona Hawaii Stake, Philip A. Harris prayed to know what the Lord would have him accomplish during his service. He recounted: "One night I dreamt there was to be a temple in Kona. I woke and told my wife. . . . I took my dream to be a direction for me as a stake president that I was to [help] my people to become temple worthy and temple ready."

Knowing the logistics of building a large temple in Kona, he thought that the dream simply meant the people were to be spiritually prepared, not that there would be an actual temple in Kona. Then President Gordon B. Hinckley announced that a number of small temples would be built. And soon, a temple was announced for Kona. "I knew then that in my lifetime I would see the temple here that I had seen in my dream."[1]

Despite the announcement that a temple would be built in Kona, many involved in the process questioned whether the Kailua village planning and design committee would give the Church permission to build the temple. To help the cause, Kona Hawaii Temple architect John Pharis asked President Harris if he could arrange a showing of community support. Nearly three hundred faithful Saints and friends showed up at the planning hearing dressed in their Sunday best. John Pharis described the event: "The place was bursting at the seams. The whole room filled. People were outside the windows looking in. You could barely walk through—the corridor was full, and

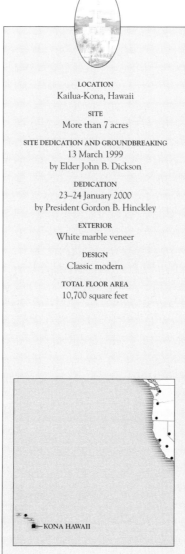

LOCATION
Kailua-Kona, Hawaii

SITE
More than 7 acres

SITE DEDICATION AND GROUNDBREAKING
13 March 1999
by Elder John B. Dickson

DEDICATION
23–24 January 2000
by President Gordon B. Hinckley

EXTERIOR
White marble veneer

DESIGN
Classic modern

TOTAL FLOOR AREA
10,700 square feet

KONA HAWAII

the sidewalks were packed full of people." It really sent a powerful message of support.[2] The committee members were astonished at the support the proposal had generated. When word got out that the proposal had passed, everyone in attendance cheered.[3]

Ground was broken for the Kona Hawaii Temple on 13 March 1999 on a clear, sunny morning. Some twelve hundred people, including Church members, Church and community leaders, and other guests, gathered in the nearby stake center for the groundbreaking services. A combined choir from the Hilo and Kona stakes, dressed in white and accented with colorful island leis, provided music. In a touching moment, Primary children were asked to help turn the dirt and willingly performed that service.

Throughout the construction process, many people had incredible spiritual experiences. For example, Myron Lindsey was repositioning a mobile crane one day when the weight it was carrying began to topple the machine. Just when it would have tipped over and possibly killed or severely injured workers below the crane, it righted itself and became stable. Others felt strongly the influence and even presence of those who had gone before and who were intensely interested in the progress of the temple. While Mark Kealamakia was working in the baptismal font area, he felt the strong presence of some "very old people." Although he didn't actually see them, he felt they may have been the early settlers of the island who had never had the fulness of the gospel and wanted their temple ordinances performed for them.[4]

These experiences and others made the Hawaiian Saints eager to attend the temple and return regularly after its completion.

Kona Hawaii Temple

May thy blessings attend all who labor within these walls, both those who will administer the ordinances and those who will receive them. May the loftiest ideals of their faith be realized. May a spirit of love and peace, a spirit in harmony with thee, be felt by all who serve here in whatever capacity.

—FROM THE DEDICATORY PRAYER

Kona
HAWAII

The fasting and prayers of the Saints helped miracles to happen during the construction of the temple. Construction workers feared that the crane they had to use to lift the nine-thousand-pound spire into place was not going to work. They asked all involved to fast and pray that all would go well. As the spire was finally being raised, the crane started to bow. The spire cleared the roof by only a foot, but it was enough to position the spire and relieve the crane of its burden. After the task was safely completed, the men involved sat down for their lunch break and offered a prayer of gratitude for their Heavenly Father's help.[5]

In an interview following the first dedicatory session, President Harris commented on the open house and the wonderful feelings it brought to those who attended. "Families were impressed with the spirit of the celestial room. Mothers would stop and embrace their children. . . . There's a feeling and a spirit that have come over the people because of this temple. It has had a tremendous effect not only with the members but also with the others who have sensed the Spirit."[6]

The dedication of the temple was marked by feelings of joy and gratitude. President Harris felt that in addition to prayer and song, there was an even better way for the Saints to show their gratitude for the blessing of the new temple. "I think our way of expressing thanks to the Lord for providing this temple is for us to wear it out from use. That's what we endeavor to do."[7]

The beauty of the temple is enhanced by the sugar-cane

Hidden in the foreground are the eight main islands of the state of Hawaii. To the right of the temple is a full-length image of the Savior Jesus Christ.

leaf decorations on benches outside and inside the temple. Architect John Pharis was inspired to create these patterns as he was reading the parable of the wheat and the tares. Because wheat is not a native island plant, he felt it would look out of place in the temple. Then he thought of the sugar cane and its similarities to wheat, and he incorporated that island plant into his design.[8]

To add vibrant color to the grounds for the temple dedication, hundreds of beautiful red poinsettias, still in their pots, were positioned in front of the temple. President Gordon B. Hinckley dedicated the Kona Hawaii Temple on 23 January 2000. Privileged to be in attendance, I will never forget participating in the dedication of the Kona Temple; it was one of the most spiritual experiences of my life. Following the dedicatory prayer and Hosanna Shout, the members in the temple stood and joined in singing the sacred hymn, 'The Spirit of God.' I have never heard the hymn sung with such emotion and power. I am certain the temple walls must have been shaking.

After the dedicatory services, more than a thousand Saints gathered in front of the temple to wait for President Hinckley to leave the building. As he made his way from the temple, they began singing reverently, "We Thank Thee, O God, for a Prophet." As the prophet waved before getting into his car, the multitude, as if on cue, began singing the traditional farewell song "Aloha oe." An unforgettable spirit of gratitude and love embraced all who were there.

May a spirit of love and peace, a spirit in harmony with thee, be felt by all who serve here

Ciudad Juárez México Temple

May thy people feel constrained in their hearts to come here frequently and engage in the service which will be performed here. May they leave with gratitude and appreciation for the wonderful opportunity that is theirs.

—FROM THE DEDICATORY PRAYER

The Ciudad Juarez Mexico Temple, whose exterior is faced with white marble quarried in Mexico, is a blessing to Latter-day Saints on both sides of the United States–Mexico border. This temple is one of the few smaller temples not built next to a chapel. It is located instead behind a high school and a public park near downtown Juarez. Ciudad Juarez, Mexico's fourth largest city, is located across the Rio Grande River, less than thirty miles from El Paso, Texas. The temple was built in Ciudad Juarez rather than El Paso because it is relatively easy for citizens of the United States to travel from El Paso into Mexico, but it is very difficult for most Mexican citizens to travel into the United States.

Members living in the Ciudad Juarez stakes had previously been part of the Mexico City Mexico Temple district. When it was announced in May 1998 that Ciudad Juarez would have a temple of its own, many of the members thought the news too good to be true, believing the announcement to be a publication error. The members thought Ciudad Juarez had been confused with Colonia Juarez, a small Latter-day Saint community located approximately two hundred miles to the south. Leticia Guitierrez de Orozco, the Ciudad Juarez temple historian, described her reaction: "At first it was difficult to accept the fact that there was no mistake in the announcement because we never believed a temple here would be possible."

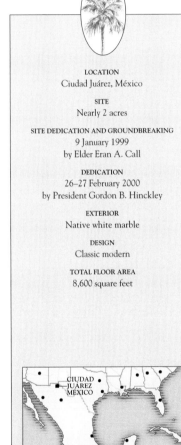

LOCATION
Ciudad Juárez, México

SITE
Nearly 2 acres

SITE DEDICATION AND GROUNDBREAKING
9 January 1999
by Elder Eran A. Call

DEDICATION
26–27 February 2000
by President Gordon B. Hinckley

EXTERIOR
Native white marble

DESIGN
Classic modern

TOTAL FLOOR AREA
8,600 square feet

She said that when the members were assured that the temple was going to be built in Ciudad Juarez, everyone was overcome with emotion and began to rejoice.[1]

From the beginning of the temple construction process, it was noted that the temple would bring together members of two nations and cultures. Presiding at the temple's groundbreaking services on 9 January 1999, Elder Eran A. Call of the Seventy, president of the Mexico North Area, commented, "In this temple district, we have members on both sides of the border. This will bring a uniting and joining of members of both communities. This temple is a great thing for members [in Mexico and] in the United States."[2]

As the dedication of the temple approached, members of both communities helped to assure that any brothers and sisters in need had temple clothing. Members donated extra or new clothing or loaned their own.

Many of the Mexican members made their own temple clothing. Groups of sisters from El Paso traveled across the border to help the Mexican sisters make temple slippers for themselves in Relief Society. While serving as temple construction missionaries, Elder Richard Skidmore and Sister Bon Adell Skidmore witnessed the loving cooperation of the cultures. "We feel like there has been more than a temple built here. We have witnessed a mingling of cultures and a sharing of ideas."[3]

As the temple neared completion, some construction supervisors were worried about getting the landscaping finished in the little time that remained. But Elder Skidmore said he learned a lesson during the temple's construction: "The Lord knew that the temple needed to be finished, and he knew the efforts that everyone had made. A miracle occurred every day, one after another, to get things done on time."[4]

Many Church members assisted in the completion of the landscaping. About forty members from Colonia Juarez brought their farming equipment and spent an entire day helping with the landscaping. During the final weeks of construction, groups from both the United States and Mexico worked on the temple site daily, cleaning both the interior and exterior of the temple, washing windows, wiping down the exterior walls, and accomplishing last-minute tasks. It was calculated that members donated more than fifty thousand hours on the Ciudad Juarez Mexico Temple.[5]

Following the completion of the temple, a few days before leaving Ciudad Juarez, Elder Skidmore reflected: "The crowning event is watching the members use their new temple. Just to know that now many places in the world have that opportunity to take part in temple blessings without having to go for a week at a time to attend the temple. People who have lived near temples all of their lives may have taken their nearby temples for granted.

"I think that the thing that impresses me more than anything else is how excited and eager [the members here] are to have a temple within an hour's drive. The humility and eagerness is very unique."[6]

May they leave with gratitude and appreciation for the wonderful opportunity that is theirs

Hermosillo Sonora México Temple

[This temple] is sacred to us, the place where holy ordinances will be administered for both the living and the dead. Here will be exercised the only authority on earth which reaches beyond the veil of death and is efficacious in the worlds beyond. How thankful we are to have in our midst this sacred and beautiful edifice.

—FROM THE DEDICATORY PRAYER

The Hermosillo Sonora Mexico Temple is located in an affluent area in the beautiful town of Pitic, an Indian word that means "where two rivers meet." The word *Hermosillo* means "land of beauty." And all who visit the temple here in Pitic agree that the temple enhances the land's beauty.

The Church has owned property, including the temple site, in Hermosillo since 1964. The land on which the temple now stands was once home to the Mexico Hermosillo Mission offices.[1] Latter-day Saints living nearby were previously included in the Mexico City Mexico Temple district. For many, making the arduous excursion to Mexico City required up to thirty-six hours each way by car or bus and four hundred thousand pesos (about $400 U.S.) per person. Such a sum was burdensome to come up with, given that the average person in Mexico earns about fifty to one hundred pesos a day. Even with sufficient funds for the trip, it was often difficult for members to take a week off work to make the journey.

Families desiring to attend the temple together to be sealed had to make great sacrifices to reach that goal. Traveling eight hours northward to the Mesa Arizona Temple was a

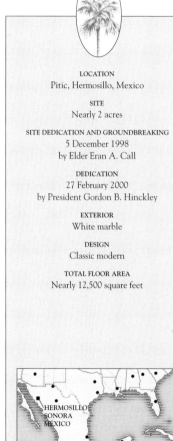

LOCATION
Pitic, Hermosillo, Mexico

SITE
Nearly 2 acres

SITE DEDICATION AND GROUNDBREAKING
5 December 1998
by Elder Eran A. Call

DEDICATION
27 February 2000
by President Gordon B. Hinckley

EXTERIOR
White marble

DESIGN
Classic modern

TOTAL FLOOR AREA
Nearly 12,500 square feet

HERMOSILLO SONORA MEXICO

somewhat shorter and less expensive trip, but the expense and difficulty of obtaining passports and visas still prevented many Mexican members from traveling to Arizona.[2]

Moncelo Guerro, a faithful longtime member in Hermosillo, shared his feelings about the new temple. "It was hard to raise money to travel to the temple," he said. "Whenever we had things to sell, we sold them. Now, we are full of happiness to have a temple here and we will be able to visit it."[3]

When President Gordon B. Hinckley visited the city of Hermosillo in March 1998, he told the members that if they would continue to be faithful, they would have a temple in or near their city.[4] During his visit to Hermosillo, President Hinckley personally chose where the temple was to be built. Upon his arrival he visited some of the property that the Church already owned, including the location where the temple now stands. After speaking at a regional conference, President Hinckley asked if he could visit the location again. Local Church leaders were later informed by mail that a temple would be built on this site.[5]

The temple's announcement brought a time of rejoicing. Many of the local members had a great desire to assist in some way in the building of the new temple. Members in Hermosillo donated their time and talents to beautify the unattractive boulevard that ran along the front of the temple. Church architects drew up plans, then members implemented the plans, creating beautiful and inviting gardens. Herardo Rivera, Hermosillo Sonora Mexico Temple historian, said, "We would work in the evenings and at night, whenever we could, and we left the spot very precious and beautiful. . . . It has given us great joy to know that we have participated in something that has to do with the temple."[6] The attractive gardens provide a drastic contrast to the previous street conditions. This service beautified the temple's surroundings and was greatly appreciated by the city and the temple's neighbors.[7]

As construction progressed, a brick mason and carpenter began taking the missionary discussions. By the time the temple was dedicated, the two were converted and baptized. "One of these men said that during the construction, supervisors from Salt Lake would come and say, 'That is not good enough, you have to knock it down; You have to destroy it and return and do it again,'" said Hugo Montoya, a member of the Hermosillo Mexico Pitic Stake. "The men began to realize that they were involved with something very special. They began to be more careful and asked 'Why? What is it that we are building?' They began to ask more questions, then received the missionaries and were converted."[8]

Following the placement of the temple's spire in July 1999, a unique event was experienced by those working at the site. Many construction workers were on the roof when a severe and quickly moving thunderstorm approached. "As they were trying to get down, a lightning bolt came down, but it did not hit the temple," said Brother Rivera. "The lightning hit a spire on top of the chapel right next to the temple. The height of the temple's metal spire resting on the temple reached sixty-nine feet. The neighboring chapel's spire has a metal spire that reaches only twenty feet. . . . Everyone made it to safety. This was a major event that impacted everyone."[9]

"It was a miracle," added Brother Montoya.[10]

To accommodate the large numbers of people attending the temple's open house, touring hours were extended until 11 P.M. each day. On the final day of the open house, there were so many people that the temple opened early and did not close until midnight. "We noticed many who left the temple had tears on their faces because of the peace that they felt," said Brother Rivera. "We hope and we pray that these people will come closer to the Savior and listen to His words."[11]

The dedication of the temple on 27 February 2000 was an unheralded milestone for President Hinckley. In his long pursuit of promoting temple building and temple worship, that dedicatory service marked the fiftieth temple he had dedicated or rededicated.

*How thankful we are to have in our midst
this sacred and beautiful edifice*

Albuquerque New Mexico Temple

Located on the northeast edge of Albuquerque, the Albuquerque New Mexico Temple serves Latter-day Saints in New Mexico, Arizona, and Colorado. The site is situated in the heart of the residential neighborhood of North Albuquerque Acres. From the temple grounds, visitors can see a panoramic view of the metro-Albuquerque area, the Rio Grande Valley, and the Sandia Mountains. Fifteen months after its groundbreaking, the temple was dedicated on 5 March 2000, becoming the first temple in the Land of Enchantment.

Typically, the first public announcement of a temple comes directly from the Church's First Presidency in a regional or general conference setting. But in an effort to build good public and civic relations, the Church announced plans for a temple in Albuquerque through the local media first and then to the general Church membership a day later.

On a Thursday evening before general conference in April 1997, bishops and stake presidents were informed of the temple announcement and asked not to spread word until 5:30 the following morning. The news media in the region had already been informed of the Church's intention to build a temple in Albuquerque. Media representatives were also asked not to release the information until the following morning. All media outlets honored the Church's request, breaking the Albuquerque temple news simultaneously with local TV and newspaper coverage.

Friday evening Melchizedek Priesthood holders from three wards located near the temple site were asked to knock on every door in the neighborhood to inform residents about the temple and answer questions. A packet was presented that explained the purpose of temples and how other

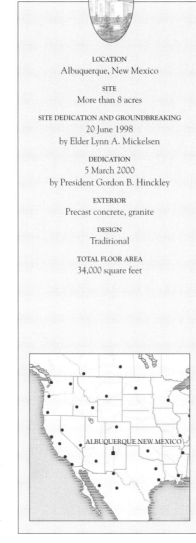

LOCATION
Albuquerque, New Mexico

SITE
More than 8 acres

SITE DEDICATION AND GROUNDBREAKING
20 June 1998
by Elder Lynn A. Mickelsen

DEDICATION
5 March 2000
by President Gordon B. Hinckley

EXTERIOR
Precast concrete, granite

DESIGN
Traditional

TOTAL FLOOR AREA
34,000 square feet

ALBUQUERQUE NEW MEXICO

temples have positively impacted surrounding communities. Many of the residents invited the men inside; some asked questions about the temple and the Church for twenty minutes or more. The neighbors appreciated the personal attention. This proactive approach created a supportive environment for the temple's construction.

The following day, during Saturday morning's session of general conference, President Hinckley informed the general Church membership that property had been obtained in Albuquerque for the building of a temple.

Youth of four New Mexico stakes prepared the temple site for groundbreaking. The teens brought shovels, rakes, and gloves to rid the site of sagebrush, garbage, and cholla plants. Weeds were then mowed and the ground made safe for those attending the groundbreaking ceremony. One young man who had just turned in his missionary papers realized the blessing of having a temple nearby and being worthy to attend it. "We need to clean all the cactuses out of our lives before we can go to the temple," he said.[1] At the groundbreaking ceremony—attended by more than sixty-five hundred Church members—many of the youth who had been at the cleanup participated in the youth choir.

As construction on the temple began, thirty-six year residents Tony and Ann Knudsen began their temple construction mission. In addition to overseeing the construction of the temple, the Knudsens traveled throughout the temple district speaking about the temple. Unfortunately, Sister Knudsen passed away during her time of service on the temple. Her influence, however, is still felt throughout the area. At the temple open house, a nonmember gave Brother Knudsen a

Albuquerque New
Mexico Temple

*Bless all who serve here, be they officiators or patrons, that they
may do so with reverence and with respect and love for thee. May
the incomparable Atonement of thy Beloved Son come to have
greater meaning and may their understanding increase as they
pursue the work of salvation which is based on the gift of thy Son
in behalf of all mankind. May their minds be lifted to visions of
eternity and of thy great plan of happiness for thy children.*

—FROM THE DEDICATORY PRAYER

Albuquerque

Chad Hawkins © 2000

card that praised his wife's service. "It told me how much she affected his life," Brother Knudsen said.[2]

Because the area is a desert where water is a scarce commodity, the grounds of the Albuquerque New Mexico Temple have xeric (dry or desert-like) landscaping. All of the plants require little water but provide a picturesque setting.

The temple's beautiful exterior is an indigenous color called desert rose. As the desert sun shines on the temple, the color seems to vary depending on the time of day. The upper portion of the temple is formed out of precast concrete. The concrete portions were manufactured in Utah and then trucked to the temple site in Albuquerque. It took more than one hundred trips to bring all of the panels to the site.

Each colored panel is eight inches thick. Exhaustive measures were taken to ensure that the colored panels matched each other perfectly. To take out subtle variations in the installed panels, a crew worked for four months sandblasting the panels and washing them down with acid. Elder Tony Knudsen, a temple construction missionary, described the work as "a painstaking process. They washed every one of those things with a sponge."[3] The temple's base is covered with Texas pearl granite, which contrasts beautifully with the lighter-colored upper portion of the edifice.

Native American influence is immediately apparent within the temple. In the entryway are two Navajo tapestries on opposite walls; two more are found in the stairways. The longest tapestry measures three feet by ten feet. One of them displays thirty-five vibrant colors that are all derived from natural vegetable dyes. Commissioned by the Church, an elderly Navajo woman made the temple's tapestries by hand. It is such

Hidden in the mountains in this depiction of the Albuquerque New Mexico Temple is an image of Jesus Christ as the Good Shepherd. His flock of sheep is found in the clouds and among the mountain peaks. The tall stone monument honoring the Mormon Battalion is subtly included in the lower right corner.

a laborious and complicated task that she was able to complete an average of only six inches in two days.

Native American pottery is found throughout the temple. Original oil paintings depict the Rio Grande River and other landscapes typical of the region. The colors in the wallpaper and paint show natural earth tones.

The temple has ten groups of windows, six on the west, and two on the north and south. Each window group is made up of twelve smaller windows, for a total of 120 small window openings. Each one of these smaller windows features a simple Native American border. Within the windows in the celestial room are six stylized handwoven baskets.

On the east side of the temple are ordinance rooms, a chapel, sealing rooms, and the celestial room. Contrasted by the darker cherry woods on the west side, all of the woodwork on the east side is painted white. The crown moldings, the decorative molding on the walls, and the doors are painted white.

The beauty of the celestial room is enhanced by its nine-foot-tall, 1,750 pound Austrian crystal chandelier. The ceiling is decorated by a beautifully detailed gold leaf design that an artist took four days to paint. Two matching mirrors on two facing walls reach to the thirty-foot ceiling. Standing in the middle and looking into the reflecting mirrors gives one an impression of eternity.

In dedicating the temple, President Hinckley prayed, "May [the temple] be a house of quiet contemplation concerning the eternal nature of life and of Thy divine plan for Thy sons and daughters as they walk the road of immortality and eternal life."[4]

May their minds be lifted to visions of eternity

Oaxaca México Temple

Bless those who come as patrons, that they may come with clean hands and pure hearts to do the work for which this sacred structure has been designed. When they leave here, having served thee according to thy pattern, may they return to their homes with an added sense of their great responsibilities as husbands and wives, and as parents who have a binding responsibility to bring up their children in light and truth.

— FROM THE DEDICATORY PRAYER

Most of the state of Oaxaca (pronounced "wah-HAH-kah"), located in southeastern Mexico, includes a mountain range that is home to some of the highest peaks and volcanoes in the country. Below these great mountains lie the Oaxaca Valley and the city of Oaxaca. The temple, widely appreciated as one of the most beautiful buildings in the city, is located on a major boulevard near a university in the Candiani sector of Oaxaca. With more than three million residents, this centuries-old city is known for its colonial architecture and religious traditions.

The archaeologically rich region—known as "land of the temples" because of its many ancient ruins—is situated on the relatively narrow strip of land near the southeastern end of Mexico. Just outside the city of Oaxaca are the ancient Monte Alban ruins; the state of Oaxaca was a center of ancient Mesoamerican cultures.

Because earthquakes are an ever-present possibility in this area of Mexico, the temple was built on pilings to make it as earthquake proof as possible. Two major earthquakes tested the temple before its construction was even complete. The first, a

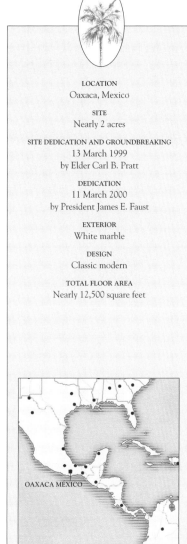

LOCATION
Oaxaca, Mexico

SITE
Nearly 2 acres

SITE DEDICATION AND GROUNDBREAKING
13 March 1999
by Elder Carl B. Pratt

DEDICATION
11 March 2000
by President James E. Faust

EXTERIOR
White marble

DESIGN
Classic modern

TOTAL FLOOR AREA
Nearly 12,500 square feet

OAXACA MEXICO

6.5 quake with its epicenter two hundred miles north of Oaxaca, occurred in July 1999 as the temple's footings were being put into place. The next earthquake was much closer and more severe. On 30 September, as the temple's exterior walls were nearing completion, a three-minute, 7.6 earthquake struck.

The temple's project manager, Jay Erekson, described the event. "As we were running out of the temple, the ground was moving up and down six to eight inches. I stood there and watched as the windows went out of square in both directions. The temple's tower was whipping back and forth four or five feet. As I watched it happen, I started to cry because I thought, 'Our temple is ruined.' I thought that we would have to tear it down and start over again."

More than one hundred buildings in the city were destroyed by the quake or damaged to the degree that they were later condemned. After the disaster, instruments were used to check every angle and line of the temple. "When we were through, we discovered that the temple had not moved a millimeter out of square or out of plumb. It was a miracle," said Brother Erekson.[1]

After the building was completed and furnishings and paintings placed throughout, once-irreverent construction workers gained new respect for the temple. "The whole mood in the temple changed," noticed Brother Erekson. "Prior to that time, guys would yell down the hall to each other and run back and forth. But once the furnishings were in, and the workers noticed the paintings of the Savior on the wall, the mood of all the workers changed. Without any instigation, they began to walk, not run, and they would talk only in a whisper. It was something that came from inside of them."[2]

More than ten thousand visitors toured the temple during its open house. One guest commented, "One feels a peace there, a tranquillity. It is heavenly!" A member said, with tears in his eyes, that he knew that "the Lord loves us very much, and having this temple in our city now makes it seem He has come closer to us."[3] Following the open house, full-time missionaries began visiting a thousand people who had requested more information about the gospel.

Although the Oaxaca Mexico Temple has the same architectural design as other smaller temples, many of its decorative features are unique to the area and culture. Temple designers made special efforts to visit the area and become acquainted with its people, customs, and culture. Their research is reflected in the temple's unique Mexican decor. For example, two original oil paintings of local landscapes are prominently displayed inside. One depicts a nearby lake of historical significance and the other the northern mountains of Oaxaca. A colorful handwoven rug, made with natural dyes, is hung in the temple's foyer.

The Church's seventy-fourth operating temple—Mexico's fifth—was dedicated 11 March 2000 in four sessions by President James E. Faust, second counselor in the First Presidency. It was the first temple dedicated by President Faust. Speaking in behalf of local members, he said in the dedicatory prayer, "We have longed for the day when a house of the Lord would be built nearer to us that we might come here often and worship Thee in spirit and in truth, and receive those ordinances, for both the living and the dead, which lead to immortality and eternal life through the great Atonement wrought by our Redeemer, Thy Beloved Son."[4]

The temple has provided new possibilities for service among local members, eighteen thousand of whom attended its dedication. It has opened the door for frequent temple attendance for members whose obedience and dedication was demonstrated through the years by their willingness to expend their time and resources in traveling to the nearest temple in Mexico City. Now they are able to spend their time *within* the temple rather than traveling to and from the temple for days.

Howard G. Schmidt, who was a temple sealer in the Colonia Juárez Chihuahua Mexico Temple before being called as the Oaxaca Mexico Temple president, said many have volunteered to work in the temple.

One longtime member who serves as a temple worker is Cleotilde Alvarez de Melchor, a widowed mother of thirteen children. Sister Melchor remembers when men, women, and children worked to build the first Oaxaca meetinghouse. Members sold their televisions, watches, jewelry, and food to pay for the building. From that sacrifice, she said, "We have had more blessings than I can enumerate," one of which is the new temple.[5]

. . . come with clean hands and pure hearts to do the work for which this sacred structure has been designed

Tuxtla Gutiérrez México Temple

Father, as thy sons and daughters assembled in this thy holy house, we look to thee with love as we do to thy Son. We pray that we may always remember the covenants we have made with thee. We pray that we may grow in thy favor, and partake of thy divine spirit.

—FROM THE DEDICATORY PRAYER

Sparkling white marble and crisp, clean lines make the temple a visible landmark in Tuxtla Gutierrez, the capital city of Mexico's southernmost state, Chiapas, which is bordered on the east by the forests of Guatemala. The region has fascinated archaeologists for generations. Hundreds of ancient ruins and artifacts found in the area indicate that it was home to a highly developed culture between 500 and 300 B.C. The city—now home to more than three hundred thousand—is nestled in a valley among the mountains that cover much of Mexico's isthmus. In 1957, on a mountain overlooking the city, Elder Howard W. Hunter, of the Quorum of the Twelve Apostles, dedicated this area for the preaching of the gospel.

Local Church members rejoiced when the First Presidency announced in March 1999 that a temple would be built in Tuxtla Gutierrez. Seven-year-old Ingrid Fabiola Martinez Barredo was so excited that she told everyone she knew. "Temples are where dads and moms can be married for eternity!" she said. "Temples are where families can be sealed together forever!"[1] When Ingrid was five, she and her parents had traveled eighteen hours on a crowded bus to the Mexico

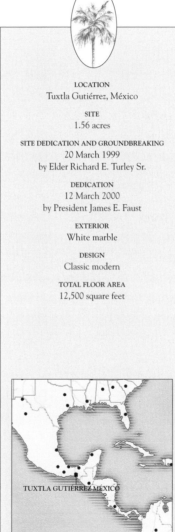

LOCATION
Tuxtla Gutiérrez, México

SITE
1.56 acres

SITE DEDICATION AND GROUNDBREAKING
20 March 1999
by Elder Richard E. Turley Sr.

DEDICATION
12 March 2000
by President James E. Faust

EXTERIOR
White marble

DESIGN
Classic modern

TOTAL FLOOR AREA
12,500 square feet

TUXTLA GUTIÉRREZ MÉXICO

City Mexico Temple to be sealed as an eternal family. It is no wonder she rejoiced at the idea of a temple in her own "backyard."

Like Ingrid and her family, members in the area have always been faithful in attending the temple despite inconvenient circumstances. Prior to the dedication of the Mexico City Mexico Temple, members living in Tuxtla would travel some twenty-two hundred miles to the Mesa Arizona Temple to perform ordinance work and be sealed to their spouses. Enrique Sanchez Casillas, Tuxtla Gutierrez Mexico Temple president, served as district president during this time. He recalled, "In order to finance the annual trips to Arizona, members would often sell their possessions, including land, cars, furniture, or typewriters. In those days we could only attend the temple once a year. We had to travel four or five days and nights non-stop to Mesa. All of our children would come along with us. In a bus there may have been forty adults and twenty to forty kids—every one of us had a child. It was a real group effort."[2]

When the Mexico City Mexico Temple was dedicated in 1983, members continued to make stake temple excursions every three months. With the dedication of the temple in Tuxtla—an hour-long trip for most—members now have the opportunity to visit the house of the Lord as often as they like.

On 20 March 1999, Elder Richard E. Turley Sr. of the Seventy and first counselor in the Mexico South Area presidency, said that "new life in the springtime" had come as ground was broken for the Tuxtla Gutierrez Mexico Temple. Speaking at the groundbreaking ceremony, Elder Turley observed that "the greatest gift we have received on this earth is the Atonement of the Lord Jesus Christ. But another great gift from the Lord is to have the essential keys to do temple work, which is essential to prepare the world for the Second Coming of the Lord, and to help us gain eternal life with our Heavenly Father."[3] Among the 297 Latter-day Saints attending the groundbreaking were many third-generation members of the Church.

When construction began, a group of masonry construction workers arrived from a little town called San Lucas. After working for several weeks, the workers knew they were building a temple but did not understand the significance if it. While working in the temple, these construction workers became acquainted with the full-time missionaries and accepted them into their homes to hear the gospel. Four workers and their families, totaling sixteen people, accepted the gospel and were baptized members of the Church. These families then made plans to be sealed in the temple they helped to construct.[4]

Local members contributed to the temple by helping to landscape the grounds, planting trees and flowers in the area. Indians living in nearby San Cristobal made traditional, hand-embroidered blouses that are displayed on the walls of the temple's entry room. Handmade wool rugs of indigenous colors and patterns are also on display.

When the building was completed and dedicated on 12 March 2000, residents were grateful to have such a lovely building in their town. More than eight thousand people attended the open house. As the public left the temple, they used words like "amazing" and "unbelievable" to describe their experience. Many agreed that the white marble temple was the most beautiful building in the entire city, saying, "We need more buildings like this; it is wonderful!"[5] Nearly one thousand referrals were received during the open house, and some four thousand members attended the temple's four dedicatory sessions.

We pray that we may grow in thy favor, and partake of thy divine spirit

Louisville Kentucky Temple

Located on a forested hill about twelve miles northeast of Louisville, the Louisville Kentucky Temple stands next to the Crestwood Ward chapel. Although the basic design is similar to that of other small temples, the celestial room in the Louisville Kentucky Temple is slightly larger, which makes the temple appear larger.

From the earliest stages of the temple's construction, it was made clear to contractors that only the best of materials and workmanship would be accepted. As a reminder of the significance of the work they were doing, an image of Jesus Christ was hung in the construction trailer. Beneath the picture were the words, "This is who we are working for; this is the Savior, our Redeemer."

As construction progressed and the roof was completed, this picture and message were moved inside the temple lobby. Elder Marvin Prestridge, a construction missionary, described the effect the picture had on workers. "It set the tone for how we felt about the temple. It made quite an impression on the crew. They understood why we wanted the high quality we did."[1]

Even a city building inspector joked about the high quality of the temple. He said he would never have to worry about the temple because the Church had much stricter building codes than the city.[2]

The stunning whiteness of the temple's marble exterior is the result of a laborious selection process. As the polished, Danby Vermont marble arrived on site, Elder Prestridge selected only the whitest, rejecting more than 40 percent of the incoming stone. Elder Prestridge estimates that he handled just under two hundred thousand pounds of marble.[3]

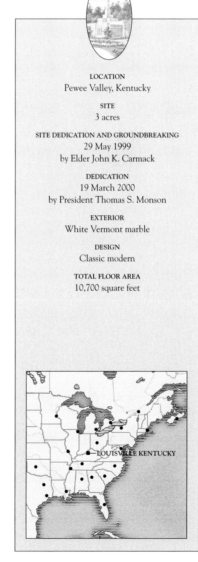

LOCATION
Pewee Valley, Kentucky

SITE
3 acres

SITE DEDICATION AND GROUNDBREAKING
29 May 1999
by Elder John K. Carmack

DEDICATION
19 March 2000
by President Thomas S. Monson

EXTERIOR
White Vermont marble

DESIGN
Classic modern

TOTAL FLOOR AREA
10,700 square feet

One faithful and energetic construction worker on the project was not an employee of the general contractor and never received payment for his services. Woodford "Woody" Hatton, a stake patriarch, volunteered his time to work on the temple nearly every day from the time the foundation was poured until the landscaping was completed. The only days he did not work on the site of the Louisville Kentucky Temple were the days he served in the St. Louis Missouri Temple as a sealer. The seventy-five-year-old did anything he was asked to do, including pushing wheelbarrows full of dirt and concrete, sweeping floors, picking up trash, and helping with framing.

Elder Prestridge described Brother Hatton as "'the man who knows.' He was able to explain things in a very simple and lovely way, so that people who did not know anything about the gospel could really understand.

"Brother Hatton loved to answer questions about the temple. He loves the temple—he is a part of this temple, and the temple is a part of him."[4]

Young women from local stakes had a memorable experience hanging crystals on the temple's chandeliers. Working in shifts, the young sisters were awed by what they were doing. As they assembled the chandeliers, they joined in singing songs about the temple.

"They had very beautiful high soprano voices, and it made you think there were groups of angels singing in the temple," said Sister Karla Packer Prestridge, a temple construction missionary and Elder Prestridge's wife. When the chandelier was raised into its permanent position in the celestial room, she continued, "many of the girls said, 'When I get married in

Louisville Kentucky Temple

May this house stand as an expression of thy love for thy children. May the peace of the Lord be here. May there be quiet and reverence. May this be a house of worship wherein thy holy name and that of thy Son are spoken in praise unto thee and unto him.

—FROM THE DEDICATORY PRAYER

Louisville

this temple, I can come and say that I helped with the crystals on that chandelier.'"[5]

Valerie Blackwell contributed to the temple project by serving long hours as the temple committee public affairs director. Sister Blackwell recounted how quickly the temple construction was organized and completed. She compared the project with the parable of the ten virgins:

"When the announcement [of this new temple] was made, everyone was completely surprised, and the time for preparation was past," she said. "We were either with or without oil in our lamps. We were called into service immediately, without the luxury of a lot of scripture reading or personal preparation. We had to do what we had to do in an incredibly short amount of time—this temple was built in about nine months from the time of its groundbreaking. We now look up at the temple and say to ourselves, 'This is the Lord's work undoubtedly. We are happy to have had even a drop of oil in our lamps so that we could help pull this off.'"[6]

Project superintendent Don Poulsen also felt deeply honored to take part in the temple's construction. Commenting on blessings that had transpired during construction, Brother

The image hidden in this drawing is of the Savior kneeling in prayer.

Poulsen said, "In this season of temple building, I do not think it is a coincidence that the United States has had one of the warmest winters in recorded history. Call it what you want, but I think the Lord controls it all. From groundbreaking until there was a roof on the temple, we lost fewer than five days to weather." Another blessing came after an adhesive necessary for exterior marble installation was out of stock throughout the East. "I prayed, asking for direction from my Heavenly Father," said Brother Poulsen. "After spending half a day on the phone, I found some. It was shipped overnight, and we only lost one day of construction."[7]

Brother Poulsen's son, Ben, worked on the project to earn money for his mission. When the temple was nearly completed, Ben joined his father in the cab of the crane and helped place the statue of the angel Moroni on the temple's spire, an unforgettable experience for both father and son.

As his calling to assist in the temple's construction came to an end, Elder Prestridge said, "I think that this is true, not just about this temple but about all temples: the Lord built this temple; we just helped. We are just his hands on the earth, but he built the temple. The Spirit was there, right from the very first."[8]

Palmyra New York Temple

Nestled on a hillside, the Palmyra New York Temple overlooks the Sacred Grove. "I regard this temple as perhaps the most significant, in one respect," President Gordon B. Hinckley said at the spring 1999 groundbreaking, "in the entire Church. This is where it all began. . . . From this place, this work has spread over the earth to more than 160 nations."[1]

The temple is built within the boundaries of the original one hundred acres purchased by the Smith family in 1818. Preparing the hillside for the temple site required that nearly half a million cubic yards of dirt be excavated from the hill. "We literally moved a small mountain," said the temple architect, David Richards. The hillside had to be leveled without disturbing a rock wall just east of where the temple was to be built. "It is believed that the rock wall was laid up there by the Smiths as they cleared their field," said Brother Richards. "They probably took the rocks out of the dirt and piled them up along their property boundary."[2]

The white granite for the exterior was specifically selected and finished to give the temple its exquisite brightness. It was quarried near Sharon, Vermont, where Joseph Smith was born. "That is why this granite was chosen instead of marble," says Brother Richards.[3]

Brother Richards's architectural design included engraved symbols on the temple exterior. Sun, moon, and star stones detail the exterior temple walls. Stones on the perimeter of the temple depict twenty-one different phases of the moon at moonrise in two-week intervals. These phases begin on the center of the temple's south side, above a stained glass window depicting the tree of life. The date of this moon phase represents 6 April 2000, the date of the temple's dedication. The

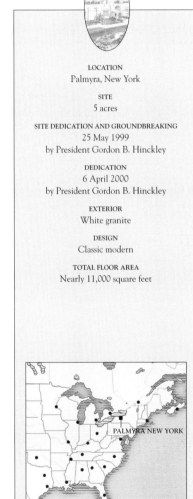

LOCATION
Palmyra, New York

SITE
5 acres

SITE DEDICATION AND GROUNDBREAKING
25 May 1999
by President Gordon B. Hinckley

DEDICATION
6 April 2000
by President Gordon B. Hinckley

EXTERIOR
White granite

DESIGN
Classic modern

TOTAL FLOOR AREA
Nearly 11,000 square feet

PALMYRA NEW YORK

moonstone found on the center of the temple's west side represents 27 June 1844, the date of the Prophet Joseph's martyrdom. "We oriented the phases so that moonstone would face due west to the Sacred Grove," Brother Richards explained.[4]

The sun and star stones of the temple are on the spire. There are four sunstones, each one facing a cardinal direction of the compass. Each sunstone has thirty-three rays of light, representing the number of years of the Savior's mortal existence. Higher on the spire are three stars adorning each of its four sides, totaling twelve stars. This design refers to the symbolic meanings represented by the numbers three and twelve.

Adding to the beauty and spirit of the Palmyra New York Temple are intricate works of handcrafted stained glass art. Equaling the awe-inspiring beauty of the art glass are the spiritual messages and stories behind the glass. Tom Holdman and a crew of eight completed in just over four months what under normal circumstances would have required a year. They constructed twenty-seven exterior windows, the front doors and side panels, an octagonal baptistry skylight, and a mural window depicting Joseph Smith's first vision. Adding beauty to the trees depicted in the windows are sixty-five hundred handmade leaves with beveled edges. In all, the glass designs required sixteen thousand individually cut pieces and more than a mile of lead to hold the pieces in place.

"The First Vision work alone contains over fourteen hundred intricate pieces of glass," says Brother Holdman. "All of the items in this rendition point to the Father and the Son. Branches, Joseph's arm, Joseph's hat, rays of light—all bring the viewer's eye to the Father and the Son."[5] Originally,

Palmyra New York Temple

May the sacred work that will be accomplished here be a constant reminder of thy love for thy children of all generations and of the provision thou hast made for their eternal progress and happiness. This house speaks of the everlasting covenant between thee and thy children. All that will take place herein will be concerned with the things of eternity. It stands as a monument to all the world of the certain immortality of the human soul.

—FROM THE DEDICATORY PRAYER

Palmyra

Brother Holdman was asked to create only the First Vision window. But desiring to continue the theme of the Sacred Grove, he proposed that stained glass be added throughout the temple.

Both the architect and President Hinckley agreed that it would be appropriate if the trees in the stained glass windows gave visitors the impression of being in the Sacred Grove; however, because of the strict budget, a private donor was needed to pay for the windows. The first person Brother Holdman called replied, "Two weeks ago we were in the celestial room of the Mount Timpanogos Temple and felt impressed that we should donate money for the Palmyra Temple."[6]

Brother Holdman included spiritual messages in his glass designs. "All of the grove trees are made of clear and white glass," he explained, "because when Heavenly Father and Jesus Christ were in the grove, all of their light would have washed out the color in the trees."[7]

The entryway to the temple has two sets of doors, both of which are inlaid with tree designs to give the feeling of entering a forest. Within the front doors is a panel containing the tree of knowledge. The baptistry skylight contains twelve trees, symbolic of the twelve tribes of Israel. The leaves on the trees represent the posterity of the twelve tribes.

In the celestial room mural window are seven trees, the seventh being the tree of life. The seven trees represent the seven days of the Creation. Within the tree of life are twelve

A hidden image of the young Joseph Smith is drawn in the lower left, and the vision of the Father and the Son is represented in the upper right. These figures are patterned after those portrayed in the stained glass within the Palmyra New York Temple.

pieces of clear glass representing the fruit found on the tree. The west side of the temple, which faces the Sacred Grove, has windows with trees that are clear, allowing an unobstructed view of the grove.

Saints within the temple district were given the opportunity to help with the project. Primary children prepared personal inscriptions on small stones that were to be used in the foundation. Youth participated by clearing weeds, vines, and small trees on the grounds. Relief Society sisters crocheted squares that were then connected to form seven cloths for the altars. Three thousand hours of service were required to make these cloths. They "represent each sister's best work, her desire to serve the Lord," said Sandy Caton, who supervised the project.[8]

The Palmyra New York Temple was dedicated 6 April 2000, exactly one hundred seventy years after the Church was organized on 6 April 1830. Never before in this dispensation have so many members been able to witness the dedication of a temple.

When the dates were announced, it was also announced that the dedication would be broadcast from the temple in Palmyra to the Salt Lake Tabernacle. The response was tremendous. After ticket requests for the broadcast topped two hundred thousand, the First Presidency decided to broadcast the dedication to all satellite-equipped stake centers in North America. It was estimated that the total number of Latter-day Saints in attendance at the dedication was 1.5 million.[9]

This house speaks of the everlasting covenant between thee and thy children

Fresno California Temple

The Fresno California Temple, which neighbors a local stake center, is on property that was formerly part of twelve thousand acres of fig orchards. In the early 1900s, the area was known as Fig Garden, and boasted one of the largest concentrations of figs in the world. Fresno, in central San Joaquin Valley, is one of the largest food-producing regions in the United States.

Preliminary plans for the Fresno California Temple originated in 1997, after President Gordon B. Hinckley announced in October conference the concept of smaller temples. The presidency of the Fresno California West Stake immediately wrote to President Hinckley, suggesting to him the location where the temple now stands. The letter explained how Fresno was ready for a temple: Latter-day Saints in the area had a longstanding reputation for having the highest temple attendance in the Oakland California Temple district, despite having to travel some two hundred miles to do so.[1]

In the fall of 1998, Church representatives went to Fresno to look into the possibility of building a temple there. Efforts were made to get approval from city planners, local residents, and the city council. According to the director of the Church's temple construction department, this was the fastest approval of a temple from conception to obtaining a building permit in the history of the Church. Much of that success was due to the support of the city and local residents. Years before, people in the area were not nearly as receptive to construction of the stake center near which the temple was built. Because of that, similar opposition was expected with the building of the temple. It never materialized, however, because the presence of the stake center had eventually established a positive precedent of Latter-day Saint influence in the neighborhood.

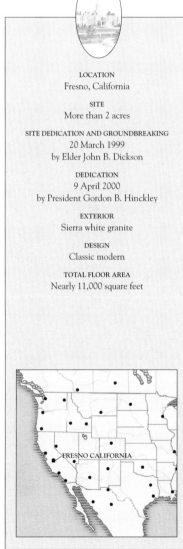

LOCATION
Fresno, California

SITE
More than 2 acres

SITE DEDICATION AND GROUNDBREAKING
20 March 1999
by Elder John B. Dickson

DEDICATION
9 April 2000
by President Gordon B. Hinckley

EXTERIOR
Sierra white granite

DESIGN
Classic modern

TOTAL FLOOR AREA
Nearly 11,000 square feet

FRESNO CALIFORNIA

To ensure continued good public relations, local Church leadership organized a proactive door-to-door approach to address any concerns or questions about the temple from the community. Of the ninety-one residents contacted, eighty-five said they supported the building of the temple. More than nine hundred citizens attended the city council's neighborhood meeting, organized to discuss the proposed temple and its effect on the community. At the conclusion of this meeting, all but one expressed support for the temple project. This lone dissenter was eventually won over and even participated in the groundbreaking. The cooperative support furthered the temple's progress without delay. During the 1999 Christmas season, Church youth showed their appreciation to nearly three hundred neighbors living near the temple by going door-to-door caroling.[2]

Mature olives trees, chosen both for their Christian symbolism and for their importance as a local agricultural crop, beautify the approach to the front of the temple. The Sierra white granite of the temple exterior was chosen because it is the same as that of the Oakland California Temple. Latter-day Saints in the Fresno area have attended that temple since its dedication in 1964 and have long been familiar with its appearance. It was hoped that the use of the same recognizable granite would quickly make the new temple feel "like home" for Fresno members.[3]

Continuing that impression on the inside, the celestial room was enlarged slightly from the standard plan for smaller temples to accommodate a larger number of anticipated patrons. Two original oil paintings rendered by local artists also beautify the temple's interior. One of these, painted by Mark Gudmundsen, is a scene of nearby Yosemite Valley. The other,

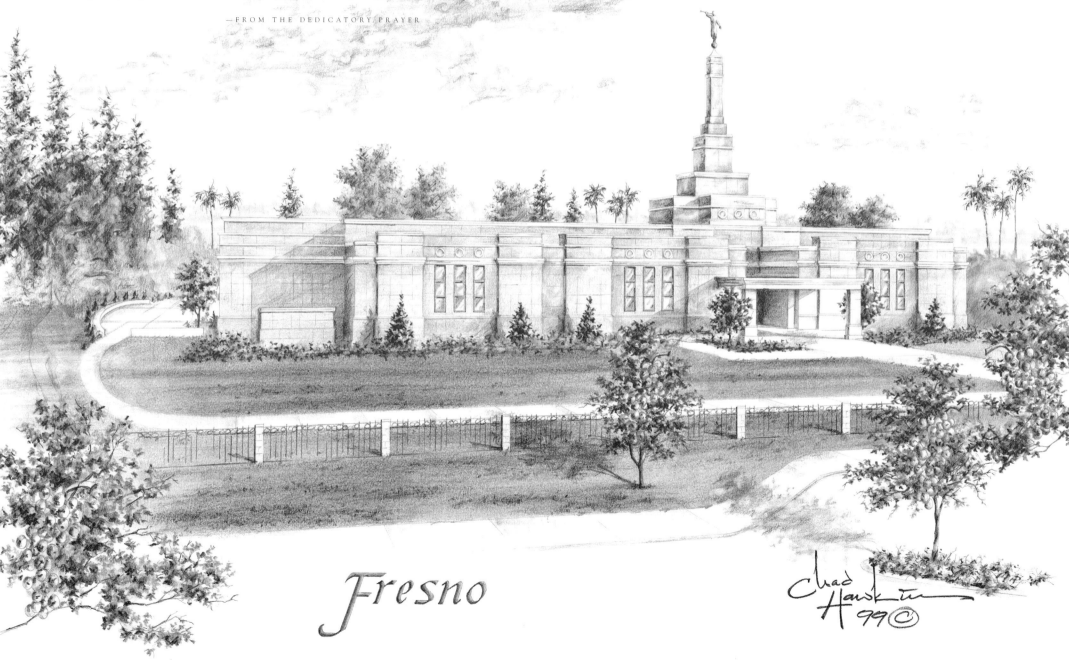

Fresno California Temple

Wilt thou bless all who will serve within this sacred structure. They will come here to assist in bringing to pass thy work and thy glory, even the immortality and eternal life of man. May they not weary in well doing. May they be blessed with strength and vitality to carry on the rigorous activity which lies before them.

—FROM THE DEDICATORY PRAYER

Fresno

Chad Hawkins '99 ©

painted by David Dalton, depicts several familiar features of the San Joaquin Valley, including oak trees, rolling foothills beneath the Sierra Mountains, and lush vineyards. Brother Dalton's great-grandfather used his skills as a woodworker to beautify the Cardston Alberta Temple. Remembering his ancestor's contributions, Brother Dalton said, "In a way I felt that I was carrying on a tradition by donating my talents to the temple."[4]

At the open house, tours were planned for leaders of other religious denominations in Fresno. Members of the North America West Area presidency and local area authority seventies conducted most of these tours. James R. Maxwell, president of the Fresno West Stake, was asked to conduct several tours for local religious leaders unable to make the original tour dates. At the conclusion of one tour, "the pastors of the two largest congregations in Fresno took me aside and expressed their interest in fostering positive, cooperative relationships," said President Maxwell.

"Another minister who arrived to take the temple's public tour was very concerned about the amount the Church had spent on the temple. However, following the tour he said, 'When I was in that temple, I felt the presence of God. To give people a chance to come somewhere and feel the presence of God has to be something of very great value. While you have

The Fresno area is rich in beautiful vineyards. Hidden images of the Savior and clusters of grapes symbolize that Christ is the Master of the Vineyard.

spent a lot, what you have acquired with that expenditure is truly worth a great deal.'"[5] During the eight-day open house, more than fifty-one thousand visitors toured the temple.

The temple was dedicated on 9 April 2000 by President Gordon B. Hinckley. Elder M. Russell Ballard of the Quorum of the Twelve Apostles and Elder William R. Bradford of the Seventy also attended. "What a beautiful morning!" President Hinckley announced to about twelve thousand people who were gathered outside for the cornerstone ceremony. "I've never been in Fresno on a more beautiful morning."[6]

Ten thousand Saints attended the four dedicatory sessions. Among them were Higinio Rodriguez and his family, who were thrilled to visit after the dedication with their former bishop, Bryan Pratt.

Brother Pratt had been the bishop when Higinio and his family investigated and joined the Church. "It took a long time," Brother Rodriguez remembered. "I was not converted by the elders; I was converted by Alma [in the Book of Mormon]." Brother Pratt gladly took a photograph of the Rodriguez family in front of the newly dedicated temple that stands as a symbol of a different kind of growth in the fertile valley.[7]

They will come here to assist in bringing to pass thy work and thy glory

Medford Oregon Temple

The Medford Oregon Temple is situated in the community of Central Point in the beautiful Rogue River Valley. Four miles northwest of Medford and thirty-five miles north of the California border, the temple is Oregon's second—the first being in Portland. The sacred edifice reflects the building of the lives and testimonies of those involved with its construction and operation, from the contractor who laid the concrete to the Church members who serve in the temple.

In 1924, Elder Melvin J. Ballard of the Quorum of the Twelve Apostles visited the nearby city of Grants Pass to speak at a conference. During his remarks, he promised that someday a temple would be built in the Rogue River Valley. Seventy-six years later the Medford Oregon Temple was dedicated, fulfilling that promise.[1]

Surrounding the temple grounds are farmlands, a creek, and residential neighborhoods. Nearby is the Central Point Stake center. Years ago, the Church acquired the property on which the stake center is located, intending to build on five acres and sell the remainder. But Bishop Rosecrans, the agent bishop and eventually patriarch of the Central Point Stake, felt strongly that the land should be kept, and it was used for some time as a community garden. That extra acreage now provides an ideal setting for the temple.

A prayer meeting was held every morning before work began during construction. The main petition was that the workers would not become casual about the spirit that existed at the temple site. The result was a strong unity among all who worked there.

Elder Ross Woodward, who served as a temple construction missionary, said, "There was a wonderful spirit about the work we were doing, which permeated the hearts of the workers. All workers, both members and nonmembers, took pride in building the temple."[2]

During construction, a beautiful painting of a recently completed temple was placed on an easel at the temple's entryway. Along the bottom of the painting was the saying, "May everyone laboring herein feel peace in their lives as they help build this temple to our Father in Heaven and the Savior Jesus Christ." In another area was a small architectural rendering of the Medford Oregon Temple with a statement that read, "Together we are building a temple," reminding workers of their goal.

Because they were building the house of the Lord, the workers tried to be perfect in their labors. One worker was told that everything on the temple had to be as exact as if he were "building a piano."[3]

Building the temple was a particularly significant experience for one construction worker, not a Church member, who said, "I have worked on almost every kind of project in my life, and last year I prayed that someday I could help build a church. This temple is really an answer to prayer."[4]

The Medford Oregon Temple district spans a large area of northern California and southern Oregon. Local leaders wanted each of the nearly twenty-nine thousand Church members living in the district to feel invested in the new temple. They knew that when it was completed, much of the Saints' time and effort would be needed to keep it busy, so they used the construction period to motivate members to "lengthen their stride" in Church and temple service.

One project that helped accomplish that goal involved

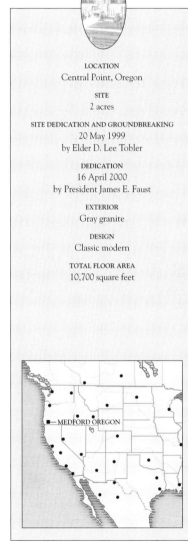

LOCATION
Central Point, Oregon

SITE
2 acres

SITE DEDICATION AND GROUNDBREAKING
20 May 1999
by Elder D. Lee Tobler

DEDICATION
16 April 2000
by President James E. Faust

EXTERIOR
Gray granite

DESIGN
Classic modern

TOTAL FLOOR AREA
10,700 square feet

MEDFORD OREGON

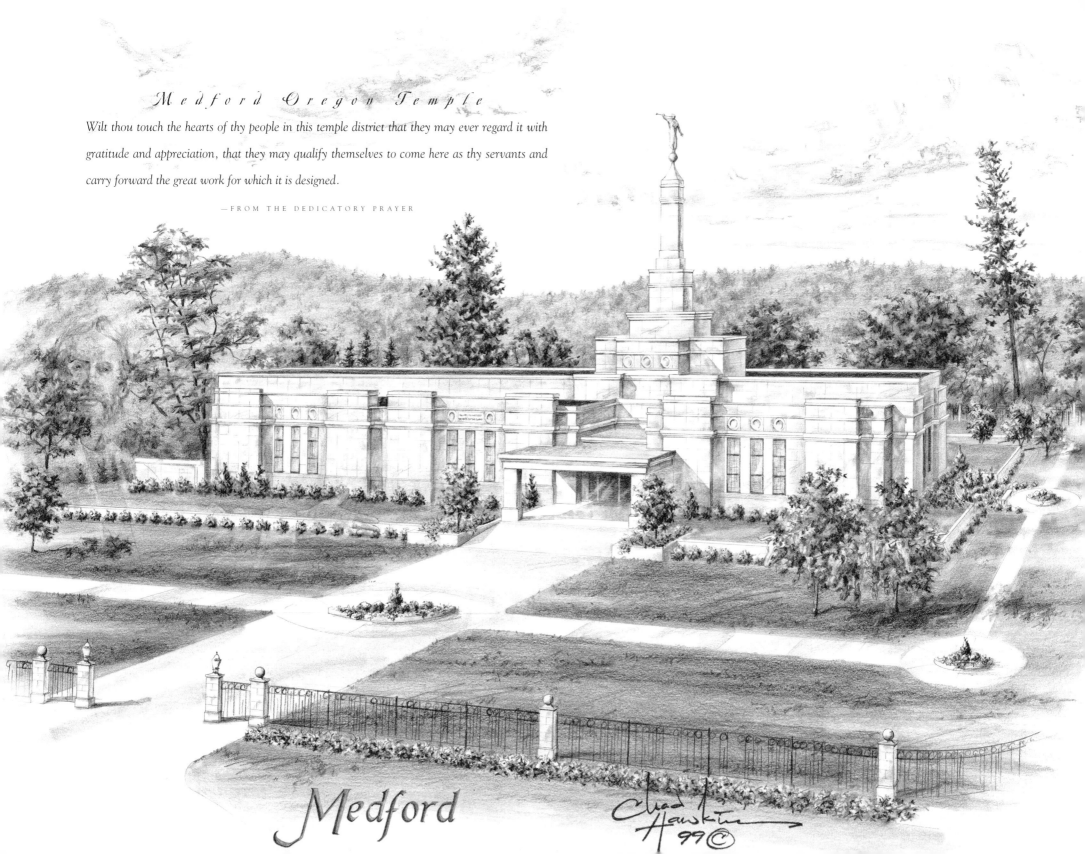

Medford Oregon Temple

Wilt thou touch the hearts of thy people in this temple district that they may ever regard it with gratitude and appreciation, that they may qualify themselves to come here as thy servants and carry forward the great work for which it is designed.

—FROM THE DEDICATORY PRAYER

Medford

gathering many rounded stones, which Church members cleaned and sealed with varnish. Upon each stone was then written "Lengthening their stride" and the names of the stakes, wards, and branches of the temple district. Before the cement was poured to form the foundation, these special stones were carefully positioned beneath the place where the celestial room would be built.

Continuing to encourage the Saints to lengthen their stride, members of area stakes asked me to draw the new temple. Thousands of prints of the drawing were distributed to remind adults and youth to prepare themselves to enter the house of the Lord.

The entrance to the temple features a water fountain cascading over a one-ton block of granite left over from construction of the Conference Center in Salt Lake City. To keep the building project within its established budget, the water fountain was funded locally and assembled using donated labor.

Nearly forty-six thousand people attended the seven-day open house, triple the number anticipated. The outstanding turnout was largely due to publicity efforts made by the temple

Hidden among the trees is an image of the Savior and, near the baptistry, the images of four oxen.

committee. Three television networks ran daily updates about the progress being made on the temple. Published in nineteen area newspapers, a sixteen-page insert contained an invitation to the open house, historical and doctrinal information about the Church, and a copy of "The Family: A Proclamation to the World." A quarter of a million inserts were printed and distributed.

One nonmember visitor from California had read about the open house in the newspaper and said to her husband, "This is an opportunity for an educational experience we may never have again." Together they decided to tour the temple. Afterward, the woman commented that she "just shivered" as she walked through the edifice, "due to the sweet feeling inside."[5]

Among the contents of the time capsule placed in the temple's cornerstone is the Medford Oregon Temple history, which covers everything from the groundbreaking for the temple to its dedication. Included in this history is an excerpt of a letter written by a local Catholic priest after he attended the open house. "Thank you very much for your kindness and hospitality," read the letter, "and may God bless you and bring all of us—indeed all of His children—into the Father's eternal kingdom."[6]

. . . that they may qualify themselves to come here as thy servants and carry forward the great work for which it is designed

Memphis Tennessee Temple

The Memphis Tennessee Temple is located northeast of Memphis in the suburb of Bartlett, near the banks of the Mississippi River. The property on which the temple stands was previously used for growing cotton and soybeans. Nearby historical sites, including several homes dating back to the Civil War, give visitors a glimpse into Southern life.

The Church had humble beginnings in Tennessee. Elder Wilford Woodruff was the first missionary who visited Memphis to preach the restored gospel. Traveling by foot and canoe from Liberty, Missouri, Elder Woodruff arrived dirty, penniless, and alone. His companion had returned home, but Elder Woodruff carried on, and the exhaustion of three months' travel did not deter him from going into Josiah Jackson's inn to preach for an hour and a half.[1]

The life of the early Saints in Memphis and the mid South was marked by persecution and suffering, and yet in spite of that, the Church has continued to grow. Only a month after the Memphis Tennessee Temple was dedicated, the state became home to yet another dedicated temple—in Nashville.

When the temple site near Memphis was first acquired by the Church, it was intended for the building of the Memphis North Stake center. Only three acres were necessary for the new stake center, but the site totaled more than six acres.

Former Memphis North Stake president David Denton remembered approving the property's purchase. "I was hesitant to purchase the site because of the excess acreage. After pondering for some time on the property acquisition, my counselors and I agreed that the extra property would be a benefit to the new stake center."[2] This extra property eventually because the site for a house of the Lord.

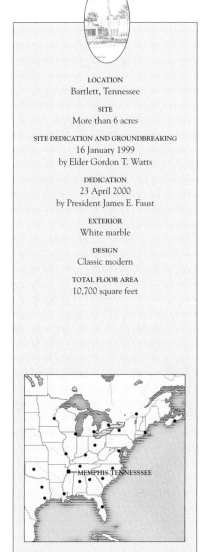

LOCATION
Bartlett, Tennessee

SITE
More than 6 acres

SITE DEDICATION AND GROUNDBREAKING
16 January 1999
by Elder Gordon T. Watts

DEDICATION
23 April 2000
by President James E. Faust

EXTERIOR
White marble

DESIGN
Classic modern

TOTAL FLOOR AREA
10,700 square feet

MEMPHIS TENNESSEE

Through the years, Church members in the Memphis area have been assigned to four different temple districts, including Mesa, Arizona; Washington D. C.; Atlanta, Georgia; and St. Louis, Missouri. The long trips to these distant temples were difficult for the Saints.

When the Nashville Tennessee Temple was announced, Latter-day Saints in the Memphis area felt their dreams of having a temple close to home had finally come true. They were overcome when, only a short time later, another announcement was made that a temple would be built right in Memphis.

Church members in some stakes in what would be the new temple district prepared for the temple by focusing on family history research. The Church's Internet genealogy resources and its *FamilySearch*™ program were explained in family history seminars and then used by members to prepare their ancestors' information for temple work. In 1999 nearly two thousand people used the resources provided, logging more than twenty-five hundred hours on the genealogical computers in these stakes.[3]

Although the Memphis Tennessee Temple uses the same basic design as the other smaller temples, its plans contain more than two hundred revisions. One of the most significant is the lowered and slightly shortened art glass windows. Because of this change, visitors both inside and outside the temple can see the windows in their full splendor. To contrast with them, the windows in the baptistry and celestial room were left at their original height and position.[4]

Every effort was made to construct the temple as quickly as possible. Favorable weather conditions were a tremendous

Memphis Tennessee Temple

Father, we thank thee for this temple. It is an answer to our prayers. It will enrich the lives of countless thousands who will here seek blessings for themselves and stand as proxies in behalf of those who have passed beyond. May hearts leap with joy, and may smiles of satisfaction come to the faces of all who labor herein as they carry forward thy work of salvation and exaltation.

—FROM THE DEDICATORY PRAYER

Memphis

aid in reaching building goals. Sister Trenna Anderson, a temple construction missionary, said:

"When the wet weather came, it always seemed to be during the night or on the weekends. I can remember only three days during the six-month construction period that it rained during construction hours.

"Often the storms would approach the temple from the west, head over the Mississippi River, and then go around us."[5]

One memorable milestone was the placement of the statue of the angel Moroni. The statue was positioned on a Saturday, and all of the workers arriving to help with the statue that day donated their time. About six hundred onlookers gathered along the fence, armed with cameras and video recorders.

The watchers spontaneously joined in singing "The Spirit of God" as the crane hoisted the statue toward the spire. After the statue was successfully placed, the construction worker responsible for raising the statue removed his hard hat in salute.[6]

Detailed beauty can be found in every corner of the temple, from the statue of the angel Moroni and the exterior

Hidden near the temple's entrance is an image of the Savior. Images of four oxen are hidden in the shrubbery outside the baptistry.

walls to the warm whites, ivories, and light beige colors throughout the interior.

Adorning the walls are several oil paintings and a framed quilt. Exquisite chairs add grace and ornamentation to the temple's sealing and celestial rooms. On the backs of the chairs are beautifully carved gold colored leaves. This pattern on the chairs harmonizes with the leaf pattern repeated on ceilings and in the carpets in the sealing rooms.

During Brother David Denton's forty-five years of local Church service, he has been instrumental in preparing the region for a temple. When the open house concluded, he said:

"I suppose that it may be difficult for people who have lived in the proximity of a temple all their lives to understand what the temple means to members living in this area of the world.

"Having a temple so close to home means we now do not have to travel such long distances. So much time has been wasted in travel. Now we can better spend our time doing the work inside the temple.

"It really is marvelous what has been accomplished for people around the world."[7]

May hearts leap with joy, and may smiles of satisfaction come to the faces of all who labor herein

Reno Nevada Temple

Fifteen miles from the California border, the Reno Nevada Temple is the second temple in the Silver State. Surrounding the temple are retaining walls that blend with its environment. Some of the walls are of indigenous stone, and others are made of concrete tinted a desert sand color.

In 1997, after President Gordon B. Hinckley announced the concept of building smaller temples, Reno stakes were among the first to request a temple and then receive approval.

When local leaders are looking for a suitable location for a smaller temple, they give first consideration to Church-owned property near a stake center. If no such property is available, they then see if land adjacent to a stake center can be purchased. If neither of these options is viable, they then consider other sites that might be appropriate for a house of the Lord.

Because the first two options were not feasible in Reno, a committee was organized to find property suitable for a "stand-alone" temple. Eventually, a peaceful site that provides a panoramic view of the city and valley was obtained.[1]

At the groundbreaking ceremony on 24 July 1999, Elder Rex D. Pinegar of the Seventy encouraged the members to complete the temple in the scheduled six months. Project superintendent Vernon C. Forbush said, "We were able to complete this temple because of the united cooperation of members and nonmembers. Many of the contractors have told me on different occasions that they have felt the spirit of the temple and they know that it is a special place. We found ourselves doing things far above our ability. . . .

"If there is one thing that needs to be emphasized, it's the

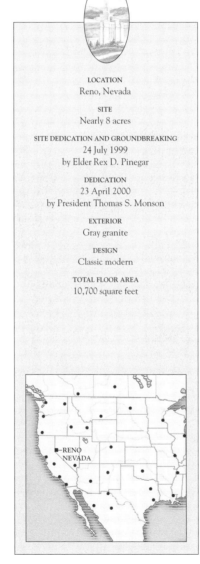

LOCATION
Reno, Nevada

SITE
Nearly 8 acres

SITE DEDICATION AND GROUNDBREAKING
24 July 1999
by Elder Rex D. Pinegar

DEDICATION
23 April 2000
by President Thomas S. Monson

EXTERIOR
Gray granite

DESIGN
Classic modern

TOTAL FLOOR AREA
10,700 square feet

spirit of service—that is what got this temple finished in the time in which it was finished."[2]

From the earliest stages of construction, the temple's architect made it clear to all workers that only the highest quality of materials and workmanship was acceptable. He explained to workers, "You are going to do things you never thought you were going to do. We do things almost perfectly."

Although speed was a constant factor in the construction, the quality of workmanship was never sacrificed.[3]

In an effort to foster positive relations with the temple's neighbors, Church members were asked to refrain from driving to the temple site during construction. With such overwhelming enthusiasm for the new temple, obeying this counsel was indeed a sacrifice for members.

Local Latter-day Saints willingly donated their time and talents to the temple's construction. For example, members of a small branch installed the site's flagpole, stake presidencies and bishoprics put in the oxen for the baptismal font, and a youth group cleaned the font.[4]

Although the Reno Nevada Temple has the same floor plan as most of the other smaller temples, a vestibule was added and the doorway moved to the north. This prevents the constant westerly winds of Reno from entering the temple.

There is also an almost imperceptible difference in the statue of the angel Moroni on this temple. It is not finished with traditional gold leafing. The company that painted the pipes of the organ in the Conference Center in Salt Lake City used the same technology to paint the fiberglass statue a golden color. This method was chosen because of the paint's durability in steady winds.

Reno Nevada Temple

Dear Father, bless all who have made possible this beautiful structure.

May they gain satisfaction from the knowledge that they have had a part

in creating this sacred edifice. May they recognize that it is no longer

simply a building but rather a house consecrated unto thee and thy

beloved Son, a place of holiness, a sanctuary of faith.

—FROM THE DEDICATORY PRAYER

Reno

Chad Hawkins © 2000

Some opposition is frequently associated with the construction of a temple, and the temple in Reno was no exception. Opposition had to be addressed from the temple's inception to its completion.

During the open house, one temple worker said, "We have had countless examples of resistance to the temple, from groundbreaking until just an hour ago. The adversary does not want temples built, and that has been very obvious on this job."[5]

But Church leaders noted that just as there are influences against the temple's progress, so there are also righteous powers beyond the veil seeing to its successful completion.[6]

Before the dedication of the Reno Nevada Temple, the Saints in the area were part of the Oakland California Temple district. The four-hour journey through the Sierras and Donner Pass could be very treacherous in winter. The unpredictable weather made the months of March through November the only reliably safe time to visit the temple in Oakland. One member commented, "What a unique thing it will be for us to be able to visit the temple throughout the year."[7]

An image of the Savior is hidden in the scenery at the left.

Months before the temple in Reno was dedicated, the blessings of the temple were already touching the lives of many Church members. They prepared themselves for the temple by meeting with their bishops and stake presidents and committing themselves to temple attendance.

Bishops in all the stakes reported many temple recommend appointments for people who had not been to the temple in years. One stake president observed, "We are having people coming out of the woodwork, getting their lives in order so they can come to the dedication and then participate in temple service.

"This has created a lot of work for us—work we love to have."[8]

Members of one stake prepared themselves for the temple by committing to read the Book of Mormon in its entirety by the time the temple was finished. They were asked to mark every verse that referred to the Savior and his mission. During this process, the Saints strengthened their testimonies and gained a better understanding of why the Book of Mormon is called another testament of Jesus Christ.[9]

. . . a house consecrated unto thee and thy beloved Son,

a place of holiness, a sanctuary of faith

Cochabamba Bolivia Temple

Cochabamba, Bolivia, is in a fairly temperate environment, nearly eight thousand feet above sea level at the base of the Andes. Though Cochabamba has suffered occasional lengthy periods of drought, the coming of a house of the Lord has inundated Church members there with all the blessings that a temple affords.

The temple itself sits on the northern side of the city. On a hill near the temple stands a tall statue of Jesus Christ. The morning and evening sun alike illuminate this statue, as well as the statue of the angel Moroni atop the temple spire, to create a dramatic presence for residents of Cochabamba. The scene is a daily reminder of the tranquility and stability that the Lord of all offers to a sometimes turbulent country.

On 21 January 1995, Elder Mario Guzman, an area authority seventy, received a telephone call from Elder Julio E. Davila of the South America North Area presidency inviting him to attend a special meeting. "None of us present had any idea why the meeting had been called," said Elder Guzman. "Elder Davila was very nervous. He kept asking, 'Has the fax come?' Twenty minutes passed; then someone handed him a fax. 'This

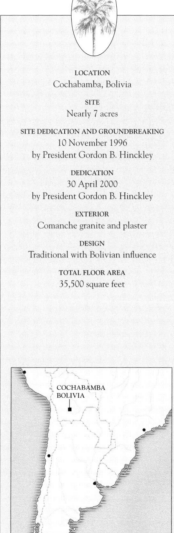

LOCATION
Cochabamba, Bolivia

SITE
Nearly 7 acres

SITE DEDICATION AND GROUNDBREAKING
10 November 1996
by President Gordon B. Hinckley

DEDICATION
30 April 2000
by President Gordon B. Hinckley

EXTERIOR
Comanche granite and plaster

DESIGN
Traditional with Bolivian influence

TOTAL FLOOR AREA
35,500 square feet

COCHABAMBA
BOLIVIA

comes from the First Presidency,' he told us, and read: 'A temple has been approved for Cochabamba, Bolivia.' A profound silence fell. Us? A temple? We had no words to say. We all began to cry."[1]

Soon the news of a temple in Bolivia spread among the members of the Church. Brother Rene Cabrerra, the local Church distribution center manager, echoed the feelings of many when he said, "To have a temple in Cochabamba is to have a temple in the heart of Bolivia, where all the members throughout Bolivia have relatively easy access by bus."[2]

That announcement of a temple for Bolivia took place in January 1995. Just under two years later, on 10 November 1996, President Gordon B. Hinckley arrived to preside over the groundbreaking ceremony. One of Cochabamba's long dry spells was hanging over the area, but the rain finally came just a few hours before he arrived. Latter-day Saints from throughout the country had traveled to attend this momentous ceremony, and they felt it no great sacrifice to stand in the pouring rain for hours to await their prophet to begin construction on a temple of God.

President Hinckley addressed approximately four thousand attendees by beginning, "My beloved and wet brothers and sisters." The downpour shortened the groundbreaking ceremony, but those who were there said later that neither the rain nor the shortness of the ceremony detracted from the significance of the prophet's visit.[3]

During that somewhat abbreviated and wet groundbreaking ceremony, President Hinckley issued a challenge: "Get a temple recommend now," he said. "Be worthy of a temple recommend now. If you are not worthy, get yourselves worthy. You won't be able to go to the temple here for at least two years. But let that temple recommend be a reminder of that to which you look forward."[4]

Members of the four stakes in Cochabamba became especially dedicated to accepting and obeying that counsel. One ward at a time was invited to tour the temple construction site each Saturday to feel the spirit attendant on the site and to envision the day when they might return worthily to perform ordinances for themselves and their deceased ancestors.

Ivan Gutierrez, president of the Jaihuayco Bolivia Stake, commented: "We are preparing the people. We encourage them to be ready spiritually. We have a goal to put a picture of the temple in every home. We have identified those who do not have temple recommends. We visit them and help them set goals for themselves. As a result, great changes are coming into the lives of the people."[5]

Two weeks of open house were scheduled in early April 2000 with the hope that tens of thousands of people would attend before the dedication on 30 April. Political unrest, however, was looming, and rebellion was touched off by an increase in utilities prices, causing demonstrations and anxiety throughout the country. Bolivia's president declared a state of emergency on 8 April 2000, and police were sent into the streets with anti-riot gear, tear gas, and rubber bullets to help quiet things down. Because of obvious safety concerns, the time for the open house was reduced from two weeks to one and the dedication from two days to one. The reduced time allotted for the Saints to take part in these activities created larger groups participating in the remaining open house and dedication ceremonies. Despite the changes, Church officials were pleased with attendance.

According to Brother Enrique O. Huerta of the Cochabamba Bolivia Universidad Stake: "We were supposed to be under martial law for ninety days, but it was lifted after thirteen days. We anticipated 50,000 visitors in two weeks of open house but instead we got 65,570 in one week. Twenty thousand people came in one day. They were lined up for blocks and stayed until midnight."[6]

The family of Antonio and Gloria Ayaviri have a testimony of temple attendance. "Raising children is much easier now that we have the gospel and temple blessings in our lives," Antonio stated. "In our home we have a piece of heaven. We have learned that the way to receive blessings—the way to run our home—is to serve the Lord first."[7]

May they recognize their Redeemer and be faithful and true Saints of the Most High

Tampico México Temple

Strengthen thy Church wherever it may be established. Bless this great nation of Mexico.

. . . May thy work grow in this nation in a miraculous and marvelous way.

—FROM THE DEDICATORY PRAYER

Tampico, Mexico, is an industrial city on central Mexico's Gulf Coast. The temple is built on a hill that many people nearby have long thought of as sacred. It is thus appropriate that a house of the Lord be located there. The temple attracts the attention and respect of many Tampico residents.

The property on which the temple stands was purchased by the Church in the 1950s. The first building to be constructed there was the Tampico Madero Stake center. Then, in 1967, the Church added a school. Academics were not the only benefits of becoming a student at the school—children attending this highly rated school participated in early-morning seminary at the nearby stake center. The school functioned for seventeen years before being converted in 1984 into offices for the Mexico Tampico Mission.

After the announcement of a temple for this area, a thorough search for possible locations ensued. Several were identified and considered, but the First Presidency ultimately felt inspired that the temple should be built on the site of the mission offices, which were consequently relocated and the building razed.[1]

For some, the announcement of a temple for this city was the fulfillment of long-felt spiritual inclinations. Nearly twenty years earlier Church officials had discussed the possibility of selling the property. In the end, the property was retained, in

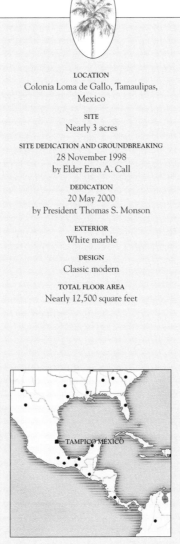

LOCATION
Colonia Loma de Gallo, Tamaulipas, Mexico

SITE
Nearly 3 acres

SITE DEDICATION AND GROUNDBREAKING
28 November 1998
by Elder Eran A. Call

DEDICATION
20 May 2000
by President Thomas S. Monson

EXTERIOR
White marble

DESIGN
Classic modern

TOTAL FLOOR AREA
Nearly 12,500 square feet

no small measure due to the persuasive beliefs of stake president Roberto de Leon Perales, who humbly witnessed, "One day a temple will be built here."[2]

To involve local leadership in bringing about the successful construction of a temple and its integration into the community, the Church organized a temple committee to assist in various assignments. Roberto Cruz was overwhelmed when asked to serve on that committee as the public affairs director. "I am a humble shoemaker," he said, "and I wondered, 'Why wasn't someone with more experience or more intellect called to this position?' But I have learned from this experience that the Lord qualifies whom He calls, and He has been there to help."[3]

His wife, Ana Bertha, represented their combined commitment and hard work when she said, "We have joined our hearts, souls and strength together in this work, but it is still humbling to say: 'Lord, this is Thy House.'"[4]

Latter-day Saints living in the Tampico Mexico Temple district are no strangers to committed temple service. Though a trip to the nearest temple—the Mexico City Mexico Temple—was a long twelve hours by bus, most temple recommend holders attended two or three times each year. Their dedication brought great blessings not only to those sacrificing to take these temple trips but also to those who observed them doing so. Many less-active members were influenced by the spirit and enthusiasm for the temple that these faithful members showed, enough that they made themselves worthy to join their ranks in receiving temple recommends.

Brother Rodolfo Avalos, project supervisor of the temple construction, commented that the construction crew had to meet two difficult challenges to complete the project successfully. First were the high construction standards required for building a house of the Lord. Second was the need to properly translate the plans, which had been developed in English in Salt Lake City. Fortunately, with the help of the Lord, these challenges were met quite successfully, along with a number of others, such as heavy rains and scorching heat.

On one occasion the temple committee felt prompted to double night security because of unsafe conditions in a nearby community. That night, very late, ruffians tried to jump the fence, but the additional security forces were able to stop them from entering the temple site.[5]

Jose Ponce, patriarch in the Tampico Mexico Bosque Stake, served as branch president outside Tampico fifteen years before the temple was dedicated. He reflected on his calling as the branch president and the growth of the Church in just a generation. "I was so excited that we could fill every teaching position in the branch, only to realize that those callings left us without any students. Now seeing the Church grow to the point where we can build a temple is a joyous blessing."[6]

Even though the Saints in Tampico already had an outstanding temple attendance record, there is no question that having their own temple nearby is making temple blessings more accessible. And that is very important. "The temple is a light," says Manuel Camacho of the Madero stake, "an enormous light for Tampico and the world."[7]

May thy work grow in this nation

in a miraculous and marvelous way

Nashville Tennessee Temple

Franklin, Tennessee, was not the original choice, nor even the second choice, for the site of the temple first announced in 1994, but this is the place where the Nashville Tennessee Temple found its home six years later. This part of the country is known as the Bible Belt, Nashville being considered the "belt buckle." Religion plays a significant role in the culture of middle Tennessee, sometimes to the advantage of members of The Church of Jesus Christ of Latter-day Saints and sometimes not. And so, despite considerable opposition, the need for a temple in the area was satisfied through the faith and perseverance of local Church members and general Church leadership. Now a dedicated house of the Lord is blessing lives in the Nashville, Tennessee, area.

In the spring of 1994, President Howard W. Hunter, president of the Quorum of the Twelve Apostles, felt inspired to consider building a temple in central Tennessee. President Gordon B. Hinckley and President Thomas S. Monson, counselors in the First Presidency, traveled to Nashville in April that year and selected a tentative site in Forest Hills, south of Nashville. When the Church requested that the site be rezoned for religious use, the city council denied the request. Not all nonmembers, however, were against the notion of a Latter-day Saint temple in their neighborhood. Jacqueline Srouji, for example, wrote in a letter to the editor of a major Tennessee newspaper:

"Although I have never been in one, I have seen Mormon temples during my travels throughout the world. These are structures of unusual spiritual and physical beauty. My only hope is that our Tennessee Mormons will have the same strong character as their pioneer ancestors to withstand whatever

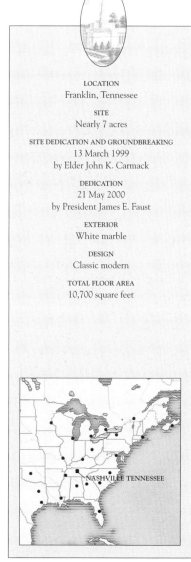

LOCATION
Franklin, Tennessee

SITE
Nearly 7 acres

SITE DEDICATION AND GROUNDBREAKING
13 March 1999
by Elder John K. Carmack

DEDICATION
21 May 2000
by President James E. Faust

EXTERIOR
White marble

DESIGN
Classic modern

TOTAL FLOOR AREA
10,700 square feet

NASHVILLE TENNESSEE

opposition is sent until their beautiful temple is finally built."[1] In January 1995, President Thomas S. Monson spoke at a regional conference at the Grand Ole Opry house. During his address, he assured the Saints that the Brethren were praying for their success and that despite the struggle, Nashville would have a temple.

A second site in Forest Hills was selected in July 1995. Although there was newfound support from some local congregations of other faiths and an organized effort to educate residents around the proposed site on what the addition of a temple would mean to their neighborhood, the planning commission once again denied the rezoning request.

In April 1998, the Church announced its plan to build a smaller temple next to the stake center in Franklin. This land, part of a tract owned by the Church, was already zoned for religious purposes. After overcoming minor obstacles in Franklin, the temple project was given permission to proceed.

On 13 March 1999, approximately fifteen hundred members from central Tennessee and southern Kentucky ignored uncomfortable weather conditions during the temple's groundbreaking ceremony. Drenching rains complicated the ceremonies by requiring officials to hold an umbrella in one hand and a shovel in the other. The muddy shovelfuls of dirt seemed to symbolize five years of struggle.

Hundreds of Laurels who lived in the temple district participated in "crystal parties," in which they assembled the crystal chandeliers for the celestial room and the sealing rooms. For those involved, it was a memorable experience to polish and place the crystals on the chandeliers. After finishing their work, the young women took part in a tour and discussion with Sister Barbara Blake, a temple construction

Nashville Tennessee Temple

This sacred structure stands as a monument before the world of our belief in the immortality of the human soul and that a great work is going forward on the other side of the veil to bring blessings to those who will accept the ordinances which will be performed in their behalf in this thy house.

—FROM THE DEDICATORY PRAYER

Nashville

missionary. Sister Blake paused in the brides' room to allow the girls an opportunity to reflect on their own goal of a temple marriage.

Other local Saints also had significant opportunities for service during the construction period. For example, when the decision was made to plant new sod around the neighboring stake center to match the sod of the temple grounds, the assistance of eighty men was requested. Not surprisingly, 140 people came to fill the request, which was done quickly and well. Because their work was finished in less time than anticipated, they stayed to help with other tasks as well. This attitude was typical of the Saints' commitment to their dream of a temple.[2]

Though challenges presented themselves almost daily, so too were solutions found—sometimes seemingly at the last minute but found nonetheless. These challenges ranged from carpet that was improperly installed to chairs that arrived without the bolts necessary to assemble them. The chairs that arrived without bolts were for the endowment rooms and were thus important fixtures in the temple. After searching all over town, temple construction missionary Elder Leo Udy located the necessary hundred specialty bolts and spent half the night painting them to match the chairs. He said, "At the last minute the Lord provided."[3] Though solving such problems often required faith and significant amounts of hard work and extra hours, the temple was successfully built to the typical high standards.

At times, opposition came not from construction

The image of the Savior is hidden at the right of the temple; his face and hands seem part of the temple and the distant trees.

difficulties but from local citizens. The Spirit eventually came to rest on many of those who raised objections. One outspoken opponent had just such a change of heart. When he was invited to tour the temple during its open house, he responded, "After all the problems I caused you, I never expected to receive such an invitation. I am surprised that you would care or remember me this way. Thank you! I would love to tour your temple."[4]

The temple's new president, Buryl G. McClurg, has been involved with the temple from the beginning. While serving as stake president, he played a key role in purchasing the land now used for the stake center and temple, and he helped get approval from county commissioners to build the temple. He did whatever was needed at the time, whether it was dislodging a large rock that was blocking the stake center sewer line or using steel wool to scrub concrete spatters from the fence surrounding the temple site. When asked to make a statement that would be permanently recorded in the temple's cornerstone, President McClurg responded:

"The gospel is true today; it will be true tomorrow. Although we had some struggles in making this happen, the glory is quite unparalleled in terms of what you can do to make something like this become a reality. . . . As the stone rolls forth, there will be many temples, hundreds and hundreds of temples. . . . Join hands, love the Lord, be true and faithful, never veer from that which is right, because Satan's influence cannot overpower the Lord's Spirit."[5]

This sacred structure stands as a monument before the world of our belief in the immortality of the human soul

Villahermosa México Temple

Hear the prayers of thy people whenever they plead with thee in their troubles. Give unto them peace in their hearts and the assurance that thou art watching over them. May they come here, dressing in white, to commune with thee and to participate in those ordinances which will bring to them blessings for their eternal exaltation and for the exaltation of uncounted numbers beyond the veil of death.

—FROM THE DEDICATORY PRAYER

Villahermosa, the capital of the state of Tabasco, is located in southeastern Mexico. Situated on the Grijalva River, the community has become a regional commercial and manufacturing center. The temple itself, built on a site near the coast of Mexico's isthmus, will someday also have a stake center to the west of it.

The property on which the temple was built has been owned by the Church for many years and was the site of a meetinghouse, which had to be removed to make way for the temple. Ground was broken on 9 January 1999, under the direction of Elder Richard E. Turley Sr. of the Seventy and first counselor in the Mexico South Area Presidency.

Only about two hundred people—mostly local leaders and their families—attended the ceremony because there was simply not enough room for more. Elder Turley bore testimony of the Savior and his mission to "bring to pass the immortality and eternal life of man" (Moses 1:39). He reminded the Saints that it is only through the Savior and his atonement

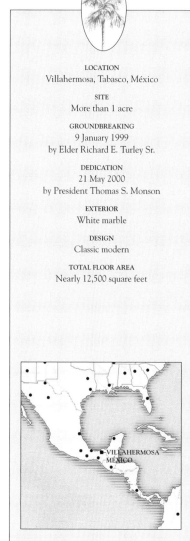

LOCATION
Villahermosa, Tabasco, México

SITE
More than 1 acre

GROUNDBREAKING
9 January 1999
by Elder Richard E. Turley Sr.

DEDICATION
21 May 2000
by President Thomas S. Monson

EXTERIOR
White marble

DESIGN
Classic modern

TOTAL FLOOR AREA
Nearly 12,500 square feet

VILLAHERMOSA
MEXICO

that we can receive exaltation. "This is why," Elder Turley said, "temples are, along with the Atonement, the greatest gift to mankind as well as the greatest tool to prepare the earth for the Second Coming of the Savior." He told the Saints that they "must now develop within their homes a culture of temple attendance and participation. It is our hope that every member home in the temple district will eventually have a picture of the temple to remind them and their children of the opportunities that can be theirs. If you are faithful," he said, "the spirituality of the members will increase. There will be a measurable impact on the whole community through the faithfulness of the people and the beauty of the temple and its surroundings."[1]

As with other temples built in Mexico, most of the construction was done by hand. Boards were cut, steel was cut and bent, and cement was mixed by hand—often with homemade tools. To make the cement, water was poured into sand and gravel and then mixed on the ground with a shovel. Although a cement pump truck was used to pour the concrete on the roof, most cement was transported to the appropriate area in five-gallon buckets. Workers put in long hours in the sun but remained dedicated to their task. Only when the finishing work on the temple was being completed was a power saw brought on site.

The unforeseen height of the water table caused minor difficulties when the hole was dug for the baptismal font, but an extra pump was installed to prevent any water damage. The climate of the Mexican isthmus does not require any type of heating system, but eight air conditioning units were installed to add to the comfort of the patrons.[2]

The interior colors of the temple, floral arrangements, and

commissioned artwork were selected to represent the region. One original painting depicts well-known waterfalls sixty miles from Villahermosa. The other portrays a prominent river south of the city.[3] Adding to the temple's exterior beauty is its Blanco Guardiano marble from Torreon, Mexico.

Gracing the grounds of the temple are several ceiba trees, including one tree near the temple's entrance with branches that tower above the building. Ceiba trees are protected by the government so strictly that it is illegal to cut them down in the state of Tabasco. According to Mayan legend, the tree is sacred and symbolizes the need to stay rooted deeply in good Mexican soil while reaching towards the heavens. For these reasons, the temple's landscaping centers on these important trees.[4]

On 21 May 2000, President Thomas S. Monson dedicated the Villahermosa Mexico Temple in a series of four dedicatory sessions with nearly four thousand Church members in attendance. He was visibly moved by the love and excitement on the faces and in the voices of the local Saints.

It was a marvelous day of rejoicing and thanksgiving as more than twenty-eight thousand Latter-day Saints in eight stakes and two districts received a temple to call their own. Their feelings were aptly expressed by Samuel Oteo, a longtime member of the Church, when he humbly said, "I have prayed often for a temple in this part of Mexico. Today, I am very, very happy and grateful to my Heavenly Father."[5]

May they come here,
dressing in white,
to commune with thee

Montréal Québec Temple

Bless us to be worthy always of coming to this thy house. Save us from evil and doubt.

Bless us with righteousness and faith. May thy holy Spirit be felt by all who come within

these walls. May old men dream dreams and young men see visions as they

contemplate the wonder and majesty of thy divine and eternal plan for the

salvation and exaltation of thy sons and daughters of all generations.

— FROM THE DEDICATORY PRAYER

Montreal, Quebec, which lies on the banks of the St. Lawrence River, is a city of contrasts. Old-world charm mixes comfortably with skyscrapers and hurried business-people. It is home to some of the oldest settlements on the continent and is visited by an army of tourists from throughout the world. Many residents of Montreal are bilingual, speaking both French and English. Building a temple in this Canadian city worked to unite the people, tradition, and future of this beautiful and varied land.

The engraving on the Montreal Quebec Temple's corner-stone reads, "Edifiè en L'an 2000," or "Erected in 2000." But the history of the Church in this part of Canada began long before that historic year. And the people who live there remember that history well.

Shortly after the organization of the Church in 1830, the first Latter-day Saint missionaries traveled to Quebec, or Lower Canada, as it was then known. During the early years of the Church, many Canadian converts emigrated to Utah, so it wasn't until 1919 that the Canadian Mission was organized. In 1930 the first English-speaking branch was

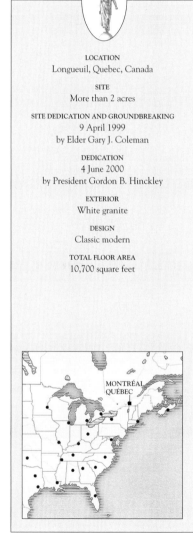

LOCATION
Longueuil, Quebec, Canada

SITE
More than 2 acres

SITE DEDICATION AND GROUNDBREAKING
9 April 1999
by Elder Gary J. Coleman

DEDICATION
4 June 2000
by President Gordon B. Hinckley

EXTERIOR
White granite

DESIGN
Classic modern

TOTAL FLOOR AREA
10,700 square feet

MONTRÉAL
QUÉBEC

organized in Montreal. A meetinghouse was purchased in 1942, and it served local members for thirty years. While serving as president of the Canadian Mission, President Thomas S. Monson sent the first six French-speaking missionaries to Quebec in 1961. In 1978, the Montreal Quebec Stake, the first French-speaking stake in North America, was created. As these events took place, the hope of a temple grew.

So it was with much rejoicing that the Saints in Montreal greeted President Gordon B. Hinckley's 6 August 1998 announcement that a temple would be built in their city. Seven months later, four hundred and fifty invited guests took part in the 9 April 1999 groundbreaking for the Montreal Quebec Temple. The services were held in the empty garage of a vacated automobile dealership, which was later demolished to make way for the temple.[1]

A little more than a year later, from 20 May to 27 May 2000, the temple's week-long open house attracted nearly ten thousand visitors. The temple was then dedicated in four sessions on Sunday, 4 June 2000, by President Gordon B. Hinckley. The sixth temple to be built in Canada, the Montreal Quebec Temple serves Church members living in the Canadian provinces of Quebec and Ontario and the state of Vermont in the United States.

The temple's location is a great blessing to local members. For decades, faithful Saints in Quebec traveled great distances to serve in the temple. English-speaking members drove forty-five hours to the Cardston Alberta Temple, and French-speaking members traveled to the Bern Switzerland Temple. The construction of temples in Washington, D. C., and Toronto, Ontario, Canada, brought temple worship closer, but travel even to these locations was long and difficult. Georges Bourget, second counselor in the first Montreal Quebec Temple presidency, explained the members' tradition of temple service and their willingness to sacrifice. "We in this area are a temple-loving people, and we were known for our faithfulness in attending the temple," he said. "I think that's one of the reasons we were able to receive a temple, even though the Church is relatively small here."[2]

This faithfulness was evident in December 1992, when members of the Montreal Quebec Stake showed their commitment to temple service by keeping an appointment to be in the Toronto Ontario Temple despite a heavy snowfall that kept them on the road for twelve hours—one way. On that stormy day, noted a member of the temple presidency, "only members from the Montreal Quebec Stake crossed the white curtain of snow around the temple" to serve in the Lord's house.

The following year, members of the same stake set a goal regarding their temple attendance. Stake president Michel J. Carter, in a 1993 stake priesthood meeting, said, "Brethren, to better prepare for upcoming stake conference, let us as a stake go together to the temple in numbers large enough to perform saving ordinances for an *entire ward* beyond the veil." What President Carter had in mind was to perform all the ordinance work for six hundred individuals. Many stake members were already researching family names, and many of the six hundred individuals for whom ordinances were performed were ancestors of stake members. During one three-day visit to the Toronto Ontario Temple, stake members achieved their goal.[3]

But even those who had never experienced nor heard of the Montreal Saints' tradition of temple service felt the excitement of the new temple in their midst. From the time of its announcement until its dedication, the temple helped increase public awareness of the Church in Montreal. Local leaders used all avenues of the media and took advantage of every opportunity to explain the importance of temples and to publicize Church beliefs. Montreal stake president Sterling H. Dietze related that during an interview with a local radio station, the interviewer commented, "It's really amazing how attached your Church seems to be to a building—almost like the ancient Jews [to the temple at Jerusalem]." The interview was the perfect chance for President Dietze to explain the heritage and importance of temple worship. He made it clear that although this attachment "is to a building, . . . it's more than the building."[4]

The knowledge that a temple is more than a building has motivated ninety-one-year-old Church member Jeanne Clement to participate faithfully in temple work ever since her conversion to the gospel of Jesus Christ. "Before I was baptized," she said, "I wondered how God would do justice to those who died without being baptized. When I joined the Church, I realized how simple it is—we are baptized for them."

Through the years this lifelong resident of Montreal has worked to compile family names back to 1529. In the past she traveled twelve hours to the Washington D. C. Temple and then later nearly seven hours to the Toronto Ontario Temple to complete the ordinance work for those family members. With the dedication of the Montreal Quebec Temple, her journey was cut to only thirty-five minutes. Because she was accustomed to traveling to the temple, staying for four days, and doing as many ordinances during each of those four days as possible, Sister Clement realized it would be an adjustment for her to have a temple so close. But her commitment to the future of temple work in Montreal is evident in her response: "I wonder what we'll do," she said. "We won't go for a week, just for a day. I hope I will be able to go once a week."[5]

Bless us with righteousness and faith

San José Costa Rica Temple

Accept of our love for thee and for our Redeemer. Help us to walk the straight and narrow road which leads to life eternal. May the specter of death hold no fears for those who have received the ordinances of this house. May all walk in obedience before thee, and wilt thou touch their minds and hearts by thy power to a new awakening of faith and responsibility.

— FROM THE DEDICATORY PRAYER

San Jose is the capital of Costa Rica and the nation's largest city. In one particularly picturesque part of the city stands a landmark that attracts faithful Saints from all over this Central American country and offers much more than just a beautiful view. The San Jose Costa Rica Temple represents to Latter-day Saints the promise of an eternal vista.

The temple, whose walls are covered with Blanco Guardiano marble from Torreon, Mexico, is located in San Antonio, a suburb of San Jose. It is the first temple in southern Central America and the first small temple in all of Central America.

The Church is relatively young in this part of Latin America, and Costa Rican members still aspire to meet the challenge given by Elder Spencer W. Kimball when he dedicated Central America for the preaching of the gospel in 1952. He declared that the time had come for the people to "rise in majesty and strength and power to their ultimate destiny."[1] Costa Rica has proven to be a land ready for gospel growth, as Church membership has grown from thirty-eight hundred in 1977 to thirty-five thousand in the year 2000.[2]

With this rich history of growth, Latter-day Saint Costa

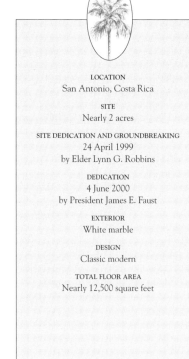

LOCATION
San Antonio, Costa Rica

SITE
Nearly 2 acres

SITE DEDICATION AND GROUNDBREAKING
24 April 1999
by Elder Lynn G. Robbins

DEDICATION
4 June 2000
by President James E. Faust

EXTERIOR
White marble

DESIGN
Classic modern

TOTAL FLOOR AREA
Nearly 12,500 square feet

SAN JOSÉ COSTA RICA

Ricans look forward to continued growth and strengthening that will inevitably take place with a temple in their country. Henry Obando, who was baptized in 1981 and later became president of the La Sabana Costa Rica Stake, recalled an occasion when another Church leader remarked that the pioneering members in Costa Rica "were like children cutting their teeth on the gospel feast." With the dedication of the temple, President Obando believes that time has passed. "Now we are ready to eat meat," he said.[3]

Before the completion of the San Jose Costa Rica Temple, Elder Enrique R. Falabella, an area authority seventy, shared his thoughts on the members' sacrifice to attend the nearest temple, at that time the Guatemala City Guatemala Temple. "I believe that Costa Ricans love the temple," he said. "Even though it is expensive to travel to the Guatemala City Temple—often the cost is twice the monthly income— members still make the effort."[4]

The sacrifice referred to by Elder Falabella was evident long before the Guatemala City Guatemala Temple was built. In January 1976, eighty-four Latter-day Saints, including forty-six from Costa Rica, traveled by bus eight thousand miles round-trip to attend the Mesa Arizona Temple. Misael and Maria Alfaro, who had been baptized in 1956, saved their money to make the excursion with all eight of their children.

"A short time before they were to leave, Brother Alfaro lost the money he had saved for the trip. When he told his wife, they wept, then prayed for help to raise the needed money. A shoemaker, Brother Alfaro took all of his handmade shoes to a neighboring town and sold them for whatever he could get. When he returned home, still short of the needed amount, he sold his car. 'The blessings of being sealed together in the temple will last forever,' he says. 'It was worth our sacrifice.'"[5]

Attending the temple became a little less difficult with the construction and dedication of the temple in Guatemala City. Costa Rican members, however, continued to make whatever sacrifices were necessary to attend the temple. Their sacrifices stand as a legacy to the Church in Costa Rica. For example, Dennis and Rosa Guillen of Limon, Costa Rica, have eleven children. To support his family, Brother Guillen sold Sno-cones, fried chicken, and fried bananas from a small stand. After three of their daughters had served missions, the family saved money to attend the Guatemala City Guatemala Temple. The *Ensign* reported his humble efforts:

"Asked how he earned enough money for three missions, and now the temple, Brother Guillen pauses. Tears form in his eyes and his voice trembles as he says slowly, '*Trabajé duro*. [I worked hard.] *Trabajé duro*. *Entonces poco a poco*. [Then little by little.] *Poco a poco*.' His words stop, but not his tears.

"'We can only afford to take three of our children,' Sister Guillen explained. 'When we return, we will save our money again until we can take a few more of our children. Someday all of us will be sealed together for eternity.'"[6]

Such trips were greatly simplified with the dedication of the San Jose Costa Rica Temple on Sunday, 4 June 2000, by President James E. Faust,

second counselor in the First Presidency. Heavy rains preceded the dedicatory services, forcing the closure of the airport. But the rains subsided and the sun broke through for the dedicatory services, which some four thousand Saints attended.

One of them was Norbei Vierti, who traveled eleven hours with his family from Panama, which is part of the San Jose Costa Rica Temple district. Brother Vierti made the trip to hear President Faust's counsel, to participate in a dedicatory session, and most important, to be sealed to his wife and two children as soon as the temple opened. "The sacrifice of coming to the temple will result in many blessings," Brother Vierti said. "I've been looking to this day since the day I was married. Today, I'm very happy."[7]

Even with their joy at the temple dedication, these members recognized that with blessings come sacred responsibilities. Nicaraguan member Martin Rios, who joined the Church twenty-six years before, explained, "It is a great blessing to have a second temple in Central America and a challenge from the Lord to us to lengthen our stride."[8]

Stake president Henry Obando says that another temple in Latin America is simply one more historic step in realizing the eternal blessings promised to Heavenly Father's faithful children. "The temple has already made such a difference in our Church units," he said. "Now there are two kinds of members: those who are ready for the temple, and those who are getting themselves ready for the temple."[9]

May all walk in obedience before thee, and wilt thou touch their minds and hearts

Fukuoka Japan Temple

Dear Father, thy work has been established across the world in very many areas. Wilt thou inspire all who serve therein, whatever may be their duty, be it large or small. May they find joy in their service.

— FROM THE DEDICATORY PRAYER

Fukuoka, Japan, is located in the northern part of the island of Kyushu, some six hundred twenty miles southwest of Tokyo. Japan's closest major port to mainland Asia, Fukuoka has a population of 1.3 million. Not far from the bustle of this burgeoning metropolis, however, are forested hills containing a zoo and botanical gardens. Among these lush green hills is the Fukuoka Japan Temple. In the midst of one of Japan's largest and busiest centers, the Lord's house provides peace and reverence for those who go within its doors to serve and for those who look to it as a landmark.

In 1975, in Tokyo, President Spencer W. Kimball made the historic announcement of the Tokyo Japan Temple: "We will build a temple to our God in Japan for the people of Asia. The first temple in this eastern land will be built in Tokyo, and we shall hope that it will serve the needs of the Saints in Asia until we can grow large enough and strong enough to build other temples in other areas in this land."[1] The 11 June 2000 dedication of the Fukuoka Japan Temple is evidence that the Church has grown "large enough" and "strong enough" to warrant the "other temples" President Kimball foresaw.

The Fukuoka Japan Temple is designed much like other small temples, with a few slight variations. The temple's exterior is made of two types of granite from China—Empress

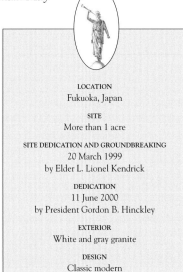

LOCATION
Fukuoka, Japan

SITE
More than 1 acre

SITE DEDICATION AND GROUNDBREAKING
20 March 1999
by Elder L. Lionel Kendrick

DEDICATION
11 June 2000
by President Gordon B. Hinckley

EXTERIOR
White and gray granite

DESIGN
Classic modern

TOTAL FLOOR AREA
10,800 square feet

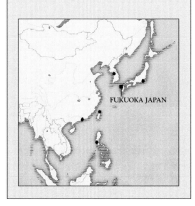

FUKUOKA JAPAN

White and Majestic Gray. In an area where the price of land is exorbitantly high, the temple uses with as much efficiency as possible nearly all of the property's space. The building's lower level includes parking space, a mission home, mission offices, and an apartment for the temple president.[2]

The construction of this unique, multiuse structure on a relatively small piece of property brought challenges. Workers lacked space to store materials and equipment at the building location. A solution was found when workers realized the neighboring zoo was closed on Mondays; they then arranged to use the zoo's parking lot to temporarily store equipment and supplies. Monday subsequently became the busiest and most crucial day of the week during the temple construction.[3]

The temple is also unusual in that its entire two-story structure is made of concrete and steel. "Not a two-by-four was used in the entire building," said temple construction missionary Elder Charles H. Blackburn. Concrete and steel were chosen to make the structure virtually earthquake proof; these materials also saved on costs because of the high price of wood in the area. The sidewalks, driveways, and parking areas make extensive use of tile.[4]

The land on which the temple is built is of historic significance to Latter-day Saints in Fukuoka. Pioneering Church members remember when the Church obtained the property for a meetinghouse. The site was then "out in the boondocks," said Eugene M. Kitamura, area director of temporal affairs for the Church and a native of Fukuoka. At that time the road to the area was not paved, and, Brother Kitamura explained, those walking to church through the rain were lucky if they didn't lose their shoes in the mud. Later a mission home also occupied what has become the temple site.[5]

The Fukuoka ward meetinghouse is now located a few blocks away, the mission home has been incorporated into the new building, and the temple itself is blessing the lives of Church members in the temple district by making temple worship accessible to more members than ever before. Brother Kitamura remembers the journeys members used to make to the Laie Hawaii Temple and the sacrifices those trips required. The Laie Hawaii Temple was the closest temple until the 1980 dedication of the Tokyo Japan Temple.[6]

Members rejoiced at the closeness of the temple when ground was broken for the Fukuoka Japan Temple on 20 March 1999. Presiding at the groundbreaking was Elder L. Lionel Kendrick of the Seventy and president of the Asia North Area. "When a temple is built in an area it lessens the evil influences of the adversary. It brings blessings to the area and to its people," said Elder Kendrick. "These blessings come not only to the members of the Church but also to all those who live in the bounds of the temple district."[7]

As Elder Kendrick promised, the temple has been a blessing to its district. While the temple was being constructed, reported Elder Gary Matsuda, area authority seventy and vice-chairman of the temple committee, nearly two hundred members returned to Church activity. Although many of their efforts were self-started, these newly activated members were strengthened by priesthood and auxiliary leaders working to prepare members to attend the temple.[8]

Members gained strength as they fasted and prayed every month to offer thanks for the temple and to petition for its construction to proceed without difficulty. Construction did proceed according to plan, and a week before the dedication, a three-day open house was attended by more than forty-eight hundred people, including many nonmembers who wished to learn more about the Church.

"Before I came to the open house," commented one visitor, "I determined that I would not change my preconceived ideas about this Christian church. As I walked through the temple, I repeated this to myself over and over. But when I entered the celestial room, I felt my preconceptions change."[9]

Although it took place during the region's rainy season, the dedication of the Fukuoka Japan Temple on 11 June 2000 was warm and dry. President Gordon B. Hinckley, who directed the Church's work in Asia for many years and has visited there numerous times, dedicated the temple in four sessions. The timing of the dedication of the second temple in Japan was also appropriate, as the year 2000 marked the fiftieth anniversary of the beginning of missionary work in Japan.

Temple construction missionary Elder Charles Blackburn shared his experience in helping to build the temple and his growing love for the Japanese people. He began his mission unable to speak Japanese, he explained. This obstacle was overcome with quick pencil sketches, bilingual Church members, and full-time missionaries who acted as interpreters. With these aids, he was able to communicate with the workers, and they and Elder Blackburn developed respect for one another—a respect that helped them achieve their goal of building a house of the Lord.

"They are an honest, gracious, and sincere people," Elder Blackburn said, referring not only to members of the Church but to all who worked to build the temple. "They were so anxious to please and be kind. I can see why the Lord would bless these choice people with a temple."[10]

Wilt thou inspire all who serve therein, whatever may be their duty

Adelaide Australia Temple

All that is done here will be in recognition of the immortality of the human soul. Because of the atoning sacrifice of our Redeemer, thy beloved Son, the great gift of everlasting life is made available to us, as well as to the generations who have gone before us. We are blessed by thy great plan of happiness. Help us to live worthy of the blessings thou hast promised those who walk in obedience to thy commandments and hold thy name sacred before the world.

—FROM THE DEDICATORY PRAYER

A modern city situated on the Torrens River and made up of broad streets, large squares, and extensive parks, Adelaide is the capital and chief city of the state of South Australia. The Adelaide Australia Temple, with an exterior of snow-white granite from Campolonghi, Italy, is located just a few miles from the Adelaide city center. This temple—and the others in Australia—are a tangible sign and a direct result of the growth of the Church in that nation. The last national census in Australia identified The Church of Jesus Christ of Latter-day Saints as the fastest growing Christian faith in the country.[1]

This growth comes as no surprise to the more than fifteen hundred Saints who heard Elder Bruce R. McConkie of the Quorum of the Twelve Apostles speak after the groundbreaking services for the Sydney Australia Temple in 1982. Elder McConkie's comments helped them begin to prepare for the day when the Lord's house would be in their midst. He affirmed to the Australian Saints that other temples would be built as Church membership grew in their land. "There is no

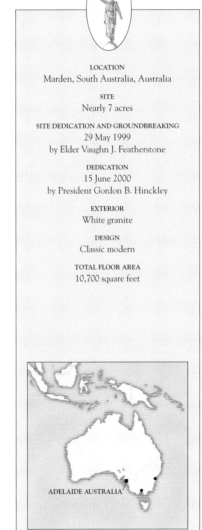

LOCATION
Marden, South Australia, Australia

SITE
Nearly 7 acres

SITE DEDICATION AND GROUNDBREAKING
29 May 1999
by Elder Vaughn J. Featherstone

DEDICATION
15 June 2000
by President Gordon B. Hinckley

EXTERIOR
White granite

DESIGN
Classic modern

TOTAL FLOOR AREA
10,700 square feet

ADELAIDE AUSTRALIA

reason why we can't have temples in Adelaide, Melbourne, Brisbane, Perth, or wherever the number of Saints justifies it," Elder McConkie declared.[2]

President Gordon B. Hinckley traveled to Adelaide in 1997, where twenty-eight hundred members from three stakes gathered to hear him speak on 13 May. His visit to the area was the first by a Church president in twenty-one years. Although the members in Adelaide lived far from the closest temple, the prophet spoke of temple work. "I hope every man in this congregation has taken his wife to the house of the Lord. Work for the temple and the sealing ordinances," he said. "Take your companion and your children if you can, there to be joined under a covenant that time cannot destroy and death cannot break."[3]

Two short years later, on 17 March 1999, the Adelaide Australia Temple was announced. And two months after that, almost five hundred people gathered at the temple site on 29 May 1999 for the groundbreaking of the Adelaide Australia Temple. Elder Vaughn J. Featherstone of the Seventy and president of the Australia–New Zealand Area presided at the services. He gave credit to the Church members in Adelaide for faithfully serving the Lord as they awaited the day in which a temple would be closer to home. He talked of the Saints who had traveled between fifteen and twenty hours each way to attend the temple in Sydney. For their efforts, he said, "they surely merit a temple in their midst."[4]

While the Adelaide Australia Temple was still under construction, Rhelma Badger, a resident of the city, found herself preparing for a significant life change. Her daughter, Kerrie, who had been baptized a member of the Church a few months earlier, invited Rhelma to join the youth at a Mutual activity. The activity happened to be a tour of the temple site, and Kerrie wanted her mother to see it, even though it was unfinished. Rhelma's husband was also a member of the Church, but she herself attended another Christian church.

Rhelma was surprised by the experience. "I felt so warm as we went into the baptismal area and then the sealing room," she said. "I went home and asked God to tell me what to do and for help to be able to tell my parents that I wanted to join [my husband's] church."

Rhelma's parents had always opposed their daughter joining the Church, but not long after Rhelma's visit to the temple, they called her and, without explanation for the change, encouraged her to be baptized. With that obstacle removed, Rhelma Badger was soon baptized a member of the Church.[5]

Sister Badger was one of many who were affected by the construction of the new temple. The entire community was intrigued by the temple after substantial media coverage made local citizens aware of its presence. As a result of advertisements on radio and in newspapers, as well as personal invitations from Church members, many people were prepared to tour the temple; nearly fifty thousand of them took advantage of the opportunity. The number is remarkably high considering the relatively small number—twelve thousand—of Church members in the temple district.[6]

The dedication of the Adelaide and Melbourne Australia Temples

and the planned construction of two more in Perth and Brisbane are fulfillments of many years of preparation by Australian Latter-day Saints. "Formerly, many of our members had to overcome Australia's famed 'tyranny of distance' to attend the Sydney temple," remarked Elder Bruce C. Hafen of the Seventy and president of the Australia–New Zealand Area. "Where previously a temple visit was just an occasional encounter, now the Saints throughout Australia will have an opportunity for a lifetime of temple experiences."[7]

The dedication of the Adelaide Australia Temple was also the fulfillment of another kind of preparation. For the first time in Church history, four temples were ready for dedication almost simultaneously. On an extended trip that included meetings with the Saints and other events in addition to the temple dedications, President Gordon B. Hinckley dedicated the Fukuoka Japan Temple on 11 June 2000, the Adelaide Australia Temple on 15 June 2000, the Melbourne Australia Temple on 16 June 2000, and the Suva Fiji Temple on 18 June 2000.

While making this historic trip, President Hinckley reminisced about his previous experiences in Australia. "We traveled through this great land and came to feel the large distances which Church members have to travel to visit the House of the Lord," he said. "I know it is a long way from Adelaide and Perth to Sydney. Within a year, there will be five temples where there was just one. What a great season in the life of the Church in Australia."[8]

We are blessed by thy great plan of happiness. Help us to live worthy of the blessings thou hast promised

Melbourne Australia Temple

Before the Melbourne Australia Temple was built, local Saints faithfully visited the Sydney Autralia Temple. Members making this ten- or twelve-hour journey would often leave Friday evening and travel all night, arriving at the temple by 6 o'clock Saturday morning. After serving for the entire day in the temple, they would leave in the evening, arriving home early Sunday morning in time to sleep a few hours before attending their church meetings.

"For 16 years we have traveled the 1,500 miles round trip to the Sydney temple and before that many members of the Church here had to sacrifice—sometimes their house, car and other possessions—so they could afford to make the journey to the New Zealand Temple," said Melbourne Australia Pakenham Stake president Murray Lobley at the temple's dedication. "We are now no longer enslaved by the tyranny of distance. We have been truly blessed to have a temple built in Melbourne."[1]

The first efforts to find a suitable spot for a temple in Melbourne, a city in southeastern Australia and the capital of the state of Victoria, were made in 1997 when President Gordon B. Hinckley announced that he was planning a trip to Australia and New Zealand to visit the Saints. Before President Hinckley's arrival, Elder Bruce C. Hafen of the Seventy, first counselor in the Australia–New Zealand Area presidency, was asked to identify locations in Melbourne and Brisbane as possible temple sites. It was not until after his visit to Australia that President Hinckley outlined the program to build smaller temples.

Overwhelming joy followed initial feelings of amazement among Melbourne Saints when the temple—to be built on

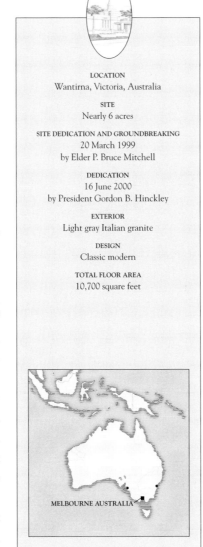

LOCATION
Wantirna, Victoria, Australia

SITE
Nearly 6 acres

SITE DEDICATION AND GROUNDBREAKING
20 March 1999
by Elder P. Bruce Mitchell

DEDICATION
16 June 2000
by President Gordon B. Hinckley

EXTERIOR
Light gray Italian granite

DESIGN
Classic modern

TOTAL FLOOR AREA
10,700 square feet

MELBOURNE AUSTRALIA

property adjacent to the Maroondah stake center—was first announced. That joy was particularly obvious among those who had helped establish the Church sufficiently for a temple to be built in Melbourne, the second largest metropolitan area in Australia, second only to Sydney.

The nearly four hundred participants at the groundbreaking service held on 20 March 1999 also greeted the temple's formal beginning with joy. "It's no surprise that we are commencing a temple here, at this time," said Elder P. Bruce Mitchell, an area authority seventy and second counselor in the Australia–New Zealand Area presidency. Elder Mitchell assured members that their faithfulness in attending the Sydney Australia Temple had not gone unnoticed by the Lord. He honored those who had so many times made the long trip to Sydney. He quoted Elder John A. Widtsoe of the Quorum of the Twelve Apostles: "When we go through the temple for other people we taste the sweet joy of saviorhood and our stature becomes more like the Savior Jesus Christ who died to save us all."[2]

When Sister Edna Ord of Melbourne's Northcote Ward heard the announcement of the temple, her response was one of joy but not one of surprise. "Oh, yes, isn't it marvelous," she said. "When I heard the announcement, I said, 'Oh, Elder McConkie, you were right.'" Eighty-four-year-old Sister Ord had served for eighteen years as secretary to the mission presidents in Melbourne. She remembered when Elder Bruce R. McConkie, later a member of the Quorum of the Twelve Apostles, was mission president in Australia and had said to her, "I promise you, Edna, you will have a temple in Melbourne."[3]

Melbourne Australia Temple

[This temple] is now vested with a peculiar and wonderful sanctity. Henceforth it will be open only to those who are properly recommended as worthy to enter its portals. As they come here, we pray that thou wilt endow them with special blessings, with sacred covenants, with wondrous promises that only thou canst give. May they know that they walk through sacred halls. May they always act reverently as thy guests. May they leave rejoicing, standing taller as sons and daughters of God, with strengthened resolve to walk in thy paths.

—FROM THE DEDICATORY PRAYER

Chad Hawkins
©2000

Melbourne

A temple in Melbourne was foreseen at least forty years before, by Elder Spencer W. Kimball of the Quorum of the Twelve Apostles. When the Melbourne Australia Stake was formed in October 1960, Elder Spencer W. Kimball ordained local member Frank Davenport a seventy. Elder Kimball blessed Brother Davenport that he "would have his temple in Melbourne."

Sixteen years later, in 1976, as part of a high council assignment, Brother Davenport was given the task of finding suitable land on which to build a stake center. His initial site selections were met with stiff opposition from residents. In a meeting with a city council, Brother Davenport felt impressed to invite them to propose a location for the new Church building. Within hours, the council contacted him with an invitation to meet with them again. They offered a beautiful orchard property, and Church leaders gladly accepted. The stake center and, many years later, the Melbourne Australia Temple were built on that orchard site.

When construction on the temple began, workers ran into a few unexpected challenges. During the excavation, several old chemical drums were uncovered. This discovery caused concern that some of the soil might be contaminated and therefore unsafe. Excavation was halted until experts could test soil samples, but it was ultimately determined that the soil was not hazardous and posed no threat to construction workers or to the temple project. Another interesting development helped workers make up lost time. On several occasions, the building union called a strike that affected the locations of the

Among the trees and foliage in this drawing of the Melbourne Australia Temple is a full-length image of the Savior nviting us to receive the blessings found in temple service. The familiar shape of the continent of Australia is hidden among the trees behind the temple.

contractor's other projects but not the area where the temple site was. Under those conditions, the contractor reassigned workers from the affected sites to the temple project without causing any difficulty with the union. The extra workers helped keep the temple project on its tight building schedule.

The more than twenty-eight thousand visitors to the temple's week-long open house admired the temple's exterior, which is an attractive light gray Italian granite, as well as the beauty and peace of the temple's interior. Some participants in the temple project were given the chance to experience an even greater kind of peace and joy.

Temple construction missionaries Neil and Beverly Ann Langley oversaw the temple's construction and had a profound influence on most of the workers. Their experience in the construction trade and their willingness to help were a great benefit to the project. As Christmas approached in 1999, Elder and Sister Langley carefully gift wrapped forty copies of the Book of Mormon and presented them to the workers before the holiday break. The books were appreciated by the recipients.

The Melbourne Australia Temple was dedicated by President Gordon B. Hinckley on 16 June 2000. "The number of friends we are making in the community because of the temple is just overwhelming," said Pakenham stake president Murray Lobley. "The lives of tens of thousands within the Church and without will continue to be touched by the temple—here in Melbourne and beyond."[4]

May they leave rejoicing, standing taller as sons and daughters of God, with strengthened resolve to walk in thy paths

Suva Fiji Temple

We pray, dear Father, that these beautiful islands may be blessed with peace, that there shall be no abridgment of the great freedom of worship afforded by the government of this land. May thy Saints be recognized as good citizens and may thy work grow and flourish in this favored part of thy vineyard.

—FROM THE DEDICATORY PRAYER

In October 1997, President Gordon B. Hinckley visited Fiji, an independent republic in the southern Pacific Ocean composed of more than three hundred islands, one hundred of which are inhabited. At a meeting of the Saints during that visit, President Hinckley asked whoever in the congregation desired a temple in Fiji to raise his or her hand. Every hand shot into the air.[1] Excitement was even greater not long afterward when, during April 1998 general conference, President Hinckley officially announced the Suva Fiji Temple.

The history of the Church in the island nation is not long, but it is eventful. Missionary work officially began in Fiji in 1954. When President David O. McKay visited there 1955, he told a small gathering of Saints that the time had come to build up the kingdom of God in their homeland. He emphasized the importance of being an example, of participating in member-missionary work, and of performing service.

President McKay authorized the building in Fiji of a large meetinghouse with all of the standard features, including a kitchen, a cultural hall with a stage, multiple classrooms, and so on. At the dedication of the chapel in 1958, President

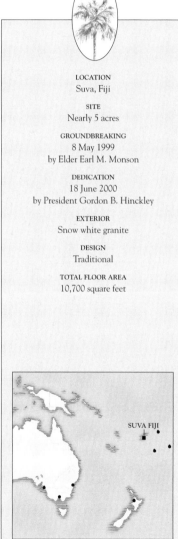

LOCATION
Suva, Fiji

SITE
Nearly 5 acres

GROUNDBREAKING
8 May 1999
by Elder Earl M. Monson

DEDICATION
18 June 2000
by President Gordon B. Hinckley

EXTERIOR
Snow white granite

DESIGN
Traditional

TOTAL FLOOR AREA
10,700 square feet

SUVA FIJI

McKay told Church members that they would soon grow into their building—and even outgrow it.[2]

This prophecy was quickly fulfilled, and at the time of the groundbreaking for the temple in May 1999, Fiji was home to eighteen chapels and two Church-operated schools.

Before the completion of the Suva Fiji Temple, Saints in the temple district—which includes Fiji and the nearby island nations of Vanuatu, New Caledonia, Kiribati, Nauru, and Tuvalu—traveled to Tonga, Samoa, or New Zealand to attend the temple. These trips were long and expensive, and many Saints had limited resources. One family sold their home to raise the funds so they could travel to New Zealand to be sealed. Other faithful Church members likewise sacrificed whatever was necessary to achieve their goal of receiving the temple ordinances.[3]

Members in the temple district may now attend much more conveniently. Their beautiful temple is located at one of the highest points in Suva, the capital of Fiji, and overlooks the Pacific Ocean on three sides. The granite exterior walls create a striking contrast to the lush green vegetation that surrounds the building.

The site was identified by President Hinckley in October 1997 as the preferred location for the temple. The owners of the property were originally willing to sell it but later took it off the market. Though Church leaders made several attempts to acquire it, it was no longer available. Eventually, leaders identified three other possible sites and were about to take them to the general authorities for approval. Then, explained Elder Quentin L. Cook of the Seventy, and president of the Pacific Islands Area, "The original owner called and said that the property would be sold to the Church and at a very reasonable price."[4]

During the dedicatory services, Elder Cook explained that once the site was obtained and construction had begun, workers discovered several underground concrete bunkers. Elder Cook read from a history of the area written by Elder Allen Christensen, who had served as the executive secretary for the Pacific Islands Area presidency, that the bunkers "had been erected during World War II for the defense of Suva." Elder Cook declared, "Where once stood structures erected to resist [invasion] will now stand a fortress of faith, a House of the Lord . . . where the blessings of eternity can be given to the faithful."[5]

The peaceful setting of the temple belies the unwanted excitement that surrounded the temple's opening. On 19 May 2000, a few weeks before the planned open house and dedication, amidst ethnic tensions, armed rebels took several government officials hostage. Because of safety concerns in the volatile political climate, the temple open house received limited publicity. Even then, the six-day event brought more than sixteen thousand members of the public and three hundred community leaders to tour the temple.[6]

Temple guides noticed that attending the open house often brought visible relief to the worried citizens of Fiji. "As we took them through the temple, we saw the cares of the world melt away and, by the time they reached the celestial room, you could tell that they were experiencing something very special," said Elder Cook, who conducted tours for community leaders.

Sister Lolene Adams, an organizer of the open house, shared one particularly touching experience: "Three high-ranking military men came through and were very quiet and reserved when they viewed the introductory video. I spoke with the second-in-command and asked how he felt when he looked in the reflections in the mirrors in the celestial room. He said he had studied eternal life for many years and had never understood it, but when he looked in the mirrors it all came clear to him and he was excited." The senior officer asked if it would be possible to bring the full military council to tour the temple. "Because of the strife in Fiji," Sister Adams explained, "he felt that the temple was a place they could come and close out the outside world . . . and find peace."[7]

Despite the political unrest, President Gordon B. Hinckley dedicated the Suva Fiji Temple on 18 June 2000. Believing that holding the usual four dedicatory services might be unwise, the First Presidency decided on one small dedicatory session attended mostly by members of the local temple committee and their families. Mindful of the difficulties in the land, President Hinckley petitioned for peace in the temple's dedicatory prayer. "We pray, dear Father," he said, "that these beautiful islands may be blessed with peace, that there shall be no abridgment of the great freedom of worship afforded by the government of this land."[8]

President Hinckley described his feelings after this unusual dedication. "There was a great outpouring of the Spirit," he said, "matched by the feeling of good fellowship among those in attendance." Others commented that the unity of Church members greatly outweighed the political and ethnic division in the country, as evidenced by the love shown by Saints of all ethnic groups at the temple dedication.[9]

Although many were disappointed at being unable to attend the long-awaited dedication, the services increased the Fijian Saints' excitement at being able to receive the sacred temple ordinances in their own land.

. . . may thy work grow and flourish in this favored part of thy vineyard

Mérida México Temple

Latter-day Saints living in Merida, Mexico, capital of the state of Yucatan, are acutely aware of current archaeological research. One meetinghouse displays on its bulletin board an article describing strong similarities between civilizations in Mexico and ancient Middle Eastern–Judaic civilizations. The article, written by scholars who are not Latter-day Saints, is just one indication that the history of Merida, located in the center of Mesoamerica and home to important archaeological sites, may date back to Book of Mormon times. "We love the Book of Mormon; we can *feel* the Book of Mormon," said Miguel Tun, a branch president in Ticul, a town sixty miles from Merida.[1]

Merida, home to the ninety-second temple of the Church, is part of the Yucatan Peninsula, which projects into the Atlantic Ocean and separates the Gulf of Mexico from the Caribbean Sea. Founded by the Spanish in 1542, Merida sits atop an ancient Mayan city. A goodly number of Church members in this peninsula rich in history meet in dozens of chapels and now flock to a temple of the Lord.

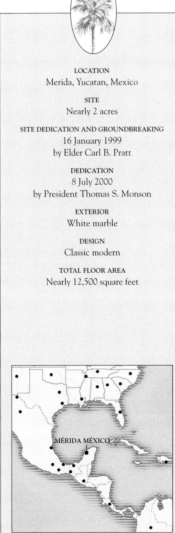

LOCATION
Merida, Yucatan, Mexico

SITE
Nearly 2 acres

SITE DEDICATION AND GROUNDBREAKING
16 January 1999
by Elder Carl B. Pratt

DEDICATION
8 July 2000
by President Thomas S. Monson

EXTERIOR
White marble

DESIGN
Classic modern

TOTAL FLOOR AREA
Nearly 12,500 square feet

MÉRIDA MÉXICO

The building of a temple came as a great blessing to the faithful members who had labored to build the Church in their area. In 1989, when Elder Carlos H. Amado of the Seventy organized the third stake in Merida, he asked local priesthood leaders to be ready to organize another stake by the same time the following year. "We took this as a challenge," said Joaquin Eduardo Carrillo, president of the newly formed Merida Mexico Centro Stake. "The stake presidents and mission president began working very hard on this." On 10 June 1990, their efforts resulted in a fourth stake in Merida. It was created one day before the one-year deadline.[2]

This amazing growth rate is just one example of what these faithful Saints have done to prepare themselves for a house of the Lord.

In an area near the famous Uxmal and Chichen Itza Mayan ruins on the Yucatan Peninsula, Elder Carl B. Pratt of the Seventy and president of the Mexico South Area presided at the ceremonial groundbreaking for the temple on 16 January 1999. Elder Pratt told the more than five hundred members who had gathered for the event: "We want to establish a culture of temple attendance. From sacrifice comes blessings. I know that the construction of this temple will add to the strength of the home; it will add to the love of husbands and wives; it will add to the peace in the Yucatan Peninsula." He also told the Saints that the maintenance of the temple would become their responsibility, and he promised Aaronic Priesthood holders that they would have the task and blessing of caring for the gardens on the temple grounds.[3]

The time they now spend to care for their temple is indeed a blessing, not a sacrifice, to these faithful Saints who used to make long, costly excursions to the temple in Mexico City. The temple in Guatemala City, Guatemala, is actually closer geographically for these Saints, but to reach it, Church members had to cross an international border, a jungle, and several mountain ranges. These obstacles made the one-thousand-mile trip to the Mexico City Mexico Temple an easier option.[4]

Yet this journey was very costly, and many sacrificed for years to pay their travel expenses. They did so because they know that temple blessings are priceless. Some longtime members even gratefully endured two-week trips to the Mesa Arizona Temple. "Many sacrifices marked those temple trips to Mesa," said Jose Andres Parra, a pioneer Church member in Merida. "Sometimes it would take four days to travel to the temple. Then we would spend four days in the temple and another four days to return to our homes."[5]

Another pioneer Church member, Celia Carrillo, who was baptized in 1959, described a journey to the temple in Mexico City on a train infested with mice that "scurried across my feet as we traveled." On a later temple trip, Sister Carrillo was with a group of Saints on a rented bus when the driver lost control on an isolated section of highway and the bus ended up in a gully.

"I didn't want to open my eyes for fear some of the members had been killed," Sister Carrillo said. Fortunately, the passengers' injuries were minor, but as they climbed out of the bus, they were confronted with robbers preparing to get whatever they could from the stranded bus riders. Suddenly, and without explanation for their change of mind, the robbers quickly left the scene. Nearby villagers offered assistance and medical care.

"We talked then about returning to Merida and forgetting about the temple, but we all said, 'Let's continue on,'" Sister Carrillo said.[6]

Although many of these hardships are now in the past, they will never be forgotten. Remembering these sacrifices increases the Saints' gratitude for their temple.

The Merida Mexico Temple is located in the old section of the city, where the roads are narrow and the history of the area has been preserved. When Church leaders proposed building a temple there, city planners required that aesthetic and historic consistency be maintained, so designers included a wall in front of the temple that harmonizes with existing structures. But the old did give way to the new when the stake center, mission office, and seminary building on the temple site were removed. The future of the Church is manifest here: the remaining property is large enough for a stake center to be built when the time is right.[7]

The Merida Mexico Temple, faced with Blanco Guardiano marble from Torreon, Mexico, was dedicated in four sessions on 8 July 2000 by President Thomas S. Monson, first counselor in the First Presidency. For Domingo Renan Perez Maldonado, president of the Merida Mexico Itzimna Stake, the event was a fulfillment of prophecy. He had been hoping for a temple to be built near his home ever since he served as an interpreter to Elder David B. Haight of the Quorum of the Twelve Apostles during a 1979 visit to the Yucatan Peninsula.

"The apostle told us a temple would be built here someday," he said. "This temple will be a place of spiritual light for everybody."[8]

May we ever carry in our hearts a great sense of gratitude for its presence in this our land and city

Veracruz México Temple

It is a magnificent blessing to have this holy house in our midst, to which we may come, to be endowed by thee from on high, to make covenants with thee, to be sealed together as families under thy divine plan. Sanctify it to our good, dear Father. May we always look upon it as the house of the Lord, with holiness unto thee.

—FROM THE DEDICATORY PRAYER

On 28 January 1996, President Gordon B. Hinckley spoke to nine thousand Church members gathered for a regional conference in Veracruz, Mexico. He reminded listeners of a visit he had made to Veracruz in 1978, when there was only one stake of the Church there. The Church has grown substantially in the intervening years, he remarked; the large crowd gathered to hear him speak that day was evidence of the growth. Through an interpreter, he told the congregation of Saints, "The more often you go [to the temple], the more certainly you will know of the truth of this great work in the house of the Lord." In an earlier meeting, with more than one thousand local priesthood leaders in attendance, President Hinckley had reminded leaders of their stewardship over the spiritual growth of their brothers and sisters in the gospel. "You have responsibility for the work of the Lord in this great area," he said. "It will stand or move forward according to what you do. . . . We are all in this together, to build the kingdom of God in the earth; and if we work together, nothing can stop us."[1]

Nothing has stopped them. Their efforts resulted in the announcement of the Veracruz Mexico Temple on 14 April 1999, three short years after President Hinckley's counsel to Church leaders and members in Veracruz.

LOCATION
Veracruz, Mexico

SITE
More than 3 acres

SITE DEDICATION AND GROUNDBREAKING
29 May 1999
by Elder Carl B. Pratt

DEDICATION
9 July 2000
by President Thomas S. Monson

EXTERIOR
White marble

DESIGN
Classic modern

TOTAL FLOOR AREA
Nearly 12,500 square feet

VERACRUZ MÉXICO

On 29 May 1999, many of those same stake and ward leaders and their families attended the groundbreaking for the new temple. Services were held at the temple site outside Veracruz, an important seaport in eastern Mexico dating back to the sixteenth century. Elder Carl B. Pratt of the Seventy presided at the occasion and during his remarks acknowledged the early Saints in Veracruz, who had faithfully sacrificed to travel to the temple in Mesa, Arizona. Because members understood the importance of temple worship, they had been willing to make any necessary sacrifices with an attitude that helped secure the blessings of the Lord. Their example prepared the members for this day of building a temple nearby, Elder Pratt said. "We are in the true Church," he continued. "We are preparing the earth for the Second Coming, and with the temple we will be better prepared to do so."[2]

The members may have been prepared for the temple's construction, but there was still work to be done among government officials and citizens of Veracruz. Under pressure from the public, city officials hesitated to give the temple project supervisors a license to begin construction. For months, Church leaders made unsuccessful weekly attempts to acquire the license. Finally, Rodolfo "Rudy" Avalos, the project supervisor, met with the mayor. With his support, city officials finally granted the license, and construction on the project began.[3]

The construction of the temple was not completed without difficulty, but again the Lord's guiding hand was evident. On one occasion, workers were digging a deep trench to accommodate a sewer line. During the digging, the trench unexpectedly caved in and completely buried two men. "We could not find them for a few seconds," Brother Avalos explained. "We were finally able to uncover their heads, which allowed them to breathe while we dug them out. It was a blessing no one was killed."[4] All who were present that day realized a fatal accident had been prevented, and they acknowledged the Lord's blessings upon their work.

A watchful heavenly eye also helped workers the day the angel Moroni statue was placed atop the temple. Workers and Church leaders were concerned about the weather. "It had been raining heavily, and I asked the workers and bishops to pray that the rain would cease," Brother Avalos explained. "It is extremely dangerous to place the angel on the metal spire when it is raining because of electrical currents." But, he continued, "as we prepared to raise the angel, it immediately stopped raining. Once the statue was in position, the rain began to fall again."[5] Workers were able to complete this task on time and maintain their tight construction schedule.

With the construction completed, the dedication of the Veracruz temple was scheduled for 9 July 2000. Shortly before the dedication, Church officials learned of a large all-terrain vehicle and motorcycle rally scheduled to take place near the temple on the morning of the dedicatory services. That event, with its crowds and loud engines, was planned for a location less than fifty yards from the temple grounds. Both it and the temple cornerstone ceremony were to begin at 9 A.M. Dedication organizers were concerned and wondered how to maintain the reverent feeling appropriate for placing the cornerstone of a house of the Lord. But Sunday morning, the day of the dedication, arrived with rain showers significant enough to cancel all the scheduled off-road vehicle events. Ron Weekes, media specialist for the dedication, observed, "I know that the hand of the Lord was involved with what transpired."

In his opening comments during the first of the four sessions, President Thomas S. Monson, first counselor in the First Presidency, who presided and who gave the dedicatory prayer, acknowledged the hand of the Lord in making sure the dedication of the Veracruz Mexico Temple could be carried out in the spirit it deserved.[6]

Latter-day Saints in Mexico may forever recall the year 2000 as the year of Mexican temples. Two temples were operating in Mexico when the year began, and eight new temples were dedicated in that country during 2000. Two more temples have been announced—for Guadalajara and Monterrey. This phenomenal increase has made it possible for almost every Church member in Mexico to reach a temple within a four-hour drive.[7]

The great increase in temple building has not gone unnoticed by the citizens of Mexico. Many citizens consider the temples to be the most beautiful buildings in their cities. Jay Erekson, project manager for the Oaxaca Mexico Temple, commented: "We set an entirely new standard in quality for buildings in Mexico by building these temples the way we have built them. In recent history, there has never been anything like them in terms of the quality of workmanship achieved in these temples."[8]

And after years of sacrifice to attend the temple, great increases in temple building have certainly not gone unnoticed by Latter-day Saints in Mexico. These grateful Church members are showing their appreciation by being a temple-attending and a temple-loving people. Rodolfo Avalos, project supervisor for the Veracruz Mexico Temples, summed up the feelings of many: "It is a very wonderful process to prepare temples for the Lord. I am grateful for these opportunities. I have grown from all I have experienced."[9]

It is a magnificent blessing to have this holy house in our midst

Baton Rouge Louisiana Temple

Baton Rouge Louisiana Stake president Brent D. Rawson received a telephone call during the summer of 1998 from the Church Temple Department. The caller told him that evaluations were underway for the possible construction of a temple in the Baton Rouge area and asked him for his assistance. President Rawson measured the ground immediately behind the Baton Rouge stake center and behind another local meetinghouse, confirming that there was ample land on either site to accommodate a small temple.

After receiving this research, Elder Monte J. Brough of the Seventy and president of the North America Southeast Area was asked to make a recommendation. Elder Brough suggested the site where the temple now stands because of the "sweet peaceful feelings" he had while observing the wooded area at the base of the hill behind the stake center. He later told President Rawson that he knew this was the place where the Lord would have one of his temples built. The recommendation was endorsed by the Temple Department and approved by the First Presidency.[1]

The temple sits at the base of a small hill and is only sixteen feet above sea level. It is the first house of the Lord to be built in the Louisiana-Mississippi area. Despite its big-city setting, visitors to the temple are impressed by its natural and picturesque surroundings. Directly northeast of the temple boundaries is a nature preserve, and raccoons, armadillos, opossums, and waterfowl are frequently seen.

The peacefulness of its location is important to local Church members, but more important is the accessibility it gives them to the ordinances of the Lord's house. As one of the fastest growing cities in Louisiana, Baton Rouge is also home

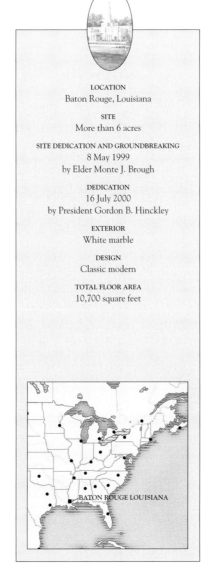

LOCATION
Baton Rouge, Louisiana

SITE
More than 6 acres

SITE DEDICATION AND GROUNDBREAKING
8 May 1999
by Elder Monte J. Brough

DEDICATION
16 July 2000
by President Gordon B. Hinckley

EXTERIOR
White marble

DESIGN
Classic modern

TOTAL FLOOR AREA
10,700 square feet

BATON ROUGE LOUISIANA

to a growing Latter-day Saint population. President Rawson articulated the feelings of local members who had traveled long distances to attend the temple. "Dallas, the closest temple, was nine and a half hours away for some of our people," he said. "To have a facility here is something people have only dreamed about." He concluded, "It's a dream come true for many people of the Church."[2]

Members rejoiced in this fulfillment of a dream on 14 October 1998, when they received a letter from the First Presidency announcing the temple. They again rejoiced when ground was broken on 8 May 1999, many arriving hours early for the groundbreaking. The sun shone brightly on this historic day in typically humid Louisiana, and temperatures soared above eighty degrees. But the Latter-day Saints remained undaunted, and approximately twenty-five hundred people gathered to witness the event.

During the groundbreaking ceremonies, Elder Brough encouraged members to remember their obligations to their Heavenly Father. "May He help us understand our responsibility to [ensure] that this temple won't be empty," Elder Brough said.[3]

Elder Brough spoke of his former assignment in the Church Family History Department and explained that workers and volunteers were microfilming records that could provide temples with six hundred million names per year. The temples in operation at that time, however, were completing ordinance work for six million people per year. Still, President Gordon B. Hinckley asked the Family History Department to keep up their pace of preserving and gathering these important records.[4]

Baton Rouge
Louisiana Temple

Grant unto thy Saints a vision of the great and eternal work for
which it has been constructed. May thy people come here frequently
and be refreshed by a knowledge of thine eternal and everlasting
purposes in behalf of thy children of all generations. Wilt thou smile
upon them from thy dwelling place on high and cause their thoughts
to reach up to thee and to thy beloved Son who, through the gift of
his life, brought salvation unto all of thy sons and daughters, and
the opportunity of exaltation to all who walk in obedience to thy
commandments.

—FROM THE DEDICATORY PRAYER

Baton Rouge

Chad Hawkins
© 2000

The department's ability to gather such a large number of names, Elder Brough said, is a fulfillment of Malachi's prophecy that the hearts of the children will turn to their fathers. "Last year," Elder Brough said, "the Family History Department filmed in many different countries, gathering millions of names. At current rates, we have collected enough names to keep the temples busy for a long time." With the building of more temples, he concluded, "we really have no excuse" but to keep working.[5]

As the Baton Rouge Louisiana Temple neared completion, a last-minute decision was made to add three ceiling medallions to the interior. When the medallions arrived, workers noticed that the one intended for the celestial room was damaged. The project manager, Marc Lundin, immediately began searching for a replacement, only to find that the original supplier and all the other dealers he could find were out of stock. Even the manufacturer was unable to provide another one.

Finally, with the help of the Internet, Marc located a dealer in Atlanta, Georgia, who had one left. Marc gave him the address of the temple in Baton Rouge, and the dealer remarked, "My church is getting ready to dedicate a building in Baton Rouge." Marc quickly asked, "What church would that be?" When the dealer responded, "The LDS Church," Marc was happy to tell him that they were both referring to the very same building, adding that the medallion would be placed in the celestial room. Marc then asked what the price of the medallion would be, and J. Doyle Henderson, the Latter-day Saint who happened to have the only remaining one available, said he was grateful to have the opportunity to donate the medallion to the temple.[6]

Hidden in this drawing of the Baton Rouge Louisiana Temple is a full-length image of the Savior inviting us to attend the temple and experience the blessings found in serving herein.

The medallion was one of the many donations members made to building the temple. When the marble veneer for the temple's exterior walls was shipped to the construction site from Vermont, one of the eighteen-wheel delivery trucks arrived after the construction crew had left. Only the foreman, Max Quayle, was still on the site to receive the shipment of ten crates of marble, each weighing three-quarters of a ton. Brother Quayle unloaded two crates, and then a hydraulic line on the forklift broke.

The truck driver needed to get back on the road quickly, so the only solution seemed to be to unload the truck by hand. A few phone calls were made, and within fifteen minutes twenty-five young Latter-day Saints were there, ready to assist with the seemingly insurmountable task. They unloaded the remaining eight crates, approximately fifteen thousand pounds of marble. The young men went the extra mile by placing the marble, piece by piece, around the temple where workers could use it as it was needed. After that they freed the truck, which was stuck on a pile of sand.

Although it was a night of very hard labor, it was work that made the Baton Rouge Louisiana Temple even more of a blessing to the young men who participated. The marble story—their contribution to building their temple—will be one they share with their children in years to come.[7]

The final chapter in the building of the temple occurred on 16 July 2000 when President Gordon B. Hinckley dedicated the temple, making it possible for the Saints to pass down stories of frequent temple attendance and the blessings that accompany that work.

May thy people come here frequently

Oklahoma City Oklahoma Temple

In March 1999, Church members in Oklahoma City learned that a temple would be constructed next to their meetinghouse when stake president Gary J. Newman asked in a sacrament meeting, "Would any of you mind giving up your baseball field for a temple?"[1]

Years earlier, when the Church had purchased the property for that meetinghouse, the sellers had donated an additional parcel of land. A meetinghouse was built on the property, and members often enjoyed a baseball game on the donated portion. With gratitude for the Lord's blessings, they rejoiced in the proposal to put the land to another, more sacred use.

Invitations to the groundbreaking ceremonies on 3 July 1999 were kept to a minimum to avoid disrupting the surrounding neighborhood. During the groundbreaking, David L. Lawton, president of the Oklahoma City Oklahoma South Stake, spoke of a tornado that had devastated much of their stake just two months earlier. "I feel, in looking back, that there was a great purpose of the Lord in the tornado: (1) It strengthened us—helped us all remember how temporary the things of this world are. [They are] not to be relied on. (2) It . . . temper[ed] opposition to our temple. More than 100,000 Latter-day Saint hours of volunteer labor were given in behalf of those whose homes and businesses and schools and churches were ravaged. The 8,000 members giving a helping hand in the community made others view the Mormons in a different light."[2]

Elder Rex D. Pinegar of the Seventy and president of the North America Southwest Area also referred to the tornado disaster during his address: "As we drove through the area of its swath, we saw signs on top of the rubble. . . . 'We've been crushed but we're not out', 'Temporarily out of service.' . . . As

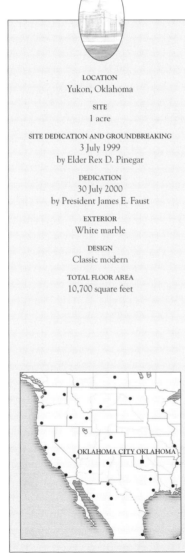

LOCATION
Yukon, Oklahoma

SITE
1 acre

SITE DEDICATION AND GROUNDBREAKING
3 July 1999
by Elder Rex D. Pinegar

DEDICATION
30 July 2000
by President James E. Faust

EXTERIOR
White marble

DESIGN
Classic modern

TOTAL FLOOR AREA
10,700 square feet

OKLAHOMA CITY OKLAHOMA

we scanned the area, we saw nothing standing but the people. A sign on a demolished home read: 'In God we trust.'" These signs, Elder Pinegar said, displayed the character of the members and the community living in the vicinity of the planned Oklahoma City temple.[3]

Although it was devastating, many local Latter-day Saints agreed that the tornado helped prepare the way for the temple. The Church's aid in cleanup and relief efforts had a dramatic effect on the community's perception of the Church. Leaders and workers were able to proceed with their building plans because there was no substantial obstacle or any notable opposition toward building the temple.[4]

The design for the temple did have to be altered slightly for the temple to fit the selected site, however. Architects adjusted the floor plan of the Oklahoma City Oklahoma Temple by mirroring the original plan. Instead of entering toward the right end of the building, patrons go through an entrance on the left. Once inside, they find the baptistry on the left instead of the right as in most other small temples.

At 9 A.M. on 9 March 2000, a milestone in the construction was reached when the steeple and the statue of the angel Moroni were raised and placed on top of the temple. These events brought tears to the eyes of those in attendance. James R. Engebretsen, president of the Oklahoma Oklahoma City Mission, had instructed his missionaries to attend in order to assist in crowd control. Church members, however, had obeyed their leaders' request to stay away out of respect for the temple's neighbors and their privacy. Ironically, the missionaries sent to control the crowd became the crowd.[5]

Many of those same local Church members arrived almost immediately, however, when the contractor responsible for

Oklahoma City Oklahoma Temple

Dear Father, we thank thee for this thy sacred house. We have longed for it. We are grateful that this day has come. It is wonderful to have this temple in our midst, where we may partake of the ordinances of the everlasting gospel made possible through the bestowal of the fulness of the priesthood.

—FROM THE DEDICATORY PRAYER

Oklahoma City

laying the sod did not keep his commitments. A bishop made some phone calls, and within an hour, more than 150 members were on the site laying sod. One member with a tractor graded the site until 2 A.M.

Efforts to beautify the temple grounds were a success, and the subsequent fourteen-day open house was attended by more than forty thousand visitors. The open house itself differed in its approach from previous ones. Organizers experimented with replacing the traditional self-guided, silent tours with tours in which a guide explained the rooms the tour covered. At first, half the tours were self-guided and half were not. But the guided tours were clearly more successful, and organizers soon arranged for all the remaining tours to include assistance from a guide. In the end, the open house resulted in the placing of fifteen hundred copies of the Book of Mormon and receiving thirty-eight missionary referrals. The guided tours were so successful that they were adopted for use in open houses at other temples.[6]

The success of the open house is particularly evident in an experience told by President Newman:

"To me the greatest blessing of the open house was when a lady shared with me that she had only heard bad about the Mormons and that all she saw in the temple was good. Her perception of the Church and temples has changed forever; it will never be the same. We made many friends during the open house."[7]

An image of the Savior is hidden on the wall of the temple, beckoning us to partake of the blessings of temple service.

The completed white marble Oklahoma City Oklahoma Temple complements its country atmosphere, standing among tall green trees near a golf course and a quiet residential area in northwest Oklahoma City. At night, the temple can be seen from great distances.

The building's peaceful and dramatic beauty has impressed many in the temple district, which encompasses an area once known as Indian Territory. In the 1840s, thousands of Native Americans were forced from their homes in the cold of winter. They found refuge in Oklahoma. Their march, called the "Trail of Tears," was filled with sickness and death. Oklahoma City temple president H. Jerrel Chesney described the emotional significance of having a temple in this part of the country. "After being driven and suffering as they did, after the government then designated this as the official home of the Lamanite people, now the gospel is here for them with the full benefits."[8] Many members living in the temple district are descendants of those who were forced here and live on the same land as their ancestors.

The temple was dedicated on 30 July 2000 by President James E. Faust, second counselor in the First Presidency. Anne Pemberton, a Latter-day Saint and a member of the Delaware tribe, commented: "It's home. . . . [The temple] is sacred and on sacred ground. Our ancestors have waited. They rejoice in this day."[9]

It is wonderful to have this temple in our midst

Caracas Venezuela Temple

Venezuela's varied geography ranges from Amazon rain forests to high mountain peaks to balmy beaches. Caracas, its capital, is located twenty-seven hundred feet above sea level and is blessed with temperatures at a nearly constant seventy degrees Fahrenheit.

On 2 November 1966, Elder Marion G. Romney of the Quorum of the Twelve Apostles dedicated the country for the preaching of the gospel. Within weeks four missionaries from the Costa Rica mission were sent to Venezuela. They found the work hard and the growth slow in the beginning.

Nonetheless, strong individuals and families began entering the waters of baptism. In less than eight years Church membership in this beautiful land had grown to nearly four thousand.

In 1974 the first Latter-day Saint meetinghouse was constructed. In the mid-1980s, twenty years after the entrance of missionaries into the country, Church membership had reached nearly twenty-five thousand in five stakes and eight districts.

In a session of general conference on 30 September 1995, President Gordon B. Hinckley announced plans to construct a temple in Venezuela. Immediately after this announcement, the search for an appropriate building site was begun. Several properties were identified and considered over the next eighteen months. But because of circumstances ranging from extremely high prices to zoning restrictions that would not allow religious use of the land, no suitable location was found.

Despite discouraging setbacks, the prophet did not lose sight of the goal. On 5 April 1997, President Gordon B.

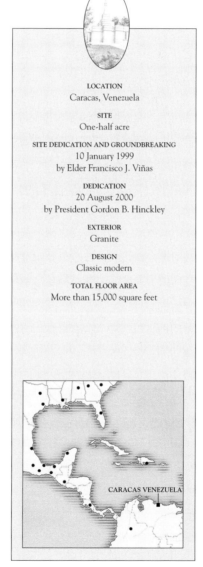

LOCATION
Caracas, Venezuela

SITE
One-half acre

SITE DEDICATION AND GROUNDBREAKING
10 January 1999
by Elder Francisco J. Viñas

DEDICATION
20 August 2000
by President Gordon B. Hinckley

EXTERIOR
Granite

DESIGN
Classic modern

TOTAL FLOOR AREA
More than 15,000 square feet

CARACAS VENEZUELA

Hinckley again stated in general conference, "The search for a suitable property continues in Venezuela."[1]

When President Hinckley announced and explained the concept of smaller temples, new options opened up in Venezuela, and representatives of the Church reexamined existing holdings in the country. Finally, the decision was made to build a house of the Lord in the city of Caracas on a lot the Church had owned since 1977.[2]

Groundbreaking ceremonies were held Sunday, 10 January 1999, with approximately three hundred people crowded into the Caurimare ward chapel in Caracas to hear their leaders speak at the services. Construction began soon thereafter.

Several unforeseen obstructions blocked progress on the temple construction. For example, when digging the foundation, excavators discovered an underground spring. Once the water was diverted, excavation could continue. The digging, however, caused two landslides. Both occurred after hours when there were no workers in harm's way, but the second landslide did cause some damage—eight tons of earth and materials were shifted in the slide.

Construction supervisor Duane Cheney stated: "In all my experience as a builder, never have I had the problems that I have seen in temple construction, but besides the fact that the adversary works with power and strength, the feeling that fills me is that all will work out well.

"In fact the Lord, Jesus Christ himself, directs this project and has helped us and will continue doing so."[3]

Although the design of the Caracas Venezuela Temple follows the general plan for small temples, the topography of the building site required a few changes that actually increased the

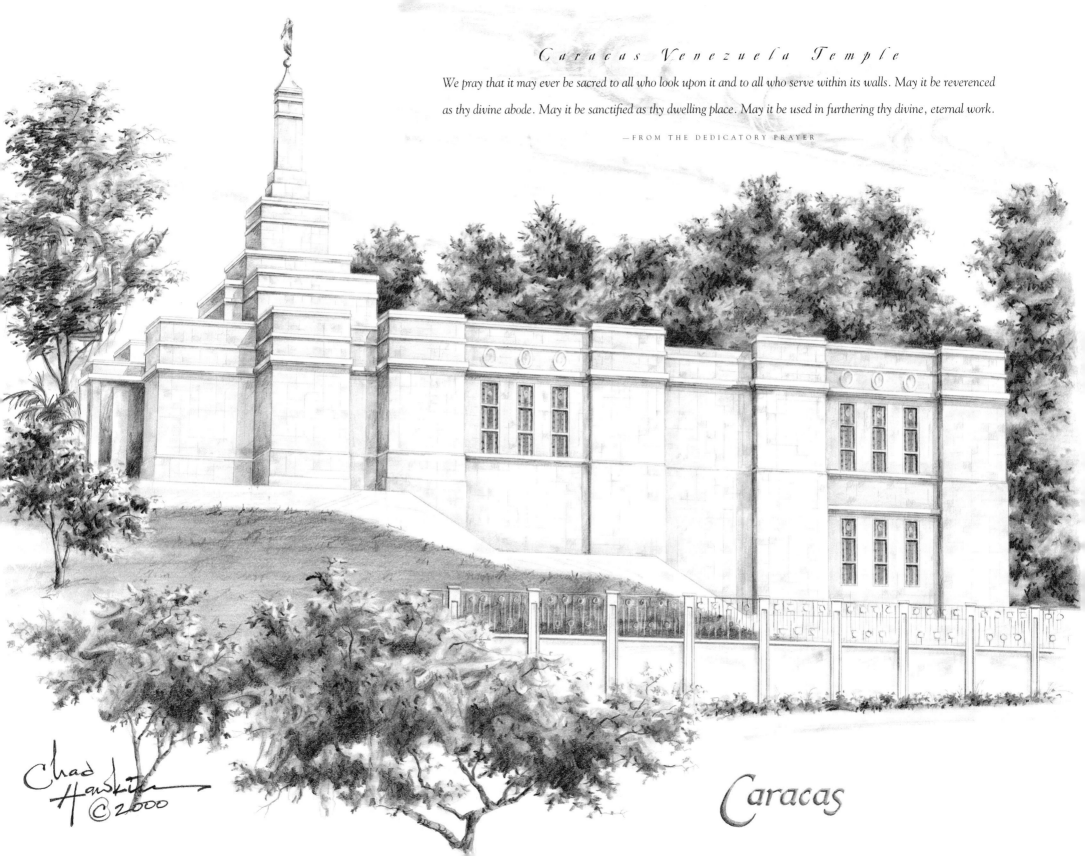

Caracas Venezuela Temple

We pray that it may ever be sacred to all who look upon it and to all who serve within its walls. May it be reverenced as thy divine abode. May it be sanctified as thy dwelling place. May it be used in furthering thy divine, eternal work.

—FROM THE DEDICATORY PRAYER

Caracas

Chad Hawkins
© 2000

total square footage. To ensure that the baptismal font was lower than other parts of the temple, a second floor was added. The consequent rearrangement of the floor plan allowed for a larger entry and lobby.

The interior design and decor of the Caracas Venezuela Temple is the result of loving service by local Saints. The lamps and chandeliers, chosen for their beauty and luminosity and imported from Spain, were assembled in part by volunteers. Nine young women and their mothers and grandmothers carefully placed nearly five thousand crystal pieces in the lamps and chandeliers for the sealing rooms and the celestial room.

Two sisters who are artists created paintings for the temple that represent the country of Venezuela.

The exterior of the temple is granite, imported from Spain and cut and polished in Venezuela. The polished surface gleams almost mirrorlike in the sunshine.

Nearly six thousand Latter-day Saints from the temple district attended the four dedicatory sessions presided over by

Left of the temple is hidden an image of the Savior. Images of oxen, reminiscent of the baptismal font, are hidden in the foreground.

President Gordon B. Hinckley. Perhaps the most important counsel he gave the Saints was never to let a day pass without holding a current temple recommend. Members were obviously deeply moved by the presence and counsel of the living prophet.

At the conclusion of the day's events, President Hinckley, his wife, Sister Marjorie Hinckley, and the others of their party climbed into the waiting cars. As they drove from the temple grounds, thousands of Venezuelan Saints saluted the procession, waving white handkerchiefs and singing in their own language "We Thank Thee, O God, for a Prophet."[4]

President Ruiz of the Caracas Venezuela Stake summed up the feeling among the Saints toward this new house of the Lord as he reminded the people that temples bring blessings—and new responsibilities:

"The Venezuelan temple will leave our people spiritually refined," he said. "Our people are going to change. Venezuela is going to change."[5]

We pray that it may ever be sacred to all who look upon it

Houston Texas Temple

Houston, Texas, the fourth largest city in the United States, is home to the ninety-seventh temple of The Church of Jesus Christ of Latter-day Saints. The Church members who live in this area know that it was only through the Spirit of the Lord, combined with years of preparation on the part of local members, that the pathway was made clear for the construction of a house of the Lord.

On 19 February 1997, the search for a temple site began. Houston realtor Steve Cook, a faithful member of the Church who had assisted representatives of the Church in purchasing real estate in the past, was asked to help find the site. Several potential sites were located, but Brother Cook's top choice belonged to a prominent real estate developer who had no desire to sell. The developer had, in fact, received offers from other parties but was holding that prime location in reserve for a project of his own. Brother Cook worked to build a trusting relationship with this developer and maintained an interest in the site. A different religious organization had previously treated the developer dishonestly, and he was extremely cautious as a result.

Brother Cook continued to meet with the property owner and, in time, the owner realized he could trust the Church. This developer had faced financial ruin in the 1980s and had humbly knelt in prayer, asking for God's intervention. Circumstances changed, and he survived the challenge. In an effort to show gratitude for that answered prayer, he decided that he should sell the land for the "Mormon cathedral." Not surprisingly, this soul-searching decision happened on the same weekend that President Gordon B. Hinckley chose this site from among the several possibilities proposed to him.[1]

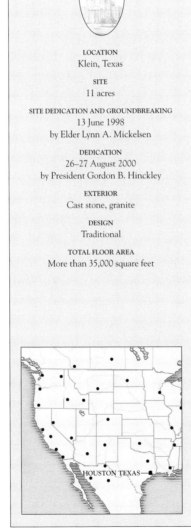

LOCATION
Klein, Texas

SITE
11 acres

SITE DEDICATION AND GROUNDBREAKING
13 June 1998
by Elder Lynn A. Mickelsen

DEDICATION
26–27 August 2000
by President Gordon B. Hinckley

EXTERIOR
Cast stone, granite

DESIGN
Traditional

TOTAL FLOOR AREA
More than 35,000 square feet

HOUSTON TEXAS

The Houston Texas Temple was originally intended to resemble the temple in Billings, Montana, but the plans were altered to provide an architectural design and plan more harmonious with local buildings.

Brother Steve Cook shared some thoughts about his involvement with the temple: "It was astounding to me to witness the miracles that continually occurred in achieving the Lord's purposes and seeing people's hearts changed. Additionally, it was humbling to see the Lord exercise His influence in such a pragmatic way; he moves and touches men's hearts to accomplish His purposes."[2]

A plumber working on the job had his heart changed in a significant way. Before he started to work on the temple, he "smoked like a chimney and every other word was a swear word." Because construction workers on the temple site followed strict rules about not smoking and swearing, it was hard for this man to control his language. His behavior did not change only on the temple site, however; he changed his habits on other jobs as well.[3]

For years Latter-day Saints in Houston had been developing improved community relations among their neighbors and also with people who ended up acting as key decision makers on city and community boards that approved various aspects of the construction project. What opposition remained was ineffective and went largely unnoticed. In the most open show of resistance, members of opposition groups positioned themselves outside the temple grounds during the public open house to hand out deceptive material about the Church. Relatively little literature made it to the hands of members, however, for they were more concerned about ensuring that

Houston Texas Temple

With living proxies acting in behalf of those who are dead, baptisms will be performed, ordinances and covenants will be administered, and the great crowning sealing of husbands and wives, parents and children will take place. How glorious and complete is thy plan for the salvation and exaltation of thy children of all generations. How tremendous is our obligation to carry forward this great vicarious work in their behalf.

—FROM THE DEDICATORY PRAYER

HOUSTON TEXAS TEMPLE
THE CHURCH OF JESUS CHRIST OF LATTER-DAY SAINTS

the protestors had sufficient food and water to endure the challenging Texas heat.

Even the temple's landscaping was a testimony of the spiritual preparation of the Saints in the area. Several months before the temple was announced, Brother Richard Gieseke, a local nursery owner, had a very vivid dream of gardens surrounding a beautiful temple. Because of the power and detail of the dream, Brother Gieseke felt impressed to begin collecting plants and trees and grow them for the temple. Soon miraculous events began occurring in his business to allow him to purchase and grow plants and trees of outstanding quality and beauty. In August 1998, for example, he received a call from a construction foreman, offering him thirty large crape myrtles that were about to be destroyed by a bulldozer. In one-hundred-degree heat, four twenty-five-foot myrtles in ground as hard as concrete were carefully excavated. These myrtles now stand at the front of the temple's entryway, their unusual white flowers contrasting beautifully with the temple's gray granite exterior.

Crape myrtles also surround a beautiful garden on the north side of the temple. The garden has a fountain and benches as well as a meandering brick walkway that leads along the edge of the natural foliage. As the walkway moves closer to the temple the plants become more formal.[4]

When Brother Gieseke heard the announcement for the Houston Texas Temple, he immediately contacted his stake president about donating plants for the landscaping. Members of the temple committee were delighted with the beauty and

An image of the Savior kneeling in prayer, hidden in the landscape in the left-hand side of the drawing, is a reminder of the importance of his atonement.

quality of the plants and trees offered by Brother Gieseke and used them to create elegant and unique gardens for the temple.

Geometric designs form the basis of many elements created for the Houston Texas Temple, including the grounds, the exterior, and the interior. Of all the geometric forms used, the circle—which has no beginning or end—is perhaps the most prominent.[5]

The temple has a total of 120 stained glass windows, all imported from Germany. They range in size from small ovals to the multipaneled window in the celestial room, which measures more than thirty feet in height. Each first-level window contains almost two hundred individual pieces of stained glass held in place by a polished, highly reflective, silver-toned lead.[6]

Fearing that the work of placing the statue of the angel Moroni might damage the finished granite exterior of the temple if the wind blew or the crane operator made an error, contractors planned to position the sculpture early in the construction process. But attaching the angel to the top of the spire was not easy. On the day the statue was to be placed, hornets swarmed the spire. So, armed with insecticide spray and in front of an audience of motorists stopped nearby, three workers ascended in the basket of the crane along with the sculpture. Fortunately, the hornets stayed below the basket, and the angel was placed without the workers being stung.[7]

The Houston Texas Temple serves an estimated forty-four thousand members in the temple district, which roughly encompasses the southern half of Texas.

How glorious and complete is thy plan for the salvation and exaltation of thy children of all generations

Birmingham Alabama Temple

In early September 2000, Alabama became home to the ninety-eighth temple of The Church of Jesus Christ of Latter-day Saints. The Birmingham Alabama Temple, which took just eleven months from groundbreaking to dedication to build, is located in the Birmingham suburb of Gardendale, where it sits on a heavily wooded hill across the street from the Gardendale Branch meetinghouse. Interestingly, the temple is on Mount Olive Boulevard.

In December 1998, the Church announced that it would like to build a temple next to the meetinghouse in Indian Springs, Alabama. Tests on the site, however, revealed that the earth there was too unstable to permit the construction; in addition, the community did not react favorably toward the proposition. Another site was located and investigated, but again obstacles arose that prevented the project from beginning. Finally, in April 1999, the First Presidency of the Church approved a site in Gardendale, chosen by President Gordon B. Hinckley. The Church had actually purchased the property in the early 1990s and had promptly constructed a small meetinghouse on it. The remaining ground was very adequate for a small temple of the Lord.

Gardendale is a conservative, family-oriented area. The residents oppose such potentially negative influences as movie theaters and businesses that would sell alcohol, and they have thus far prevented those entities from encroaching into the community. Town leaders welcomed the temple project, however, believing that the Church, its values, and beautiful temple would be assets to the community.

Before construction on the temple could begin, a building permit was required. To obtain the permit, the Church had to

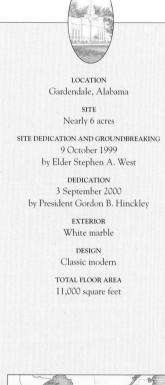

LOCATION
Gardendale, Alabama

SITE
Nearly 6 acres

SITE DEDICATION AND GROUNDBREAKING
9 October 1999
by Elder Stephen A. West

DEDICATION
3 September 2000
by President Gordon B. Hinckley

EXTERIOR
White marble

DESIGN
Classic modern

TOTAL FLOOR AREA
11,000 square feet

BIRMINGHAM
ALABAMA

ensure that the temple's sewer line could be attached to an existing county sewer line. This was a challenge because the sewer line was on the other side of two major roadways. Both state and county permits had to be granted before the Church could dig beneath the two roads. Applications were made, impact fees paid, and the Church received all of the required building permits.

Temple construction missionary Dale L. Arave was a key figure in acquiring the permits. He recalled: "As we were going down the road one day, I had just about given up on getting a sewer permit when I thought, 'Let's go over to the court house one more time and perhaps we can work something out.' I went to the courthouse and spoke with the man that I needed to talk to, and I found him in a friendly mood. He said, 'If you give me your plans I will stamp them and we will get it done.' I happened to have the plans in my car and got them stamped. And with that approval I was able to get the building permit the same day. It was miraculous the way it happened, and that is one of the reasons why we believe that the Lord wants the temple in Gardendale."[1]

On 9 October 1999, the heavens seemed to open up for the twenty-three hundred Latter-day Saints attending the groundbreaking ceremony. In his remarks, Elder Stephen A. West of the Seventy and second counselor in the North America Southeast Area presidency told those huddled under the multitude of umbrellas: "When we drove in about an hour before this meeting was to start, we saw already hundreds of people here, umbrellas up. And my wife and I started to cry. We were touched by your faith." Elder West said that life takes sacrifice. "You are sacrificing here as you come today, as you sit in the rain. And it will take sacrifice to come to the temple. It

Birmingham Alabama Temple

May only those who are worthy before thee enter its portals to serve thee in righteousness. Imbue all who participate within these walls with a great overpowering sense of the importance of that which they do. May that which they do for themselves, in accepting the ordinances of this house, strengthen their lives, give purpose to their existence, make of them better husbands and wives, parents and children. May the solemnities of eternity rest upon them and bring to them an understanding of the efficacy of the work they do in behalf of the dead.

—FROM THE DEDICATORY PRAYER

BIRMINGHAM ALABAMA TEMPLE
THE CHURCH OF JESUS CHRIST OF LATTER DAY SAINTS

Chad Hawkins
© 2000

will take commitment and it will take belief. It will require of each of us that we live worthy of having a temple recommend. . . . Yet it really is not a sacrifice—it really is a blessing."[2]

More than twenty-one thousand visitors toured the temple during the week-long open house. Although a small group of activists demonstrated against the temple's presence, neighbors actually increased their support of the temple as a result. Many residents were appalled by such a lack of hospitality for the Church. "It just seems in very poor taste," said Ed Sellers of Gardendale. "If you don't agree with them, then don't go to their church."[3]

The influence of the Spirit was felt by those working to build the temple. While adding the finishing touches to the temple, construction workers were preparing to cut a large piece of marble. Then one of them felt impressed to ask whether the marble was supposed to be used for the surface of the recommend desk. When the workers examined it more closely, they discovered that it was indeed the piece for the desk.[4]

An image of the Savior is hidden at the left of the temple.

Less than a year after the groundbreaking, on 3 September 2000, President Gordon B. Hinckley presided at all four sessions of the dedication of the Church's ninety-eighth temple, including the traditional cornerstone ceremony. As he had in so many places in recent months, President Hinckley approached the cornerstone of the temple with a trowel and a small amount of mortar.

"I'll take a little mud here and try to move this along now so you don't have to stand too long out in the Alabama sun," said the prophet. And when others, including children, were invited to follow his lead in sealing the cornerstone with additional mortar, he quipped, "Just like making a cake, except put more on the crack and less on the floor."[5]

Alabama's first temple serves twenty thousand Latter-day Saints in Alabama and Florida. As with most temples, it has not come without years of commitment and faith preparing the way. The same spirit of commitment and faith fills the hearts of worthy members who come here to serve and partake of the blessings of the temple.

Imbue all who participate within these walls with a great overpowering sense of the importance of that which they do

Santo Domingo Dominican Republic Temple

Dear Father, we thank thee that thy divine plan hast made provision for all of thy sons and daughters, regardless of when they walked the earth, to move forward on the road to immortality and eternal life. All will receive the blessings of the resurrection that come of the atonement of thy beloved Son, whom thou gavest to the world that all who believe in him may not perish but have everlasting life. Glorious is the opportunity for growth and exaltation through obedience to the laws and commandments of the gospel of Jesus Christ.

—FROM THE DEDICATORY PRAYER

Located in the southern part of the Dominican Republic, Santo Domingo is the country's largest city, chief seaport, and capital. Founded in 1496 by Bartholomew Columbus, brother of Christopher Columbus, the city is the oldest European settlement existing in the New World. The temple is located on a rise in the western part of Santo Domingo beside a park for the National Music Conservatory. Overlooking the waters of the Caribbean Sea, the Santo Domingo Dominican Republic Temple is fast becoming a beacon of strength for members throughout the Caribbean.

Many Dominican Saints believe that Juan Pablo Duarte, an early patriot and liberator, was inspired because he carried a banner with the words "God, Land, and Liberty" written on it (see Alma 46:11–14). Yet, the formal connection between the Church and the Dominican Republic is relatively recent. On 7 December 1978, Elder M. Russell Ballard of the First Quorum of the Seventy dedicated the country for the preaching of the gospel. In that same year, two Latter-day Saint

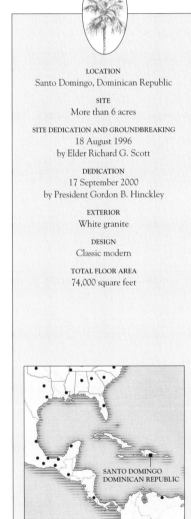

LOCATION
Santo Domingo, Dominican Republic

SITE
More than 6 acres

SITE DEDICATION AND GROUNDBREAKING
18 August 1996
by Elder Richard G. Scott

DEDICATION
17 September 2000
by President Gordon B. Hinckley

EXTERIOR
White granite

DESIGN
Classic modern

TOTAL FLOOR AREA
74,000 square feet

SANTO DOMINGO
DOMINICAN REPUBLIC

families—totally independent of each other—moved to the Dominican Republic and became acquainted. Slowly they began to share the gospel with friends and associates, and a fire of growth was kindled.

In 1979, more than three hundred fifty people were baptized. In 1981, the first mission was organized, and the LDS population reached twenty-five hundred members. When the country's first stake was organized in 1986, membership had grown to eleven thousand. In 1998, Church membership had reached more than sixty thousand, just twenty years after those two pioneering families entered the country and began talking to their neighbors about a previously unknown religion.

Despite the challenges of a fairly strong class division based on economics, Church members in the Dominican Republic perform acts of true charity for all their brothers and sisters who are in need. When one member's child became ill, he was able to pay for the medical bills but couldn't afford medicine. Several ward members helped to supply the medicine the child needed. One night, Sister Ana Mercedes Torres returned from a trip to the Guatemala City Guatemala Temple to find that her house had burned down. "The members helped me with clothes, with everything," she says. "They were there that very night and are still continuing to help."[1]

As with many regions of the world, financial struggles make it difficult for some families to go to the temple. Although several Dominican families have visited temples in the United States, most have attended temples in Guatemala, Peru, or elsewhere in South America. Affording any of these trips may require months and sometimes years of saving.

"Inflation in this country makes it extremely difficult to save," said Fausto Ventura, first counselor in the Santo Domingo Mission. "I could afford to take my family to the temple in the United States, but for the average Dominican family, that's impossible."[2]

Before the temple in Santo Domingo was built, only 5 percent of families in the Church there had been able to receive the ordinances of the temple. Although few could go, they still maintained a vision of eternity, participated in temple seminars, and hoped for a temple of their own someday.

The humble prayers of the faithful were answered when ground was broken for the first temple in the Caribbean area on 18 August 1996 by Elder Richard G. Scott of the Quorum of the Twelve. Some four thousand members attended the ceremony. The difficult task of excavation was overcome by patience and hard work. The task was largely accomplished by jackhammers and hand labor after attempts with bulldozers and other equipment proved futile in the hard coral rock.

In 1997 President Jose Castro of the Santo Domingo Dominican Republic Stake explained how local members were preparing for service in the temple. He said, "We are working in the area of obtaining family history information for temple work. Members are to receive help from stake family history specialists. Our goal is to have at least 170,000 names

available when the temple doors open." In preparation for the temple, he noted, "In the year 1996, we took 10 excursions to the Lima Peru Temple. Also another group traveled to the Orlando Florida Temple. In 1997, we have made plans and will take nine trips to Peru and other trips to other temples. The members who are preparing themselves for the temple are serving as missionaries and look forward to being temple workers. Their enthusiasm is very, very great."[3]

The temple district serves thirty-five stakes, including seven stakes spread throughout the Caribbean area. The temple has four ordinance rooms and four sealing rooms and was built according to the Church's customary high standards for materials and workmanship. But more than that, the temple serves as a source of strength to a rising generation of youth who are striving to live a high moral standard in a culture where marriage itself is looked upon as something of an unnecessary oddity. The occasional tropical storm or hurricane that sweeps across the island country causes little damage compared to the ravages of social drinking and sexual impurity that constantly barrage Church members in this country of ten million people. If Latter-day Saints will commit to live lives worthy of temple attendance, and as youth prepare to enter the temple free from serious moral transgression, great blessings await them, blessings that they have not yet begun to imagine.

Glorious is the opportunity for growth and exaltation through obedience to the laws and commandments of the gospel of Jesus Christ

Boston Massachusetts Temple

Boston, Massachusetts, a city rich in American history, has strong spiritual ties to The Church of Jesus Christ of Latter-day Saints. Joseph and Hyrum Smith and their ancestors lived in New England; and several generations preceding both their parents lived in Boston from 1640 to 1790. New England was the birthplace of other early Church leaders—including Brigham Young, Heber C. Kimball, Wilford Woodruff, and Orson Hyde—as well. Now, the Church's one-hundredth temple stands as a beacon of truth and spiritual freedom on the granite of Belmont Hill, just twenty-five miles west of Boston itself.

The course that led to the construction of a house of the Lord in this location was not easy; the difficulties, in fact, were befitting of the rocky soil that dominates much of New England's coastline. The story began in 1995 when the Church announced that a location for a temple in the Hartford, Connecticut, area was being sought. Part of that search was detailed in the biography of President Gordon B. Hinckley:

"After a day of looking at property in New York and Connecticut, [President Hinckley] was still unsettled. The next day, in a luncheon meeting with stake presidents in the Boston area, President Hinckley spoke candidly with them concerning the challenge of determining a location for a temple in the East. 'Brethren, I am frustrated,' he admitted. 'We have looked high and low around the Hartford, Connecticut, area for property, and nothing has developed. Do any of you have any suggestions?' President Kenneth G. Hutchins of the Boston Stake volunteered that he believed the Church owned a prime piece of property on a hill overlooking Boston that had never been developed. At that,

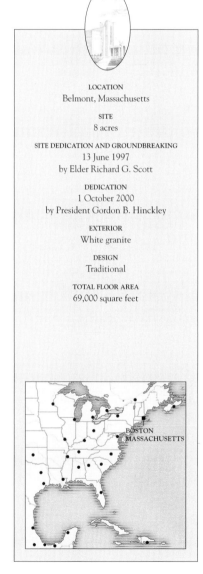

LOCATION
Belmont, Massachusetts

SITE
8 acres

SITE DEDICATION AND GROUNDBREAKING
13 June 1997
by Elder Richard G. Scott

DEDICATION
1 October 2000
by President Gordon B. Hinckley

EXTERIOR
White granite

DESIGN
Traditional

TOTAL FLOOR AREA
69,000 square feet

President Hinckley turned the meeting over to Elder Neal A. Maxwell, who was traveling with him, and immediately left to inspect the site. Later that evening President Hinckley recorded what happened when he walked about the property: 'As I stood there I had an electric feeling that this is the place, that the Lord inspired its acquisition and its retention. Very few seemed to know anything about it. . . . I think I know why I have had such a very difficult time determining the situation concerning Hartford. I have prayed about it. I have come here three or four times. I have studied maps and tables of membership. With all of this I have not had a strong confirmation. I felt a confirmation as I stood in Belmont on this property this afternoon. This is the place for a House of the Lord in the New England area.'"[1]

Despite the prophet's having received a confirming witness that this was the place to build the Lord's temple, challenges plagued the Church's efforts for more than four years. Even as the temple was dedicated, the Church faced legal suits regarding its design and size. To accommodate earlier requirements and community wishes, the Church reduced the temple's size by 50 percent; more than a third of the remaining area is built below ground level. Originally designed to have six spires, the temple will now have only one, pending the outcome of the legal proceedings. Despite the array of white steeples and belfries that dot the New England landscape, individuals who live in the neighborhood of the temple have challenged the Church's right to build the structure as planned. At the dedicatory services, President Hinckley commented: "It's time we had a temple in Boston. We're so glad it's here. We wish the steeple were on it. I regret that it isn't. But we can get along without it

Boston Massachusetts Temple

We pray that thy people in this temple district may make themselves worthy of every blessing to be found here. May they come, pure in heart and clean in hand, to the house of the Lord with gratitude in their hearts for the marvelous blessings to be gained here. . . . May they sense the wonders of the blessings of eternity to be gained here and here alone.

—FROM THE DEDICATORY PRAYER

while awaiting the outcome of the legal action. In the meantime, we'll go forward performing the ordinance work of this sacred house."[2]

As the temple became a reality, myriad efforts were made to build trust and a positive feeling in the community. Trees were planted on the grounds to block the light that neighbors complained would bother them. During construction itself, great pains were taken to ensure a minimal effect on the surrounding environment. For example, a sound-proofing box was constructed and hoisted by crane over the jackhammer as the granite was drilled for the temple's footings. To minimize dust, a water truck drove constantly about the site, dampening the ground. Large earthen walls were created to block the wind from blowing dust into neighboring yards. Construction trucks were washed before leaving the site to prevent them from scattering rocks and debris on public streets. All of these efforts aided in softening many skeptical hearts in the community.[3]

Regarding the finished temple, William Monahan, chair of the Belmont board of selectmen, said, "It's a beautiful edifice. They've taken a piece of ledge, total rock, and made it into a striking garden, with 20,000 shrubs and I don't know how many flowering bushes. Twenty years ago, if someone said they were going to build there, you would have said it was impossible."[4]

An image of the Savior is hidden in a tree to the left, emphasizing that Jesus Christ is the focus of temple ordinances. Another hidden image is the proposed spire, blending into the clouds above the temple.

The temple's exterior is composed of Italian Olympia white granite, carefully placed as if it were a giant 3-D puzzle. Imported from Sardinia, an Italian island in the Mediterranean Sea, the granite was shaped to fit specific places on the temple walls. Each piece was anchored to its own spot with stainless steel anchors bolted to the block. Like a puzzle, each piece supports another piece.[5]

The road to the finished temple, like the history in which the area is steeped, has not been easy. Plans for a temple in Boston were announced in the fall of 1995, and the groundbreaking ceremony came nearly two years later, in the summer of 1997. Construction began in August 1997 and was completed in September 2000. The open house, which began even before construction was completed, was held 29 August through 23 September 2000 and was attended by more than eighty-two thousand people.

President Hinckley presided at the dedication, with nearly seventeen thousand Latter-day Saints attending the four sessions on Sunday, 1 October. At the introduction of the temple's dedicatory prayer, President Hinckley said, "We are assembled to dedicate this thy holy house. It is a special occasion. This temple becomes the 100th operating temple of thy Church. We have looked forward to this occasion. We have prayed for this day."[6]

May they sense the wonders of the blessings of eternity

Facts about the First 100 Temples

The Bountiful Utah Temple is the only temple whose site was personally chosen by President Ezra Taft Benson and the only temple whose site was selected with all three members of the First Presidency present.[1]

The Laie Hawaii Temple was the first temple dedicated outside the continental United States (in 1919; Hawaii entered the Union on 21 August 1959 as the fiftieth state).

The tallest temple is the Washington D. C. Temple, standing at 288 feet.

The Oakland California Temple is the only temple with five spires, which are perforated and covered in blue glass mosaic and gold leaf. The Oriental look of the temple reflects the presence of Asian communities in the area.

For many years after its dedication, the Manti Utah Temple had an arched tunnel below the east tower, and many people remember driving through it. The passage has since been closed.[2]

On the exterior of the Laie Hawaii Temple are 123 nearly life-size figures depicting God's dealings with his children in four great dispensations from the time of Adam to the present: the Old Testament, the Book of Mormon, the New Testament (followed by the Apostasy), and the Restoration.

Skilled craftsmen, many of whom came from Norway, built an upside-down boat for the roof trusses of the Manti Utah Temple.[3]

The San Diego California Temple has gardens and trees on its roof. Patrons leaving the celestial room may enjoy the glass-enclosed gardens and look up to the statue of the angel Moroni.

World War II affected three temples: postponing construction on the Los Angeles California Temple, paving the way to purchase a temple site for the Oakland California Temple, and causing workmen on the Idaho Falls Idaho Temple to join the armed forces.

The Bern Switzerland Temple was the first in which English was not the principal language.

Friezes on the four sides of the Mesa Arizona Temple depict the fulfillment of Isaiah's prophecy that in the latter days the Lord would "set up an ensign for the nations" to gather "the remnant of his people" from "the four corners of the earth" and "the islands of the sea" (Isaiah 11:11–12).

The Tokyo Japan Temple was the first to be built in a nation whose predominant religion is not Christian.

Four temples have been commemorated on postal stamps or as postal cancellations: the Salt Lake Temple (in 1980 and 1993), the Stockholm Sweden Temple (in 1985), the Apia Samoa Temple (in 1988), and the Nuku'alofa Tonga Temple (in 1991).[4]

The Seoul South Korea Temple was the first Latter-day Saint temple built on the mainland of Asia.

The cornerstone box of the Oakland California Temple contains periodicals describing the twenty-three–orbit flight around the world of Astronaut Gordon Cooper.[5]

The temple with the smallest site is the Hong Kong China Temple (.3 acres).

The temples with the largest sites are the Hamilton New Zealand Temple and college grounds (86 acres), the Washington D. C. Temple (52 acres), and the London England Temple (32 acres).

The Vernal Utah Temple is the only one of the first one hundred temples built from an already-existing structure, the eighty-seven-year-old Uintah Stake Tabernacle.

The Monticello Utah Temple was the first completed of the smaller temples conceived by President Gordon B. Hinckley.

His Highness Malietoa Tunumafili II of Samoa and King Taufa'ahau Tupou IV of Tonga participated in the groundbreaking ceremonies of the temples in their respective countries.[6]

The cornerstone for a temple in Independence, Missouri, was laid and the site dedicated 3 August 1831 by Joseph Smith.[7]

The terraced appearance of the Mesa Arizona Temple is similar to that of the Temple of Herod as well as to ancient temples in the Americas.

An early welfare project was connected with building the Logan Utah Temple. A one-hundred-acre welfare farm was established nearby to provide fruit, vegetables, and meat for the temple workmen.

Ordinances for the Founding Fathers of the United States were performed in the St. George Utah Temple.

A tower on the Manti Utah Temple was struck by lightning and burned for more than three hours but caused only minimal damage. Spectators said it was the slowest-burning fire they had ever seen.[8]

A temple site was dedicated and cornerstones laid in Far West, Missouri, in July 1838. Because of persecution and the Saints' expulsion from the state, the temple was not erected, but the cornerstones may still be seen.

The Church suspended construction of the Stockholm Sweden Temple for more than a year so that archaeological relics could be excavated from ancient Viking graves, dating from 600 B.C. to A.D. 200, discovered on the temple site. Stockholm's mayor noted, "Had it not been for the temple, we would never have discovered the relics."[9]

The Chicago Illinois Temple is located near a 140-acre natural reserve noted for the pristine condition of its grassland prairie, variety of trees, and wildflowers. To harmonize with this natural beauty and to enhance the quiet serenity of the temple, the Church perpetuated the native landscaping on the temple grounds.

The cornerstone box of the Orlando Florida Temple contains a limited-edition animation cel of Jiminy Cricket, who symbolizes conscience, from the classic 1940 Disney film, *Pinocchio*. The cel of *Pinocchio* was chosen for donation by Walt Disney and Company because of the spiritual theme of the story of a wooden puppet who goes through the process of sin, repentance, and sacrifice to become a "real boy."[10]

The exterior of the Oakland California Temple features two sculpted panels, one depicting Jesus ministering in Palestine and the other ministering to the Nephites in the land Bountiful.

The Laie Hawaii Temple was built of concrete made from crushed lava rock obtained near the temple site.

The builders of the St. George Utah Temple set its foundation rock with a cannon originally made in France and used by the armies of Napoleon.[11]

The Nauvoo Temple featured a weathervane of an angel "flying" in a horizontal position.

The Bern Switzerland Temple was the first Latter-day Saint temple built in Europe.

The Saints in the area were asked to raise one million dollars for the Los Angeles California Temple. More than $1.6 million was contributed in less than three months.[12]

Paintings adorning the grand stairway of the Mesa Arizona Temple remind patrons that this is a place for the Lamanites of the Southwest and Mexico to perform their temple work. This temple is affectionately known as the Lamanite temple.

The Relief Society had its beginnings when a group of women in the Church volunteered to sew clothing for the men working on the Nauvoo Temple.

The Portland Oregon Temple was built on approximately seven acres of Church property purchased in the 1960s for a junior college.[13]

In total floor area, the four largest temples are the Salt Lake Temple (253,015 square feet), the Los Angeles California Temple (190,614 square feet), the Washington D. C. Temple (160,000 square feet), and the Jordan River Utah Temple (153,641 square feet).

A microfiche sheet containing the names of all the nearly eleven thousand Primary children in the San Diego California Temple district was placed in the cornerstone of the temple.[14]

Despite the threat of a typhoon, more than two thousand Church members attended groundbreaking ceremonies for the Manila Philippines Temple on 25 August 1982. The site was dedicated by President Gordon B. Hinckley.

Three temples were built with no towers or spires, suggesting ancient temples in the Americas: the Mesa Arizona Temple, the Cardston Alberta Temple, and the Laie Hawaii Temple.

Traditionally, cornerstone boxes are opened after one hundred years. When the cornerstone box in the foundation of the Salt Lake Temple was opened in 1993, the papers it contained were water damaged and could not be salvaged; however, a set of Latter-day Saint gold coins was in good condition and is now kept in the Church archives.

After lightning destroyed the original spire of the St. George Utah Temple, the tower was rebuilt higher to be more in proportion with the rest of the building.

Among the archaeological discoveries in the area around the Tuxtla Gutierrez Mexico Temple were carved monuments used as calendars, stone boxes, wheel-made pottery, cement, a true arch, and incense burners. One stele, or upright stone, discovered in 1959, is carved with representations of the sons of an ancestral couple absorbing and perhaps recording their knowledge of a tree of life. These artifacts originated with a highly developed culture between 500 and 300 B.C.

The original plan of the Washington D. C. Temple was a hexagon with six equal sides. At each of the six corners was a tower also having six sides.[15]

Relief Society sisters helped cut, fit, and sew the carpet for each room of the Logan Utah Temple. Rag-tearing sessions were held almost every day as the women brought their rags, tore them into strips, and then threw them into heaps. When the pile was large enough, the women sat in a circle, carefully selected the colors, sewed the rags together, and rolled the long strips into balls. The balls were taken to the weaving machine, and the completed product came off the loom in large rolls that took two men to lift.[16]

The first temple to offer the temple ordinances in a language other than English was the Mesa Arizona Temple—Spanish, in 1945.

The Monticello Utah Temple is the only temple to have had a statue of the angel Moroni colored white. Within a year, the white statue was replaced with a larger and more visible gold-leafed one.

Of the twenty largest temples (in square feet), eighteen are in the United States. The other two are the Mexico City Mexico Temple (the fifth largest, at 117,113 square feet) and the Cardston Alberta Temple (the thirteenth largest, at 89,405 square feet).

Hundreds of rattlesnakes had to be cleared from the Manti Utah Temple site before construction could begin.[17]

The Hamilton New Zealand Temple, dedicated in 1956, was the first temple south of the equator.

President Heber C. Kimball described the dedication of the temple site at Adam-ondi-Ahman: "The Saints—preparing to defend themselves from the mob, who were threatening the destruction of our people. Men, women, and children were fleeing to that place for safety from every direction; their houses and property were burned and they had to flee half naked, crying and frightened nigh unto death, to save their lives. While there we laid out a city on a high elevated piece of land, and set the stakes for the four corners of a temple block, which was dedicated, Brigham Young being mouth, There were from three to five hundred men present on the occasion, under arms."[18]

To represent the influence of the NASA space organization in the Orlando Florida Temple district, the box in the cornerstone of the temple contains patches worn in space by Latter-day Saint astronaut Don Lind and United States Senator Jake Garn. Accompanying Senator Garn's patch is an autographed copy of his book, *Why I Believe*.[19]

Hundreds of Latter-day Saints cleared away overgrown banana trees to prepare the site for the groundbreaking of the São Paulo Brazil Temple.

The property that became the site of the Tokyo Japan Temple was devastated by two bombs during World War II.[20]

The Freiberg Germany Temple was the first to be built in a Communist-ruled nation. The dedication of the temple marked the beginning of a new era of Church growth in other Communist countries.

Unlike most spiral staircases, which wind around a central support column, those in the Manti Utah Temple are open in the center. Each story of the temple is reached by one complete revolution of the stairway. The curved panels and perfectly executed banisters of imported black walnut are a marvel of workmanship.[21]

The architecture of the Nauvoo Temple influenced that of the St. George Utah Temple and the St. Louis Missouri Temple.

Designed to protect the temple grounds and its beautiful landscaping from deer and other wild animals, the painted, galvanized-steel fence around the perimeter of the Bountiful Utah Temple ranges from 8 feet to 10 feet 8 inches in height.

Inspiration for the design of the San Diego California Temple came from the Washington D. C. and Salt Lake Temples.

The statue of the angel Moroni on the Jordan River Utah Temple is 20 feet tall; on the Washington D. C. Temple, 18 feet; on the Los Angeles Temple, 15 feet 5 inches tall; on the Salt Lake Temple, 12 feet 5 inches.

In the cornerstone of the Cardston Alberta Temple is an airtight copper box containing a picture of Joseph Smith and a lock of his hair.

The architects of the Mesa Arizona Temple had recently designed the Utah State Capitol Building.

With enthusiastic support from local Saints, a twelve-foot statue of the angel Moroni was added to the Idaho Falls Idaho Temple thirty-eight years after the temple was dedicated.

The first temple to include separate creation, garden, world, terrestrial, and celestial rooms was the Logan Utah Temple. St. George had one large instruction room on each of its two floors until the remodeling of 1938.

The São Paulo Brazil Temple was the first temple in South America.

During renovation of the Laie Hawaii Temple and its grounds, more than two hundred graves were discovered behind the temple. A near-jungle was removed, and the forgotten graves of early pioneer Church members were restored.

A much-anticipated event occurs annually at the Sydney Australia Temple when numerous plovers, beautiful gray and white birds with yellow head cones and long legs, arrive to lay their eggs after flying thousands of miles. The birds, which mate for life, nest directly on the lawn, each pair within about two feet of its original spot, so a special effort is made to mow around them. Fine screens have been installed over nearby storm drains to prevent heavy rains from washing away the eggs or chicks.[22]

When dedicated in January 1999, the Anchorage Alaska Temple became the northernmost temple in the world and also the smallest in square footage.

The four temples with the largest open-house attendance were the Bountiful Utah Temple (870,000), the Washington D. C. Temple (758,328, wearing out the carpet in the main annex), and the Los Angeles California and San Diego California Temples (700,000 each).

Of the first one hundred temples, fifteen do not have a statue of the angel Moroni: St. George Utah, Logan Utah, Manti Utah, Laie Hawaii, Cardston Alberta, Mesa Arizona, Hamilton New Zealand, Bern Switzerland, London England, Oakland California, Ogden Utah, Provo Utah, Tokyo Japan, São Paulo Brazil, and Freiberg Germany.

The first four temples to feature a statue of the angel Moroni were the Nauvoo, Salt Lake, Los Angeles California, and Washington D. C. Temples.

The total weight of gold leaf required to cover a seven-foot statue of the angel Moroni is 1.5 ounces.[23]

Three Church structures other than temples have had a full-sized statue of the angel Moroni: (1) In the 1930s a statue was placed 160 feet above the ground atop the Washington D. C. chapel. (2) In 1935 a statue was commissioned to adorn a thirty-foot monument at the Hill Cumorah in New York. The sculptor, Torlief Knaphus, made seven sketches and then hiked to Salt Lake City's Ensign Peak, where he prayed to know which of his sketches was acceptable to the Lord. Brother Knaphus said he saw a finger of light point to a particular sketch that he felt impressed Church leaders would choose, and they did.[24] (3) A statue was made for the Church's pavilion during the New York World's Fair of 1965. This statue was later used in the movie *Legacy* and in the video *Mountain of the Lord*.[25]

The Washington D. C. Temple was the first to be faced with marble.[26]

Three temples have been dedicated on 6 April: St. George Utah (1877), Salt Lake (1893), and Palmyra New York (2000).

A forty-ton water truck whose parking brake failed or was not engaged plunged five hundred yards down a brush-covered hillside during construction of the Bountiful Utah Temple and crashed into a house below. The residents of the home learned of the accident when they drove up and saw police cars and fire trucks. "It was a miracle no one was home," the homeowner said. The truck demolished the kitchen before dropping through the floor into the basement.[27]

The Laie Hawaii Temple was once painted a pale green so it would better blend with the surrounding landscape.[28]

The oxen used for the baptismal font of the Vernal Utah Temple were on display for more than twenty years in the South Visitors' Center on Temple Square in Salt Lake City.[29]

Germany was the first country other than the United States to have more than one temple.

These three temples have the smallest area in square feet: Freiberg Germany Temple (7,840), Monticello Utah Temple (7,000), and Anchorage Alaska Temple (6,800).

An estimated 1.2 million members attended the dedication of the Palmyra New York Temple, which was broadcast to every satellite-equipped stake center in North America.[30]

The sunstone on the Palmyra New York Temple has thirty-three rays of light, representing the age of the Savior at his death.[31]

The Hermosillo Sonora Mexico Temple was the fiftieth temple that President Gordon B. Hinckley dedicated or rededicated.

Baptisms for the dead were performed in the St. George Utah Temple for the first time on 9 January 1877; endowments for the dead were begun two days later. President Wilford Woodruff described that occasion as "the first time endowments for the dead had been given in any temple in this dispensation."[32]

For nearly one hundred years, an angel atop the Salem Evangelical and Reformed Church has towered over the city of Cincinnati, Ohio. Little do passersby realize that this same angel likely once graced the Nauvoo Temple.[33]

The Hong Kong China Temple has the world's largest temple district.

Motion picture company MGM and film producer Cecil B. DeMille assisted greatly in the design of the audiovisual system in the Bern Switzerland Temple.[34]

Former astronaut Don Lind served in the presidency of the Portland Oregon Temple.

On 20 and 21 May 2000, for the first time, three temples were dedicated in one weekend: the Tampico Mexico Temple, the Nashville Tennessee Temple, and the Villahermosa Mexico Temple.

The Salt Lake Temple was the first to have a vertical statue of the angel Moroni.

With rain predicted for the groundbreaking of the Dallas Texas Temple, attendees borrowed large umbrellas from a nearby golf clubhouse. When the rain began to fall and people opened the umbrellas, they noticed that the umbrellas were decorated with advertisements for alcoholic beverages. The umbrellas were quickly replaced.[35]

The president of the Church signed every temple recommend until 1891, when this responsibility was given to bishops and stake presidents.[36]

As the finishing touches were being added to the Toronto Ontario Temple, a labor strike idled construction workers for six weeks. Union leaders allowed a few members to do finishing work inside the temple as unpaid, voluntary workers.[37]

Soon after the dedication of the Santiago Chile Temple, an earthquake registering 8.5 on the Richter scale hit the city. Other than minor cracks in the plaster, however, the quake damaged only the statue of the angel Moroni, whose trumpet was found in a flowerbed. A long crane from a fire truck restored the trumpet to its proper position.[38]

The statue of the angel Moroni was placed on the St. Paul Minnesota Temple on the 176th anniversary of the day Moroni first appeared to Joseph Smith.[39]

The government of Mexico changed its laws so a Catholic mass could be conducted in that country by the pope. This change opened the door for Church officials to ask again about constructing the Mexico City Temple.[40]

The St. Paul Minnesota Temple was the first to be dedicated in the year 2000 (on January 9). Engraved on the cornerstone are the words "ERECTED 1999–DEDICATED JANUARY 2000."

The first time two temples were dedicated on the same day was 14 November 1999: the Halifax Nova Scotia Temple and the Regina Saskatchewan Temple. This was also the first time since 1846 that a general authority not in the First Presidency dedicated a temple. On the same day that President Hinckley dedicated the Halifax Nova Scotia Temple, President Boyd K. Packer, acting president of the Quorum of the Twelve Apostles, dedicated the Regina Saskatchewan Temple.[41]

Six temples have annual pageants nearby: Logan Utah, Manti Utah, Mesa Arizona, Palmyra New York, Oakland California, and Washington D. C.

Several temples are located near a missionary training center: Bogota Colombia, Buenos Aires Argentina, Cochabamba Bolivia, Guatemala City Guatemala, Hamilton New Zealand, Lima Peru, Preston England, Madrid Spain, Manila Philippines, Mexico City Mexico, Provo Utah, Santo Domingo Dominican Republic, Santiago Chile, São Paulo Brazil, Seoul South Korea, and Tokyo Japan.

Several temples have visitors' centers on or near the temple grounds: Hamilton New Zealand, Idaho Falls Idaho, Laie Hawaii, Los Angeles California, Mesa Arizona, Mexico City Mexico, Oakland California, Palmyra New York, Salt Lake City, St. George Utah, and Washington D. C.

The Santo Domingo Dominican Republic Temple was built in a city founded in 1496 by Bartholomew Columbus, brother of Christopher Columbus. The city is the oldest European settlement still existing in the New World.

When the site of the Suva Fiji Temple was being prepared for construction, workers discovered several large underground concrete bunkers that had been established as a defense during World War II.[42]

Notes

PREFACE, page viii

1. McConkie, *Mormon Doctrine*, 781.
2. Hinckley, *Ensign*, November 1985.
3. *1999–2000 Church Almanac*, 480.
4. Harris, interview.
5. Hunter, "Temple-Motivated People."

KIRTLAND TEMPLE, page 1

1. Robison, *First Mormon Temple*, 8.
2. Tullidge, *Life of Joseph, the Prophet*, 189; *Church History*, 291.
3. Morello, "Faith Brought This Temple," 3, 13.
4. *Church History*, 292.
5. Cowan, *Temples to Dot the Earth*, 27.
6. Newell and Avery, "Sweet Counsel and Seas of Tribulation," 155.
7. Robison, *First Mormon Temple*, 79.
8. Robison, *First Mormon Temple*, 19.
9. Talmage, *House of the Lord*, 99.
10. Smith, *History of the Church*, 2:428.

NAUVOO TEMPLE, page 4

1. Colvin, "Historical Study," 68.
2. Cannon, *Gems of Reminiscence*, 173–75.
3. Corbett, *Mary Fielding Smith*, 155.
4. Talmage, *House of the Lord*, 109.
5. *History of Relief Society*, 18.
6. McGavin, *Nauvoo Temple*, 45.
7. *Millennial Star* 5 (December 1844): 104.
8. Brown, "Sacred Departments," 374.
9. Conference Report, April 1999, 117.

ST. GEORGE UTAH TEMPLE, page 7

1. DeMille, *St. George Temple*, 21.
2. Lundwall, *Temples of the Most High*, 81.
3. Lundwall, *Temples of the Most High*, 78; DeMille, *St. George Temple*, 27–28.
4. "Latter-day Temples," 31.
5. Lundwall, *Temples of the Most High*, 79.
6. Lundwall, *Temples of the Most High*, 79.
7. Talmage, *House of the Lord*, 181.

8. DeMille, *St. George Temple*, 87–88.
9. Conference Report, April 1898, 89–90.
10. Woodruff, *Journal*, entries of 21–24 August 1877.
11. Conference Report, April 1898, 89.

LOGAN UTAH TEMPLE, page 10

1. Ricks, *History of a Valley*, 282.
2. Olsen, *Logan Temple*, 6.
3. Lundwall, *Temples of the Most High*, 98.
4. Richards, "Latter-day Temples," 19.
5. Olsen, *Logan Temple*, 73.
6. Olsen, *Logan Temple*, 75–76.
7. Olsen, *Logan Temple*, 152–53.
8. Olsen, *Logan Temple*, 166.
9. Olsen, *Logan Temple*, 166.
10. *Logan Temple* [pamphlet], 14.

MANTI UTAH TEMPLE, page 13

1. "Spiritual Manifestations," 521.
2. Whitney, *Life of Heber C. Kimball*, 436.
3. *Manti Temple*, 5.
4. *Manti Temple*, 25.
5. *Manti Temple*, 104.
6. "Genealogical and Temple Work," 148.
7. "Dedication of the Manti Temple," 405.
8. Lundwall, *Temples of the Most High*, 116.
9. *Manti Temple*, 131.
10. *Manti Temple*, 118.

SALT LAKE TEMPLE, page 16

1. Young, *Journal of Discourses*, 1:133.
2. Holzapfel, *Every Stone a Sermon*, 9.
3. Holzapfel, *Every Stone a Sermon*, 9.
4. Young, *Journal of Discourses*, 10:254.
5. Jackson, "Saints in the Shadow of Mount Timpanogos," 96.
6. Hunter, "I Saw Another Angel Fly," 30.
7. Hinckley, Conference Report, October 1995, 93.
8. Gibbons, *Dynamic Disciples*, 127–28; Snow, "Remarkable Manifestation."

LAIE HAWAII TEMPLE, page 20

1. Spurrier, "Hawaii Temple," 29.
2. Spurrier, "Hawaii Temple," 31.
3. Pope, *About the Temple in Hawaii*, 149–50.
4. Conference Report, October 1917, 80; Cowan, *Temples to Dot the Earth*, 128–29.
5. Cowan, *Temples to Dot the Earth*, 130.
6. "Dedicatory Prayer," 283.
7. Spurrier, "Hawaii Temple," 33.
8. Spurrier, "Hawaii Temple," 33.
9. Stoker, "Their Faith," 6.

CARDSTON ALBERTA TEMPLE, page 23

1. Conference Report, April 1901, 69.
2. Wood, *Alberta Temple*, 25–26.
3. Wood, *Alberta Temple*, 27.
4. Wood, *Alberta Temple*, 35.
5. Wood, *Alberta Temple*, 44.
6. Wood, *Alberta Temple*, 50–59.
7. Wood, *Alberta Temple*, 102–3.
8. Wood, *Alberta Temple*, 64.
9. *History of the Mormon Church in Canada*, 74.
10. Wood, *Alberta Temple*, 74.
11. Wood, *Alberta Temple*, 93.
12. Wood, *Alberta Temple*, 173; Cowan, *Temples to Dot the Earth*, 126.

MESA ARIZONA TEMPLE, page 26

1. McClintock, *Mormon Settlement in Arizona*, 223.
2. LeSueur, "Story Told by the Frieze," 19.
3. Lundwall, *Temples of the Most High*, 170.
4. Lundwall, *Temples of the Most High*, 181.
5. Cowan, *Latter-day Saint Century*, 152.
6. Adair, "Mesa Easter Pageant," 4.
7. Adair, "Mesa Temple Christmas Display," 11.
8. Ettenborough, "Mesa Temple Lighting."

IDAHO FALLS IDAHO TEMPLE, page 29

1. Lundwall, *Temples of the Most High*, 191.
2. Cowan, *Temples to Dot the Earth*, 142.
3. Dockstader, " 'Temple by the River' Jubilee," 11.
4. Cowan, *Temples to Dot the Earth*, 142.
5. Lundwall, *Temples of the Most High*, 191.
6. Lundwall, *Temples of the Most High*, 193.
7. Dockstader, "Sacred Structure," 11.
8. Cowan, *Temples to Dot the Earth*, 143.
9. Cowan, *Temples to Dot the Earth*, 143–44.
10. "Statue of Angel Is Placed," 7.
11. Conference Report, April 1993, 51.
12. Felt, "On the Bright Side," 2.

BERN SWITZERLAND TEMPLE, page 32

1. Smith, "Gospel unto All Nations," 332.
2. "Latter-day Temples," 30.
3. "Latter-day Temples," 30.
4. "Dedicatory Addresses," 847.
5. Kirby, "History of the Swiss Temple," 8.
6. "Blessings of House of the Lord."
7. Josephson, "Temple Is Risen," 624–25.
8. Josephson, "Temple Is Risen," 625.
9. Kirby, "History of the Swiss Temple," 16–17.
10. Kirby, "History of the Swiss Temple, 17–18.
11. Kirby, "History of the Swiss Temple," 18.
12. Josephson, "Temple Is Risen," 685–86.
13. "Dedicatory Addresses," 795.
14. Conference Report, September 1955, 7.
15. "LDS Officials Rededicate Swiss Temple"; Avant, "Thousands Tour London and Swiss Temples."

LOS ANGELES CALIFORNIA TEMPLE, page 35

1. "Latter-day Temples," 30.
2. "Latter-day Temples," 30.

3. Lundwall, *Temples of the Most High*, 205–7.
4. Cowan, *Temples to Dot the Earth*, 153.
5. Cowan, *Temples to Dot the Earth*, 153.
6. Lundwall, *Temples of the Most High*, 206.
7. Lundwall, *Temples of the Most High*, 209.
8. Cowan, *Temples to Dot the Earth*, 156.
9. Hunter, "I Saw Another Angel Fly," 34.
10. Cowan, *Temples to Dot the Earth*, 155.
11. Cowan, *Temples to Dot the Earth*, 156.
12. Poole, "Lights Symbolize the Savior's Birth," 12.
13. "Grounds at Los Angeles Temple," 6.
14. Hart, "I'm Here!"

HAMILTON NEW ZEALAND TEMPLE, page 38

1. Hunt, *Zion in New Zealand*, 9.
2. Cowley, "Maori Chief," 696.
3. Hunt, *Zion in New Zealand*, 81.
4. Hunt, *Zion in New Zealand*, 81.
5. Howe, "Temple in the South Pacific," 811–13.
6. *Mormon Temple, Temple View* (brochure), 13–14.
7. Allred, "Great Labor of Love," 226–29.
8. Cowan, *Temples to Dot the Earth*, 166.
9. Hunt, *Zion in New Zealand*, 87.
10. Hunt, *Zion in New Zealand*, 82.
11. Mendenhall, "Temple in New Zealand," 492.
12. Hunt, *Zion in New Zealand*, 88–89.
13. Hunt, *Zion in New Zealand*, 89.
14. Hunt, *Zion in New Zealand*, 85.
15. Rudd, *Treasured Experiences*, 222–25.

LONDON ENGLAND TEMPLE, page 40

1. Warner, "Temple for Great Britain."
2. *Mormon Temple Near London*, 10.
3. Radnedge, "London Temple Has Served Members 25 Years," 12.
4. Warner, "Temple for Great Britain."
5. Radnedge, "London Temple Has Served Members 25 Years," 12.
6. Anderson, "Making of a Temple."
7. Lundwall, *Temples of the Most High*, 224.
8. Warner, "Temple for Great Britain."
9. Anderson, "Making of a Temple."

10. Lundwall, *Temples of the Most High*, 225.
11. "In Dedicatory Prayer," 3.
12. Warner, "Temple for Great Britain."
13. Avant, "Thousands Tour London and Swiss Temples."
14. Avant, "Thousands Tour London and Swiss Temples."

OAKLAND CALIFORNIA TEMPLE, page 43

1. Candland, *Ensign to the Nations*, 60.
2. Conference Report, April 1943, 6.
3. Candland, *Ensign to the Nations*, 63.
4. Burton and MacDonald, "Oakland Temple," 20.
5. Candland, *Ensign to the Nations*, 65.
6. Candland, *Ensign to the Nations*, 67–68.
7. Candland, *Ensign to the Nations*, 68–69.
8. Hart, "Heroes Emerge," 3.
9. "Temple Unscathed," 5.
10. Candland, *Ensign to the Nations*, 71.

OGDEN UTAH TEMPLE, page 46

1. Hunter, *Beneath Ben Lomond's Peak*, 52–56.
2. *Mormon Temple in Ogden, Utah*, 6.
3. Liston, "Geographical Analysis," 112.
4. "Ogden Temple," 80; Green, "Two Temples to Be Dedicated," 6–9.
5. Liston, "Geographical Analysis," 113–15.
6. Green, "Two Temples to Be Dedicated," 10–12; "Ogden Temple," 80.
7. Hipwell, *Ogden Utah Weber North Stake History*, 151.
8. Hipwell, *Ogden Utah Weber North Stake History*, 151.
9. "Temple Experiences in 'Deseret,'" 10.
10. "Ogden Temple," 80.
11. Madsen, "House of Glory."

PROVO UTAH TEMPLE, page 49

1. Bullock, affadavit.
2. Liston, "Geographical Analysis," 101–3.
3. Green, "Two Temples to Be Dedicated," 9.
4. Green, "Two Temples to Be Dedicated," 13.

5. Hart, "Mt. Timpanogos Utah Temple," 4.
6. "Temple Experiences in 'Deseret,'" 10.

WASHINGTON D. C. TEMPLE, page 52

1. Smith, "Monument to Spirituality," 7, 11.
2. Belnap and Belnap, "Washington Temple Visitors' Center."
3. Smith, "Monument to Spirituality," 7.
4. "To Build a Temple," 16.
5. Wilcox, *Washington D. C. Temple*.
6. "To Build a Temple," 19.
7. "Washington Temple Design," 3.
8. "To Build a Temple," 17.
9. "Angel Moroni Statue Chosen for Temple," 5.
10. Hunter, "I Saw Another Angel Fly," 34.
11. Belnap and Belnap, "Washington Temple Visitors' Center."
12. Barker, "Brief History."
13. Cowan, *Temples to Dot the Earth*, 177.
14. Painter and Pichaske, "Landmark."

SÃO PAULO BRAZIL TEMPLE, page 55

1. Heslop, "Area Conference in Brazil," 3.
2. Heslop, "Greater Need," 3.
3. Aidukaitis, "Temple Progresses in Brazil," 3.
4. Aidukaitis, "Temple Progresses in Brazil," 3.
5. Aidukaitis, "Temple Progresses in Brazil," 10.
6. Aidukaitis, "Temple Progresses in Brazil," 10.
7. Van Orden, "Sao Paulo Temple Cornerstone," 3, 9.
8. Van Orden, "Temple Dedication Brings Blessings," 10.
9. "In Many Countries."
10. Santiago and Archibald, "From Amazon Basin."
11. "In Many Countries."

TOKYO JAPAN TEMPLE, page 57

1. Palmer, *Church Encounters Asia*, 83.
2. Japan Area Conference Report, 4.

3. "Temple Plan Thrills Members," 5.
4. "Temple Plan Thrills Members," 5.
5. Van Orden, "Dedication of Temple," 3.
6. Van Orden, "Dedication of Temple," 3.
7. Van Orden, "Dedication of Temple," 3.
8. Van Orden, "Dedication of Temple," 3.
9. "Wait Is Worth It," 13.
10. "Temple in Japan," 16.

SEATTLE WASHINGTON TEMPLE, page 59

1. Price, "Seattle Washington Temple," 6.
2. Price, "Seattle Washington Temple," 7.
3. "Elated Saints," 93.
4. Harmon, interview.
5. Price, "Seattle Temple," 3.
6. Price, "Seattle Temple," 9.
7. Price, "Seattle Temple," 14–15.
8. Price, "Seattle Temple," 15.

JORDAN RIVER UTAH TEMPLE, page 62

1. "New Temple Planned in Utah," 3.
2. Liston, "Geographical Analysis," 127–28, 130.
3. "Jordan River Temple Architectural Design," 80.
4. "Temple Completion," 3.
5. Liston, "Geographical Analysis," 129.
6. McKay and McKay, *For His House*.
7. McKay and McKay, *For His House*.
8. McKay and McKay, *For His House*.
9. "Temple Completion," 3.
10. Van Orden, "Ground Is Broken," 3.
11. "Temple Service Extends the Spirit of Christmas."

ATLANTA GEORGIA TEMPLE, page 65

1. Avant, "Ground Broken for New Atlanta Temple," 3.
2. "Atlanta Temple Report."
3. Hunter, "I Saw Another Angel Fly," 32.
4. Willey, "Atlanta Temple Opens Doors," 3.
5. Faherty, radio editorial.
6. Conkey, interview.

7. Conkey, "Atlanta Temple Dedicated," 73.

8. "Members Volunteer," 79.

9. "Atlanta Temple Rededicated."

10. Conkey, "Atlanta Temple Dedicated," 73.

APIA SAMOA TEMPLE, page 68

1. Taylor, "Ah Mu," 47.

2. Britsch, *Unto the Islands of the Sea*, 424.

3. "Eternal Riches."

4. Britsch, *Unto the Islands of the Sea*, 424–25.

5. Britsch, *Unto the Islands of the Sea*, 425.

6. Hunter, "I Saw Another Angel Fly," 36.

7. Avant, "Members Rejoice at Samoa Rites," 5.

8. Avant, "Members Rejoice at Samoa Rites," 5.

9. "Stamp Commemorates 100 Years."

10. "Samoans Recovering," 75.

NUKU'ALOFA TONGA TEMPLE, page 70

1. Britsch, *Unto the Islands of the Sea*, 492–93.

2. Shumway, *Tongan Saints*, 166.

3. Shumway, *Tongan Saints*, 143–44.

4. Shumway, *Tongan Saints*, 195.

5. Shumway, *Tongan Saints*, 195.

6. Britsch, *Unto the Islands of the Sea*, 495.

7. Avant, "Tongans Sing, Dance," 7.

8. Britsch, *Unto the Islands of the Sea*, 497.

9. "Tongans Travel Sea," 13.

SANTIAGO CHILE TEMPLE, page 72

1. Cahill, "Latin America Area Conferences Report," 113.

2. Billikopf, "On Sacred Ground," 52–53.

3. "In Many Countries," 7.

4. "Temple Open House," 4.

5. Ayala, "Reflections."

6. Hart, "Temple Dedicated in an Oasis of Calm," 10.

7. "Temple Dedicated in Santiago," 93.

PAPEETE TAHITI TEMPLE, page 74

1. "Church Launches Worldwide Temple-Building Emphasis," 102–3.

2. Britsch, *Unto the Islands of the Sea*, 78.

3. Ellsworth and Perrin, *Seasons of Faith and Courage*, 255–56.

4. Ellsworth and Perrin, *Seasons of Faith and Courage*, 258.

5. Ellsworth and Perrin, *Seasons of Faith and Courage*, 269.

6. Ellsworth and Perrin, *Seasons of Faith and Courage*, 271–72.

7. "Tahitians Feel Spirit," 67.

8. Britsch, *Unto the Isles of the Sea*, 90; see also "Tahitians Feel Spirit," 66.

9. Britsch, *Unto the Isles of the Sea*, 86–87.

10. "Temple in Tahiti," 7.

MÉXICO CITY MÉXICO TEMPLE, page 76

1. O'Donnal, *Pioneer in Guatemala*, 283.

2. Weekes, "Mexico City Temple."

3. O'Donnal, *Pioneer in Guatemala*, 286.

4. O'Donnal, *Pioneer in Guatemala*, 288.

5. "Saints Throng to Temple," 75.

6. "Saints Throng to Temple," 75.

7. "Saints Throng to Temple," 75.

8. "Saints Throng to Temple," 75.

9. Weekes, "Mexico City Temple."

10. "Saints Throng to Temple," 74.

11. "In Many Countries," 7.

BOISE IDAHO TEMPLE, page 78

1. Cazier, "Boise Temple Dedicated," 77.

2. "Ground Is Broken," 78.

3. Thurber, interview.

4. Thurber, interview.

5. "Ground Is Broken," 78.

6. Cazier, "Boise Temple Dedicated," 77.

7. Thurber, interview.

8. Cazier, "Boise Temple Dedicated," 77.

9. "Boise Idaho Temple Mini-History."

10. Cazier, "Boise Temple Dedicated," 76–77.

11. Cazier, "Boise Temple Dedicated," 76.

SYDNEY AUSTRALIA TEMPLE, page 81

1. Bakker, "Among Australian Landmarks," 105; see also "Brief History of the Development of the Sydney Australia Temple."

2. Britsch, *Unto the Islands of the Sea*, 247.

3. "Joke Backfires," 7.

4. Britsch, *Unto the Islands of the Sea*, 248–49.

5. *Roofing Review* 28 (Spring 1984).

6. Bakker, "Among Australian Landmarks," 105.

7. Bakker, "Among Australian Landmarks," 104–5.

8. Bakker, "Among Australian Landmarks," 105.

9. Meyer, "Aborigines Gather," 5.

10. "Prayer, Determination," 16.

MANILA PHILIPPINES TEMPLE, page 84

1. Ilagan, "Brief History," 6.

2. Ilagan, "Brief History," 2.

3. Ilagan, "Brief History," 2.

4. Ilagan, "Brief History," 12.

5. Ilagan, "Brief History," 12.

6. Orquiola, "Temple Dedication Rewards Faith," 107.

7. Orquiola, "Temple Dedication Rewards Faith," 107.

8. Orquiola, "Temple Dedication Rewards Faith," 106.

9. Orquiola, "Temple Dedication Rewards Faith," 106.

10. "Houses of the Lord in Far-Away Places," 7.

DALLAS TEXAS TEMPLE, page 86

1. Cobb, "Dallas Temple Dedication," 70.

2. Hobson, *Dallas Texas Temple*, 29–30.

3. "Temple in Dallas Means Blessings," 77.

4. "Dallas Temple Is Underway," 77.

5. Hobson, *Dallas Texas Temple*, 70.

6. Hobson, *Dallas Texas Temple*, 45.

7. Hobson, *Dallas Texas Temple*, 43, 74–75.

8. Hobson, *Dallas Texas Temple*, 55.

9. "Dallas Temple Is Underway," 77.

10. Cobb, "Dallas Temple Dedication," 70.

11. Cobb, "Dallas Temple Dedication," 69.

12. Hobson, *Dallas Texas Temple*, 191.

13. Hobson, *Dallas Texas Temple*, 129.

14. Hobson, *Dallas Texas Temple*, 177.

15. Cobb, "Dallas Temple Dedication," 69.

TAIPEI TAIWAN TEMPLE, page 89

1. Jensen and Liu, "Taiwan Saints Eager," 107.

2. "Southern Far East Mission History."

3. Jensen and Liu, "Taiwan Saints Eager," 108.

4. Jensen and Liu, "Taiwan Saints Eager," 108.

5. Wallgren, interview.

6. Liu, "Taipei Taiwan Temple Dedicated," 76.

7. Liu, "Taipei Taiwan Temple Dedicated," 76.

8. Liu, "Taipei Taiwan Temple Dedicated," 75.

9. Jensen and Liu, "Taiwan Saints Eager," 108.

10. Jensen and Liu, "Taiwan Saints Eager," 108.

GUATEMALA CITY GUATEMALA TEMPLE, page 91

1. O'Donnal, *Pioneer in Guatemala*, 308.

2. O'Donnal, *Pioneer in Guatemala*, 302.

3. "Guatemala City Temple Dedicated," 77.

4. "Guatemala City Temple Dedicated," 77.

5. "Guatemala City Temple Dedicated," 77.

6. Hill, "New Facility," 3.

7. "In Many Countries," 7.

FREIBERG GERMANY TEMPLE, page 93

1. *1999–2000 Church Almanac*, 324.

2. Monson, *Faith Rewarded*, 117–18.

3. Monson, *Faith Rewarded*, 88.

4. Monson, *Faith Rewarded*, 85.

5. Monson, *Faith Rewarded*, 103.

6. "Hero in the Font," 16.

7. Biddulph, *Morning Breaks*, 180–86.

8. Monson, *Faith Rewarded*, 105.

STOCKHOLM SWEDEN TEMPLE, page 95

1. Evans, "Building of Temple," 11.
2. Evans, "Building of Temple," 11.
3. Evans, "Building of Temple," 11.
4. Palm, "Nordic Temple," 7.
5. Avant, "Temple in Sweden."
6. Johnson, *Open Doors*, 131–32.
7. Kimball, *Teachings*, 586.
8. Johnson, *Open Doors*, 133.
9. Avant, "Temple in Sweden."

CHICAGO ILLINOIS TEMPLE, page 97

1. Winfield, "Rites Begin Construction," 3.
2. Wood, "Temple a Mecca."
3. *Chicago Herald*, 13 July 1985, 1.
4. "Chicago Temple Dedicated," 72.
5. "Chicago Saints," 77.
6. "Chicago Temple Dedicated," 72.
7. "Chicago Temple Dedicated," 72.
8. Heslop, "Bright Future Seen."
9. "Chicago Temple Dedicated," 72.
10. "Chicago Temple Dedicated," 72.
11. Barton, remarks.

JOHANNESBURG SOUTH AFRICA TEMPLE, page 100

1. *Johannesburg Temple*, 5–7.
2. "Blessings of House of the Lord," 7.
3. "Johannesburg Temple Dedicated," 102.
4. "Johannesburg Temple Dedicated," 102.
5. "Gospel Pioneers."
6. Mostert, "Trip to Temple."

SEOUL SOUTH KOREA TEMPLE, page 102

1. Younger, Newby, and Le Cheminant, *For Those Who Dare to Dream*, 11.
2. Younger, Newby, and Le Cheminant, *Those Who Dare to Dream*, 35.
3. Cahill, "Times of Great Blessings," 70.
4. Younger, Newby, and Le Cheminant, *For Those Who Dare to Dream*, 44.
5. Younger, Newby, and Le Cheminant, *Those Who Dare to Dream*, 44.
6. Younger, Newby, and Le Cheminant, *For Those Who Dare to Dream*, 49.

7. Younger, Newby, and Le Cheminant, *For Those Who Dare to Dream*, 54.
8. Younger, Newby, and Le Cheminant, *For Those Who Dare to Dream*, 60.
9. "Houses of the Lord in Far-Away Places."
10. Younger, Newby, and Le Cheminant, *For Those Who Dare to Dream*, 59.

LIMA PERU TEMPLE, page 104

1. "The Church in Bolivia," 79.
2. "Seven New Stakes Created," 77.
3. Holley, "Lehi's Children."
4. "In Many Countries."
5. Holley, "Lehi's Children."
6. "Lima Temple Dedication," 83.

BUENOS AIRES ARGENTINA TEMPLE, page 106

1. "Buenos Aires Temple Will Be a Focal Point," 80.
2. Ballard, "Kingdom Rolls Forth," 12.
3. "Buenos Aires Temple Fulfills Desire of Saints," 84.
4. "Buenos Aires Temple Will Be a Focal Point," 80.
5. Curbelo, "New Training Center," 5.
6. "In Many Countries."
7. Walker, "Facing the Challenge," 10.

DENVER COLORADO TEMPLE, page 108

1. Bird, *Build unto My Holy Name*, 28–29.
2. Bird, *Build unto My Holy Name*, 23.
3. Bird, *Build unto My Holy Name*, 48.
4. Bird, *Build unto My Holy Name*, 71.
5. Bird, *Build unto My Holy Name*, 53–54.
6. Bird, *Build unto My Holy Name*, 53–54.
7. Bird, *Build unto My Holy Name*, 89, 94, 120, 136.
8. Lloyd, "LDS Fill Denver Arena."
9. Stoker, "Their Faith."
10. "Look to Temple," 5.

FRANKFURT GERMANY TEMPLE, page 111

1. "Fight over Mormon Temple."

2. Harbers, "Mormon Temple in the Huguenot City?"
3. "Mormon Temple in Friedrichsdorf."
4. Harbers, "Instead of Tolerance."
5. Mourik, "Frankfurt Temple Site History."
6. Mueller, "Friedrichsdorf, a Hallowed Refuge," 54–55.
7. Mourik, "Frankfurt Temple Site History."
8. Obst, "First 35,000 Visit," 11.
9. Mueller, "Friedrichsdorf, a Hallowed Refuge," 54–55.
10. Johnson, "Eternal Road Trip."
11. "Blessings of House of the Lord."

PORTLAND OREGON TEMPLE, page 114

1. Kullberg, *Saints to the Columbia*, 108.
2. "300,000 Visitors Tour."
3. Kullberg, *Saints to the Columbia*, 111.
4. Kullberg, *Saints to the Columbia*, 113.
5. Kullberg, *Saints to the Columbia*, 103.
6. Kullberg, *Saints to the Columbia*, 104.
7. "300,000 Visitors Tour."
8. "Many Receive Sweet Blessings."
9. "Temple Is 'Gift,'" 7.
10. Avant, "Temple Dedicated," 3.
11. Hart, "I Needed to Be There."
12. Avant, "Metaphor of Life," 11.

LAS VEGAS NEVADA TEMPLE, page 117

1. "LDS in Las Vegas."
2. "Fifteen Thousand Attend," 74.
3. Hart, "Las Vegas Temple."
4. Hart, "Las Vegas Temple."
5. "November Open House."
6. "Nearly 300,000 Tour."
7. Hart, "Temple Open House Exceeds Hopes."
8. Hart, "Temple Open House Exceeds Hopes."
9. Hart, "New Temple Inspires."
10. Hart, "New Temple Inspires."
11. Tate, interview.
12. Tate, interview.
13. Tate, interview.

TORONTO ONTARIO TEMPLE, page 120

1. Van Orden, "Valiant Acts."
2. Robertson, "Toronto," 46.
3. "Toronto Temple Nears Completion."
4. "Toronto Temple Dedicated," 104.
5. "Toronto Temple Dedicated," 104.
6. "Temple: Place of Peace."
7. "City Gives Excellence Award."
8. "Toronto Temple Dedicated," 104.
9. "Apostles Testify of Temples' Importance."
10. "Toronto Temple Dedicated," 104.
11. "180 Gather to Paint Fence," 14.
12. "Apostles Testify of Temples' Importance."

SAN DIEGO CALIFORNIA TEMPLE, page 123

1. Frank, "New Mormon Temple a Treat for the Eyes," B8.
2. Frank, "New Mormon Temple a Treat for the Eyes," B8.
3. Whitman, "Rabbi Writes."
4. "Children Learn about Temple."
5. "Children Learn about Temple."
6. "Angel Moroni."
7. "Volunteers Who Cleaned," 1.
8. "Volunteers Who Cleaned," 1.
9. "Volunteers Who Cleaned," 1.
10. Van Orden, "San Diego Temple Dedication."
11. Van Orden, "San Diego Temple."
12. Van Orden, "San Diego Temple."
13. Van Orden, "San Diego Temple."
14. Van Orden, "San Diego Temple."

ORLANDO FLORIDA TEMPLE, page 126

1. Skousen, *Sunshine in the Soul*, 60.
2. Skousen, *Sunshine in the Soul*, 61.
3. Skousen, *Sunshine in the Soul*, 61.
4. Skousen, *Sunshine in the Soul*, 63–65.
5. "Temple to Bring 'Brighter Day.'"
6. "Temple to Bring 'Brighter Day.'"
7. Skousen, *Sunshine in the Soul*, 67, 71.
8. Lloyd, "Orlando Temple Opens."
9. Lloyd, "90,000 Tour Temple."

10. Jorgensen, "Orlando Florida Temple Dedicated," 66.
11. Skousen, *Sunshine in the Soul*, 80–81.
12. Avant, "Temple Is Dedicated in Sunshine State."
13. Avant, "Members Enjoy Blessings."
14. Avant, "Temple Is Dedicated in Sunshine State."

BOUNTIFUL UTAH TEMPLE, page 129

1. Barlow, *Bountiful Utah Temple Site History*, 1.
2. Barlow, *Bountiful Utah Temple Site History*, 52–53.
3. Griffiths, "Bountiful Utah Temple."
4. "Temple Experiences in 'Deseret.'"
5. Griffiths, "Bountiful Utah Temple."
6. "'Elegance to Complement the Spirit.'"
7. "'Elegance to Complement the Spirit.'"
8. Parkinson, "Newly Completed Temple."
9. "Bountiful Utah Temple Dedicated," 74.
10. "Bountiful Utah Temple Dedicated," 74.
11. "Bountiful Utah Temple Dedicatory Prayer," 75.
12. "200,000 Attend Dedicatory Sessions."

HONG KONG CHINA TEMPLE, page 132

1. Avant, "Hong Kong Temple Dedicated."
2. "Where the Twain Meet."
3. "Where the Twain Meet."
4. "Where the Twain Meet."
5. "Guests Feel Peace at Open House."
6. "Where the Twain Meet."
7. Avant, "Hong Kong Temple Dedicated."
8. "Where the Twain Meet."
9. "Where the Twain Meet."
10. Avant, "Hong Kong Temple Dedicated."
11. Avant, "Hong Kong Temple Dedicated."

MOUNT TIMPANOGOS UTAH TEMPLE, page 134

1. "American Fork Site."
2. Hart, "Mt. Timpanogos Utah Temple," 4.
3. Hart, "Mt. Timpanogos Utah Temple," 4.
4. Weaver, "157,917 Attend Dedication."

ST. LOUIS MISSOURI TEMPLE, page 137

1. "St. Louis Temple Book of Remembrance," 23.
2. Hart, "Ground Is Broken on Cold Day."
3. Hart, "Ground Is Broken on Cold Day."
4. Hart, "Ground Is Broken on Cold Day."
5. Lloyd, "Church Dedicates Its 50th Temple."
6. Lloyd, "Church Dedicates Its 50th Temple."
7. Lloyd, "Church Dedicates Its 50th Temple."

VERNAL UTAH TEMPLE, page 140

1. Lloyd, "Vernal Temple Doors."
2. "Temple Experiences in 'Deseret.'"
3. "Temple Experiences in 'Deseret.'"
4. Irving and Barton, *From Tabernacle to Temple*, 32–33, 34.
5. Hart, "Transformation Begins."
6. Irving and Barton, *From Tabernacle to Temple*, 38, 40.
7. Irving and Barton, *From Tabernacle to Temple*, 40.
8. Lloyd, "Vernal Temple Doors."
9. Lloyd, "Vernal Temple Doors."
10. Irving and Barton, *From Tabernacle to Temple*, 61–62, 63, 64.

PRESTON ENGLAND TEMPLE, page 143

1. *1999–2000 Church Almanac*, 399.
2. "Preston Temple Modern Classical Design."
3. Avant, "Blessings of House of the Lord."
4. Avant, "Blessings of House of the Lord."

5. Cannon, "Dressing Temple Grounds in Green."
6. "Temple Experiences in 'Deseret.'"
7. Huether, "Special Technique," 6.
8. Sears, interview.
9. "20,000 See Statue Lifted."
10. Weaver, "157,917 Attend Dedication."
11. Van Orden, "Mount Timpanogos Temple Dedicated."

5. Lloyd, "Open House Begins."
6. "Multitudes Throng Preston Temple."
7. Lloyd, "Open House Begins."
8. "Multitudes Throng Preston Temple."
9. Avant, "Hearts Brim Full."
10. Avant, "Temple Is Great Symbol."
11. Avant, "Hearts Brim Full."
12. Avant, "Temple Is Great Symbol."
13. Avant, "Temple Is Great Symbol."

MONTICELLO UTAH TEMPLE, page 146

1. Reay, *Incredible Passage*.
2. Lloyd, "Ground Broken."
3. Lloyd, "Ground Broken."
4. http://www.hubwest.com/monticellotemple/Monticello_Temple_marble.html
5. http://www.hubwest.com/monticellotemple/Monticello_Temple_marble.html
6. Lloyd, "20,000 Tour New Temple."
7. *Blue Mountain Panorama*.
8. Van Orden, "Inspiration Came for Smaller Temples."

ANCHORAGE ALASKA TEMPLE, page 149

1. Nichols, *History of the Acquisition*.
2. Jasper and Lommel, *Gathering of Saints*, 320.
3. Jasper and Lommel, *Gathering of Saints*, 320.
4. Liungman, *Dictionary of Symbols*, 318.
5. "Architect Gives Newest Temple."
6. *Ogden Standard-Examiner*, 23 June 1999.
7. Dockstader, "Northernmost Temple Dedicated."
8. "Work Goes On."
9. Dockstader, "Northernmost Temple Dedicated."
10. Nichols, *Experiences in the Temple Baptistry*.

COLONIA JUÁREZ CHIHUAHUA MÉXICO TEMPLE, page 152

1. "Colonia Juárez Temple Dedication."
2. "Temple Started for Mexico Colonies."
3. Whetten, "Colonia Juárez Temple Groundbreaking."

4. Skidmore and Skidmore, interview.
5. Skidmore and Skidmore, interview.
6. Hart, "Newest Temple in Mexico."
7. "Colonia Juárez Temple Dedication."
8. Hart, "Newest Temple in Mexico."

MADRID SPAIN TEMPLE, page 154

1. "Saints in Spain."
2. "Ground Broken for Temple in Madrid."
3. "Saints in Spain."
4. Harmon, "Sacred Edifice."
5. Avant, "President Hinckley in Spain."
6. "Saints in Spain."
7. "Temple Dedicated in Madrid."
8. "President Hinckley Dedicates Madrid Spain Temple."
9. "Construction Well Under Way on Madrid Temple."
10. "Saints in Spain."

BOGOTÁ COLOMBIA TEMPLE, page 157

1. Hart, "Gift of Inner Peace."
2. Aulesita, interview.
3. Aulesita, interview.
4. "Work Begins on Colombia Temple."
5. "Work Begins on Colombia Temple."

GUAYAQUIL ECUADOR TEMPLE, page 159

1. Aulesita, interview.
2. Hart, "Guayaquil Ecuador Temple."
3. "In Many Countries."
4. Hart, "Guayaquil Ecuador Temple."
5. Hart, "Guayaquil Ecuador Temple."
6. Hart, "Guayaquil Ecuador Temple."
7. Hart, "Guayaquil Ecuador Temple."
8. "This Is a Day of History."
9. Hart, "Guayaquil Ecuador Temple."
10. Hart, "Guayaquil Ecuador Temple."

SPOKANE WASHINGTON TEMPLE, page 161

1. McBride, "Latter-day Saints Marching."
2. Bickley, interview.
3. "Weather Clears."

4. Bickley, interview.
5. *Spokane Temple News*, June 1999.
6. Dockstader, "You Live in Greatest Age of World."
7. Dockstader, "Amid Rays of Sunshine."
8. Dockstader, "Amid Rays of Sunshine."
9. Dockstader, "'You Live in Greatest Age of World.'"

COLUMBUS OHIO TEMPLE, page 164

1. Martin and Shannon, *Columbus Ohio Temple*, 3.
2. Martin and Shannon, *Columbus Ohio Temple*, 21.
3. Stahle, "Spiritual Celebration."
4. Martin and Shannon, *Columbus Ohio Temple*, 51–52.
5. Martin and Shannon, *Columbus Ohio Temple*, 46.
6. Martin and Shannon, *Columbus Ohio Temple*, 56.
7. Stahle, "Spiritual Celebration."
8. Stahle, "Spiritual Celebration."

BISMARCK NORTH DAKOTA TEMPLE, page 167

1. Cheney, "Miracles of the Bismarck North Dakota Temple Site."
2. Cheney, "Miracles of the Bismarck North Dakota Temple Site."
3. Cheney, "Miracles of the Bismarck North Dakota Temple Site."
4. Kruckenberg, "Ground Broken."
5. Kruckenberg, "Ground Broken."
6. Johnson, "Art Worth Hanging."
7. Posted on <www.familyforever.com/temples>.
8. Van Orden, "Shortening the Vast Distances."
9. Van Orden, "Shortening the Vast Distances."
10. Dahlgren, interview.

COLUMBIA SOUTH CAROLINA TEMPLE, page 170

1. Munday, "Mormons Offer Glimpse."
2. "Columbia South Carolina Temple."

3. "Columbia South Carolina Temple."
4. Smith, interview.
5. Franklin-Moore, "South Carolina Temple."
6. Lloyd, "New Temple in a 'Place of History.'"
7. Lloyd, "New Temple in a 'Place of History.'"
8. Koyle, interview.
9. "Temple Sustains Couple in Trial," 3.

DETROIT MICHIGAN TEMPLE, page 173

1. Hill, "Temple in Their Midst."
2. Hill, "Temple in Their Midst."
3. "Ground Broken for Two New Temples."
4. Hill, "Temple in Their Midst."
5. "Ground Broken for Two New Temples."
6. Cady, "Angel Moroni Statue."
7. Brown and Brown, interview.
8. Brown and Brown, interview.
9. Michalek, "Detroit Open House."
10. *Detroit Temple Times.*
11. *Detroit Temple Times.*

HALIFAX NOVA SCOTIA TEMPLE, page 176

1. Hinckley, *Ensign*, November 1997.
2. Stahle, "Historic Sabbath."
3. "Thousands Attend."
4. Kruckenberg, "Announcements of New Holy Edifices."
5. "'What a Happy Day.'"
6. "'What a Happy Day.'"
7. "Thousands Attend."
8. Stahle, "Historic Sabbath."
9. Stahle, "Historic Sabbath."

REGINA SASKATCHEWAN TEMPLE, page 178

1. Lloyd, "Ground Broken."
2. Lloyd, "Ground Broken."
3. Burch and Burch, interview.
4. Burch and Burch, interview.
5. Kruckenberg, "Regina Prairie."
6. "Plane Problem Leads to LDS First."

BILLINGS MONTANA TEMPLE, page 180

1. Larsen, "History of Billings Temple."
2. Larsen, "History of Billings Temple."
3. Pottenger, interview.
4. Mair, interview.
5. Mair, interview.

EDMONTON ALBERTA TEMPLE, page 183

1. Kruckenberg, "Announcements of New Holy Edifices."
2. "Temples Dedicated in Alberta."
3. Lloyd, "Ground Is Broken."
4. Udy and Udy, interview.
5. Udy and Udy, interview.
6. Quigley, "Temple to Call Their Own."
7. Udy and Udy, interview.
8. Quigley, "A Temple to Call Their Own."
9. Dedicatory Prayers.
10. Udy and Udy, interview.

RALEIGH NORTH CAROLINA TEMPLE, page 186

1. Dixon, "Temple Is at the 'Apex,'" 3.
2. Johnson, "Temple Project History," 1–2.
3. Johnson, "Temple Project History," 5.
4. Johnson, "Temple Project History," 10.
5. Anderson and Anderson, "Sacred Lace."
6. Leone, "Children Earn Dimes," 5.
7. Lloyd, "While Building Temple," 14.
8. Anderson and Anderson, "Sacred Lace."
9. Lloyd, "While Building Temple," 14.
10. "'May Thy Holy Spirit Constantly Dwell Herein,'" 4.

ST. PAUL MINNESOTA TEMPLE, page 189

1. Halverson, interview.
2. Kruckenberg, "Ground Broken for Temple."
3. Halverson, interview.
4. Kruckenberg, "Announcements of New Holy Edifices."
5. Howell, letter.
6. "Statues of Angel."
7. Erickson, interview.

KONA HAWAII TEMPLE, page 192.

1. Harris, interview.
2. Pharis, interview.
3. "Tremendous Support for Temple Hearing."
4. Stratton, "Kona Hawaii Temple History."
5. Stratton and Stratton, interview.
6. Dockstader, "Second Sacred Edifice," 10.
7. Dockstader, "Second Sacred Edifice," 10.
8. Pharis, interview.

CIUDAD JUÁREZ MÉXICO TEMPLE, page 195

1. Guitierrez de Orozco, interview.
2. "Temple in Ciudad Juárez."
3. Skidmore and Skidmore, interview.
4. Skidmore and Skidmore, interview.
5. Skidmore and Skidmore, interview.
6. Skidmore and Skidmore, interview.

HERMOSILLO SONORA MÉXICO TEMPLE, page 197

1. Rivera, interview.
2. Montoya, interview.
3. Hart, "Impact on Lives Begins."
4. Montoya, interview.
5. Rivera, interview.
6. Rivera, interview.
7. Montoya, interview.
8. Montoya, interview.
9. Rivera, interview.
10. Montoya, interview.
11. Rivera, interview.

ALBUQUERQUE NEW MEXICO TEMPLE, page 199

1. Ghaznavi, "Site to Behold," 14.
2. Knudsen, interview.
3. Knudsen, interview.
4. Dedicatory Prayers.

OAXACA MÉXICO TEMPLE, page 202

1. Erekson, interview.
2. Erekson, interview.
3. "Seven Temples Dedicated," 111.

4. "Seven Temples Dedicated," 110.
5. Hart, "New Horizons Open."

TUXTLA GUTIÉRREZ MÉXICO TEMPLE, page 204

1. Gardner, "Making Friends," 2.
2. Sanchez, interview.
3. "Springtime Ceremony Begins."
4. Sanchez, interview.
5. Sanchez, interview.

LOUISVILLE KENTUCKY TEMPLE, page 206

1. Prestridge and Prestridge, interview.
2. Louisville Kentucky Temple Update.
3. Prestridge and Prestridge, interview.
4. Prestridge and Prestridge, interview.
5. Prestridge and Prestridge, interview.
6. Blackwell, interview.
7. Poulsen, interview.
8. Prestridge and Prestridge, interview.

PALMYRA NEW YORK TEMPLE, page 209

1. Moore, "'Jewel' Adorns Palmyra."
2. Richards, interview.
3. Richards, interview.
4. Richards, interview.
5. Holdman, interview.
6. Holdman, interview.
7. Holdman, interview.
8. Adams, "Palmyra Temple History," 19, 21, 26–27.
9. Adams, "Palmyra Temple History," 19, 21, 26–27.

FRESNO CALIFORNIA TEMPLE, page 212

1. Maxwell, Boswell, and Ellsworth, interview.
2. Maxwell, Boswell, and Ellsworth, interview.
3. Maxwell, Boswell, and Ellsworth, interview.
4. Dalton, interview.
5. Maxwell, Boswell, and Ellsworth, interview.

6. Lloyd, "Symbol of Growth."
7. Lloyd, "Symbol of Growth."

MEDFORD OREGON TEMPLE, page 215

1. "Promise Fulfilled."
2. Woodward, interview.
3. Woodward, "Preparing the Lord's Way," 7.
4. Woodward, "Building of Men," 7.
5. Woodward, "Medford Oregon Temple History," 127.
6. Woodward, "Medford Oregon Temple History," 128.

MEMPHIS TENNESSEE TEMPLE, page 218

1. Avant, "Remembering Roots."
2. Denton, interview.
3. Anderson and Anderson, interview.
4. Denton, interview.
5. Anderson and Anderson, interview.
6. Anderson and Anderson, interview.
7. Denton, interview.

RENO NEVADA TEMPLE, page 221

1. Dyches, interview.
2. Forbush, interview.
3. Forbush, interview.
4. Forbush, interview.
5. Forbush, interview.
6. Trimble, interview.
7. Dyches, interview.
8. Trimble, interview.
9. Dyches, interview.

COCHABAMBA BOLIVIA TEMPLE, page 224

1. Olsen, "Bolivia," 22.
2. Johnston, "Worthy of the Heart of a People," 3.
3. "President Hinckley Visits South America," 72.
4. Hart, "Prophet Breaks Ground for New Temples," 3.
5. Olsen, "Bolivia," 22.

6. Johnston, "Worthy of the Heart of a People," 3.
7. Olsen, "Bolivia," 22.

TAMPICO MÉXICO TEMPLE, page 226

1. Saldivar, interview.
2. Swensen, "Sacred Hill," 4.
3. Swensen, "Sacred Hill," 4.
4. Swensen, "Sacred Hill," 4.
5. Avalos, interview.
6. Swensen, "Sacred Hill," 3.
7. Swensen, "Sacred Hill," 4.

NASHVILLE TENNESSEE TEMPLE, page 228

1. "Letter to the Editor," *Tennessean*, 26 November 1994.
2. McClurg and McClurg, interview.
3. Udy and Udy, interview.
4. Seifers, "Nashville Temple."
5. Seifers, "Nashville Temple."

VILLAHERMOSA MÉXICO TEMPLE, page 231

1. "Villahermosa Tabasco Temple," 75.
2. Maxwell and Maxwell, interview.
3. Maxwell and Maxwell, interview.
4. Swensen, "Villahermosa Temple," 3.
5. Swensen, "Villahermosa Temple," 3.

MONTRÉAL QUÉBEC TEMPLE, page 233

1. "Dream of a Temple in Quebec," 15.
2. "Five New Temples Dedicated in Four Countries," 76.
3. Brugger, "Teaming Up for Temple Work," 30.
4. Dockstader, "Montreal Temple Highlight," 4.
5. Farrington, "Wonderful News!" 16.

SAN JOSÉ COSTA RICA TEMPLE, page 235

1. Gaunt, "Costa Rica."
2. Swensen, " 'Pura Vida' Costa Rica."
3. Swensen, " 'Pura Vida' Costa Rica."

4. Gaunt, "Costa Rica," 24.
5. Gaunt, "Costa Rica," 24.
6. Gaunt, "Costa Rica," 25.
7. Swensen, "New Landmark by Shining Seas," 5.
8. Swensen, "New Landmark by Shining Seas," 5.
9. Swensen, "New Landmark by Shining Seas," 5.

FUKUOKA JAPAN TEMPLE, page 237

1. "Temple Plan Thrills Members," 5.
2. Hill, "Church Members Rejoice," 3.
3. Blackburn and Blackburn, interview.
4. Blackburn and Blackburn, interview.
5. Hill, "Church Members Rejoice," 3.
6. Hill, "Church Members Rejoice," 3.
7. Okata, "Japan's Second Temple."
8. Hill, "Church Members Rejoice," 6.
9. "Four Temples Dedicated," 72.
10. Blackburn and Blackburn, interview.

ADELAIDE AUSTRALIA TEMPLE, page 239

1. " 'Spiritual Sanctuaries,' " 5.
2. Britsch, *Unto the Islands of the Sea*, 248–49.
3. "President Hinckley Visits New Zealand, Australia, and Mexico," 76.
4. Howes, "Rain, Clouds in Adelaide," 3.
5. " 'Spiritual Sanctuaries,' " 5.
6. " 'Spiritual Sanctuaries,' " 5.
7. " 'Spiritual Sanctuaries,' " 3.
8. " 'Spiritual Sanctuaries,' " 3, 5.

MELBOURNE AUSTRALIA TEMPLE, page 241

1. " 'Spiritual Sanctuaries,' " 5.
2. Sanders, "Ground Is Broken for Melbourne Temple," 5.
3. Kruckenberg, "Announcements of New Holy Edifices," 10.
4. " 'Spiritual Sanctuaries,' " 5.

SUVA FIJI TEMPLE, page 244

1. Lesuma, "Members in Fiji," 10.

2. Britsch, *Unto the Islands of the Sea*, 504–6.
3. Lesuma, "Members in Fiji," 10.
4. "'Fortress of Faith,'" 4.
5. "'Fortress of Faith,'" 4.
6. Weaver, "Fijian LDS Temple."
7. "'Fortress of Faith,'" 4.
8. "May Be Blessed with Peace," 6.
9. "'Fortress of Faith,'" 3.

MÉRIDA MÉXICO TEMPLE, page 246

1. Warnick, "Yucatán," 10.
2. Warnick, "Yucatán," 8-9.
3. Pinelo de Ferraez, "Temple 'Will Add to Peace,'" 3.
4. Warnick, "Yucatán," 10.
5. Swensen, "Modern Temple Rises," 4.
6. Swensen, "Modern Temple Rises," 4.
7. Fife and Fife, interview.
8. Swensen, "Modern Temple Rises," 4.

VERACRUZ MÉXICO TEMPLE, page 248

1. "President Hinckley Stresses Family," 74-75.
2. "Ground Broken for Eighth Temple in Mexico," 3, 6.
3. Avalos, interview.
4. Avalos, interview.
5. Avalos, interview.
6. Weekes, interview.
7. Swensen, "New Temples in Mexico," 13.
8. Erekson, interview.
9. Avalos, interview.

BATON ROUGE LOUISIANA TEMPLE, page 250

1. Rawson, "Temple Site Selection."
2. Kay, "Dream Come True."
3. Strawn and Smith, "2,000 Attend Ceremony," 3.

4. Bounds, "Baton Rouge Temple Groundbreaking."
5. Strawn and Smith, "2,000 Attend Ceremony," 13.
6. Smith and Smith, interview.
7. Smith and Smith, interview.

OKLAHOMA CITY OKLAHOMA TEMPLE, page 253

1. Lukens, "History of the Oklahoma City Oklahoma Temple."
2. Lukens, "History of the Oklahoma City Oklahoma Temple."
3. Lukens, "History of the Oklahoma City Oklahoma Temple."
4. Newman, interview.
5. Lukens, "History of the Oklahoma City Oklahoma Temple."
6. Lukens and Lukens, interview.
7. Newman, interview.
8. Dockstader, "Sacred Building on Sacred Ground," 7.
9. Dockstader, "Sacred Building on Sacred Ground," 3.

CARACAS VENEZUELA TEMPLE, page 256

1. Hinckley, *Ensign*, May 1997.
2. Ruscitti, "Choosing the Land."
3. Ruscitti, "History of the Construction."
4. Swensen, "Venezuela Saints Rejoicing."
5. Swensen, "Venezuela Saints Rejoicing."

HOUSTON TEXAS TEMPLE, page 259

1. Cook, "Beginning of the Houston Temple."
2. Cook, "Beginning of the Houston Temple."
3. Shadler and Gill, recorded conversation.
4. "Designing the Temple Landscape."
5. "One Eternal Round."
6. "Windows of Heaven."

7. Fults and Driggs, "Angel Moroni Placement."

BIRMINGHAM ALABAMA TEMPLE, page 262

1. Arave and Arave, interview.
2. "Ground Broken for Temple in Alabama."
3. Garrison, "Critics Gather at Temple."
4. Arave, "Birmingham Alabama Temple Construction History," 6–7.
5. Garrison, "Mormon President Conducts Ceremony," 1.

SANTO DOMINGO DOMINICAN REPUBLIC TEMPLE, page 265

1. VanDenBerghe and VanDenBerghe, "Dominican Saints."
2. VanDenBerghe and VanDenBerghe, "Dominican Saints."
3. "Excitement Growing As Members Prepare."

BOSTON MASSACHUSETTS TEMPLE, page 267

1. Dew, *Go Forward with Faith*, 530.
2. Stahle, "This Has Been a Banner Year," 4.
3. Stahle, "This Has Been a Banner Year," 4.
4. Stahle, "Dedication Sunday."
5. Bobinchock, "Temple's Granite Exterior."
6. "We Dedicate It As Being Complete," 6.

FACTS ABOUT THE FIRST 100 TEMPLES, page 270

1. Barlow, *Bountiful Utah Temple Site History*, 53.
2. *Manti Temple*, 41.
3. *Manti Temple*, 28.
4. Kimball, "'Mormon' Stamps."
5. Candland, *Ensign to the Nations*, 64.

6. Britsch, *Unto the Islands of the Sea*, 425, 494.
7. Lundwall, *Temples of the Most High*, 419.
8. *Manti Temple*, 66–67.
9. Palm, "Nordic Temple."
10. Skousen, *Sunshine in the Soul*.
11. St. George Temple visitors' center brochure.
12. Lundwall, *Temples of the Most High*, 206.
13. Kullberg, *Saints to the Columbia*, 109.
14. "Children Learn about Temple."
15. Wilcox, *Washington D. C. Temple*.
16. Olsen, *Logan Temple*, 129.
17. *Manti Temple*, 1.
18. Whitney, *Life of Heber C. Kimball*, 221–22.
19. Skousen, *Sunshine in the Soul*.
20. Benson, "Tokyo Temple."
21. *Manti Temple*, 104.
22. "On the Bright Side."
23. Wallgren, interview.
24. Hunter, "I Saw Another Angel Fly," 32–33.
25. Wallgren, interview.
26. Smith, "Washington Temple."
27. Clifton, "10-Ton Water Truck."
28. Spurrier, *Mormon History in the Pacific*, 33.
29. Irving and Barton, *From Tabernacle to Temple*, 63.
30. Adams, *Palmyra Temple History*, 24.
31. Richards, interview.
32. Talmage, *House of the Lord*, 181.
33. Craig, "Mormon Angel."
34. Kirby and Cowan, "History of the Swiss Temple," 17.
35. Hobson, *Dallas Texas Temple*, 56.
36. Hunter, "Your Temple Recommend," 6.
37. "Toronto Temple Nears Completion."
38. Olsen, LDSWorldGems.
39. "Statues of Angel."
40. Weekes, "The Mexico City Temple."
41. Stahle, "Historic Sabbath in Canada."
42. "'Fortress of Faith,'" 3.

Sources

Adair, Jill B. "Mesa Easter Pageant Notes 60th Anniversary." *Church News*, 18 April 1998, 4.

———. "Mesa Temple Christmas Display Enhances Spirit of Season." *Church News*, 11 December 1999, 11.

Adams, Roger J. "Palmyra Temple History." Unpublished.

Aidukaitis, Nelson C. "Ground Is Broken for Brazil Temple." *Church News*, 27 March 1976, 3.

———. "Temple Progresses in Brazil." *Church News*, 15 January 1977, 3.

Allred, Gordon. "The Great Labor of Love." *Improvement Era* 61 (April 1958): 226–29.

"American Fork Site Selected for New Utah County Temple." *Church News*, 10 April 1993, 3.

Anderson, Donna, and Forrest Anderson. "Sacred Lace." *Raleigh Temple Times*, 2 October 1999, 8.

Anderson, Edward O. "The Making of a Temple." *Millennial Star*, September 1958, 278.

Anderson, Trenna, and DeLoy Anderson. Interview by author, 15 April 2000.

"Angel Moroni Gets Some New Gold." *San Diego Seagull*, March 1993, 6.

"Angel Moroni Statue Chosen for Temple." *Church News*, 10 July 1971, 5.

"Apostles Testify of Temples' Importance." *Church News*, 1 September 1990, 7.

Arave, Carol Colleen. "Birmingham Alabama Temple Construction History." Unpublished.

Arave, Dale L., and Carol Colleen Arave. Interview by author, 7 September 2000.

"Architect Gives Newest Temple Alaska Touches." *Anchorage Daily News*, 27 December 1998, A12.

"Atlanta Temple Rededicated after Baptistry Renovation." *Church News*, 22 November 1997, 5.

Atlanta Temple Report. Monthly bulletin distributed to Church units in the temple district.

Aulesita, Jim. Interview by author, 25 February 2000.

Avalos, Rodolfo. Interview by author translated by Adam Rigby, May 21, 2000.

Avant, Gerry. "Blessings of House of the Lord Reach Faithful in Many Lands." *Church News*, 24 September 1994, 7.

———. "Ground Broken for New Atlanta Temple," *Church News*, 14 March 1981, 3.

———. "Hearts Brim Full of Gratitude." *Church News*, 13 June 1998, 3.

———. "Hong Kong Temple Dedicated." *Church News*, 1 June 1996, 3.

———. "In Sweden, 'New Day' Brings Bright Future." *Church News*, 21 October 1995, 8.

———. "LDS Officials Rededicate Swiss Temple." *Deseret News*, 24 October 1992.

———. "Members Enjoy Blessings at Dedication." *Church News*, 15 October 1994, 5.

———. "Members Rejoice at Samoa Rites." *Church News*, 14 August 1983, 3.

———. "A Metaphor of Life: Building on Solid Foundation of Faith." *Church News*, 22 April 1995, 6.

———. "Pres. Hinckley in Spain for Dedication of Temple." *Deseret News*, 18 March 1999.

———. "Remembering Roots at Memphis Dedication." *Church News*, 29 April 2000.

———. "Temple Dedicated in Madrid, Spain." *Church News*, 27 March 1999, 3.

———. "Temple Dedicated in 'Quiet Splendor.'" *Church News*, 26 August 1989, 3.

———. "Temple in Sweden Is As Spiritual Magnet to Grateful Members." *Deseret News*, 11 November 1995, 4.

———. "Temple Is Dedicated in Sunshine State; 20,670 Attend Sessions." *Church News*, 15 October 1994, 3.

———. "Temple Is 'Great Symbol of Our Message to the World.'" *Church News*, 26 December 1998, 7.

———. "Thousands Tour London and Swiss Temples." *Church News*, 24 October 1992, 3.

———. "Tongans Sing, Dance, Weep at Dedication." *Church News*, 14 August 1983, 3.

Ayala, Viviana. "Reflections of the Temple Dedication." LDSWorldGems.

Bakker, Lynda. "Among Australian Landmarks, a House of the Lord." *Ensign*, November 1984, 104.

Ballard, M. Russell. "The Kingdom Rolls Forth in South America." *Ensign*, May 1986, 12.

Barker, Robert. "Brief History of the Washington D. C. Temple." Unpublished.

Barlow, John Paul. *Bountiful Utah Temple Site History*. Bountiful, Utah: Carr Printing, 1992.

Barton, Willard B. Remarks delivered at Chicago Illinois Temple dedication, 10 August 1985. Archives of The Church of Jesus Christ of Latter-day Saints, Salt Lake City.

Belnap, Phyllis, and Bruce Belnap. "Washington Temple Visitors Center." Unpublished.

Benson, Lee. "Tokyo Temple to Rise on Historic Site." *Church News*, 2 September 1978, 14.

Bickley, Mark. Interview by author, 14 August 1999.

Biddulph, Howard L. *The Morning Breaks: Stories of Conversion and Faith in the Former Soviet Union*. Salt Lake City: Deseret Book, 1996.

Billikopf, Gregory Encina. "On Sacred Ground." *Ensign*, January 1992, 52–53.

Bird, Twila. *Build unto My Holy Name: The Story of the Denver Temple*. Denver: Denver Colorado Area Public Communications Council, 1987.

Blackburn, Charles H., and Marjorie Blackburn. Interview by author, 25 September 2000.

Blackwell, Valerie. Interview by author, 11 March 2000.

Blue Mountain Panorama, N.p.: Blanding, Utah, n.d.

"Boise Idaho Temple Mini-History." Prepared by Boise Idaho Temple personnel.

Bounds, Dane. "Baton Rouge Temple Groundbreaking." LDSWorldGems.

"Bountiful Utah Temple Dedicated." *Ensign*, March 1995, 74.

"Bountiful Utah Temple Dedicatory Prayer." *Ensign*, March 1995, 75.

"A Brief History of the Development of the Sydney Australia Temple." Prepared by Sydney Australia Temple personnel.

Britsch, R. Lanier. *Unto the Islands of the Sea: A History of the Latter-day Saints in the Pacific*. Salt Lake City: Deseret Book, 1986.

Brown, Keith, and Lorraine Brown. Interview by author, 18 March 2000.

Brown, Lisle G. "The Sacred Departments for Temple Work in Nauvoo: The Assembly Room and the Council Chamber." *BYU Studies* 19 (Spring 1979), 361.

Brugger, Don L. "Teaming Up for Temple Work," *Ensign*, June 1995, 30.

Buehner, Carl W. *Do unto Others*. Salt Lake City: Bookcraft, 1957.

"Buenos Aires Temple Fulfills Desire of Saints." *Ensign*, March 1986, 84.

Bullock, Benjamin Hart. Affidavit, 4 August 1952. Archives of The Church of Jesus Christ of Latter-day Saints, Salt Lake City.

Burch, Sterling L., and Joy S. Burch. Interview by author, 17 September 2000.

Burton, Harold W., and W. Aird MacDonald. "The Oakland Temple." *Improvement Era*, May 1964, 380.

Cady, Jeanne. "Angel Moroni Statue Tops Detroit Temple." *Church News*, 17 July 1999, 6.

Cahill, Jerry P. "Latin America Area Conferences Report." *Ensign*, May 1977, 107.

———. "Times of Great Blessings." *Ensign*, January 1981, 70.

Candland, Evelyn. *An Ensign to the Nations: History of the Oakland Stake*. Oakland: Oakland California Stake, 1992.

Cannon, George Q. *Gems of Reminiscence*. Book 17 of *Faith Promoting Series*. Salt Lake City: George C. Lambert, 1915.

Cannon, Mike. "Dressing Temple Grounds in Green." *Church News*, 4 November 1995, 6.

Cazier, Bob. "Boise Temple Dedicated." *Ensign*, August 1984, 76.

Cheney, Lowell L. "Miracles of the Bismarck North Dakota Temple Site." Unpublished; copy in cornerstone of Bismarck North Dakota Temple.

Chicago Herald. 13 July 1985, 1.

"Chicago Saints: Reaching Out for Spiritual Blessings." *Ensign*, August 1985, 77.

"Chicago Temple Dedicated." *Ensign*, October 1985, 72.

"Children Learn about Temple, While Adding to Beauty of Grounds." *Church News*, 8 May 1993, 7.

Church History: Selections from the Encyclopedia of Mormonism. Edited by Daniel H. Ludlow. Salt Lake City: Deseret Book, 1992.

"The Church in Bolivia, Colombia, Ecuador, Peru, and Venezuela." *Ensign*, January 1997, 79.

"Church Launches Worldwide Temple-Building Emphasis with Announcement of Seven New Temples." *Ensign*, May 1980, 102–3.

"City Gives Excellence Award to Toronto Ontario Temple." *Church News*, 27 October 1990, 13.

Clifton, David. "10-Ton Water Truck Plunges into Home." *Salt Lake Tribune*, 5 June 1992, D4.

Cobb, Susan. "Dallas Temple Dedication Opens New Era for Southwestern Saints." *Ensign*, December 1984, 69.

"Colonia Juárez Temple Dedication." *Church News*, 13 March 1999, 3.

"Columbia South Carolina Temple Groundbreaking." *Ensign*, March 1999, 75.

Colvin, Don. "Historical Study of the Nauvoo Temple." Unpublished.

Conference Report. Salt Lake City: The Church of Jesus Christ of Latter-day Saints, 1899–2000.

Conkey, Donald S. "Atlanta Temple Dedicated." *Ensign*, August 1983, 72.

———. Interview by author, 15 September 2000.

"Construction Well Under Way on Madrid Temple." *Church News*, 16 November 1996, 3.

Cook, Steven R. "The Beginning of the Houston Temple: Site Selection History." Unpublished.

Corbett, Don Cecil. *Mary Fielding Smith: Daughter of Britain*. Salt Lake City: Deseret Book, 1966.

Coronel, Nestor. "Buenos Aires Temple Will Be a Focal Point for Saints." *Ensign*, January 1986, 80.

Cowan, Richard O. *The Latter-day Saint Century*, Salt Lake City: Bookcraft, 1999.

———. *Temples to Dot the Earth*. Salt Lake City: Bookcraft, 1989.

Cowley, Matthew. "Maori Chief Predicts Coming of L.D.S. Missionaries." *Improvement Era*, September 1950, 696.

Craig, Robert D. "Mormon Angel in Cincinnati." Typescript, 1964. Archives of The Church of Jesus Christ of Latter-day Saints.

Curbelo, Nestor. "New Training Center, Temple Housing Facility Dedicated in Argentina." *Church News*, 19 March 1994, 3.

Dahlgren, Robert B. Interview by author, 11 September 2000.

"Dallas Temple Is Underway." *Ensign*, April 1983, 77.

"The Dedication of the Manti Temple." *Millennial Star*, 25 June 1888, 405.

"Dedicatory Addresses Delivered at Swiss Temple Dedication." *Improvement Era*, November 1955, 795.

"Dedicatory Prayer in the Hawaiian Temple." *Improvement Era*, February 1920, 283.

Dedicatory Prayers. Archives of The Church of Jesus Christ of Latter-day Saints, Salt Lake City.

DeMille, Janice Force. *The St. George Temple: First 100 Years*. Hurricane, Utah: Homestead Publishers, 1977.

Denton, David. Interview by author, 14 April 2000.

"Designing the Temple Landscape." *Temple Times*, Cyprus Texas Stake, April 2000.

Detroit Temple Times.

Dew, Sheri L. *Go Forward with Faith: The Biography of Gordon B. Hinckley*. Salt Lake City: Deseret Book, 1996.

Dixon, Sarah. "Temple Is at the 'Apex' of N.C. LDS History." *The Raleigh Temple Times*, 2 October 1999.

Dockstader, Julie A. "Amid Rays of Sunshine, 59th Temple Dedicated." *Church News*, 28 August 1999, 3.

———. "Montreal Temple Highlight of 40 Years of Progress." *Church News*, 10 June 2000, 3.

———. "Northernmost Temple Dedicated." *Church News*, 16 January 1999, 3.

———. "A Sacred Building on Sacred Ground." *Church News*, 5 August 2000, 3.

———. "Sacred Structure Continues to Stand As 'Symbol of Purity.'" *Church News*, 23 September 1995, 11.

———. "Second Sacred Edifice in Hawaiian Islands." *Church News*, 29 January 2000.

———. "'Temple by the River' Jubilee Celebrated." *Church News*, 23 September 1995, 3.

———. "'You Live in Greatest Age of World,' Pres. Hinckley Tells Spokane Youth." *Church News*, 4 September 1999, 3.

"Dream of a Temple in Quebec Near Reality with Groundbreaking." *Church News*, 17 April 1999, 3.

Dyches, Timothy John. Interview by author, 7 April 2000.

"Elated Saints Greet New Temple Plans." *Ensign*, January 1976, 93.

"'Elegance to Complement the Spirit.'" *Church News*, 12 November 1994, 6.

Ellsworth, S. George, and Kathleen C. Perrin. *Seasons of Faith and Courage: The Church of Jesus Christ of Latter-day Saints in French Polynesia, a Sesquicentennial History, 1843–1993*. Sandy, Utah: Yves R. Perrin, 1994.

Erekson, John Jay. Interview by author, 26 September 2000.

Erickson, Galen. Interview by author, 14 September 2000.

"Eternal Riches." *Church News*, 20 January 1996, 16.

Ettenborough, Kelly. "Mesa Temple Lighting Holiday Display Today." *Arizona Republic*, 26 November 1999.

Evans, Richard. "Building of Temple in Sweden Is Greeted with 'Open Arms.'" *Church News*, 2 June 1985, 11.

"Excitement Growing As Members Prepare for Caribbean Temple." *Church News*, 11 January 1997, 3.

Faherty, Mike. WSB Radio editorial, Atlanta, Georgia, 3 May 1983.

Farrington, John A. "Wonderful News!" *Church News*, 24 April 1999, 16.

Felt, Judith M. "On the Bright Side." *Church News*, 16 September 1995, 2.

Fife, Wallace Dean, and Carolyn Fife. Interview by author, 27 September 2000.

"Fifteen Thousand Attend Las Vegas Regional Conference." *Ensign*, April 1987, 74.

"Fight over Mormon Temple." *Bild Frankfurt*, 15 December 1982. Archives of The Church of Jesus Christ of Latter-day Saints, Salt Lake City.

"Five New Temples Dedicated in Four Countries." *Ensign*, August 2000, 74.

Forbush, Vernon C. Interview by author, 7 April 2000.

"'Fortress of Faith' Prompts Brotherhood and Tears." *Church News*, 24 June 2000, 3.

"Four Temples Dedicated." *Ensign*, September 2000, 72.

Frank, Jeff. "New Mormon Temple a Treat for the Eyes." *San Diego Seagull*, 19 February 1993, B8.

Franklin-Moore, Linda. "South Carolina Temple Opens for Tours." *Church News*, 2 October 1999, 7.

Gardner, Marvin K. "Making Friends: Ingrid Fabiola Martínez Barredo of Tuxtla Gutiérrez, México," *Liahona*, March 2000, 2.

Garrison, Greg. "Critics Gather at Temple." *Birmingham News*, 24 August 2000.

———. "Mormon President Conducts Ceremony." *Birmingham News*, 4 September 2000.

Gaunt, LaRene Porter. "Costa Rica: Rising in Majesty and Strength." *Ensign*, December 1996, 22.

"Genealogical and Temple Work." *Utah Genealogical and Historical Magazine*, October 1924, 148.

Ghaznavi, Shanna. "A Site to Behold." *New Era*, November 1998, 12.

Gibbons, Francis M. *Dynamic Disciples: Prophets of God*. Salt Lake City: Deseret Book, 1996.

Grant, Heber J. Grant. Conference Report, April 1943, 6.

Green, Doyle L. "Two Temples to Be Dedicated." *Ensign*, January 1972, 6.

Griffiths, Larry. "The Bountiful Utah Temple." Fireside presentation given 14 August 1994.

"Ground Broken for Eighth Temple in Mexico." *Church News*, 12 June 1999, 3.

"Ground Broken for Temple in Alabama." *Church News*, 16 October 1999, 6.

"Ground Broken for Two New Temples." *Church News*, 17 October 1998, 3.

"Ground Is Broken for Boise Temple." *Ensign*, March 1983, 78.

"Grounds at Los Angeles Temple Ablaze in Light." *Church News*, 12 December 1998, 6.

"Guatemala City Temple Dedicated," *Ensign*, February 1985, 77.

"Guests Feel Peace at Open House in Hong Kong Temple." *Church News*, 18 May 1996, 3.

Guitierrez de Orozco, Leticia. Interview by author, translated by Adam Rigby, 29 February 2000.

Hafen, Bruce C. Statement delivered at Melbourne Australia Pakenham Stake Conference, 7 February 1999. Unpublished.

Halford, John. "The Johannesburg Temple of The Church of Jesus Christ of Latter-day Saints." Avonwold Publishing Co. Limited, August 1986. Copy in Archives of The Church of Jesus Christ of Latter-day Saints, Salt Lake City.

Halverson, Richard P. Interview by author, 16 September 2000.

Harbers, Claus. "Instead of Tolerance, Prelude to a 'Religious War.'" *Taunus Zeitung*, 15 December 1982. Archives of The Church of Jesus Christ of Latter-day Saints, Salt Lake City.

———. "Mormon Temple in the Huguenot City?" *Taunus Zeitung*, 15 December 1982. Archives of The Church of Jesus Christ of Latter-day Saints, Salt Lake City.

Harmon, Carolee L. "Sacred Edifice to 'Change Lives' of Many in Spain." *Church News*, 6 March 1999, 3.

Harmon, Kenneth R. Interview by author, 15 September 2000.

Harris, Philip. Interview by author, 22 January 2000.

Hart, John L. "Gift of Inner Peace in a Troubled Land." *Church News*, 1 May 1999, 3.

———. "Gospel Pioneers Still Making Inroads on Diverse Continent." *Church News*, 26 January 1991, 8.

———. "Ground Broken for Temple in Madrid." *Church News*, 22 June 1996, 3.

———. "Ground Is Broken on Cold Day for Temple in St. Louis, Mo." *Church News*, 6 November 1993, 3.

———. "Guayaquil Ecuador Temple Dedication: 'A Wondrous Day' for Members." *Church News*, 7 August 1999, 3.

———. "Heroes Emerge amid Devastation." *Church News*, 28 October 1989, 3.

———. "I'm Here!" *Church News*, 5 February 1994, 16.

———. "Impact on Lives Begins Even Before Completion." *Church News*, 4 March 2000, 3.

———. "'I Needed to Be There.'" *Church News*, 11 May 1996. 16.

———. "Las Vegas Temple 'A Crowning Jewel.'" *Church News*, 23 December 1989, 3.

———. "Mt. Timpanogos Utah Temple." *Church News*, 16 October 1993, 4, 3.

———. "Newest Temple in Mexico Dedicated in Its Oldest Stake." *Church News*, 13 March 1999, 3.

———. "New Horizons Open for a Faithful People." *Church News*, 18 March 2000, 3.

———. "New Temple Inspires Visitors." *Church News*, 18 November 1989, 3.

———. "Prophet Breaks Ground for New Temples." *Church News*, 23 November 1996, 3.

———. "Temple Dedicated in an Oasis of Calm." *Church News*, 25 September 1983, 10.

———. "Temple in Tahiti Emanates a Lasting Influence for Good." *Church News*, 3 December 1994, 7.

———. "Temple Open House Exceeds Hopes." *Church News*, 2 December 1989, 6.

———. "Transformation Begins for Temple." *Church News*, 20 May 1995, 3.

———. "Winter Chill No Obstacle to Warmth of Dedication of 'Beacon on a Hill.'" *Church News*, 14 January 1995.

"Hero in the Font." *Church News*, 14 February 1987, 16.

Heslop, J. M. "Area Conference in Brazil." *Church News*, 8 March 1975, 3.

———. "Bright Future Seen in Chicago Temple." *Church News*, 18 August 1985, 3.

———. "Greater Need Brings Temple's Renovation." *Church News*, 19 April 1975, 3.

Hill, Craig A. "New Facility Evidence of Growth." *Deseret News*, 18 July 1992, 3.

Hill, Greg. "Church Members Rejoice over Temple in Southern Japan." *Church News*, 17 June 2000, 3.

———. "A Temple in Their Midst." *Church News*, 30 October 1999, 3.

Hinckley, Gordon B. Conference Report, October 1995, 93.

———. *Ensign*, November 1985, 54.

———. *Ensign*, May 1997.

———. *Ensign*, October 1998, 88.

Hipwell, Ida Mae D. *Ogden Utah Weber North Stake History*. Ogden, Utah: Pabco Printing Company, 151. Archives of The Church of Jesus Christ of Latter-day Saints, Salt Lake City.

History of Relief Society, 1842–1966. Salt Lake City: General Board of the Relief Society of The Church of Jesus Christ of Latter-day Saints, 1966.

Hobson, Ivan L. *Dallas Texas Temple: An Early History*. Salt Lake City: I. L. Hobson, 1991.

Holdman, Tom. Interview by author, 5 January 2000.

Hollenbaugh, Joe. "Over 95,000 Visit New Temples in California, Oregon." *BYU NewsNet*, 5 April 2000.

Holley, Glen V. "Lehi's Children Blessed by Lima Temple." *Deseret News*, 27 January 1990, 6.

Holzapfel, Richard Neitzel. *Every Stone a Sermon*. Salt Lake City: Bookcraft, 1992.

"Houses of the Lord in Far-Away Places Cause Great Rejoicing." *Church News*, 13 August 1994, 7.

Howe, Allie. "A Temple in the South Pacific." *Improvement Era*, November 1955, 811.

Howell, Wayne M. Letter to the author, 17 September 2000.

Howes, Phillip. "Rain, Clouds in Adelaide Do Not Dampen Spirits During Groundbreaking." *Church News*, 5 June 1999, 3.

Huether, Gordon. "Special Technique Used to Create Art Glass for Temple." In *Mount Timpanogos Temple Commemorative Edition*. American Fork, Utah: Newtah News Group, 1996.

Hunt, Brian W. *Zion in New Zealand, 1854–1977*. Temple View, New Zealand: Church College of New Zealand, 1977.

Hunter, Howard W. "A Temple-Motivated People." *Ensign*, February 1995, 5.

———. "Your Temple Recommend." *New Era*, April 1995, 6.

Hunter, J. Michael. "I Saw Another Angel Fly." *Ensign*, January 2000, 30.

Hunter, Milton R., comp. *Beneath Ben Lomond's Peak*. Salt Lake City: Publishers Press, 1966.

Ilagan, Jovencio C., Sr. "A Brief History of the Church of Jesus Christ of Latter-day Saints in the Philippines." September 1984. Archives of The Church of Jesus Christ of Latter-day Saints, Salt Lake City.

"In Dedicatory Prayer, Church Leader Makes Ardent Appeal for Peace." *Church News*, 13 September 1958, 3.

"In Many Countries, Great Efforts Made to Attend the Temple." *Church News*, 25 June 1994, 7.

Irving, Kathleen M., and John D. Barton. *From Tabernacle to Temple: The Story of the Vernal Utah Temple*. Vernal, Utah: S. T. Tabernacle Enterprises, 1998.

Jackson, Lisa Ann. "Saints in the Shadow of Mount Timpanogos." *Ensign*, December 1996, 69.

Jasper, Patricia B., and Diane Lommel, eds. *A Gathering of Saints in Alaska: Temple Edition*. Anchorage: Alaska Printing, 1999.

Jensen, Richard L., and David C. H. Liu. "Taiwan Saints Eager for Temple Blessings." *Ensign*, November 1984, 107.

"Johannesburg Temple Dedicated." *Ensign*, November 1985, 102.

Johnson, Alaire. "Temple Project History," 1–2. Unpublished.

Johnson, Benjamin F. *My Life's Review*. Independence, Mo.: Zion's Printing and Publishing, 1947.

Johnson, Lisa A. "The Eternal Road Trip." *New Era*, June 1993, 29–31.

Johnson, Loretta. "Art Worth Hanging." *Minot Daily News*, 4 September 1999.

Johnson, Reid H. *Open Doors: A Documentary History*. Salt Lake City: Reid H. Johnson, 1998.

Johnston, Jerry. "Worthy of the Heart of a People." *Church News*, 13 May 2000, 3.

"Joke Backfires; Class Donates $8,040." *Church News*, 2 May 1981, 7.

"Jordan River Temple Architectural Design Announced." *Ensign*, July 1978, 80.

Jorgensen, Karen Lox. "Orlando Florida Temple Dedicated." *Ensign*, December 1994, 66.

Josephson, Marba C. "A Temple Is Risen to Our Lord." *Improvement Era*, September 1955, 624.

Journal of Discourses. 26 vols. London: Latter-day Saints' Book Depot, 1854–86.

Kay, Julie. "A Dream Come True." *The Advocate*, 3 July 1999.

Kimball, Edward L., ed. *The Teachings of Spencer W. Kimball*. Salt Lake City: Bookcraft, 1982.

Kimball, Spencer W. Japan Area Conference Report, 8 August 1975, 4.

Kimball, Stanley B. "'Mormon' Stamps Grow in Number." *Church News*, 15 January 1994, 11.

Kirby, Dale Z., and Richard O. Cowan. "The History of the Swiss Temple." July 1969. Unpublished.

Knudsen, Tony. Interview by author, 25 February 2000.

Koyle, Brent H. Interview by author, 27 September 2000.

Kruckenberg, Janet. "The Announcements of New Holy Edifices Bring Joy and Tears." *Church News*, 20 February 1999, 10.

———. "Ground Broken for Temple in Minnesota." *Church News*, 3 October 1998. 3.

———. "Ground Broken for Two More Temples." *Church News*, 24 October 1998, 3.

———. "Regina Prairie, Now a Place of Fulfilled Dreams." *Church News*, 20 November 1999, 3.

Kullberg, Lois Gustaveson. *Saints to the Columbia: A History of The Church of Jesus Christ of Latter-day Saints in Oregon and Southwestern Washington, 1850–1990*. Vancouver, Wash.: L-K Publications, 1991.

Larsen, Joan R. "History of the Billings Temple District." 1999. Unpublished.

"Las Vegas Temple—26th in Decade." *Church News*, 2 September 1989, 3.

"Latter-day Temples." *Ensign*, January 1972, 30.

"LDS in Las Vegas Have Dual Goals: Uphold Standards, Be Part of Community." *Church News*, 2 March 1991, 8.

Leone, David. "Children Earn Dimes for Learning Articles of Faith." *Apex Herald*, 2 December 1999, 5.

LeSueur, James W. "The Story Told by the Frieze of the Temple." *Genealogical and Historical Magazine of the Arizona Temple District*, July 1927.

Lesuma, Meli U. "Members in Fiji 'Bask in Joy' After Temple Announcement." *Church News*, 26 December 1998, 10.

"Lima Temple Dedication Brings Blessings to Saints in Peru, Bolivia." *Ensign*, March 1986, 83.

Liston, Garth R. "The Geographical Analysis of Mormon Temple Sites in Utah." Master's thesis, Brigham Young University, 1992.

Liu, David C. H. "Taipei Taiwan Temple Dedicated. " *Ensign*, February 1985, 75.

Liungman, Carl G. *Dictionary of Symbols*. Santa Barbara, Calif.: ABC-CLIO, 1991.

Lloyd, R. Scott. "Church Dedicates Its 50th Temple." *Church News*, 7 June 1997, 3.

———. "Ground Broken for Temple on Canada's Plains." *Church News*, 21 November 1998, 3.

———. "Ground Broken for the First of Church's New 'Small' Temples." *Church News*, 22 November 1997.

———. "Ground Is Broken for Temple in Canada, 'A Monument of Faith.'" *Church News*, 6 March 1999, 3.

———. "LDS Fill Denver Arena to Celebrate 100 Years of Church's Presence." *Church News*, 20 September 1997, 3.

———. "New Temple in a 'Place of History.'" *Church News*, 23 October 1999, 3.

———. "90,000 Tour Temple; Give Glowing Reports." *Church News*, 1 October 1994, 7.

———. "Open House Begins for Preston Temple." *Church News*, 23 May 1998, 3.

———. "Orlando Temple Opens for Tours; Thousands Attend Open House." *Church News*, 17 September 1994, 3.

———. "Second Temple Adds to Tennessee Peace." *Church News*, 27 May 2000, 3.

———. "Symbol of Growth in Fertile San Joaquin." *Church News*, 22 April 2000.

———. "20,000 Tour New Temple Prior to Its Dedication." *Church News*, 25 July 1998, 12.

———. "Vernal Temple Doors Open to Public." *Church News*, 18 October 1997, 3.

———. "While Building Temple, He Embraced the Gospel." *Church News*, 25 December 1999, 14.

The Logan Temple, 1884–1976. Logan, Utah: Logan Temple, 1976.

"'Look to Temple As a Refuge from Evil and Turmoil." *Church News*, 2 November 1986, 5.

Ludlow, Daniel H., ed. *Church History: Selections from the Encyclopedia of Mormonism*. Salt Lake City: Deseret Book, 1992.

Lukens, Marion. "History of the Oklahoma City Oklahoma Temple." Unpublished.

Lukens, Robert, and Marion Lukens, interview by author, 15 August 2000.

Lundwall, N. B., comp. *Temples of the Most High*. Salt Lake City: Bookcraft, 1966.

Madsen, Truman G. "House of Glory." Brigham Young University Ten-Stake Fireside Address, 5 March 1972.

Mair, Gale. Interview by author, 12 April 2000.

The Manti Temple. Manti, Utah: Manti Temple Centennial Committee, 1988.

"Many Receive Sweet Blessings As They Attend Holy Temples." *Church News*, 5 March 1994, 7.

Martin, David W., and Ernie J. Shannon. *The Columbus Ohio Temple*. Unpublished work. ©1999 David W. Martin and Ernie J. Shannon.

Maxwell, Jack, and Clara Maxwell. Interview by author, 25 September 2000.

Maxwell, James R., Jeffrey G. Boswell, and Gary R. Ellsworth, interview by author, 28 March 2000.

"May Be Blessed with Peace." *Church News*, 24 June 2000, 6.

"'May Thy Holy Spirit Constantly Dwell Herein.'" *Church News*, 25 December 1999, 4.

McBride, Kelly. "Latter-day Saints Marching in Mormon Church Building Houses of Worship to Reflect Growing Numbers." *The Spokesman-Review*, 29 June 1999.

McClintock, James H. *Mormon Settlement in Arizona*. Phoenix: The Manufacturing Stationers, 1921.

McClurg, Buryl G., and Diane W. McClurg. Interview by author, 13 May 2000.

McConkie, Bruce R. *Mormon Doctrine*. 2d ed. Salt Lake City: Bookcraft, 1966.

McGavin, E. Cecil. *The Nauvoo Temple*. Salt Lake City: Deseret Book, 1962.

McKay, David L., and Mildred C. McKay, comp. *For His House*. Salt Lake City: Murray Utah Stake, 1978.

McKay, David O. Conference Report, 30 September 1955, 7.

"Members Volunteer During Atlanta Olympics." *Ensign*, October 1996, 79.

Mendenhall, Wealtha S. "The Temple in New Zealand." *Relief Society Magazine* 45 (August 1958): 492.

Meyer, Amanda. "Aborigines Gather for Temple Work, Meetings." *Church News*, 5 February 1994, 5.

Michalek, Patricia. "Detroit Open House Visitors Feel 'Serenity of the Temple.'" *Church News*, 23 October 1999, 10.

Monson, Thomas S. *Faith Rewarded: A Personal Account of Prophetic Promises to the East German Saints*. Salt Lake City: Deseret Book, 1996.

Montoya, Hugo. Interview by author, translated by Adam Rigby, 29 February 2000.

Moore, Carrie A. "'Jewel' Adorns Palmyra." *Deseret News*, 5 April 2000.

Morello, Pauline. "Faith Brought This Temple." *Church News*, 19 September 1998, 3.

"Mormon Temple in Friedrichsdorf: Enrichment or Serious Danger?" *Taunus Kurier*, 15 December 1982. Archives of The Church of Jesus Christ of Latter-day Saints, Salt Lake City.

The Mormon Temple in Ogden, Utah. Brochure. Published by The Church of Jesus Christ of Latter-day Saints, 1973.

The Mormon Temple Near London, England. Brochure. Published by The Church of Jesus Christ of Latter-day Saints, 1967.

The Mormon Temple, Temple View, Hamilton, New Zealand. Pamphlet prepared by New Zealand Bureau of Information. Auckland, New Zealand: Auckland Star Commercial Printers, 1965.

Mostert, Mary. "Trip to Temple 'Special' for Kenya Family." *Church News*, 25 April 1992, 11.

Mourik, Peter. "Frankfurt Temple Site History of Purchase and Negotiations." Archives of The Church of Jesus Christ of Latter-day Saints, Salt Lake City.

Mueller, Erika F. "Friedrichsdorf, a Hallowed Refuge." *Ensign*, September 1990, 54–55.

"Multitudes Throng Preston Temple." *Church News*, 30 May 1998, 3.

Munday, David. "Mormons Offer Glimpse inside New Temple." *Post and Courier*, 26 September 1999.

"Nearly 300,000 Tour New Temple." *Church News*, 16 December 1989, 3.

Nelson, Russell M. Conference Report, April 1993, 49.

Newell, Linda King, and Valeen Tippetts Avery. "Sweet Counsel and Seas of Tribulation: The Religious Life of the Women in Kirtland." *BYU Studies* 20 (Winter 1980): 151.

Newman, Gary J. Interview by author, 5 September 2000.

"New Temple Planned in Utah." *Church News*, 4 February 1978, 3.

Nichols, Melvin R. *Experiences in the Temple Baptistry*. Anchorage: DOWL Engineers.

———. *The History of the Acquisition of the Anchorage Alaska Temple Site*. Anchorage: DOWL Engineers.

1999–2000 Church Almanac. Salt Lake City: Deseret News, 1998.

"November Open House, December Dedication Announced for Church's 43rd Temple." *Church News*, 2 September 1989, 3.

Obst, Michael. "First 35,000 Visit Public Open House at Frankfurt Temple." *Church News*, 8 August 1987, 11.

O'Donnal, John Forres. *Pioneer in Guatemala: The Personal History of John Forres O'Donnal, Including the History of The Church of Jesus Christ of Latter-day Saints in Guatemala*. Yorba Linda, Calif.: Shumway Family History Services, 1997.

Ogden Standard Examiner. 23 June 1999.

"The Ogden Temple." *Ensign*, February 1978, 80.

Okata, Takuji. "'Great Blessings' to Come from Fukuoka Edifice." *Church News*, 27 March 1999, 6.

Olsen, Judy C. "Bolivia: A Bounty of Blessings." *Ensign*, June 1999, 22.

Olsen, Nolan P. *Logan Temple: The First 100 Years*. Logan, Utah: Watkins and Sons, 1978.

Olsen, Rae Stephens Jones. LDSWorld-Gems, 2 October 1997.

"One Eternal Round—Geometric Designs for the Houston Texas Temple." *Temple Times*, Cypress Texas Stake, May 2000.

"180 Gather to Paint Fence." *Church News*, 15 July 2000, 14.

"On the Bright Side." *Church News*, 23 June 1990, 2.

Orquiola, Francis M. "Temple Dedication Rewards Faith of Filipino Saints." *Ensign*, November 1984, 106.

Painter, Donita, and Pete Pichaske. "Landmark to Most, Temple Is Sanctuary for Area's Mormons." *Northern Virginia Journal*, 8 November 1999.

Palmer, Spencer J. *The Church Encounters Asia*. Salt Lake City: Deseret Book, 1970.

Palm, Hakan. "Nordic Temple Rites 'a Pinnacle.'" *Church News*, 25 March 1984, 7.

Parker, J. Michael. "Mormons 100 Miles Closer to Temple." 4 August 2000. Unpublished.

Parkinson, Paul. "Newly Completed Temple a Sacred Symbol of Power." *Church News*, 3 November 1994.

Pharis, John. Interview by author. Kona, Hawaii, 21 January 2000.

Pinelo de Ferraez, Bianca. "Temple 'Will Add to Peace in the Yucatan Peninsula.'" *Church News*, 30 January 1999, 3.

"Plane Problem Leads to LDS First: Halifax, Regina Temple Rites Both Planned for Today." *Deseret News*, 14 November 1999.

Poole, Kit. "Lights Symbolize the Savior's Birth." *Church News*, 15 December 1990, 12.

Pope, Hyrum C. *About the Temple in Hawaii*. Hawaii, 1919.

Pottenger, Jim. Interview by author, 20 April 2000.

Poulsen, Don. Interview by author, 11 March 2000.

Pratt, Orson. "The Trial of Sidney Rigdon." *Millennial Star* 5 (December 1844): 104.

"Prayer, Determination." *Church News*, 5 September 1998, 16.

"President Hinckley Dedicates Madrid Spain Temple." *Church News*, 19 March 1999.

"President Hinckley Stresses Family, Book of Mormon." *Ensign*, April 1996, 74–76.

"President Hinckley Visits New Zealand, Australia, and Mexico." *Ensign*, August 1997, 75.

"President Hinckley Visits South America, Florida, Washington D. C." *Ensign*, February 1997, 72.

"Preston Temple Modern Classical Design." *Church News*, 29 October 1994, 3.

Prestridge, Karla Packer, and Marvin John Prestridge. Interview by author, 11 March 2000.

Price, Anna Kay. *The Seattle Washington Temple Twenty-Year Commemoration*. Brochure. 4 June 2000.

"Promise Fulfilled." *Church News*, 6 November 1999, 16.

Quigley, David. "A Temple to Call Their Own." *Edmonton Sun*, 28 November 1999.

Radnedge, Lynn. "London Temple Has Served Members 25 Years." *Church News*, 11 September 1983, 12.

Rawson, Brent D. "Temple Site Selection." Unpublished.

Reay, Lee. *Incredible Passage through the Hole-in-the-Rock*. Provo, Utah: Meadow Lane Publications, 1980.

"Returned Missionaries Throng to Ecuador Reunion." *Church News*, 4 September 1999, 7.

Richards, David. Interview by author, 24 March 2000.

Richards, George F. "Latter-day Temples." *Genealogical and Historical Magazine of the Arizona Temple District*, July 1930, 16.

Ricks, Joel E., ed. *The History of a Valley*. Logan, Utah: Cache Valley Centennial Commission, 1956.

Rivera, Herardo. Interview by author, translated by Adam Rigby, 23 February 2000.

Robertson, Richard. "Toronto: A Growing Light in the East." *Ensign*, September 1988, 46.

Robison, Elwin C. *The First Mormon Temple*. Provo: Brigham Young University Press, 1997.

Rudd, Glen L. *Treasured Experiences of Glen L. Rudd, Volume 1*. Salt Lake City: Glen L. Rudd, 1995.

Ruscitti, Flora. "Choosing the Land for the Caracas Venezuela Temple." Unpublished.

———. "History of the Construction of the Caracas Venezuela Temple: Construction Manager's Work." Unpublished.

St. George Temple Visitors' Center. Brochure, 1993.

"St. Louis Temple Book of Remembrance, 1997," N.p.: St. Louis Temple Committee, 1997.

"The Saints in Spain: A Faith Defined." KSL Television, Salt Lake City, 3–4 May 1999.

"Saints Throng to Temple in Mexico City." *Ensign*, February 1984, 74.

Saldivar, Gabriel Raymundo. Interview by author, translated by Adam Rigby, 11 August 2000.

"Samoans Recovering from Hurricane's Destruction." *Ensign*, March 1992, 75.

Sanchez Casillas, Enrique. Interview by author, 11 August 2000.

Sanders, Lindsay J. "Ground Is Broken for Melbourne Temple." *Church News*, 3 April 1999, 5.

Santiago, Uilson Felipe, and Linda Ritchie Archibald. "From Amazon Basin to Temple." *Church News*, 13 March 1993, 6.

Searle, Don L. "Ecuador." *Tambuli*, April 1993, 32.

Sears, Jerry. Interview by author, January 23, 2000.

Seifers, Ramona. "The Nashville Temple: A Written History." Unpublished.

"Seven New Stakes Created in 28 Hours in Lima, Peru." *Ensign*, April 1988, 77.

"Seven Temples Dedicated." *Ensign*, May 2000, 107.

Shadler, Lawrence, and Kevin Gill. Interview by author, June 2000.

Shumway, Eric B. *Tongan Saints: Legacy of Faith*. Laie, Hawaii: Institute for Polynesian Studies, Brigham Young University–Hawaii, 1991.

Skidmore, Richard, and Bon Adell Skidmore. Interview by author, 16 March 2000.

Skousen, Mark. *Sunshine in the Soul: One Hundred Years of the Mormon Church in Florida*. Winter Park, Fla.: Skousen Publishing, 1996.

Smith, Frank Miller. "Monument to Spirituality: Sacrifice, Dreams, and Faith Build the Washington Temple." *Ensign*, August 1974, 7.

———. "The Washington Temple." *Ensign*, January 1972, 27.

Smith, Janie. Interview by author, 27 September 2000.

Smith, Joseph. *History of The Church of Jesus Christ of Latter-day Saints*. Edited by B. H. Roberts. 7 vols. 2d ed. rev. Salt Lake City: The Church of Jesus Christ of Latter-day Saints, 1932–51.

Smith, Joseph F. "The Gospel unto All Nations." *Der Stern*, August 1906.

Smith, Weldon, and Doris Smith. Interview by author, 12 September 2000.

Snow, LeRoi C. "Remarkable Manifestation to Lorenzo Snow." *Deseret News*, 2 April 1938, 8.

"Southern Far East Mission History." LDS Church Archives, Salt Lake City.

"Spiritual Manifestations in the Manti Temple." *Millennial Star*, 13 August 1888, 520.

"'Spiritual Sanctuaries' for Faithful Adelaide, Melbourne Members." *Church News*, 24 June 2000, 3.

Spokane Temple News. June 1999.

"Springtime Ceremony Begins Temple in Southern Mexico." *Church News*, 27 March 1999, 6.

Spurrier, Joseph H. "The Hawaii Temple: A Special Place in a Special Land." Address delivered at meeting of Mormon Pacific Historical Society, 1 March 1986, BYU–Hawaii, Laie, Hawaii.

Stahle, Shaun D. "Dedication Sunday for LDS Temple." *Deseret News*, 30 September 2000.

———. "Historic Sabbath in Canada." *Church News*, 20 November 1999, 3.

———. "Spiritual Celebration Surrounds Dedication." *Church News*, 11 September 1999, 3.

———. "'This Has Been a Banner Year.'" *Church News*, 7 October 2000, 3.

"Stamp Commemorates 100 Years in Samoa." *Church News*, 9 July 1988, 3.

"Statue of Angel Is Placed atop Idaho Falls Temple." *Church News*, 11 September 1983, 7.

"Statues of Angel Top Minnesota, Hawaii Temples." *Church News*, 2 October 1999, 7.

Stoker, Kevin. "Their Faith Would Make Pioneers Proud." *Church News*, 21 January 1989, 6.

Stratton, Esther. "Kona Hawaii Temple History." Unpublished.

Stratton, Howard, and Esther Stratton. Interview by author, 22 January 2000.

Strawn, Karen, and Gayle Smith. "2,000 Attend Ceremony for Louisiana's First Edifice." *Church News*, 15 May 1999, 3.

Swensen, Jason. "Modern Temple Rises among Mayan Ruins." *Church News*, 15 July 2000, 3.

———. "A New Landmark by Shining Seas." *Church News*, 10 June 2000, 3.

———. "New Temples in Mexico Are Making Eternal Impact in Thousands of Lives." *Church News*, 12 August 2000, 3.

———. "'Pura Vida' Costa Rica: Land of Peace, Blessings." *Church News*, 8 July 2000, 8.

———. "Sacred Hill Now Site of Tampico Temple." *Church News*, 27 May 2000, 3.

———. "Venezuela Saints Rejoicing at New Caracas Temple." *Church News*, 26 August 2000, 3.

———. "Villahermosa Temple Stands like Ceiba Tree." *Church News*, 27 May 2000, 3.

Swiss-Austrian Mission Manuscript History, 6 September 1955, LDS Church Archives, Salt Lake City.

Tagg, Melvin S. *A History of the Mormon Church in Canada*. Lethbridge, Alberta: Lethbridge Herald Co., 1968.

"Tahitians Feel Spirit of Peace in New Temple." *Ensign*, December 1983, 66.

Talmage, James E. *The House of the Lord*. Salt Lake City: Deseret Book, 1968.

Tate, George. Interview by author, 5 September 2000.

Taylor, Rebecca M. "Ah Mu: Generous Samoan Saint." *Ensign*, September 1999, 47.

"Temple Completion Set for '81." *Church News*, 3 June 1978, 3.

"Temple Dedicated in Santiago, Chile." *Ensign*, November 1983, 93.

"Temple Dedications and Groundbreakings." *Ensign*, January 2000, 74.

"Temple Experiences in 'Deseret' Reflect Reverence, Warmth." *Church News*, 23 April 1994, 7.

"Temple in Ciudad Juárez Unites LDS Communities Both in Mexico and U.S." *Church News*, 23 January 1999, 3.

"Temple in Dallas Means Blessings for Southwestern Saints." *Ensign*, October 1984, 75.

"A Temple in Japan." *Church News*, 25 October 1980, 16.

"Temple Is 'Gift of a Thankful People.'" *Church News*, 26 August 1989, 7.

"Temple Open House: Joyous Tears in Chile." *Church News*, 11 September 1983, 3.

"Temple: Place of Peace, Particular Beauty." *Church News*, 11 August 1990, 3.

"Temple Plan Thrills Members." *Church News*, 23 August 1975, 5.

"Temples Dedicated in Alberta and North Carolina." *Ensign*, March 2000, 74.

"Temple Service Extends the Spirit of Christmas throughout the Year." *Church News*, 14 December 1991, 7.

"Temple Started for Mexico Colonies." *Church News*, 14 March 1998, 3.

"Temple Sustains Couple in Trial." *Church News*, 23 October 1999, 3.

"Temple to Bring 'Brighter Day' to Florida." *Church News*, 27 June 1992, 3.

"Temple Unscathed in Oakland Fire." *Church News*, 26 October 1991, 5.

The Tennessean. 26 November 1994.

"'This Is a Day of History.'" *Church News*, 7 August 1999, 10.

"Thousands Attend Temple Open Houses in Canada." *Church News*, 13 November 1999, 3.

"300,000 Visitors Tour Portland Temple." *Church News*, 15 July 1989, 3.

Thurber, Ronald W. Interview by author, 26 September 2000.

"To Build a Temple." *Ensign*, August 1974, 15.

"Tongans Travel Sea to the Temple." *Church News*, 13 August 1988, 13.

"Toronto Temple Nears Completion." *Church News*, 14 July 1990, 3.

"Tremendous Support for Temple Hearing." *The Journal*, Kona Hawaii Stake, August 1998.

Trimble, Robert A. Interview by author, 7 April 2000.

Tullidge, Edward W. *Life of Joseph, the Prophet*. New York: Tullidge and Crandall, 1878.

"20,000 See Statue Lifted atop Mount Timpanogos Temple." *Church News*, 22 July 1995, 3.

"200,000 Attend Dedicatory Sessions." *Church News*, 21 January 1995, 3.

Udy, Leo C., and Rhea Udy. Interview by author, 12 May 2000.

VanDenBerghe, Elizabeth, and Jed VanDenBerghe. "Dominican Saints." *Tambuli*, May 1991, 11.

Van Orden, Dell. "Dedication of Temple Called Historic Event." *Church News*, 8 November 1980, 3.

———. "Ground Is Broken for Temple," *Church News*, 16 June 1979, 3.

———. "Inspiration Came for Smaller Temples on Trip to Mexico." *Church News*, 1 August 1998, 3.

———. "Mount Timpanogos Temple Dedicated." *Church News*, 19 October 1996, 3.

———. "San Diego Temple Dedication: Dedication Is a Time for Rejoicing." *Church News*, 8 May 1993, 8.

———. "San Diego Temple: 45th House of the Lord Dedicated in 'Season for Temple Building.'" *Church News*, 8 May 1993, 8.

———. "São Paulo Temple Cornerstone Laid by President Romney." *Church News*, 19 March 1977, 3.

———. "Shortening the Vast Distances." *Church News*, 25 September 1999, 3.

———. "Temple Dedication Brings Blessings to Many Members." *Church News*, 11 November 1978, 5.

———. "Valiant Acts of Early LDS Are 'Forever Etched into History.'" *Church News*, 1 September 1990, 9.

———. "Well-Traveled President Visits North Dakota for the First Time Ever." *Church News*, 25 September 1999, 3.

"Villahermosa Tabasco Temple Groundbreaking." *Ensign*, April 1999, 75.

"Volunteers Who Cleaned Temple Made Sacrifices, Received Spiritual Gifts." *San Diego Seagull*, June 1993, 1.

"Wait Is Worth It for Japanese Wife." *Church News*, 31 July 1982, 13.

Walker, DeAnne. "Facing the Challenge in Argentina." *Liahona*, September 1998, 10.

Wallgren, LaVar. Interview by author, 5 January 2000.

Warner, Terry. "A Temple for Great Britain." *Millennial Star*, September 1958, 266.

Warnick, Lee. "Yucatan: Promising Future amid Ancient Ruins." *Church News*, 5 September 1992, 8.

"Washington Temple Design: 'Majestic, Timeless.'" *Church News*, 12 April 1969, 3.

"Weather Clears as 1,000 Watch Groundbreaking in Spokane." *Church News*, 24 October 1998, 3.

Weaver, Sarah Jane. "Fijian LDS Temple Is Dedicated in Small Ceremony." *Deseret News*, 19 June 2000.

———. "157,917 Attend Dedication." *Church News*, 26 October 1996, 3.

"We Dedicate It As Being Complete." *Church News*, 7 October 2000, 6.

Weekes, Ron. Interview by author, 13 September 2000.

———. "The Mexico City Temple." *LDSWorldGems*, 1999.

"'What a Happy Day' as 700 Attend Halifax Temple Ceremony." *Church News*, 17 October 1998, 3.

"Where the Twain Meet." KSL Television, Salt Lake City, 1996.

Whetten, Glen. "Colonia Juárez Temple Groundbreaking." *LDSWorldGems*, 1999.

Whitman, Patti. "A Rabbi Writes about His Impressions After a Visit to the San Diego Temple." *San Diego Seagull*, May 1993.

Whitney, Orson F. *The Life of Heber C. Kimball*. Salt Lake City: Stevens and Wallis, 1945.

Wilcox, Keith W. *The Washington D. C. Temple: A Light to the World*. N.p.: Keith W. Wilcox, 1995.

Wilkinson, Ernest L., and W. Cleon Skousen, eds. *Brigham Young University: A School of Destiny*. Provo, Utah: Brigham Young University Press, 1976.

Willey, Nancy. "Atlanta Temple Opens Doors." *Church News*, 8 May 1983, 3.

"The Windows of Heaven." *Temple Times*, Cypress Texas Stake, May 2000.

Winfield, Karen. "Rites Begin Construction of New Temple Near Chicago." *Church News*, 21 August 1983, 3.

Wood, Deborah Leigh. "Temple a Mecca for Midwest Mormons." *Chicago Tribune*, 12 June 1985.

Woodruff, Wilford. *Wilford Woodruff's Journal*. Edited by Scott G. Kenney. 9 vols. Midvale, Utah: Signature Books, 1983–84.

Wood, V. A. *The Alberta Temple: Centre and Symbol of Faith*. Calgary: Detselig Enterprises, 1989.

Woodward, Elaine. "Medford Oregon Temple History," 16 April 2000. Unpublished.

Woodward, Ross. "The Building of Men." *Central Point Stake Clarion*, 31 September 1999.

———. Interview by author, 27 September 1999.

———. "Preparing the Lord's Way." *Central Point Stake Clarion*, 31 September 1999.

"Work Begins on Colombia Temple." *Church News*, 3 June 1995, 3.

"The Work Goes On." *Church News*, 16 January 1999, 16.

Younger, Shirley-Anne, Gregg Newby, and Marylouise Le Cheminant. *For Those Who Dare to Dream*. Korea, 1990.

Index

LOOK AND FIND®

Disney

ENCHANTED

Written by Joanna Spathis
Illustrated by Art Mawhinney

Based on the screenplay written by Billy Kelly
Produced by Barry Josephson and Barry Sonnenfeld
Executive producers Chris Chase, Sunil Perkash, and Ezra Swerdlow
Directed by Kevin Lima

Published by
Louis Weber, C.E.O., Publications International, Ltd.
7373 North Cicero Avenue, Lincolnwood, Illinois 60712

Ground Floor, 59 Gloucester Place, London W1U 8JJ

Customer Service: 1-800-595-8484 or customer_service@pilbooks.com

www.pilbooks.com

p i kids is a registered trademark of Publications International, Ltd.

Look and Find is a registered trademark of Publications International, Ltd.,
in the United States and in Canada.

8 7 6 5 4 3 2 1

ISBN-13: 978-1-4127-5928-1
ISBN-10: 1-4127-5928-5

publications international, ltd.

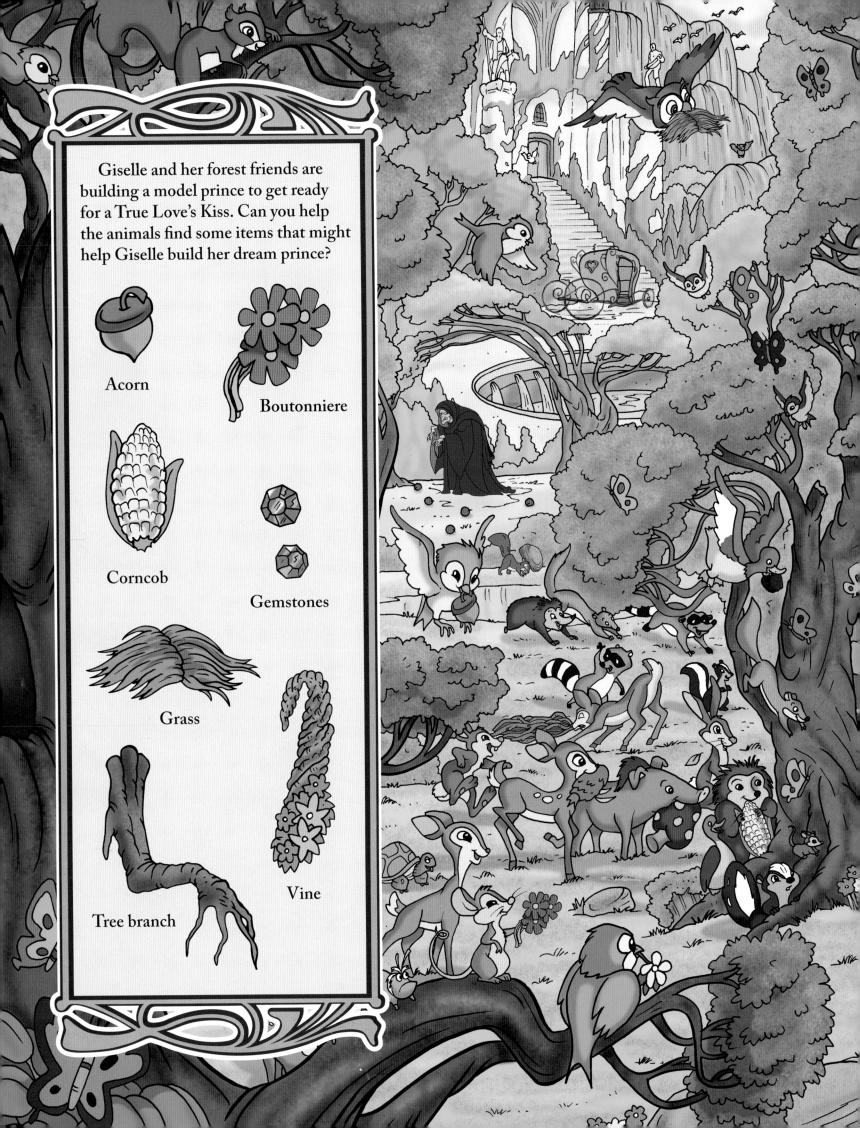

Giselle and her forest friends are building a model prince to get ready for a True Love's Kiss. Can you help the animals find some items that might help Giselle build her dream prince?

Acorn

Boutonniere

Corncob

Gemstones

Grass

Tree branch

Vine

Oh my! This kingdom is far, far away from Andalasia, indeed! Look around and find Giselle, then try to spot these other faces among the crowd.

Giselle

Robert and Morgan

Nancy

Narissa

Hot dog vendor

Singing cowboy

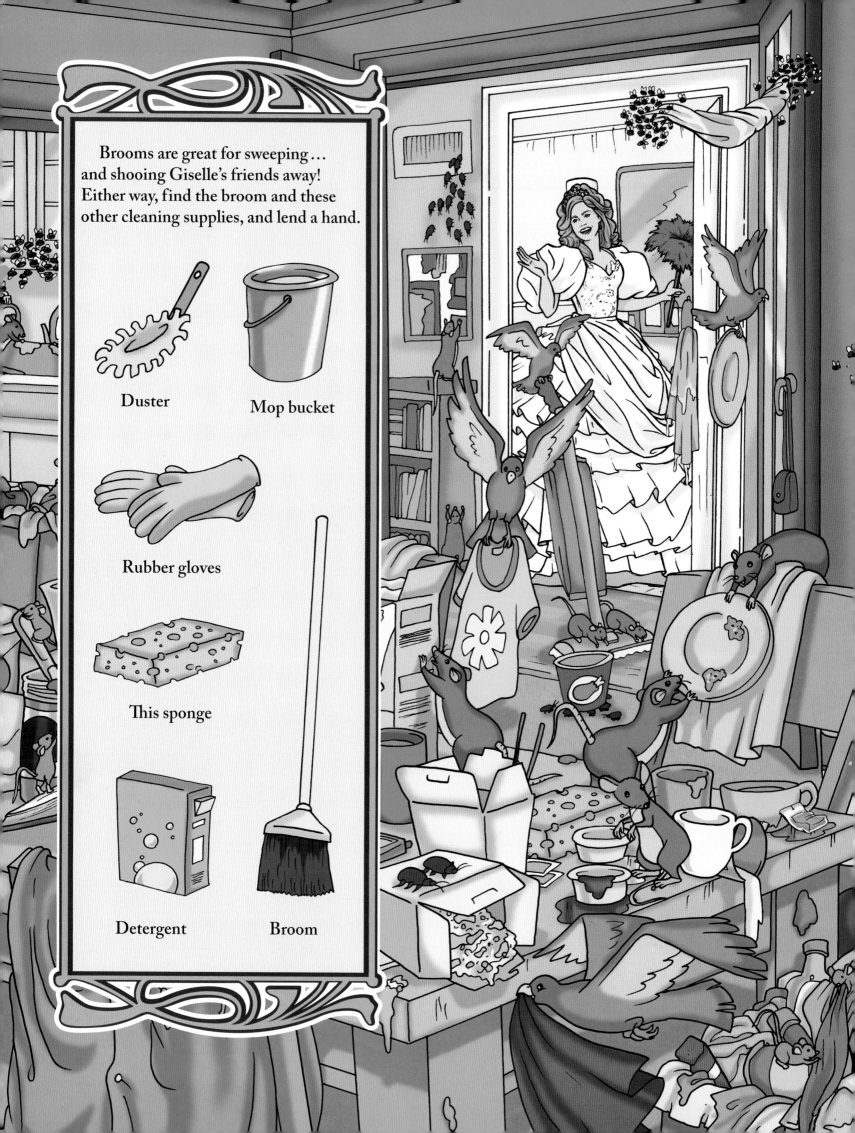

Brooms are great for sweeping...
and shooing Giselle's friends away!
Either way, find the broom and these
other cleaning supplies, and lend a hand.

Duster

Mop bucket

Rubber gloves

This sponge

Detergent

Broom

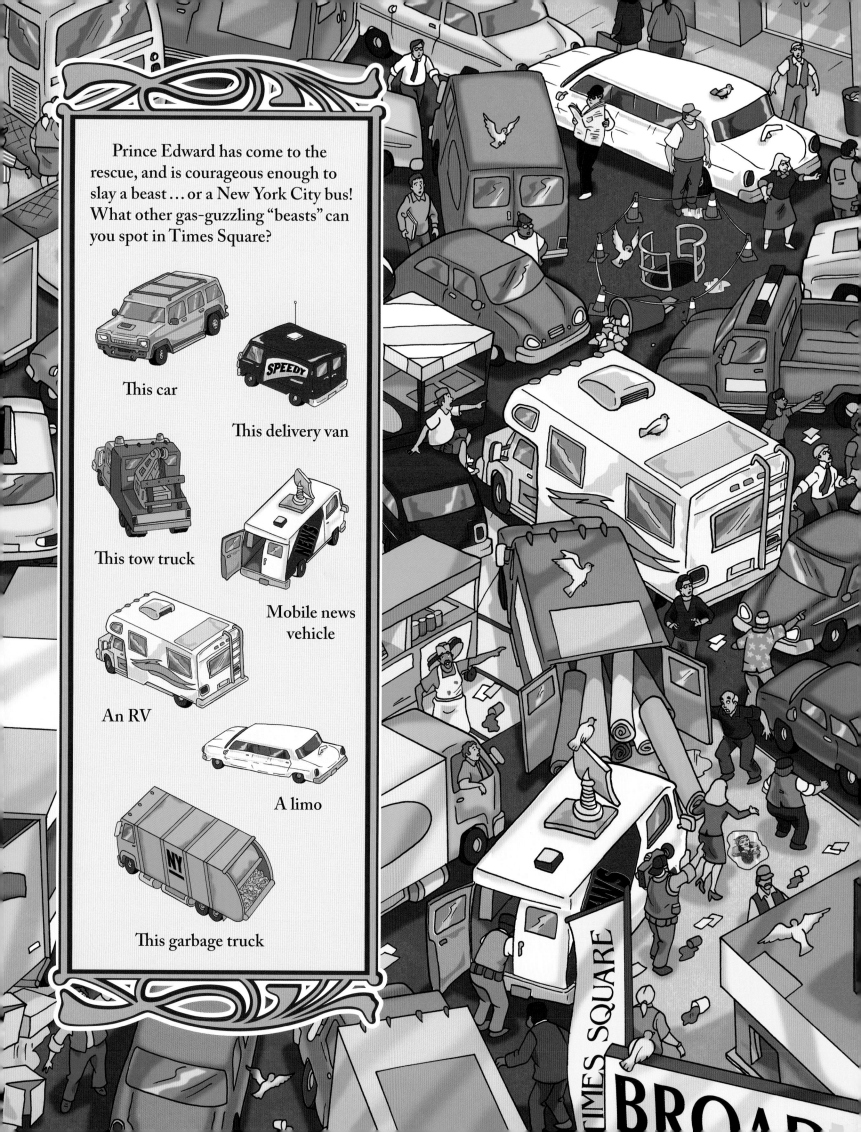

Prince Edward has come to the rescue, and is courageous enough to slay a beast … or a New York City bus! What other gas-guzzling "beasts" can you spot in Times Square?

This car

This delivery van

This tow truck

Mobile news vehicle

An RV

A limo

This garbage truck

It's common to hear music in Central Park, but today Giselle has inspired everyone to sing and dance. As you stroll through the park, look for these singing sensations:

Giselle

This vendor

This musician

This woman

This man

This man

The lords and ladies are prepared to dance the night away, but Giselle's entrance has caused many dancers to step on each other's toes. Before the waltz ends, can you find these familiar faces in the crowd?

Robert

Nathaniel

Pip

Old hag

Nancy

Edward

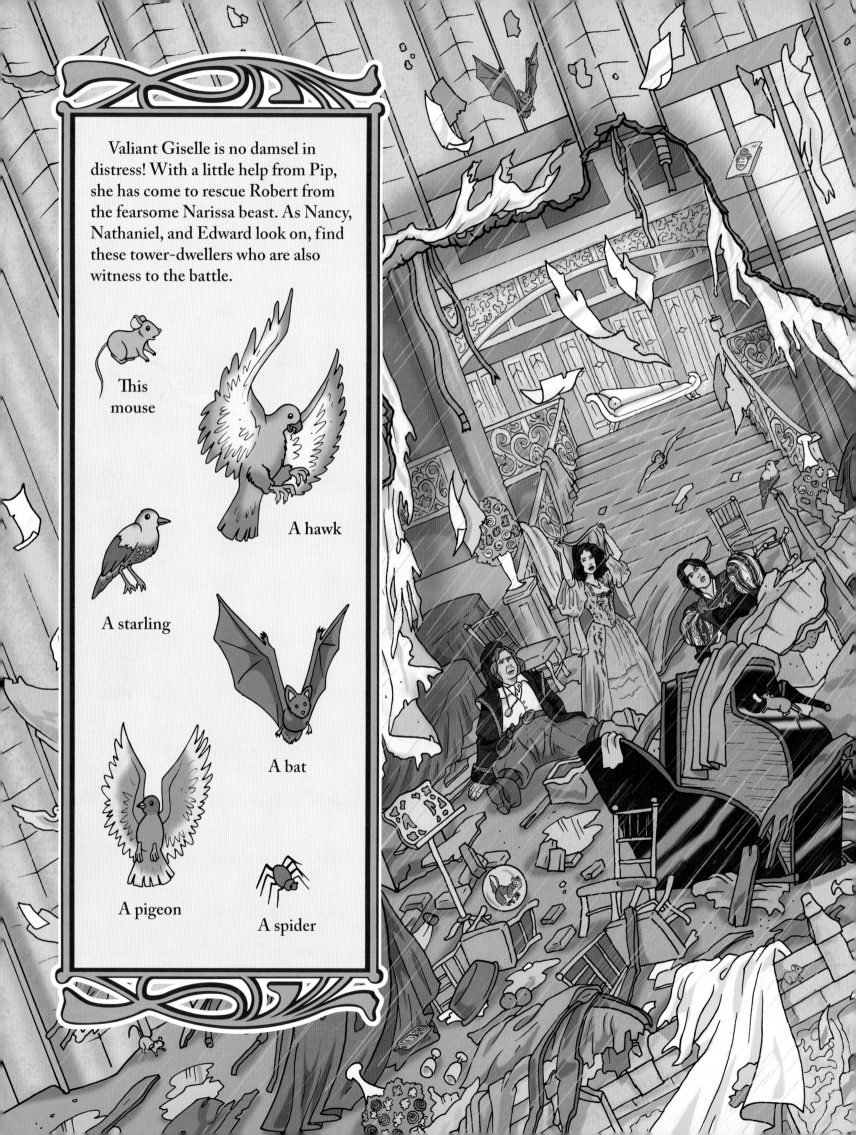

Valiant Giselle is no damsel in distress! With a little help from Pip, she has come to rescue Robert from the fearsome Narissa beast. As Nancy, Nathaniel, and Edward look on, find these tower-dwellers who are also witness to the battle.

This mouse

A hawk

A starling

A bat

A pigeon

A spider

Andalasia Fashions is open for business! Soon every little princess in the city will be decked out from head to toe in princessy things, like these:

A pair of fluttery silk wings

A ribbon wand

A flowery headband

These silk slippers

This pretty purse

This compact

All the animals are anxious to help Giselle … even these who might not be big enough for the job. Can you find these animals in Andalasia?

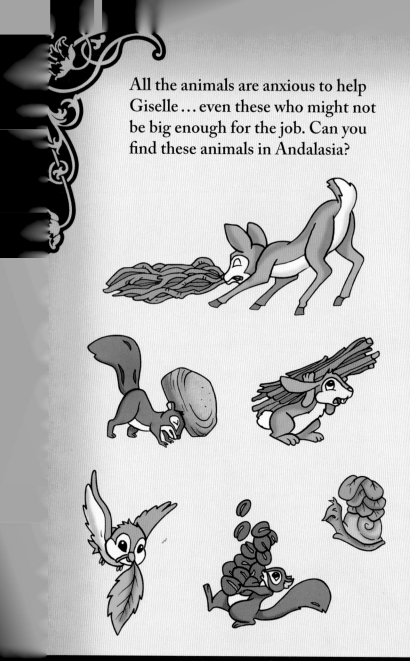

New York City might be frightening to Giselle, but other people love the Big Apple. Go back to bustling Times Square and find these examples of New York pride.

Doggie t-shirt

Bumper sticker

Backpack

Pennant

Sign

Balloon

T-shirt

Robert and Morgan's apartment is quite a mess! Tiptoe back inside and help find these untidy things:

Piece of popcorn

Old teabag

Smelly sock

Headless animal cracker

Moldy cheese

Wet towel

A crowd has gathered to watch Prince Edward slay the New York City bus. Even the pigeons are watching the action. Can you go back to the scene and spot 21 pigeons?

Back at Central Park there are a few people who haven't joined in on the fun. Can you find them and persuade them to start singing?

Giselle is wearing a pretty pair of gorgeous glass slippers, but other people are wearing fancy footwear, too. Can you find these pretty … and peculiar … pairs?

Shiny flats

Golden galoshes

Pointy-toed pumps

Platform shoes

High-tops

Ballet slippers

Furry slippers

In her rage, the Narissa beast has caused quite a mess! Look around the balcony to find these things in the debris:

One of Giselle's glass slippers

A band member's flute

Sheet music

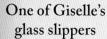

Nancy's cell phone

A violin bow

Narissa's poisoned apple

Search the fashion studio for these things:

A spool of pink thread

A lavender bow

Six pearl buttons

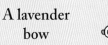

A dressmaker's dummy

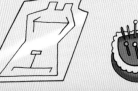

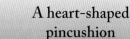

A dress pattern

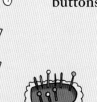

A heart-shaped pincushion

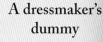